THE POET'S PLACE

First published 1991 by the Institute of Irish Studies,
The Queen's University of Belfast, University Road,
Belfast

Grateful acknowledgement for financial assistance is made to the Cultural Traditions programme of the Community Relations Council which aims to encourage acceptance and understanding of cultural diversity.

ISBN 0 85389 411 6 HB

ISBN 0 85389 408 6 PB

Printed by W.G. Baird Ltd, Antrim

The Poet's Place

Ulster literature and society
Essays in honour of John Hewitt, 1907-87

Edited by Gerald Dawe and John Wilson Foster

INSTITUTE OF IRISH STUDIES

CONTENTS

THE POET'S PLACE

Introduction

Like Yeats, John Hewitt (1907–1987) has become his admirers. But if he was a lesser poet than his great compatriot Hewitt's life and writings have become since his death what they become in the cases of very few poets of whatever stature: *common ground* on which friends, nodding acquaintances, strangers, even enemies meet to contemplate what divides and binds, threatens or ennobles them.

They do so formally (though informality is a mark of its proceedings) at the yearly John Hewitt International Summer School, held at Garron Tower on the coast of County Antrim, Northern Ireland. The first School took place in 1988 and its theme was 'An Ulster Poet and his Quest'. Inaugurated to keep green the memory of this important Ulsterman whose appeal crossed sectarian boundaries, and to celebrate his poetry in discussion and readings, the School quickly realised the wealth of cultural topics (many of them begging urgent address in a distressed province) Hewitt had left as legacy, not only in his verse but also in his essays and reviews, as well as in the comrades and contemporaries of a working life better than half a century long. Already, the School is one of the most bracing atmospheres in Ireland in which ideas about the island's past, present and future are tried and tested.

John Hewitt would have approved, we think, of our borrowing Estyn Evans' phrase 'common ground' (quoted by R.H. Buchanan in his valuable memoir of the geographer) as metaphor on this occasion. Hewitt was determined lifelong to ground his loves, awareness and identities in 'this live soil' of Ulster; like Evans, his abiding theme was 'the common people and the land itself', a decidedly democratic concern; and for him Ulster rightly existed as 'commonage' for all its inhabitants, irrespective of sect or ethnic fact (or fiction). It is true that he might have preferred the word 'freehold'— which he used to entitle one of his volumes— to commonage, since he was the Ulster Scot ('no man's pensioner') for whom tenure was to be earned by one's hard work, character and moral fibre. But it was earned too by the dead forebears buried in the native region. This was meant not to validate in retrospect an expropriatory Protestant claim to the ground of Ulster at the expense of Catholics but to advance a respectful claim of co-inhabitancy, a way, indeed, of making that 'common cause with the natives' he had his Roman colonist make in 'The Colony', the one who stayed on after the writ of the Empire had ceased to run and had begun to falter. Ulster for Hewitt, we might say, was an estate held in fee simple, without limitation of class or sect. Fittingly, the Summer School instituted a year after his death largely through the efforts of Jack McCann and Edna Longley, has attracted students and lecturers diverse in terms of denomination, social class, and political conviction.

The following essays have been culled from the first three Schools (1988–90) and inevitably the first such yield resembles a festschrift. A third of the essays (those by Gréagóir Ó Dúill, Roy McFadden, Gerald Dawe, Patricia Craig, Geraldine Watts, Tom Clyde and Terence Brown) address the writings of Hewitt. The rest do not, though even in turning to other Ulster poets and novelists (as do those by George Watson, Ivan Herbison, Adrian Rice, Eve Patten, Caomhín Mac Giolla Lith, Sophia Hillan King and Peter McDonald), they honour not just the spirit but also the expressed interests of that inquiring man. Human geography, art history, literary criticism, social anthropology, political science and natural history are all disciplines represented here whose subjects interested Hewitt as poet, curator of art, literary historian, political activist, nature-lover. R.H. Buchanan and Timothy Collins provide memoirs respectively of two Ulster figures who stand beside Hewitt to compose an impressive 20th century cultural triumvirate in the province: the geographer Estyn Evans and the naturalist Robert Lloyd Praeger. Styles, approaches and vocabularies range from the personal to the statistical, the commemorative to the analytical, but Hewitt and Ulster culture as subjects confer a family resemblance on what is otherwise an array of independent essays. (We have retained the signs of oral delivery in Buchanan's case, since the memoir of the geographer was the Estyn Evans Lecture delivered to the third School by the current Director of the Institute of Irish Studies in honour of the founding Director.)

Moreover, to know the region or province truly, Hewitt was convinced, is to know, willy-nilly, the specially related entities by which it is sustained and which it entails. These, too, were and are the poet's place. He famously called the relationship between these entities his 'hierarchy of values', and as Paul Arthur reminds us, they stretched from the province of Ulster through the island of Ireland, and the British archipelago, to the continent of Europe. There is, then, much room for thought and theme for future Hewitt Summer Schools. It has become the pattern to honour that chain of cultures by placing a cognate region under study at each School. And so there are essays here on Scottish culture (by Bernard Crick, from the second School) and Southern Irish culture (by Kevin Whelan, from the third School), with the promise of other Irish, British and European regions and cultures to come.

But because the theme of the third School was 'Turning to the Landscape', it was inevitable that the Glens of Antrim, for which Hewitt had a special love, should command attention, as well as landscape in Ulster poetry generally, and it is with these topics that this book of essays opens, with contributions from Cahal Dallat and George Watson. More than his native Belfast, which figures in his poetry far less, the Antrim glens were the first and local link in the chain of values by which Hewitt sought to give meaning through continuity to his life and writing.

The glens, the turbulent history of which is rehearsed by Dallat, are something of a microcosm through time of the loveliness and tribulations of the present-day north of Ireland, and Hewitt sought romantic escape in the former ('I have turned to the landscape because men disappoint me') and realistic challenge in the latter. Garron Tower, on a step of a fine headland above the sea, and home of the Summer School, itself rehearses the history of the vicinity and the region: built in the mid-19th century as a summer home by the Marchioness of Londonderry, it became a hotel in 1898, and a war-time sanctuary for old people in 1939—but not before being fired by the IRA in 1922—and since 1951, a Catholic school, St MacNissi's College. The loveliness of the setting has survived it all. A connoisseur of Irish paintings and prints, Hewitt knew the startling iconography of the glens and the remarkable shoreline they give on to, an iconography whose artistic and cultural importance Martyn Anglesea accounts for in his essay.

The political implications of Hewitt's 'hierarchy of values' and of his cultural outlook are the subject of several essays and are glanced at in others. Certainly his concept of regionalism is a ubiquitous guest, both announced and unannounced. The second School, 'Roots and Horizons', directly addressed regionalism (and no lecturer more pointedly than Tom Clyde), but to engage with Hewitt is always to engage at some juncture with the identity of Ulster, however open-ended that identity is interpreted. Hewitt developed his notion of regionalism in sympathetic response to its popularity among Scottish, Welsh and English poets and cultural thinkers during the 1940s, in conviction that it was especially germane to Ireland where in the North it could conceivably provide common ground between nationalist and unionist, Catholic and Protestant, firm footing under territorial claims and warring jurisdictions, capable of ultimately sustaining a federated British Isles, a federated Ireland, or a semi-autonomous Northern Ireland.

Whereas there is something somnific about the word 'regionalism' the idea that Ulster's regional identity, its 'regionality', could be forged through 'an awakened popular consciousness' was and is far more quickening and nearly revolutionary in the Europe of today. But it is more a case of discovering what is already there than of engineering what is not. To discover regionality may be, as in Kevin Whelan's researches, what is today called 'revisionism' which we take to mean no more than a justified complication (and therefore decomposition) of simple pictures of the cultural and political situation, which in Ireland means the nationalist and loyalist pictures. (In this sense, Anthony Buckley's essay is also revisionist work, displaying for us Protestant versions of history in their rhetorical and political variety.) But outside politics, Whelan takes issue with Estyn Evans to whom Whelan attributes the monolithic view of pre-20th century rural Ireland as peasant and archaic: this is fascinating because Evans, though his field was pre-partition Ireland as a whole, is popularly thought of as being in a substantive way, an Ulster geographer responsible like Hewitt for dignifying the cultural background of Ulster people as 'heritage'. Terence Brown's important reorientation of our understanding of John Hewitt's poetry, which is our last essay, reminds us that revision is as natural as reading and criticism themselves. To redefine the cultural and political status of Hewitt's Ulster seems a necessary task for us all, now and in the future.

Gerald Dawe, Galway-Dublin
John Wilson Foster, Vancouver.

CHAPTER 1

Landscape in Ulster Poetry

by

George Watson

Irish writing has been much concerned with nature, landscape and the sense of place (and I want to extend the 'landscape' of my title to include the sense of place, for reasons with will become obvious). I want to mention just once the Gaelic genre known as *dinnseanchas*, that whole corpus of poems and tales which relate the original meaning of place names and constitute a form of mythological etymology. Ulster writing has its strong relations with landscape and place, but on a somewhat more urgent level than might be suggested by the rather antiquarian flavour hanging round that definition of *dinnseanchas*. To come immediately to the point, how far is the landscape in Ulster poetry useful as, or seen as, a refuge from the hot pressures of a divided polity? The question is faced and answered with characteristic directness by John Hewitt:

> I have turned to the landscape because men disappoint me:
> I have never been compelled to turn away from the dawn
> because it carries treason behind its wakened face . . .
> I live my best in the landscape, being at ease there . . .
>
> ('*The Ram's Horn*', 1949)

Derek Mahon faces the same question with equally characteristic scepticism, in a poem called 'The Spring Vacation' (originally 'In Belfast') and dedicated to Michael Longley:

> We could all be saved by keeping an eye on the hill
> At the top of every street, for there it is,
> Eternally, if irrelevantly visible -
> But yield instead to the humorous formulae,
> The hidden menace in the knowing nod.

Hewitt's poem sees the landscape as compensation; Mahon's as lovely but irrelevant. This tone in the poetry suggests a feeling that might be put like this (with the obvious acknowledgements): 'In time, the Mournes may crumble, Cave Hill may tumble/ They're only made of clay,/ But our hate is here to stay'. Obviously, the poems suggest, said with regret. Paul Muldoon (as slippery as Hewitt is direct) raises another issue related to landscape poetry in Ulster: its thematic predictability. His 'Lunch with Pancho Villa' apparently mocks the notion of dilettantism in the writing on rural themes, when all around things fall apart, the centre cannot hold:

Look, son. Just look around you.
People are getting themselves killed
Left, right and centre
While you do what? Write rondeaux?
There's more to living in this country
Than stars and horses, pigs and trees,
Not that you'd guess it from your poems.
Do you never listen to the news?
You want to get down to something true,
Something a little nearer home.

Of course, as Muldoon knows full well behind his mask of wonderfully sustained naiveté, landscape in Ulster poetry ('stars and horses, pigs and trees') is rarely neutral, rarely simply pictorial, rarely a refuge from the 'hot pressures' of the divided society, Rather, it is freighted with an enormous weight of cultural codings, and at times even becomes the very emblem of the sectarian divide.

We might almost be better to approach the whole issue from the other end, and note how little there is of what might be called a 'pure' landscape poetry, that is, a poetry where the landscape itself seems more important than any uses (especially political, ethnic, or historical) to which the poet might want to put it. It is with great pleasure that one falls on Michael Longley's 'Carrigskeewaun', and specially a section of the poem called 'The Path' where all things that delight the eye are seen by him, and seen with that extra accuracy that only poetry provides:

With my first step I dislodge the mallards
Whose necks strain over the bog to where
Kittiwakes scrape the waves: then, the circle
Widening, lapwings, curlews, snipe until

I am left with only one swan to nudge
To the far side of its gradual disdain.

I particularly love here the way in which Longley takes the whole Yeatsian aviary, and especially the swan, and sees them, and it, in his own widening gyre, as in every sense empirically true. In 'Weather' there is the same scrupulous attention to realistic detail, but again seen from that poetic perspective where the ordinary is alchemised through the power of language into the marvellous:

I carry indoors
Two circles of blue sky,
Splinters of sunlight
As spring water tilts
And my buckets, heavy
Under the pressure of
Enormous atmosphere,
Two lakes and the islands
Enlarging constantly,
Tug at my shoulders. . .

From a rich corpus of what may be called without prejudice pure landscape poetry, I should also mention 'Spring Tide', which among other things makes me realise how much better a botanist is Michael Longley than I am, and the moving 'Mayo Monologues', where without fuss but with great power, we are made aware of the psychic price to be paid for living in the most beautiful but most remote of Ireland's landscapes.

As a kind of control quotation, to remind us all of how little our best poets' work is free from designs on the landscape, I want to cite part of a slight but effective poem by Brian Farrington called 'The Emigrant of a Hundred Townlands' (1969) which uses lots of placenames but with no sense that they constitute 'a form of mythological etymology': rather, the poem invites us simply to enjoy the plenitude of evidence that we, Celts, Normans, English, Scots, have created a map that sings:

Their names, their names they turn in my mind,
Boherapuca, Carrigaline,
Six-Mile-Bridge, Watergrasshill
Scart, Spink, Ballinakill.

They whine like fiddlers in Nad and Noone,
Nenagh, Nurney, Naul and Cloone,
Or croon like doves in Croom and Coole
Oola, Colloney, Clonacool.

Names with a distant alien ring,
Naas, Louisburgh, Glinsk or Bweeng,
Names that are Irish into the core,
Caherconlish, Magherymore.

Newtownmountkennedy, Ballyjamesduff,
Names within names, and sure enough
In Priesthaggard, Horseleap, Five-Alley-Rath
A name is a story's aftermath.

Though it's long ago and far away,
Crossmolina, Portballintrae,
Borris-in-Ossory, Ballinafad,
I'll not forget the times we had.

And, of course, there is Kavanagh. What may most strike us in this context is Seamus Heaney's praise of Kavanagh, or at least the terms in which, as ever so generous, he offered that praise. If you recall, for Heaney, the main point about Kavanagh's poetry was that it was completely free of the mystique of the national, the mythic, the tribal; that Kavanagh's work is 'premised on the rejection of nationality as a category in cultural life'; and that his placenames – Dundalk, Mucker, Inniskeen – carry no heavy etymological or cultural freighting. Heaney is surely correct in placing this emphasis on what we may call the neutrality of Kavanagh's landscape; and we see it the more clearly by the contrast with the work of the younger acolyte himself. For in Heaney's poetry, landscape is heavily determined by all sorts of cultural pressures: landscape is language, language is landscape (Anahorish, Toome, Moyola, Mossbaw, Broagh); the landscape of work is ritualised and sacramentalised in a very non-Kavanagh way; landscape becomes archetypal and archaeological ('Bogland' and all that); and Heaney's landscape is of course sectarian ('The Other Side', 'A Constable Calls'), though entirely in Heaney's courteous, compassionate, and unaggressive way.

In thus heavily interpreting the landscape, Heaney is more typical of Ulster poets than the Kavanagh – Longley – Farrington strain that I have tried to identify. And, for all their differences, Heaney and

John Hewitt are linked in this; that both see in the landscape sectarian patterns. The notion of the sectarian landscape I gratefully borrow from the seminal article by John Wilson Foster. 'The Landscape of Planter and Gael in the Poetry of John Hewitt and John Montague', which was published in 1975. For many years, Foster's opening paragraph in that essay has been for me a touchstone of sanity and encouragement:

> The urgent task facing anyone with a benevolent interest in Ulster is to explore as honestly as possible those cultural differences between Protestant and Catholic that underwrite the seemingly irrational sectarian conflict. It is less than helpful, indeed it is positively harmful, even with the best will in the world, merely to assert that beneath the orange and green camouflage Protestants and Catholics are all Irishmen and only political scoundrels prevent their mutual recognition of the fact. This is a pious delusion that short-circuits the arduous and hazardous business of trying to forge a genuine cultural synthesis (which involves recognising real antithesis).

The honesty and directness found there is what I most value also in the poetry of John Hewitt. He has written marvellous lyric poems, on subjects such as frost, owls, and stoats, and in them has occasionally hit out lines of such power – for example, 'all stripped of shadow down to bone of light' – that one wants to cheer. Still, Foster is right to imply that Hewitt's main interest for us lies in his lengthy and scrupulous debate about the position of the planter, a debate with himself set out in terms of the landscape, in well-known poems such as 'Once Alien Here', 'The Colony', 'The Glens', and 'O Country People'. Foster has done such a good analysis of these poems that I feel I can focus on just one issue pertinent to me. I want here to see myself – perhaps preposterously – as a representative of those whom Hewitt views as the dispossessed – 'the sullen Irish limping to the hills'; as one whose creed Hewitt fears as 'the lifted hand against unfettered thought'; as one whom Hewitt's colonist 'may distinguish . . . by pigmentation' and who 'breeds like flies': even allowing for his irony and poetic distancing, how can somebody from my background respond as positively as I do to Hewitt's poetry? Part of it is a recognition of the truth in the allusion to Catholic brainwashing; more importantly, what I love in Hewitt's poetry is his transparent honesty, his self-deprecating modesty, the quality of trustworthiness in the very plainness, the absence of flash in his work.

One of my favourite poems by John Hewitt must do duty for all I would like to say of his work, of his sense that the polity needs the poetry, that a man's life can have integrity despite disappointment; I suppose that what I respond to in John Hewitt is what I respond to in every Irishman or woman whose mind has not been closed by the sad accidents of our history. The poem is 'Retreaded Rhymes' (a characteristically modest title) from the *Loose Ends*, (1983), where he sums up his own sense of the quality of his poetry:

> . . . Quiet verse deliberately wrought,
> leaving the coloured crags' romantic line
> for humbler acre fairly mapped as mine;
> stranger to passion, never strongly moved
> by those emotions use has not approved. . .
>
> So ran my programme forty years ago,
> in safe iambics, *sotto voce*, slow;
> and since the butts are close, the circles wide,
> I've kept on target, and am satisfied
> when I recall behind the placid verse
> a man still stands whose attitude declares
> his loyalty to hope, unquenched belief,
> despite the incidence of age or grief
> in men's rare-hinted possibility
> of being just, compassionate and free.
>
> I struck these verses also in a set
> of plodding lines which offer comfort yet;
> though pill-propelled, unsteady in my gait,
> and conscious daily of my mortal state,
> they sing their sense forever in my head. . .

And in mine.

Nevertheless, Hewitt's poetry is implicated in what Foster has called the sectarian landscape. We will come back to that; but first and here, I want to challenge the notion that only the Irish use landscape for ideological purposes. A brief digression, intended to make us all feel better about ourselves.

English literary ideology, especially during the nineteenth century, again and again proposes the landscape as the communicator of essential historical truth. The English problem is not so much one of religious or ethnic differences, but one of differences of social class:

the class structure is then written into or read out of the landscape. Frequently, then, it is not nature that English writers look at; it is a humanised landscape which offers itself as an image of the continuity between the natural and the social. A part of George Eliot's *Adam Bede* can stand for all literary instantiations of this idea:

> The Green lay at the extremity of the village, and from it the road branched off in two directions, one leading farther up the hill by the church, and the other winding gently down towards the valley. On the side of the Green that led towards the church, the broken line of thatched cottages was continued nearly to the churchyard gate; but on the opposite north-western side, there was nothing to obstruct the view of gently swelling meadow, and wooded valley, and dark masses of distant hill. . .And directly below them the eye rested on a more advanced line of hanging woods. . .Then came the valley, where the woods grew thicker, as if they had rolled down and hurried together from the patches left smooth on the slope, that they might take the better care of the tall mansion which lifted its parapets and sent its faint blue summer smoke among them.

Here is a scene which we, as readers, are invited to view pictorially, and yet the construction of the description mimicks the social hierarchy, moving from the Green, through the village to the church and on to the mansion. And what the author does, nature does too, for the trees are in motion to protect the squire's house from public view. What we are given is a landscape, age-old, steeped in time, which underwrites social divisions. Social distinctions become natural distinctions because they are embodied in the very structure of the landscape.

So the Irish are not unique in using the landscape for various ideological purposes. What we need is to be aware of helpful and unhelpful uses of our shared landscape. I have referred to Hewitt's honesty, and to Heaney's courtesy, in their treatment of our obvious differences. I think, however, that the sectarian landscape is used in an unhelpful way in a poem which for all its undeniable power narrows the social and aesthetic range of Irish landscape poetry – John Montague's *The Rough Field*. You will remember that the poem begins with a journey from the waste land of Belfast to the sanctuary, however wasted it in turn is, of Tyrone, the ancient fiefdom of the O'Neills. There is some significant stereotyping in the poem, as for example here:

Through half of Ulster that Royal Road ran
Through Lisburn, Lurgan, Portadown,
Solid British towns, lacking local grace.

Even the women are fat: 'Headscarved housewives in bulky floral skirts/Hugged market baskets on the rexine seats' (they would be rexine, of course, rather than guaranteed genuine Children-of-Lir swansdown).

The poem can withstand a little criticism from me; and beside I want to talk more about an attitude behind the poem, rather than to give a full analysis of a longish work. I think some important issues need to be engaged, even if I start from autobiography.

I come from Portadown, which I will be the first to admit is not the Florence of the north. However, I will always remember a place we called 'the point', where the Bann river and its tributary, the Cusher, met with the northernmost part of the Newry Canal. It was only about a mile from the town, down the Tanderagee road, and over Sharkey's bog. One must avoid at all costs the emigrant's tear in the eye; but I must record my memory of what I felt when I stood at the point and looked at the skyline of my home town. There were nine factory chimneys, reflecting Portadown's relative degree of industrialisation; and I liked that, and the sense of purposeful bustle at the end of the working day – in our own small way, we had a rush hour. John Wilson Foster correctly identifies in some Catholic imaginations what might be called a Luddite strain. Portadown's railway yards and factories, the boys selling the 'Tele 6th' to people wanting a quick tea before going to one of the three cinemas – all this provided me early on with a useful inoculation against the Luddite virus. I knew, of course, that most of the workers in the linen and carpet factories were Protestants; but we played football with them. We had to: Portadown was and is an overwhelmingly Protestant town. My two elder brothers were clerical students at Maynooth (in other words, were about to become R.C. priests), but that did not really matter all that much when it came to getting the teams together. One of our most reliable regulars was Bothwell Vennard, a part-time B-man, whose description of defending Ulster from its enemies will live forever in my mind: 'Lads, it's money from America'. And at 'the point', I could see not only the skyline of my tight wee Protestant town, but also the whole range of the Mourne mountains, and I loved watching the express trains, the engines in the bright blue livery of the G.N.R., which steamed past Sharkey's bog around Moneypenny corner on their way to Newry, Goraghwood, Dundalk, Drogheda and Dublin. I liked them just as much if they were coming the other way, and if what lay ahead of them were the solid British towns of Lurgan, Moira, Lisburn and Dunmurry.

Now, at the same time, and even to a boy's mind, Portadown expressed the Ulster problem with a kind of perfect representativeness. It is thus a considerable paradox that it was the encounter with a more overtly 'Irish' culture, or perhaps more accurately, with a certain attitude to and presentation of that culture, which first shook my sense of identity (I knew exactly where I was in Portadown). My secondary school in Armagh (also, incidentally, John Montague's and Paul Muldoon's) was not only intensely nationalist, but went in with some ferocity for playing that most boring of games, wittily spoofed by Edna Longley as 'Irish, Irisher, Irishest'. There was a kind of unwritten scale, or league table, of 'Irishness', which at its simplest level was based on your town (or townland), and your name. Boys from Portadown and Lurgan started well down below boys from Aughnacloy and Crossmaglen, or from 'Beragh, Carrickmore,/Pomeroy, Fintona/- Placenames that sigh/Like a pressed melodeon', as Montague puts it in *The Rough Field*. These names were more a battle-trumpet in St. Patrick's College. If your surname was Watson, the Quinns and the O'Kanes and the O'Fiachs had a perceptible advantage (140 proof Irish). As for a first name of 'George' . . . The playing of soccer, tennis or 'English cricket' was an offence against your school, your country and your God. (I was punished for starting a small five-a-side soccer league on the grounds that I was 'corrupting the Gaelic morals of the school'). As with sports, so with language: among the boys there was a small and – I found – unpleasant group of *gaelgeoirí*, or linguistic authoritarians, who wore the gold *fainne* as a kind of threat, and regarded an interest in, say, Hardy as fairly conclusive evidence of seoninism, or West Britonism.

The learning of Irish thus and unfortunately became associated in my mind with an authoritarian nexus of nationalism, cultural morality and racial purity, which was extremely conservative and very hostile to any vision of Ireland not based on the rural, Gaelic-speaking areas of the West. If this was true Irishness, I began to doubt whether I qualified, or wanted to qualify, despite having a mother who was a native speaker of Irish from Connemara. There was no place in that Ireland for the flora and fauna of Portadown. I hope you will extend your tolerance for what may seem to be merely a set of personal memories. I hope they are more than that, I hope I can say without too much presumption and without over-dramatisation that in a small way I have known the sense of exclusion visited daily on Ulster Protestants.

I take heart from some of the points that Roy Foster made in his lecture on 'Varieties of Irishness' to the Cultural Traditions group conference in 1988:

> If there's one single unalloyed good that has come out of the overdone debates about historical 'revisionism', it's the idea of the historian as subversive. We should be seeking out the interactions, paradoxes and sub- cultures. . .(including) speculative theories of origins (like Ian Adamson's), if only to rearrange the pieces in more surprising patterns.

And he went on to say that, given the old nationalist revival ideology in which the values of the city are seen as English and the values of the country are seen as Irish, it's well past time for a change: 'What official identity has lacked up to now is the sceptical perspective of the city boys'. In the spirit of Roy Foster's remarks, I want to identify what I see as an important sub-culture, and since we in Ulster have always been obsessed with nomenclature, I am going to call this new group 'the Portadown Papes' (though I am open to offers for a better title). People from Lurgan, Lisburn, Banbridge, and Dungannon are welcome to join. What unites us is the good fortune to have been born in predominantly Protestant towns; 'good fortune' in the sense that by an accident of birth we avoided what Michael Longley has called 'cultural apartheid'. This amazed me in St. Patrick's College, where I met for the first time people who had never met a Protestant, and who thought they (the Protestants) all had horns (manufactured in Birmingham, of course). The Portadown Papes are not West Britons (if that means allegiance to Westminster); nor are they 'Castle Catholics' – a term which always suggests to me an element of class-based respectability (politics as antimacassars and the Horse Show); it's quite simply that we grew up knowing our Protestant neighbours, and if knowledge did not necessarily beget love, at least it contributed to understanding, and made us uneasy when the lads from Aughnacloy or Crossmaglen implied or stated that the desiderated unitary state could have no place for the people from 'the solid British towns'. And here, however far I may seem to have wandered from it, I return to the centrality of landscape and the sense of place in the development of a healthier polity in Ulster: landscape and the sense of place can work through the particularities of detail to subvert the idea of nation (which is, after all, even in less divided countries than ours, an enormously abstract notion). At very least, in Foster's formulation, a thoughtful reflection on the sense of place may help us to rearrange the pieces of cultural identity in more surprising patterns.

It is, after all, hard to love a country without having the rhetorical veins bulging in your biro; but it is very easy to love a place, a landscape. Even Portadown. And I think Foster is also right to ask us to listen more to the voices from that more urban background, anathematised by nationalist ideologues, voices which create compelling cityscapes with a cultural freighting very different from that of the traditional rural pieties. In this context, I salute the poetry of Ciaran Carson, which bids fair to do for Belfast what Joyce has done for Dublin. In some respects Carson sums up what I may call my pitch in favour of local studies. In a wonderful passage in his latest volume, *Belfast Confetti* (1989) called 'Schoolboys and Idlers of Pompeii', he has an affectionate account of the proceedings of the Falls Road Club, which meets on the first Thursday of every month in the Woolongong bar in Adelaide, Australia, and which reconstructs a city on the other side of the world, detailing streets and shops and houses which for the most part exist only in memory. Naming these things is the love-act and its pledge.

In general terms, indeed, a long exposure to 'country' literature and to the ideological baggage which frequently goes with it has made me more receptive to the poets of the city – and even of suburbia. I can still remember the shock of pleasure and delight I got when I first read Derek Mahon's poem, 'Glengormley', with its muted and ironic two cheers for suburbia (and for those who have tamed the terrier, trimmed the hedge and grasped the principle of the watering can). He is the last poet whom one would want to call a polemicist, but at the same time in my context he is a useful witness. As he says in a remark which is highly relevant to 'Glengormley' and to the general themes of this talk:

> The suburbs of Belfast have a peculiar relationship to the Irish cultural situation inasmuch as they're the final anathema for the traditional Irish imagination. A lot of people who are important in Irish poetry cannot accept that the Protestant suburbs in Belfast are a part of Ireland. . . At an aesthetic level they can't accept that.

Mahon's most characteristic technique, which is also his essential way of seeing, and enormously valuable in his work, is to refurbish our way of responding to the familiar by inviting us to observe it from a new or strange perspective. 'Courtyards in Delft', for example, invites us to view Glengormley, as it were, through the defamiliarising spectacles of certain Dutch paintings of the seventeenth century. Mahon is a master of tone, and as the poem develops, we become aware not of the strangeness of the comparison, but of its justness:

> I lived there as a boy and know the coal
> Glittering in its shed, late-afternoon
> Lambency informing the deal table,
> The ceiling cradled in a radiant spoon.

Another way of defining perspective is to say that it involves a sense of balance, or proportion; and Mahon is richly endowed here. So that in 'Courtyards in Delft', while he sees the limitations of the tightly corseted bourgeois lives he describes in all their trim composure ('We miss the dirty dog, the fiery gin'), he also sees qualities of orderliness and of a warm domesticity. (I like the way in which the girl in the painting suddenly moves from Delft to Belfast in the phrase where she is described as waiting 'for her man to come home for his tea'). This poem is to my mind a much more comprehending and comprehensive account of aspects of Ulster life than can be found in the scorched and parched landscapes of Tom Paulin's bitter 'Desertmartin'.

The sense of balance, even of distance, manifests itself also in those many Mahon poems where he writes almost as if from another galaxy, from somewhere beyond time. The note is there in his 'Day Trip to Donegal' where the western seascape becomes a threatening reminder, in the security of the suburbs, of elemental solitude:

> Give me a ring, goodnight, and so to bed . . .
> That night the slow sea washed against my head,
> Performing its immeasurable erosions -
> Spilling into the skull . . .

Mahon's landscapes are frequently at the edge of things, in every sense, as in the 'Apotheosis of Tins', in 'Consolations of Philosophy', in 'The Mute Phenomena' and in 'North Wind: Portrush'. He is possessed of a lively sense of the fragility and ephemerality of human existence, considered against the vastness of the galaxies and the mind-bending span of geological time. The point is made with characteristically unsettling wit in 'Rock Music', when the speaker goes for a walk on the beach the morning after a particularly noisy disco:

Rock music started up on every side –
Whisper of algae, click of stone on stone,
A thousand limpets left by the ebb-tide
Unanimous in their silent inquisition.

This perspective is alarming but also liberating – it frees us from all the enormous clutter of twentieth century material life (I sometimes think that Mahon would have made a good monk), and of course it also puts in perspective – for once the cliché is alive – the hot immediacies of Ulster political life. Mahon's work, in its balance, wit, good humour, enforces a sense of proportion on us all. Thus, even when least apparently political, it, like Guinness, is good for us. We may use about it one of his own remarks which he would be far too modest to apply to himself: 'A good poem is a paradigm of good politics'. His poetry, ironic but never chilly, distanced but compassionate, does what he said MacNeice's poetry does: it rinses the choked mud, it keeps the colours new.

Maybe all that I have been saying, with some banality, is that we should be aware that the landscape of cold Clare rock and Galway thorn is not the only landscape; and that we create our landscapes every bit as much as we are shaped by them. Our poets have played a major part in reminding us that we can invent our places, at least up to a point, and this may be a useful reminder that we could also perhaps do more to invent a better political landscape.

The general tone of all that I have said could clearly be seen to fall within what might be called the revisionist camp's views on literature, history and politics, to be an argument for pluralism. And that would be right. However, I think it only correct, in the spirit of honest enquiry emblematized by John Hewitt, and in my capacity as chairman of the Portadown Papes, to end by raising some questions about the aesthetics and politics of pluralism.

Paul Muldoon's sardonic idea of a good wee day in the country is a trip to see the Ballygawley roundabout. He is the most defiantly modernist or post-modernist of contemporary Irish poets, who rejects the very notion of origin and identity, who mocks traditional Irish poetic forms (you'll remember his scurrilous versions of the saga – 'How Cuchulain got his End' – and of the aisling, where he traces the spoor of the lovely Anorexia), who refuses the privileged or authoritative narrative voice we've come to expect in, say, Yeats or Montague or Heaney. He also refuses the familiar landscape: a relatively crude, but not unuseful, measure of how far we have come from the lake isle of Innisfree, or from Lough Beg, is given by noting that in his last three volumes, Muldoon sets poems in a tobacco shed in North Carolina, in Asturian Spain, in Minnesota, in Hope, Idaho, in the Lower East Side, in Philadelphia, Ontario, Cracow, the Amazon river, Canadian Indian territory, in a sushi bar in some American city, and in 7 Middagh St. in New York. 'Chicken Marengo! It's a far cry from the Moy'. Indeed it is.

All of this, plus his truly ingenious cross-pollination of narrative modes and genres, where Raymond Chandler rubs shoulders with Byron, or the legends of Sweeney and the Green Knight dance the intertextual gavotte with the trickster cycle of the Winnebago Indians, illustrates Muldoon's commitment to 'a pluralism of the present'. And it is often so funny – there is a lovely wit to the rhyming and similes of a poem like 'Immram':

> She was wearing what looked like a dead fox
> Over a low-cut sequinned gown,
> And went by the name of Susan, or Suzanne.
> A girl who would never pass out of fashion
> So long as there's an 'if' in California.

And yet, and yet. . .I tread a difficult line here, since I want as much as anyone to dismantle the prescriptive myths of Irishness and cultural identity. As Dillon Johnston wittily sums up those essentialist prescriptions, 'Ireland is racially Celtic, linguistically Gaelic, religiously Catholic, politically Anglophobic and republican, organizationally antinomian, sociologically clannish, aesthetically zoomorphic, and socially gregarious and alcoholic.' Naturally I applaud and enjoy writers like Muldoon who do such a good deconstructive job on the horribly familiar stereotype delineated by Johnston. I think I would enjoy him even more if I could feel that his cutting free of the past cost him a little more. There is a heartless dandy quality in Muldoon's work which will always slightly put me off, as long as there's a 'ma' in Armagh.

There is a more general problem. Pluralism is very much the flavour of the month with some of our best critics – I am thinking of Richard Kearney, Dillon Johnston, David Lloyd and Edna Longley – and given the present state of Ireland, we can all see its appeal. Down with 'Irishness'; let us agree with Edward Said that 'to leave the historical world for the metaphysics of essences like negritude, Irishness, Islam and Catholicism is . . . to abandon history'. But how about if one of those 'essences' to which our imaginations, both creative and critical, might commit themselves were to be – not an outmoded Irishness – but a reified cultural internationalism, a sort of multi-national Los Angelization of our intellectual and emotional lives?

I think of Hardy's reply to Matthew Arnold's denigration of the local and idiosyncratic: 'A certain provinciality of feeling is invaluable'. I am not arguing for a liteature focussed only on 'stars and horses, pigs and trees'. I believe in pluralism, but not a forced, programmatic pluralism which might be just as constricting in its own way as imposed Gaelicisation. I am merely suggesting that we may surely distinguish the concept of identity based on some false notion of essence and origin from the sense of identity based on lived experience, a shared and very particular landscape in both the physical and the psychological senses. Let us not throw out this particular baby with the essentialist bathwater. Cosmopolitanism as an antidote to sectarianism is praiseworthy, but as an end in itself, it must of its nature discount precisely those elements of our humanity which make us interesting to each other: our local particularity. Who really wants to converse in cultural Esperanto? To adapt some words of Yeats, we can only reach out to the universe with a gloved hand; that glove is one's own village or place, the only place one can know even a little of.

I want to end with a quotation from John Hewitt. These lines have usually been taken as reflecting his planter's sense of unease in the lack of what he can call a nation. That may be so; but which of us, north or south, Protestant or Catholic, does not in some way lack a nation? Thus, we can all say with John Hewitt:

> This is my home and country. Later on
> perhaps I'll find this nation is my own
> but here and now it is enough to love
> this faulted ledge, this map of cloud above,
> and the great sea that beats against the west
> to swamp the sun.

CHAPTER 2

The Nine Glens of Antrim

by

Cahal Dallat

I

John Hewitt first became attracted to the Glens of Antrim when his brother-in-law, Andy Millar, invited him to holiday at his summer house in Cushendall in the nineteen forties. This was to be the beginning of a fascination with the Glens which would lead Hewitt subsequently to describe the area as his 'Chosen Ground'. He returned at every opportunity for the next forty years as he tell us in his poem entitled 'The Glens of Antrim':

> I've drawn this landscape now for forty years,
> longer, if scribbles count, from lower ground. . .,
> And I have drilled my pen to draw each sign
> which peoples time and place within this frame.

The glens referred to by Hewitt as his 'Chosen Ground' were what are known locally as 'The Middle Glens' – five in number – Glenariff, Glenballyeamon, Glenaan, Glencorp and Glendun. Looking at the map of Ireland, we can see them in the northeast corner covering an area stretching from Ballycastle on the north coast to just south of the village of Glenarm. The most northerly glens, Glentaisie and Glenshesk, come together almost at the sea-shore in Ballycastle. Glendun reaches the sea at the village of Cushendun. Two glens converge at Cushendall—Glenaan and Glenballyeamon. The queen of the glens, Glenariff, sweeps down to the sea at the village of Waterfoot. Further south, the village of Carnlough lies at the foot of Glencloy, and Glenarm glen encloses the village of the same name. All the glens run down to the sea with the exception of Glencorp which connects Glendun to Glenaan.

The names of the nine glens are music to the ears as Hewitt claims in his poem 'Ulster Names': 'they move on the tongue like the lilt of a song'. In addition, many people are intrigued with the derivations of the Gaelic names. Glentaisie means the glen of Princess Taisie of the bright cheeks; Glenshesk means the glen of the sedges or reeds; Glendun means the glen of the brown river; Glencorp means the glen of the dead; Glenaan means the glen of the little fords; Glenballyeamon means the glen of Edwardstown; Glenariff means the arable glen; Glencloy means the glen of the stone ditches; Glenarm means the glen of the army.

The story of the childen of Lir belongs to the Cuchulain saga and is connected with the glens. The children of Lir were changed into white swans by their wicked stepmother, Aoife, who sentenced them to spend three hundred years swimming on the bleak and stormy sea of Moyle which washes the shores of the glens. The poet Thomas Moore tells their sad story in the 'Song of Fionnuala':

> Silent O Moyle be the roar of thy water,
> Break not, ye breezes, her chain of repose,
> While, murmuring mournfully, Lir's lonely daughter
> Tells to the night-star her sad tale of woes.

Another story from the Cuchulain sagas, that of Deirdre and the Sons of Uishneach, has a glens connection. Briefly, King Conor of Eamhain Macha (modern name, Navan Fort) was compelled by his nobles to recall Deirdre and the sons of Uishneach from exile in Scotland. They are said to have landed at Carraig Uishneach (the rock of the sons of Uishneach), near Ballycastle. The sons of Uishneach wanted to rush on to Navan but Deirdre, with a woman's intuition suspecting treachery, urged them to retreat to Rathlin to await the arrival of their friend and protector, Fergus McRoy, who had been forced under a geish (vow) to attend a banquet at Dunworry (Dun Bharaich: Barach's Fort), near Torr Head. The brothers refused to wait for Fergus and hurried on to Eamhain Macha, near Armagh, expecting King Conor to welcome them with a banquet. But the king had arranged a reception of a different kind and they were all beheaded. Deirdre threw herself on their grave and died of grief and a broken heart.

Other legendary figures connected with the glens include Finn MacCool, who mistakenly killed his faithful hound Bran at Doonfin in Glenshesk, and Ossian, the Early Christian warrior-poet, who is remembered in Glenaan, where a Neolithic court cairn in the townland of Lubitavish is traditionally believed to be his last resting place, as Hewitt wrote in his poem 'Ossian's Grave':

> The legend has it, Ossian lies
> beneath this landmark on the hill,
> asleep till Fionn and Oscar rise
> to summon his old bardic skill
> in hosting their last enterprise.

How fitting it was that in 1989 the members of the John Hewitt Summer School erected a cairn to the memory of Hewitt at this hallowed spot.

Dusty Rhodes, the tramp poet of the glens, recalls another legendary figure, the Grey Man, a Norse storm-god, who haunts Fair Head.

> Tis there at midnight's silent hour,
> The mystic Grey man glides,
> Along the top of rugged rocks,
> Or down their sloping sides.[1]

There is also mystery attached to the Vanishing Lake on the road between Ballycastle and Cushendun, so called because of its habit of suddenly emptying itself despite any obvious outlet. The old Gaelic name for the lough was 'Loch an rith amach' meaning the 'running out lough' and it was only to be expected that legends and stories should be connected with it. Locals showed little surprise when Colonel Jack McNeill and his coachman, David McNeill, were drowned in the lough in 1898. Hewitt in his poem refers to this tragedy in his poem 'Glenaan': 'Just as at Carey lough you are bound to know/The tragic story of the foundered coach'. Clearly Hewitt was listening and recording the customs and superstitions of the glens. Julia McQuillan, known as the Black Nun of Bunamargy, added to the mystery of the glens with her many prophecies which people were afraid to believe and equally afraid not to.

There is nothing legendary, however, about Tievebulliagh, the geological outcrop near Cushendall. The chalk adjacent to the volcanic plug was so affected by the intense heat that it fused and became changed into a hard and fine-grained, speckled rock, now known as Porcellanite. Early man was familiar with this rock and used it to fashion stone axes and other cutting tools. There must have been a considerable export trade in existence since many specimens of Tievebulliagh axes have been discovered in several parts of the British Isles and even further afield. The antiquity of the area is further evidenced by the numerous circular forts or raths which are to be seen throughout the landscape. These were really solitary farmsteads of fifteen hunded years ago. Other relics of the ancient past are the dolmens and megaliths erected about five thousand years ago, and the crannog or lake-dwelling in Lough na Cranagh near Fair Head. A recent excavation at Deerpark Farm, Glenarm, has revealed a slice of archaeology or history encapsulating samples of domestic life in the glens covering a period from 600 to 1100 A.D.

The glens have had a stormy history and have been the scene of many fearsome battles, as Hewitt reminds us in 'Sunset over Glenaan':

> . . . but here
> the people have such history of wars,
> that every hill-top wears its cairn of dead
> and ancient memories of turbulence,
> clan names persisting in each rocky stead.

Originally in the possession of the Earl of Ulster, they were sold to the Bissetts in the early thirteenth century. In 1242 Patrick, Earl of Athol, was murdered in his bed in his mansion at Haddington in Scotland. His house was then set on fire to destroy the evidence or to make it look like an accident. The Bissetts were suspected because they had been feuding with the earls of Athol for many years and although they were able to produce several witnesses who proclaimed their innocence, they were found guilty and condemned to banishment from Scotland. They were lucky to escape with their lives and only succeeded in saving themselves by taking a solemn oath that they would go on a crusade against the Turks and remain in the Holy Land for the rest of their lives doing penance and praying for the soul of the murdered earl. A crusade to the Holy Land, however, required a considerable sum of money so the Bissetts were given time to sell their extensive lands and their vast accumulations of stock and property.

John and Walter Bissett set out from Scotland on their journey of repentance and whether by accident or by design their ship brought them across the 'narrow sea' to Carrickfergus. Here they were met by Richard de Burgo, Earl of Ulster, who made them an offer they found it difficult to refuse. De Burgo was having difficulty in controlling the Glens of Antrim and Rathlin Island and was very glad to dispose of them to the Bissetts for ready money. Many years later

(1318) Hugh Bissett was to forfeit Rathlin for having provided a refuge for Robert Bruce of Scotland. Five generations after, the last of the Antrim Bissetts, Margery, the daughter of Eoin Bissett and Sabia O'Neill, became the sole heir to the glens.

About this time John More MacDonnell of Kintyre and Lord of the Isles was looking for a wife and he came to County Antrim to woo Margery, who has been described as 'young, high-born and handsome and an heiress to boot'. John and Margery were wed in 1399 and from that time on the glens have remained in the possession of the MacDonnells who became known as the MacDonnells of Antrim. For the next two hundred years the MacDonnells spent most of their time and energy in fighting off various claimants to their territory, particularly the McQuillans, the O'Neills and Sir Arthur Chichester.

Slieve an Orra was the site of a decisive battle between the MacDonnells and the McQuillans in 1559. The McQuillans, who were assisted by the cavalry from Clandeboy led by Hugh McPhelim O'Neill, made camp on the Orra plateau at the top of Glendun. On the night before the battle, Sorley Boy MacDonnell ordered rushes to be spread over the bog holes which lay between the hostile camps, and over which the McQuillans believed he intended to charge them at early dawn. They were treacherously led to believe that Sorley's road across the swamp had been made sufficiently secure to permit a charge of cavalry, and resolving to make the first move, persuaded Hugh O'Neill to lead the attack. The O'Neill cavalry rushed out at first light and straight into the swamp where the horses soon sank to their houghs among the thinly strewn rushes and became totally disabled whilst their riders became easy targets for the arrows and Lochaber axes of the MacDonnells. Ever after there was a saying in the glens: 'A rush bush never deceived anyone but a McQuillan'.

The MacDonnells now added the territory known as the 'Route' to the glens and so controlled the upper half of County Antrim. Shane O'Neill had proclaimed himself 'Earl of Ulster' and deciding that the MacDonnells were becoming much too powerful, determined to send them back to Scotland. In Easter week of 1565 Shane marched northwards from Armagh with two thousand men, stopping overnight at various places en route, including Dromore, Edenduffcarrick (later known as Shane's Castle) and Clough Castle on the western flank of the glens. At this stage the MacDonnells lighted warning fires on Torr Head as a signal to their kinsmen in Scotland that help was needed urgently. James MacDonnell responded immediately, crossing over and landing at Cushendun with a small force, and

Alexander promised to follow in a day or two with several hundred more, but this was a delay which was to prove very costly for the MacDonnells in terms of lives lost. Shane O'Neill was in no mood for waiting and so marching down through Glenariff he attacked and burned Red Bay castle. The MacDonnells were only a half day's march ahead of him and he pursued them to Ballycastle where at the battle of Glentaisie on 2nd May 1565 he defeated them and slew seven hundred of their number.

Two years later the same Shane O'Neill was back in the Glens of Antrim to seek help from the MacDonnells against the other Ulster clans who had joined forces against him. At first the MacDonnells received O'Neill and his thirty or so followers with great hospitality at Castle Cara, near Cushendun, and he was invited to join in the chase of the deer on the high ground above Glendun. On the third evening of his visit a banquet was arranged in his honour and there was much feasting and merry-making. The wine flowed freely, perhaps too freely, and a quarrel began between Shane's secretary, Eugene O'Hagan and a MacDonnell over a remark made about James MacDonnell's widow. A first-class row developed. Shane foolishly tried to interfere and quick as a flash the MacDonnell daggers were out. This was the moment they had been waiting for and in a very short time Shane and his followers lay dead. The MacDonnell defeat at the battle of Glentaisie had been avenged.

Many other battles and skirmishes took place as well as a couple of massacres on Rathlin Island, but eventually the MacDonnells became well established as the landlords of the glens. As time went on they began to use their famous Lochaber axes for felling trees and clearing the ground, and no doubt their swords were beaten into ploughshares. The inhabitants of the glens are descended from these war-like clans but thankfully attitudes have changed with time, and for the past three hundred years the glensfolk have been content to go about their daily occupations of farming and fishing.

The MacDonnells of Antrim had castles at Dunluce, Dunaneaney, Ballycastle and Glenarm and it was at Glenarm that they finally settled, where Sir Randal MacDonnell, first Earl of Antrim erected a castle in 1625. Anne Frances Vane Tempest Stewart, the Marchioness of Londonderry, whose mother was the Countess of Antrim, would have succeeded to the title of Earl of Antrim if she had been a male. She lived in London where she lavishly entertained England's royality and nobility but such was her love of the glens that she was determined to have a castle there which would outshine her mother's ancestral home, Glenarm Castle. When her agent, John Langtree, suggested that she build a hotel in Carnlough at which 'your Ladyship could stop when you come to visit your Estates' she readily agreed. The hotel was built and named the 'Londonderry Arms'. This did not satisfy her, however, as she still wanted something out of the ordinary. Langtree, reading her mind, then suggested that she should rebuild the clan castle at Dunluce and make it habitable but she dismissed the suggestion out of hand since it was outside the glens. When the site at Garron was proposed she was delighted. It must be said in the Tower's favour that, despite its size and height, it was sited in such a manner as not to have had any adverse impact on the visual amenity of such a highly sensitive scenic area. Garron Tower became a hotel in 1898 and in 1939 the residents of Clifton House Old Peoples' Home, Belfast were evacuated to it. In 1951 it opened as a college for boys and nowadays it is co-educational; it has also in recent years been an ideal centre for the John Hewitt International Summer School.

II

The remoteness of the glens and their inaccessibility created in their inhabitants a feeling of being apart and caused them to sense a definite affinity with their neighbours on the Scottish coast. There was a ferry running from Cushendun to Dunaverty in Scotland until 1833. In fact it was easier at one time to get to Scotland than to other parts of County Antrim. Richard Dobbs writing in 1633 and referring to a journey through the glens says:

> There are several highways but none are good for the lower ways are deep clay and the upper ways are great steep hills. From Glenarm he who would coast it to Coleraine, goes from Glenarm over the mountain to Red Bay and must have a guide, or if he keep the sea near on his right hand; it is very deep in winter, and yet some steep passages ill to ride up or down; both ways are not to be commended either in summer or winter. From Red Bay to Cushendun is very good but from thence over Carey Mountain you must have a guide to Ballycastle and you may escape—tho' the mountains seem a continual bog where a man is in danger of sinking with his horse.[2]

Because the area was cut off from the rest of the country, the indigenous population tended to be less affected by outside influences and they tended to retain the old ways of life. This was particularly evident in their customs and their speech. In the Ordnance Survey Memoirs of 1833 we read:

> They seem a distinct race from the more southern parishes, both in their features, manners and accent. They are remarkable for their honesty, theft being wholly unknown, although various kinds of property are nightly left exposed and unprotected. They are industrious and very hospitable and obliging in their dispositions, and very peaceable and well-conducted, except that they are fond of whiskey-drinking. Many neither speak nor understand the English language and all speak Irish. Those who do speak English, speak it well and free from any peculiar accent.[3]

The making of the Antrim coast road in the 1830s brought to an end the ferry service between Cushendun and Scotland. It should also have signalled the end of the isolation of the glens but old habits die hard and the area was to remain a place apart for the next hundred years. The old road along the coast from Larne to Cushendall had climbed up and over each successive headland making the journey really difficult for the traveller. Admittedly, Francis Turnly had tried to improve communications by cutting the Red Arch and making a road near the sea between Waterfoot and Cushendall: he had also blasted a way later known as 'Turnly's Cut' through a protruding crag at Garron Point. It was through the ingenuity of a Scottish engineer, William Bald, that the cliffs were blasted away down to sea-level and the rock used to make and surface a road, with the debris forming a protective battery to resist the onslaught of the sea. The underlying Lias clays, being of a slippery nature, created a serious problem for Bald as they caused the chalk and basalt cliffs to creep over the newly made road. He overcame this difficulty by building horizontal arches or, as he described it, he adopted 'the arched principle on a lateral plane'.

Nowadays we see the Antrim Coast Road as a tourist attraction but it was built as a 'grand military road' designed to open up the glens which were seen by the authorities as being a subversive area. It has since become one of the finest scenic roads in Europe and the famous travel writer H.V. Morton could describe it a hundred years later as being 'finer, to my mind, than the Grand Corniche Road in the south of France'.

Although the new road provided access to the glens in the 1830s, it was to be some time before tourists began to use it. The gentry had time and money to visit and appreciate the beauty spots of County

Antrim but the other classes were too busy trying to earn a living to have any time for scenery. Travel writers such as the Halls were beginning to notice the glens and Thackeray in his *Irish Sketch Book* (1872) claims that to describe Glenariff as 'Switzerland in miniature' is totally inadequate, for 'in joining together cataracts, valleys, rushing streams and blue mountains, with all the emphasis and picturesqueness of which type is capable, we cannot get near to a copy of Nature's sublime countenance.'[4]

Reverend George Hill, historian and librarian, draws attention to the scenic quality of the glens in his history of *The MacDonnells of Antrim* (1873):

> It is admitted, even by those who have had opportunities of visiting other lands, that the picturesque beauty of this district is in some respects, unrivalled. Each glen is found to possess its own peculiar charms, whilst throughout all, the same leading characteristics are apparent. The principal glens open on the sea at irregular intervals, along the line of coast between the little towns of Glenarm and Ballycastle, and extend inland among the hills in winding courses. A little stream finds its way down the centre of each valley to the sea, now murmuring between piles of grey rock overhung with hoary trees, and again stealing quietly onward through stretches of corn and meadowland. The overhanging slopes are generally occupied by small but well-cultivated fields, in almost every variety of shape and size, and fashioned, apparently, more by the influence of time and chance, than by any direct agency of human hands.[5]

The great variety of geological formations which exist determine, to a certain extent, the scenic beauty of the glens. These range from the very old Dalriadian schist near Ballycastle in the north-east to the geologically young rocks at Garron Point and further south. The occurrence of an underlying layer of slippery Lias clay leads to an unstable and changing topography in the cliffs along the coast road. The Old Red Sandstone occurring between Waterfoot and Cushendall, and from which Red Bay derives its name, provides a welcome change to the black and white of the basalt and limestone cliffs. This is the geological variety to which Peter Rhodes refers in his book *The Antrim Coast Road* when he writes: 'it is this succession, so beautifully displayed by the ever-changing pattern of the cliff-lined coast, that is responsible for the most striking colour contrasts which are to be seen along the Antrim Coast Road: the red desert sandstones of the Trias, the dark blue of the Lias Clays, the white of the Chalk, the black of the Basalt lavas, plugs, dykes and sills and the bright red of the interbasaltic Bed.'[6] The geology is also responsible, in addition to the variety of colours, for the interesting range of shapes varying from the statuesque features of Fair Head to the smooth, ice-worn slopes of Glenariff Glen.

Henry McNeill, who owned a coaching inn and posting establishment in Larne, was probably the first to realise the tourist potential of the glens. He organised excursions on horse-drawn waggonettes from Larne to the glens and as a result became known as 'the father of Ulster tourism'. The directors of the Northern Counties Railway decided that the Glenravel mineral railway from Ballymena to Parkmore could be used to provide a passenger service to Glenariff Glen and its fantastic waterfalls. Parliamentary permission to carry passengers was granted in 1888 and in the following year the company purchased that part of the glen in which the falls lie. A pathway was constructed along the water's edge, crossing and recrossing the river, to give splendid viewing points for the waterfalls. Near the bottom of the glen a wooden, Swiss-style tea-house was erected and here tourists could relax and enjoy afternoon tea after their strenuous walk down the glen. Day trippers from Belfast could make the journey by train to Ballymena and then by narrow-gauge train to Parkmore Station. The journey was not lacking in variety as waggonettes or long-cars conveyed them to the head of the glen. A walk of a mile or so of exciting pathways brought them down to the tea-house. After tea there was an option either to return by waggonette to Larne and train to Belfast or back by the way they had come.

III

The Irish language was still being spoken in the glens until the last quarter of the nineteenth century although the use of it had declined in most parts of Ulster. To offset this decline, the Gaelic League had been set up in 1893. The glens were seen as an area where this Gaelic revival would bear fruit and a number of enthusiasts soon became involved. It was decided to hold a great feis where people could compete in Irish dancing, traditional singing, instrumental music, story-telling and history, arts and crafts, and hurling. The feis held in Glenariff on 30th June 1904 was an outstanding success and attracted Gaels from all parts of County Antrim. Prominent among the organisers was Francis Joseph Biggar, Roger Casement, Barbara McDonnell, Margaret Dobbs, Ada McNeill, Rose Young and John Clarke. It is interesting to note that very few of those named were of the 'Nationalist' tradition. The feis was officially opened by Sir Horace Plunkett who appealed for a greater interest in Irish industries, and among the other speakers was Eoin McNeill, later to become Minister of Education in Dail Eireann. The Glens Feis has been held every year since in one of the nine glens and there is no doubt that it has played some part in preserving the distinctive culture and traditions of the glens.

Hewitt had obviously been interested in this cultural revival, as he writes about some of the participants in his poem 'Fame':

> 'Och aye, ye mean the young Miss Higginson
> stayed with Miss Ada round by Cushendun.
> She was a decent girl. I seen her when
> they held the first big feis here at the Bay,
> and Roger Casement brought the Rathlin men.
> She writ a book of pomes, I heard them say.'[7]

The glens area is often pictured as a natural, almost legendary, landscape and yet it has to be remembered that most of what we see and enjoy has been the result of man's labour. The fascinating patchwork of field-patterns is the result of man's attempts to earn a living from a terrain which could hardly be described in modern parlance as 'user-friendly'. Noticeable among these field patterns are the ladder farms which form an interesting network on the sloping sides of Glenariff. The clusters of whitewashed cottages with which the landscape is peppered are sometimes known as clachans and in days gone by they were occupied by the kin group or extended family of grandfather, father and sons. The Gaelic name for the cluster was 'baile', which appears in so many of our placenames of townlands, villages and towns in its Anglicised form of 'bally'. Also connected with the clachan or 'bally' was the 'booley' or summer dairy. Under the rundale or run-rig system the land was held in common and in order to ensure that everyone got a fair share, the infield was parcelled out in strips of good, middling and poor land. It was both impractical and impossible to fence these strips, so as soon as the crops were planted in the spring it was necessary to move all the farm animals to the upland pasture or summer-grazing as it was called. The animals remained all through the summer in the 'booley' and young boys spent the season herding them. Most of the milk from the cows in the booley was made into milk products such as cheese or gruthin (a curds and butter mixture) for use during the winter months. Remains of booley-huts can still be seen in the glens, and placenames such as

Crocknaboley, Ballybooley, Drumavoley and Tievebulliagh remain to remind us that the practice of transhumance was not always confined to Switzerland and Norway.

As families grew the farms were sub-divided to accommodate sons and grandsons and the eventual outcome was that the resulting units were no longer economically viable. This was one of the factors which led to the massive emigration which took place in the eighteenth and nineteenth centuries.

The seemingly random way in which the small cottages are scattered over the landscape might lead one to believe that they had been built without any plan or thought. That was not the case; a supply of clean water in the form of a spring-well or running stream was sought out. Shelter was also very important and most of all it was essential to avoid building on or near the fairies' paths. Because it was a place apart old methods continued to be used long after things had changed in other places. Potatoes were still being planted in lazy-beds; oats were still being sown from a bag apron and harvested with the sickle and scythe and threshed with the flail and winnowing sheet. These methods were superseded by the corn-fiddle, the swing plough, the two-horse reaper and the one-horse threshing machine. Eventually the tractor took over from the horse but it is interesting to notice how much land previously cultivated by the spade is too steep to be ploughed by the tractor. Remains of cultivation rigs or lazy beds can still be seen on the high ground throughout the glens.

It is significant that the Glens of Antrim have been classified as an area of outstanding natural beauty by the Department of the Environment for Northern Ireland and that Cushendun, Cushendall, Carnlough, Glenarm and most of Ballycastle have been designated as Conservation areas. Some of the charm of Cushendun lies in the group of houses built in the style of a Cornish village by the celebrated Welsh architect Clough Williams Ellis in 1912 and named Maud Cottages after Maud Bolitho, the Cornish wife of Lord Cushendun. Rockport Lodge at the east end of the village was once the home of Moira O'Neill whose *Songs of the Glens of Antrim* captures the simple lifestyles and pleasures of glensfolk. Cushendall's focal point is its Curfew Tower erected by Francis Turnly in 1820. Hewitt's poem 'The Curfew Tower' refers to it:

> That Curfew Tower in Cushendall
> stands oddly individual,
> a square stone tower, a hill beyond,
> rising where the four roads joined

which here we call the Diamond:
not Norman, no vast edifice
ivied with epic centuries,
but dull and plain, anonymous,
a little castle, a tall house.

The picturesque stone bridge over the River Dall has been the meeting place for the villagers for well over a hundred years. Carnlough has its Londonderry Arms Hotel, to which reference has already been made, and the attractive white limestone bridge built in 1854 to carry the mineral railway over the road to the sheltered harbour which dates from the same time. Glenarm's appeal stems from its barbican and castle as well as its narrow streets; Ballycastle's tree-lined Quay Road and Georgian houses are worthy of conservation.

For a description of the changing scenery of the Glens of Antrim we cannot do better than turn to the travel writer, H.V. Morton, who wrote in 1930: 'I do not know of eight miles of road anywhere in the British Isles which can show more varied or entrancing beauty. There are hills the height of mountains, lowlands and highlands, glens and waterfalls, with slow rivers slipping through them, fairy-like woodlands, broad pasture lands, sudden stretches of Irish bog, and, always, either in sight or within hearing, the sea thundering on rocks or sweeping in long waves over yellow sands.[8]

CHAPTER 3

The Iconography of the Antrim Coast

by

Martyn Anglesea

Nowadays we take pictorial landscape imagery for granted, but this was not always so. Landscape painting did not evolve spontaneously or for no reason. It was for economic advantage on the part of expanding mercantile powers that cartography was developed for the use of mariners, travellers, and especially traders. In spite of the intrinsic beauty of landscape, the pictorial depiction of a particular landscape had primarily a significance in pride of ownership felt by a potential patron. Such is the message of numerous European portraits of kings and nobles posing grandly before their houses and estates, and which confirm their power and standing.

This would apply only to civilized, tamed, well-cultivated landscape that would produce wealth, and, as in the classical landscape of Claude Lorraine, symbolise the good estate management of a settled aristocracy ruling a contented peasantry. The wilder, bleaker, poorer tracts of terrain—the Alps, Scandinavia, Scotland, Wales—were a very different matter. These places were horrid and dangerous, infested by savages and bandits, and without any economic stimulus there was no point in producing pictorial images of them. And yet the stimulus might sometimes be found. Since the seventeenth century, the physical features of a particular region of Ireland—the Antrim Coast—have been realised pictorially for several reasons: military strategy, scientific enquiry, poetic expression, artistic saleability and political symbolism.

I

In Ulster the seventeenth century was a period of continuous strife. In the context of O'Neill's and O'Donnell's war against Queen Elizabeth, their defeat and flight, and the subsequent colonisation of

Ulster with English and Scottish Protestant planters surrounded by a hostile Catholic native Irish, the province was a wild frontier. Therefore it is not surprising that the few early drawings of Ulster topography are military 'plotts' of beleaguered forts and walled towns: the Elizabethan bird's eye view of Enniskillen Castle, Richard Bartlett's similar view of Armagh (1600), John Dunstall's view of Carrickfergus (1612), or Thomas Raven's view of Charlemont Fort (1624). The resettlement of Ireland during Cromwell's Commonwealth carried in its wake the first systematic survey of Ireland as a whole, William Petty's 'Down Survey', when the country was mapped accurately for the first time. Petty made his survey between 1654 and 1659, but his atlas, *Hibernia Delineatio*, was not published until 1685. The military engineer Thomas Phillip's *Military Survey of Ireland*, undertaken that same year, includes a 'ground plaine of Carrick Fergus with the strengthening of the Castle if thought necessary', as well as a perspective drawing in the corner, showing the town, castle and Sir Arthur Chichester's house 'Joymount' – the only known picture of it. If Phillips's recommendations for the improvement of the fortifications of Irish ports had been carried out, and they had then been occupied by Jacobites, William of Orange and his generals would have had much more difficulty conquering Ireland.[1]

The Williamite Wars ended with the treaty of Limerick in October 1691. Following this the hopes of the Irish Catholics were crushed, and Ireland was provided with an uneasy peace under a Protestant ascendancy. In this climate a demand for topographical illustration could come from the rising urban, mercantile classes, who were primarily interested in facts, geographical, economic and scientific, which would give them information for future economic development. The foundations had already been laid by Petty. It is at this time that the most remarkable natural feature of the Antrim Coast – the Giant's Causeway – first enters the literature.[2] I do not claim any knowledge of the background of the Causeway in Irish legend, or of how far back its associations with Fionn Mac Cuaill may go. Certainly the nearby fortresses of Dunluce and Dunseverick have been occupied since very ancient times. However, the Causeway is not marked on any of the early maps of Ireland, and does not figure in Petty's survey. The first mention of it in print is a letter from Sir Richard Bulkeley, Fellow of Trinity College, Dublin, to Sir Martin Lister, President of the Royal Society in London, dated 24 April 1693 and published in the Royal Society's *Philosophical Transactions* of that year. Bulkeley had not visited the site, and relied on a description supplied to him by an unnamed Cambridge graduate who had visited the Causeway with the Bishop of Derry during the previous summer. Consequently his account is rather inaccurate; for instance, he described the columns as vertical 'cylinders', all of a piece without any jointing. The next year, 1694, Bishop Samuel Foley of Down and Connor, who had visited the site, corrected Bulkeley's mistakes, publishing his own account in the *Philosophical Transactions* together with a long series of 'queries' by Dr Thomas Molyneux (1661-1733). This is illustrated by an engraving which is the earliest known picture of the Giant's Causeway. The drawing, a crude and misleading bird's eye view, was made by Christopher Cole of Coleraine, described by Foley as a 'collector in those parts'. Foley adds: 'He tells me he has not drawn the Causeway as a Prospect, nor as a Survey or Plaatform, which he thought would not answer his design, and that he has no other name for it but a Draught, which he took after this sort: He supposed the Hills and Causeway &c., Epitomised to the same height and bigness the Draught shews them, and this he fancied the most Intelligible way to express it'. Evidently Cole was an amateurish draughtsman struggling with a difficult subject which had never before been translated into graphic language. A letter from Cole among the Molyneux Papers in Trinity College Library suggests that he was aware of his limitations: 'The discripcon of the Cawsie dos not Please me Ile Draw it better by next Post & send it up with some thing Els that I designe for the Society'.

Though he did not visit the Causeway site until 1708, Thomas Molyneux devoted himself to a serious geological study of 'this mighty large pile of stony columns'. Realising the shortcomings of Cole's 'Draught', he set about commissioning a better one: 'Perceiving then I could not so well rely on the Draught of the Giant's Causeway that was first taken, and printed about four years since. . ..as, being by the Hand of one who was no extraordinary Artist, tho' the best that could then be had; I proposed the last summer to some Philosophical Gentlemen here in Dublin, that we should imploy, at the common charge, one Mr Sandys, a good Master in Designing and Drawing of Prospects, to go into the North of Ireland, and upon the Place take the genuine and accurate Figure of the whole Rock, with the natural Posture of the Hills and Country about it for some distance. Accordingly we sent him away with such instructions as I drew up for him, and he returned soon after with a fair and beautiful Draught very expressive of each Particular we desired; an exact Copy of which my Brother lately sent over to the Royal Society'.

The engraving after this drawing appeared, without any accompany text, in the *Philosophical Transactions* of December 1697. The draughtsman, Edwin Sandys (d.1708), was a Dublin engraver and cartographer. The engraving, however, would have been done in London by an engraver entirely unfamiliar with the subject. As the original drawing is lost, we have no idea how accurate Sandys' work was, but the engraved result leaves much to be desired. The Reverend William Hamilton, an able geologist writing in 1786, scoffed at it: 'Neither the talents nor fidelity of the artist seem to have been at all suited to the purpose of a philosophical landscape . . . in this true prospect, the painter has very much indulged his own imagination at the expense of his employers, insomuch that several tall pillars, in the steep banks of this fanciful scene, appear loaded with luxuriant branches, skirting the wild and rocky bay of Port Noffer with the gay exhibition of stately forest trees. In the background he discovered a parcel of rude and useless materials which his magic pencil soon transformed into comfortable dwelling houses; and for chimneys he has happily introduced some detached pillars of basaltes, which, from their peculiar situation, and the name given to them by the peasants of the country, naturally excited the attenton of this extraordinary artist. And thus were concluded the labours of the last century concerning this curious work of nature'.[3] Molyneux eventually visited the Causeway in 1708, taking with him the engraving after Sandys' drawing to compare on the spot. He observed: 'The Draught is pretty well as to the Cawsey itself, but not so Exact in the face of the Hill and the Organs or Looms as it should be; and indeed it does not represent ye Cawsey itself to run from the Hill as it does. I think it would be as necessary to have a plan of it as well as a prospect'.

This 'necessity' was not to be fulfilled for forty years, but the result was splendid. A Dubliner named Susanna Drury, of whom we know very little, visited the Causeway in 1740, and, according to Mrs Delany, 'lived three months near the place, and went almost every day'. In Hamilton's words 'Mrs Susanna Drury made two very beautiful and correct paintings of the Giant's Causeway, which obtained the premium appointed for the encouragement of arts in Ireland; and these drawings being soon after engraved by the hand of an eminent artist, and published, the attention of the world was once again directed toward this antiquated subject'. The pair of paintings won the premium of 25 pounds from the Dublin Society in 1740, and three years later they were engraved in London by Francois Vivares, one of the best of the many French Huguenot refugees who practically took over the engraving trade in London. Two versions are known, painted in gouache on vellum, not quite identical; one pair belongs to the Knight of Glin in Co. Limerick, the other pair was bought by the

Ulster Museum in 1971 and has recently been conserved. Drury's West Prospect of the Giant's Causeway, while sharing an identical viewpoint with Sandys' engraving, gives us much more accurate information about the appearance of the columns, the texture of the rock, and the configuration of the cliffs. It represents a major step forward in topographical and geological illustration. Susanna Drury had a real eye for basalt. Though she has taken some minor compositional liberties for pictorial purposes, the essential character of the site has been satisfactorily presented in graphic terms for the very first time.

The prints, as important in the history of topography as in the history of earth sciences, were circulated throughout Europe, and their beautiful quality gave them a place in the dispute among savants as to the nature of rocks themselves. This dispute is known as the Neptunist-Vulcanist controversy. The Neptunist faction was the conservative side. They believed in the accepted theory, dating back to the time of Thales, ca.500 BC, that all rocks, including granite and basalt, were chemical precipitates from some vast primaeval ocean. The leader of this school was Abraham Gottlob Werner, a teacher of great personality and influence, who in 1775 was appointed Professor of Mining at Freiberg in Saxony. The radical side was the Vulcanist faction, led by the French geologist Nicolas Desmarest, who believed that granite and basalt were extrusive volcanic lavas. In 1763 Desmarest identified in the Auvergne region of central France a sheet of columnar basalt and showed that it had flowed from the breached wall of what was obviously a volcanic cone; in 1771 he applied the same theory to the Giant's Causeway, using the Vivares engravings after Susanna Drury as his basis. He assumed that the hillside of Aird Snout was a volcanic cone, and that the Causeway lavas had flowed from it. Nevertheless, Desmarest's Vulcanist theory was eventually proved to be basically correct, though later modified by the Plutonist school, led by Professor James Hutton of Edinburgh, the father of modern petrology. The old Neptunist school did not go down without a fight, however. Its last stand was on the beach at Portrush. Here, the 'Portrush Rock' appeared to be a sheet of basalt full of ammonite fossils, and thus obviously aquatic in origin. It was subsequently identified as hornfels rather than basalt. But the Reverend Dr William Richardson, Rector of Clonfeacle, used it as late as 1808 to defend the Neptunist standpoint, with Scriptural authority, long after such ideas had lost ground in continental Europe.

One of the earlier Neptunists, Dr Richard Pococke (1704–65), who eventually became Bishop of Ossory and later Bishop of Meath, and who was famous mainly for his travels in the Middle East, visited the Causeway in 1747 and wrote: 'This Head does not appear at first so grand as it is represented in the views engraved of it; but when one comes to walk upon it, and consider it more attentively, it appears to be a stupendous Production of Nature'. He revisited it on his Irish tour in 1752, when he stayed with a man named Duncan at Ballymagarry, near Portrush. On this occasion Susanna Drury's brother, presumably the Dublin miniature painter Franklin Drury (d.1771), none of whose paintings is at present identified, helped Pococke by making models and maps. Pococke sent his description of the Causeway to the Royal Society in May 1753, sending with it '2 models of two stones represented in cork by Mr Drury'. A month later Pococke again wrote to the Royal Society from Dublin: 'This day Dr Drury brought me two maps of the Causeway, one a view from the top of the cliff, and the measures as he pac'd; the other from my measures by a line: in which the letters answer to those in the engraving after his sister's drawing. I have sent them to you, as Mr Folkes [sic: Martin Ffolkes, PRS] some time ago desired to know how far the Causeway extended into the sea. I have also sent you four drawings by Mr Drury, of two curious stones, which I brought to Dublin'. The two maps, engraved by J Mynde, were published in the *Philosophical Transactions* along with Pococke's letter.

II

In the field of eighteenth-century watercolour painting, the word 'amateur' is not necessarily a derogatory term. One of the most interesting of the many amateur draughtsmen and caricaturists of the late eighteenth century was John Nixon (ca.1750–1818). He was a son of Robert Nixon of Uphall near Linlithgow and Tokenhouse Yard, London, a merchant who traded with Ireland, and whose business John inherited along with his brother Richard. He seems to have had extensive business contacts in the north of Ireland. There is a photograph of a lost watercolour of Belfast from Friar's Bush Graveyard, of about 1781, in the R.J. Welch collection in the Ulster Museum, and Nixon visited Ireland nearly every year between 1785 and 1798, when presumably he was deterred by the aborted rebellion of the United Irishmen. In 1791 he accompanied the antiquarian Francis Grose to Ireland. The following year, he visited Bath with his friend Thomas Rowlandson, under whose influence Nixon became a very competent draughtsman. Henry Angelo says 'he could sketch a portrait, with a few scratches of his pencil, of a party whom he had not seen for twenty years, but with such marked traits of resemblance, as to be known at a glance'. Nixon's travels elsewhere were wide: he went to St Omer in 1783, to the Netherlands in 1784, to Scotland in 1790 and perhaps 1791, and to Paris during the break in the Napoleonic Wars in 1802–4. He also made annual tours in the south of England. He was a special juryman at the Guildhall and a Captain in the Guildhall Volunteers, was treasurer of the Sublime Society of Beefsteaks, and socialised with (and caricatured) actors and musicians. About 1973 Christie's in London obtained a very large collection of John Nixon drawings from the Huguenot Hospital of La Providence, now in Rochester, Kent, and they appeared in sales for some years.[4] The Ulster Museum was able to buy quite a number of these, including The Giant's Chair at the Causeway, County of Antrim (1790). The Giant's Chair is an isolated basalt stack. Aird Snout and the Giant's Loom can be seen in the middle distance, and the Skerries off Portrush in the far distance. Two local peasants are gathering seaweed, and what appears to be an artist sketching may be Nixon himself. The Ulster Museum's Department of Local History has the following Antrim Coast watercolours by John Nixon: *Rocky Headland, probably on the North Antrim Coast* (1782), *Carrickfergus taken from the Larne Road to Belfast* (1783), *Larne Harbour, Co Antrim* (1785), *The White House near the Cave Hills, Belfast, The White Rocks near Portrush and Glenarm, Co Antrim*. This last is one of the rare views of the Georgian Glenarm Castle, before it was baronialised by William Vitruvius Morrison in the 1820s.

Many of the professional topographical draughtsmen of the eighteenth century had to augment their income by working as drawing-masters, either in schools or in private practice. A good example of a peripatetic drawing master is John James Barralet (ca.1747–1815). Of Dublin Huguenot stock, Barralet was trained at the Dublin Society's School of Art and became a drawing master in Dublin, going to London about 1770. He returned to Dublin in 1779, and accompanied Gabriel Beranger on tours making antiquarian sketches for Francis Grose in Wicklow and Wexford in 1780. In 1982 the Ulster Museum acquired eight very interesting drawings, mostly in sepia, of Glenarm and its vicinity. They were bought in a paper folder inscribed 'Views of – from – or near / Glenarm – in 1787-88-89 -/ Mostly by Mr Barrales [sic] / artist and drawing master'. That they are not all by the same hand is confirmed by the fact that two of the dated drawings are dated 1796, a year after Barralet emigrated to Philadelphia. But the series gives ample evidence that Barralet worked at Glenarm during his perambulations as a drawing master. The remaining drawings in the group are presumably by Barralet pupils since they contain stylistic similarities, particularly in the handling of foliage. One drawing of Glenarm Harbour shows the corner of Glenarm Church on the left, and a working lime-kiln on the hillside on the right. This hillside has now almost been quarried away by lime workings. Another is entitled 'Marchioness of Antrim's Cottage, Glenarm Deer Park'. The Marquessate of Antrim became extinct on the death of the 6th Earl and 2nd Marquess on 29 July 1791. His widow, the Marchioness, lived on until 1801, and she appears to have had this garden retreat built in the form of a picturesque gothick 'cottage ornee'. Another is inscribed on the verso: 'North East View of Garron Point in the County of Antrim. Belvoir February / 2nd. 1794'. (The Knight of Glin has suggested that since Barralet did some work for the Duke of Rutland when he was Lord Lieutenant of Ireland, the name 'Belvoir' might refer to his Castle in Leicestershire rather than to Belvoir House in Belfast.) This shows the old coast road – the Foran Path – descending steeply on the north side of Garron Point, which in the 18th century was a formidable hazard for coaches travelling on the Antrim Coast. The old road climbed over the headlands. In 1801, Francis Turnly of Drumnasole near Garron Point bought the village of Cushendall, but continued to live at Drumnasole. In 1822, to ease his daily journey over Garron Point, he cut a road through the chalk to avoid the steep Foran Path. Still later, in 1833, William Bald built the present coast road as a military road to keep the lawless glensmen under control. Emigrating to America in 1795, Barralet settled in Philadelphia, where Redgrave states: 'though at first a great beau, he is said to have fallen into slovenly habits'. Iolo Williams's description of him as 'an inept and heavy handed, if ambitious artist' seems to be challenged by the quality of these Glenarm drawings.[5]

The north side of Belfast Lough is, of course, part of the Antrim Coast. An artist of considerable talent, Donald Stewart, who painted several quite ambitious watercolours of the Belfast shipyards during the first decade of the nineteenth century, is now a puzzlingly obscure figure. He may have been the 'D. Stewart' who exhibited in the Belfast Association of Artists in 1836. Armagh County Museum has a series of twenty-five small topographical drawings by him, including one of Fair Head. But the watercolours of Ritchie's Dock and the still rural slopes of Cave Hill, done between 1805 and 1810, are full of fascinating detail. Four are in the Ulster Museum and one belongs to the Belfast Harbour Office.[6] Engravings after Stewart also provided illustrations to William Hamilton Drummond's remarkable topographical poem, *The Giant's Causeway* (Belfast 1811), which unites imagery of mythical legend and of current scientific dispute.[7] They were reused to illustrate Hamilton's *Letters concerning the Northern Coast of the County of Antrim* in 1822.

This period between the disastrous 1798 Rebellion and the First Parliamentary Reform Act of 1830 is a most interesting one in the cultural history of Belfast. In a political vacuum, the industrious citizens resorted to radicalism and useful knowledge, culminating in the Belfast Natural History and Philosophical Society, founded in 1821. A tantalising piece of information is given by Anne Plumptre, an English Lady who toured Ireland in 1814 and 1815. On arriving in Belfast, she was given by Hamilton Rowan a letter of introduction to Dr James Macdonnell, one of the town's leading physicians, and an amateur mineralogist (also one of the Macdonnells of the Glens). 'In his possession I saw a collection of drawings of all the most remarkable points round the coast of Antrim, taken by an Italian, who went out repeatedly in a boat along the coast for this purpose. I examined them now with very great pleasure, as giving me an excellent idea of what I was going to see: I saw them with redoubled pleasure at my return to Belfast after having visited the several spots. They are taken with perfect accuracy, exhibiting a series of wonders of which those who have not seen any thing of the kind cannot form an idea'.[8] Incidentally, it was also in this decade that William Conybeare (later Dean of Westminster) and William Buckland (later first Professor of Geology at Oxford) published their *Descriptive Notes referring to the Outline of Sections presented by a Part of the Coasts of Antrim and Derry* (1816), illustrated by beautifully drawn and hand-coloured geological sections.[9]

To rediscover the series of Antrim Coast drawings by the unknown Italian would be a major find. We are fortunate, however, in having in the Ulster Museum a series of 113 watercolours of the Antrim Coast from Belfast to Portrush, painted in 1828 by a young man who was to become the leading Belfast landscape painter of the nineteenth century, Andrew Nicholl (1804–86). It is perhaps no coincidence that one of his early patrons was Dr James Macdonnell. These Antrim Coast views were painted when Nicholl was in his early twenties, apprenticed as a compositor with the Belfast printer Francis Dalzell Finlay, founder of *The Northern Whig*. There is a charming naivete and crispness about them reminiscent of aquatint illustrations. Nicholl's style underwent a radical change about 1830, when his most important patron, the politician James Emerson Tennent, took him to London.[10] There he copied Old Master paintings in the

Dulwich College Gallery, and was influenced by the living English painters Peter de Wint, Turner and Copley Fielding. His painting thus became more sophisticated, losing its untutored naivete. With this in mind it is instructive to compare early watercolours by Nicholl from the 1828 Antrim Coast series, with later, mature watercolour paintings by the same artist. For instance, there is the early *Giant's Causeway from the Stookans*, and a much larger later view from the same point, painted about 1840. In the earlier watercolour, the Causeway is presented literally and soberly, with no hint of the romantic exaggeration in style that Nicholl was later to acquire. The three strange little fashionably-dressed figures, placed dead centre in the foreground with their backs to the spectator, recall the work that Caspar David Friedrich was producing in Dresden at the same date, but this is, of course, purely coincidental. In contrast, *The Giant's Causeway from the West*, a watercolour of Nicholl's maturity, as well as being larger, is very different. In this view the height of the cliffs and of the Grand Causeway itself is greatly exaggerated, but Nicholl has acquired an impressive repertoire of atmospheric effects. The old woman selling whiskey by the fresh water spring ('The Giant's Well'), on the right, was a local character around the 1840s. Many tourists, including Thackeray, bought whiskey from her. Presumably the whiskey came from the Bushmills Distillery nearby, which claims to be the oldest distillery in existence.

Similarly, there are several early views of Dunluce Castle in the 1828 series which contrast completely with Nicholl's later, much larger and more dramatic watercolour of Dunluce. As Nicholl seldom dated his later work, his chronology is difficult, but I feel it is fairly safe to date this about 1840. In common with the contemporary traditions of romantic painting, Nicholl has now sacrificed topographical verisimilitude in favour of poetical expression. A number of landscapes with flowers in the foreground make Nicholl's most original and attractive productions. They probably all date from the 1830s when Nicholl was living in Dublin. Little attention should be paid to the signature with its 'RHA', as these letters appear on many of Nicholl's watercolours and were probably added later, not necessarily by Nicholl himself. Nicholl was not elected a full RHA until 1860. Examples of this type of Nicholl watercolour include one with Carrickfergus Castle, which was with the Leicester Galleries, London, in 1968; one with a view of The White Rocks at Portrush, belonging to the Knight of Glin; and one with a view of Downhill, Co Londonderry. In a private collection (reproduced on the cover of the Rosc exhibition catalogue *Irish Art of the 19th Century*, Cork,

Crawford Municipal Art Gallery Oct-Dec 1971). This shift from basic topography to romantic expression is seen also in the incomplete set of prints in which Nicholl collaborated: *Picturesque Sketches of some of the finest Landscape and Coast Scenery of Ireland from drawings by G. Petrie RHA, A. Nicholl and H. O'Neill*, published by W.F. Wakeman in Dublin in 1835. Nicholl was also an important member of the team of artists who illustrated the three-volume travel book *Ireland, its Scenery, Character etc*, by Mr and Mrs Samuel Carter Hall, published 1841–43. This contains over thirty-one engravings after Nicholl.

After 1840 Andrew Nicholl spent much of his time in London, and between 1846 and 1850 he worked as a drawing master in Colombo, Emerson Tennent, his patron, having been appointed Colonial Secretary for Ceylon. He left many former pupils behind in Belfast. It is likely that the foremost drawing master working in Belfast during Nicholl's absence was James Howard Burgess (ca.1817–90), who also worked on Halls' Ireland. At some time, probably in the 1850s or 1860s, Marcus Ward in Belfast published *Illustrations of the North of Ireland and Guide to the Giant's Causeway, from drawings made expressly for the work, by J.Howard Burgess, and containing a Guide Map, directions to Tourists, descriptions of Views and Tables of Distances*, with a lithographed title-page, and illustrations in steel-engraving. The Ulster Museum has a pastel of the Giant's Causeway by Burgess, and an impressive view of Waterfoot, taken from Red Bay Castle, looking up Glenariff, in which unfortunately the tinted paper has darkened, leaving the Chinese-white highlights standing out more stridently than the artist intended.

I think it is safe to claim that the most talented of Andrew Nicholl's many amateur pupils was Dr James Moore (1819–83), a medical graduate of Edinburgh who became a consultant surgeon at what was then called the Belfast Royal Hospital. Moore was a prolific watercolour sketcher from his student days, when he knew the Edinburgh painters, especially Sam Bough, with whom he kept a lifelong correspondence. The Ulster Museum has 14 albums containing 409 watercolour sketches, made all over Britain and part of Europe between 1836 and 1882. Moore exhibited large gallery-watercolours in Belfast and Dublin, and was elected an Honorary RHA in 1868. But the small spontaneous sketches appeal much more to contemporary taste as well as being topographically interesting. Unlike Nicholl, Dr Moore was in the habit of meticulously dating his work, sometimes even down to the time it took him to complete the sketch. He has been described (by John Vinycomb in 1907) as 'certainly the most thoroughly realistic and truthful portrayer of Nature that Belfast has produced, professional or otherwise'. He was at the height of his artistic powers around 1856, when he painted a beautiful small watercolour study of Glenarm, displaying a sense of recession and damp atmosphere with an effortless assurance never matched by his master Nicholl. Some of Moore's sketches of the 1840s and 50s seem even to anticipate the 'moving crowd' paintings made by Monet and Renoir in the 1870s, and one is tempted to wonder whether, on any of his numerous professional medical trips to Paris, he ever encountered the Impressionists. Moore also painted some lively views of Fair Head, Ballycastle and the Giant's Causeway, which remind us that he was yet another amateur geologist, and a member of the Wernerian Society of Edinburgh University.[11]

From the late 18th century a number of English artists had come to Ireland in search of picturesque subject matter, as they had gone to Wales, the Lake District and Scotland. Ireland's two main areas for the 'picturesque tour' were Wicklow (easy reach of Dublin) and Killarney, but a few adventurous personalities found their way to the northern coast. Francis Towne's pupils, Sir George Bulteel Fisher and John Baverstock Knight, visited and sketched the Antrim Coast about 1800. In the mid-nineteenth century, William Andrews Nesfield made some very spirited gouache paintings in the region of the Causeway and Dunluce Castle. Clarkson Stanfield must have visited the area; the Ulster Museum has a small oil painting by him, *The Stack Rock*, dated 1861. A significant image of the Antrim Coast produced by an English artist in the nineteenth century is the Ulster Museum's large watercolour of Glenarm by Henry Gastineau, dated 1859. Gastineau (1791/2–1876), like W.H. Bartlett, Thomas Creswick and others, was one of the English artists who provided illustrations for Halls' *Ireland* in the early 1840s. This view of Glenarm is the best example the Museum has of the Victorian 'gallery watercolour', in its heavy gilt frame, having an effect which is shamelessly imitative of oil-painting, particularly of Turner's Italian views such as the *Bay of Baiae*. The view is taken from the old road from Larne to Glenarm, entering the village steeply down the street known as 'the Vennel'. Though all the buildings are identifiable, Gastineau has taken liberties with the topography, and bathed the whole scene in hazy, shimmering Italianate light. It is interesting to contrast this with James Moore's soberly factual watercolour sketch from the same viewpoint.

It would be unthinkable to discuss the iconography of the Antrim Coast without mentioning the remarkable photographs taken by the

Belfast photographer Robert John Welch (1859–1956). From an early age, Welch travelled throughout Ireland with his father, also a professional photographer, who died in 1875 leaving his son as the family breadwinner. Thus Welch had to forego his ambition of entering Queen's University and taking a degree. However, the collection of negatives he gradually built up should be regarded as one of Ireland's National Treasures. Bequeathed by Welch to the Belfast Naturalists' Field Club, of which he was a devoted lifelong member, the collection of photographs was passed to the Ulster Museum. The subjects cover a wide range – antiquities, folk-life, buildings, industry, botany and geology. It is principally the geological photographs which concern us here. Taken mainly during the 1880s and 1890s with a cumbersome full-plate camera, Welch's sharp images of Fair Head and the Causeway have never been bettered, and are still used as illustrations for geological textbooks. There is one close up study of the tesselated pavement of the Causeway, with sea water lying in the depressions, which gives the lie to the popular supposition that the Causeway consists of regular hexagons. There is also a photograph of the cliffs of Port Noffer with the red lateritic inter-basaltic bed picked out in red ink. But perhaps the image which catches the imagination is one of Welch himself, perched precariously in his stockinged feet on the isolated basalt column which straddles the Grey Man's Path above Fair Head. This was taken about 1892, Welch having bribed a local village boy to remove the lens-cap and take the exposure.[12]

From the foundation of the Belfast Ramblers' Sketching Club in 1879, and that club's gradual metamorphosis until its emergence as the Royal Ulster Academy of Arts in 1950[13], there has been no lack of pictorial material portraying the coast and glens of Antrim. Indeed, one may say that there has been a surfeit. The reason is clear. Ulster has produced a prosperous middle class with money to spare, and who require pictures to decorate their homes. With such variety of natural scenery on the doorstep, who needs to look farther afield? Painters such as the Carey brothers, James Humbert Craig, Frank McKelvey, Maurice Wilks and many more found their material in the Glens of Antrim as well as Donegal and the Mournes, all favourite holidaying places (and country cottage locations) for the Belfast bourgeoisie. I am not denigrating this sort of painting. Craig, McKelvey and their kind were very able craftsmen-painters. What they painted was immediately understandable to the public they targeted, posing no intellectual challenge. Their material was pleasant, relaxing and easily saleable, and artists have to make a living. But such painting easily fell into an oft-repeated convention. Some painters, influenced by international modernism, tried to escape from this. John Luke in the 1930s painted some studies in the neighbourhood of Larne and Glynn which are strongly influenced by the primary colours of the French fauves. Romeo Toogood, who taught at the Art School in Belfast, produced a memorable and still-popular sunlit painting of Dan Nancy's Brae, Cushendall, in 1933. Later, in the 1950s, the versatile Colin Middleton painted some near abstract paintings inspired by the scenery and buildings of Carnlough. These images extend the iconographic possibilities of the region.

It is curious that during the last two decades of the most scientifically advanced age in the history of the world, some artists have been eager to look for symbolism in the landscape features of the Antrim Coast, particularly in the Giant's Causeway. In 1974 the highly influential German sculptor, teacher, performance artist and cult-figure Joseph Beuys (1921–86), one of the founders of the Green Party, visited Northern Ireland in conjunction with an exhibition[14], and gave a three-hour lecture in the Ulster Museum. I was present at this, seated directly behind Francis Stuart, the novelist, and the late John Hewitt, who seemed unimpressed. As part of this same visit Beuys, wearing his invariable trilby hat and long fur-lined overcoat, was filmed walking on the columns of the Giant's Causeway, a memorable image. Beuys saw in the Causeway columns a symbol of political integration for the divided people of Ulster. Such a simplified symbol of intersecting regular hexagons is used as a logo by the trade union to which I as a museum curator belong, the Northern Ireland Public Service Alliance (NIPSA). Well-meaning as is the intention, the symbol is superficial and unscientific. In physical terms the Causeway columns represent a crack-pattern – disintegration rather than integration. This is realised by a much younger painter, Mickey Donnelly, who has for some time been using the Giant's Causeway in his paintings – often on a large scale – primarily for its symbolic significance. Alongside other popular Ulster insignia of division – red hands, shamrocks, Easter lilies, Orange lilies – the message of disintegration appears inevitable. Donnelly, however, also recognises and is fascinated by the inherent ambiguity of symbols. The Easter lily, for instance, is an ancient symbol of male potency as well as an emotive Nationalist emblem. All this goes to illustrate, once again, the complexity of iconographic possibilities that this richly pictorial landscape can inspire.

CHAPTER 4

Settlement and Society in Eighteenth-Century Ireland

by

Kevin Whelan

'Is ar scath a chile a mhaireann na daoine'

The eighteenth century has long been neglected by historical geographers. No doubt this is largely due to the fact that it is a century which lacks major benchmark surveys, comparable to the Civil or Down Survey maps for the seventeenth, and the Griffiths Valuation and Ordnance Survey maps for the nineteenth. Accordingly, although detailed analyses now exist for these two centuries, the eighteenth century is largely a silent one in historical geographical discourses. Yet its significance is undeniable: Cullen observes that 'The Irish man-made landscape is essentially one of the eighteenth century.'[1]

This essay is a preliminary attempt to bridge the hiatus, and special attention is paid to linking up the seventeenth- and nineteenth-century work. The focus is sharply on the interrelationship between society and settlement, especially as this is revealed in the landscape. Settlement is treated here in a broad sense as a text, a multi-layered document, full of human intentionality, a culture code which embodies different levels of meaning. Couched in these terms, the study of settlement can move away from the cold facts of land and landscape and engage with a much warmer and broader spectrum of meanings. In this view settlement is both medium and message, site and symbol, terrain and text.

To penetrate the eighteenth and nineteenth centuries we must begin by discarding two of the most venerable concepts in Irish historical geography, particularly associated with Estyn Evans. Firstly, he cast Irish society in the eighteenth and nineteenth centuries into a monolithic 'peasant framework'. Inevitably, this formulation biased work on Ireland towards the small farm world of the Atlantic fringe and west Ulster which best approximated the 'peasant model'. A second formulation was that this 'peasant' world was fundamentally a timeless one, a little tradition which endured through the centuries and underlying continuities of which lay with remote prehistory. Thus by intensive fieldwork in modern western, especially north-western, areas, one could recover intact an immemorial, aboriginal settlement pattern. Prolific, persuasive and accessible, Evans' work popularised this conceptualisation of Irish society, especially in the West, as an ancient peasant survival, a great European refuge area on the rim of the continent, preserving forms which had long disappeared at the centre. By studying these timeless survivals in the modern world, one could trace the whole sweep of Irish settlement from its genetic origins in prehistory.

The clachan or rundale village in the nineteenth century was especially to be found in these marginal refuge areas, typically in mountain ranges, bogs, peninsulas and other lonely, isolated and poor areas. Examined in general terms, the distribution of clachans was one of eastern and southern removal, northern and especially western survival. In this sense, the west retained the oldest and most basic elements in the Irish settlement network, and provided a living museum of what conditions had once been like all over the country. Evans could therefore make statements like the following: 'Conventional history is at a loss where, as in the west of Ireland, history and prehistory seem to co-exist and all time is foreshortened into a living present'; 'For many years, I have studied archaeological and ethnographic evidence for the early diffusion and secular persistence of a cultural pattern which had its origins in pre-Celtic antiquity and which proved capable of absorbing and assimilating new elements brought in by successive intrusions, whether Celtic warriors, Christian missionary or Anglo-Norman Knight'.[2]

Those postulations by Evans and his followers have been undermined by more recent work. In a devastating critique, John Andrews challenged the anthropogeographic methodology because of its fundamentally ahistoric chronological approach, its ethnic stereotyping and its unwarranted assumption (rather than demonstration) of millennial continuities.[3] Simultaneously, a series of papers by Tom Jones Hughes quietly killed the 'peasant model' of pre-famine Ireland. He showed that the peasant scenario elided class differences by ignoring the intense social stratification of pre-famine Irish life. Jones Hughes substituted an approach which highlighted the regional dynamics and settlement effects of this social stratigraphy. In so doing, he established (long before the idea became fashionable among historians) that pre-famine Ireland was not an undifferentiated mass of unrelieved poverty and that class, itself determined by broader economic forces, was the key to understanding settlement history in the post-seventeenth-century period. In one of the most incisive paragraphs ever published in Irish historical geography, Jones Hughes commented on Evans' favoured far-west fringes:

> Yet we must not overemphasise the significance of these places as the ultimate conservatories of Gaelic culture at least as far as the material aspects of that culture are concerned. Collectively they represented one of the poorest and most inaccessible parts of western Europe and it is certain that most of them only experienced close and permanent settlement by farming people at a very late date and that these late colonisers were probably refugees evicted from adjoining more desirable regions. Consequently, during the eighteenth and nineteenth centuries, these barren lands were savagely carved up into diminutive lots to satisfy the most primitive needs of despairing communities, so that we must look in vain here for any surviving traces of the genetic elements of the modern Irish rural landscape.[4]

From the ruins of these earlier conceptualisations, it is imperative to build a new model of the nature of the historical geography of eighteenth-century Ireland. The framework of such a model can be built from an interlocking series of regional archetypes based on economic, social and settlement criteria. These archetypes—recurring themes in the text of landscape—allow a more nuanced approach to the study of the period. Five archetypes emerge: pastoral with cattle fattening and dairying components, tillage, small farm, proto-industrial, and urban.

Archetype One: Pastoralism

The pastoral tradition in Ireland has been primarily orientated towards cattle, although sheep have been locally and periodically important. Ireland has a comparative European advantage of fat cattle production. Accordingly, once the focus of sea-borne trade moved decisively towards the Atlantic in the seventeenth century, Ireland's role in the provisions trade blossomed. It was simultaneously integrated into the expanding English mercantilist economy, and the rapid development of the north Atlantic commercial world opened rapacious markets for livestock products. These twin markets generated an export-orientated agricultural sector. The English market was catered to by the export of live cattle and created few forward or backward linkages. The Atlantic market was for beef and butter, products which sustained economic diversification.

Permanent pasture in Ireland, closely tied to a limestone base, had twin cores in north-east Leinster and in inner Connaught (mid-Roscommon on the celebrated plains of Boyle, east Mayo and east Galway). In between the two cores there was a third zone, waxing and waning in response to price fluctuations and located in the confused midland counties, where good and bad land alternated promiscuously in the bogs and meadows of Offaly, Longford and Westmeath. This fattening area pulsed and subsided from its heartlands, allowing the identification of aggressive and recessive phases in the history of Irish pastoralism.

Before the re-orientations of the Irish woollen industry by English mercantilist acts in the late seventeenth century, sheep were expanding on the dry pastures of counties Tipperary, Roscommon, east Galway and Carlow; by the 1760s, the surge in tillage was pushing the ewes and the bullocks back into more restricted areas. In the post-Napoleonic period, the bullock reasserted itself. In settlement terms, the seventeenth- and early eighteenth-century pastoral expansion had erosive effects on old village structures in the areas which it was colonising. The concentration of deserted villages in the pastoral transition zone hints that the desertion phase was in this period (not the late medieval as has been frequently suggested). Deserted sites are concentrated precisely in this pastoral expansion zone—a triangle linking counties Limerick, Carlow and Roscommon.

The transition from an intensive tillage to an extensive pastoral economy may have dissolved old villages. Displacement of village-based tillage farmers (scullogues or gneevers in seventeenth-century parlance) was achieved via the leasing mechanism; if cattle prices were sufficiently high, grazing could simply outbid tillage. From as far away as county Sligo, Charles O'Hara provides a clinical dissection of this process in the 1720s. 'By the year 1720, the demands for store cattle for the south had reached us, and the breeding business grew more profitable. Many villages were turned off and the lands which they had occupy'd stocked with cattle. Some of these village tenants took mountain farms but many more went off and I shall fix 1726 for the period of the change for it was in that year that the graziers encouraged by the markets first raised the price of land in order to cant the cottagers out of their farms'.[5] From County Mayo at the end of the eighteenth century, McParlan observed that 'grazing drives the natives away from the fertile fields into the swamps and mountains'.[6]

In the cattle fattening areas, the grazier holdings became the cornerstone of leasing policy and therefore of the settlement pattern. A grazier (frequently an absentee) held a very large grassland farm, poorly enclosed, devoted solely to cattle fattening. A resident herdsman looked after the cattle. As leases were assigned by the townland, graziers usually held a townland, or series of townlands, in this manner. At the apogee of their success, Tipperary graziers like the McCarthys in the Glen of Aherlow held almost 14,000 acres and the Sculls of the Golden area held twenty townlands in this fashion.[7]

Given its extensive mode of land use, the grazier economy created a desolate landscape with an attenuated social structure and only rudimentary settlement forms, where the lonely box-Georgian grazier houses were punctuated by the crude cabins of the herdsmen. These grazier holdings developed on the better limestone soils and were frequently juxtaposed with small farms, cluster-based settlements on adjacent marginal hilly or boggy ground. This pattern, evident in the 1749 census of the diocese of Elphin, was driven by the ruthless efficiency of the leasing mechanism. In this manner, the Irish paradox of an inverse relationship between population pressure and good land was established.

The close juxtaposition of the two systems also helps explain why houghing (the maiming of cattle) became prevalent as a form of social protest—a moral economy pitting itself against a commercial one. The first agrarian secret society in Ireland, the Houghers, evolved precisely in this fashion, in the east Connaught area undergoing the transition from plough to cow in the early eighteenth century. Be that as it may, the silent, empty world of grazing bullocks was one of the most striking regional variants in eighteenth-century Ireland elsewhere so often a noisy, crowded, complex society.

The areas of fat cattle production in Connaught and Leinster were predominantly geared to supplying live cattle to the English market. By contrast, Atlantic markets swallowed Irish beef and butter. There were two components in Irish-American trade, one directed to the West Indies, the other to the North American mainland. Once the Caribbean islands moved to a widespread sugar monoculture in the mid-1660s, provisions had to be imported to feed the planters. The Munster provision trade between 1670 and 1720 was the main source of food. The Barbados governor in 1675 observed about Ireland that it was 'from thence we feed so many mouths as must be used in the management of the sugaries'.[8] In the Caribbean trade, Ireland's comparative advantage lay in its ability to organise the agricultural resources into sophisticated food producing and packaging industries that effectively complemented the West Indian sugar industry, itself the most aggressively expanding sector of the colonial economy. This was augmented by the growth of the victualling trades and the shipment of beef and butter, both to the continent and to the Atlantic economies.

All these developments exerted a positive influence on dairying and cattle rearing and the export trade fostered the rise of an indigenous mercantile class. These flows reinforced the major ports of the east and south, especially Cork and Waterford, which commanded rich, wide hinterlands, accessible by navigable river systems.[9] Both ports were at the cutting edge of the Atlantic economy, which allowed them to achieve a deep market penetration across every stratum of rural society in their riverine hinterland. These hinterlands became the most prosperous agricultural regions in eighteenth- and early nineteenth-century Ireland, accompanied by the six-fold growth of rents between 1700 and 1800, the commercialisation of dairying and cattle rearing, and by the sharpening and deepening of the social stratigraphy.

The dairyman system was the distinctive feature of the rural economy of mid-Munster, especially in the Lee and Blackwater valleys, and was developed around the Cork butter market, one of the largest in contemporary Europe. Commercialised dairying in this region can be traced from the 1660s, although it is still unclear whether the dairyman system itself is of Gaelic or west country English origin. The system involved the practice of leasing twenty to forty cows to dairymen, in return for a butter rent. The dairymen disposed of calves and had some other perquisites, to make the venture profitable for him. Like the graziers, the dairy owner was a head tenant, and at the apex of the system could be a *fear míle bó* (a man of 1,000 cows). The celebrated Art O'Laoghaire is a good example of the social and cultural milieu of this social layer. In its phase of aggressive expansion in the mid-eighteenth century, dairying displaced the joint tenancy, small tillage farmers (or gneevers in Munster terminology), and Rev. James Mockler, a Protestant clergyman, described the process in 1775.[10]

The influence of dairying peaked between 1750 and 1770, literally losing ground thereafter to a resurgent commercialised tillage farming. Dairying enjoyed a second efflorescence in the late nineteenth century in the same area, based on the spread of co-operative dairying. In general, the mid-Munster dairying zone from the seventeenth to the twentieth centuries has been a resilient and innovative area, a backbone of radical conservatism which underpinned the emerging nation-forming class.[11]

However, it is important with both the fattening and dairying components of commercialised pastoralism not to reify these archetypes, nor to privilege their autonomy. Both zones had numerous and essential linkages to the small farm world which lay beyond or above them. Calves were the currency of exchange; they were gradually filtered east and south as they grew older. The intense commercialisation of these transactions is manifested in the prevalence of cattle fairs, which linked up the rearing and the fattening dairy area. The largest fairs—Ballinasloe (one of the three largest in Europe), Banagher, Athlone, Mullingar, Knockcroghery—were those best positioned to act as hinges: numerous minor ones (1,500 fair sites were operational at some stage between 1600 and 1800) lubricated the west-east movement. As commercialisation intensified under the hothouse effect of the Atlantic provisions trade, fair sites mushroomed. Fairs were crucial in articulating a nationwide economy.

The essential symbiotic linkages between small farm and large farm also effectively demolished the old 'two Irelands' concept, based with mistaken clarity on the differentiation between a commercialised 'east' and a subsistence 'west' in the pre-famine Irish economy. If such an idea had any conceptual validity, it was in a vertical (social) not horizontal (spatial) stratification.

Archetype Two—Tillage

The second great archetype is tillage—essentially mixed farm but with a specialisation in intensive commercial tillage. Built out of the environmentally favoured Anglo-Norman coastlands, the tillage zone waxed strongly in the second half of the eighteenth century, kickstarted by bounties on the transport of flour to Dublin (from 1758) and then accelerating as European demand soared in the Napoleonic period.

By the late eighteenth century, the tillage zone was concentrated in the south-east of the country, largely within a triangle linking Cork, Dundalk and Wexford. In the pre-mechanised era, tillage farms, as a labour intensive mode of production, were much smaller than their pastoral counterparts. Tillage areas therefore had a tighter settlement framework, with a fine mesh of farms, fields, fences, villages and towns. In old tillage areas, this settlement infrastructure predated the eighteenth century. In 1683, an observer described the

Barony of Forth in south County Wexford. 'The whole Barony at a distance viewed in times of harvest represents a well cultivated garden, with diversified plots.'[12] Given more complex economic functions, tillage areas had a fuller social structure than their skeletal pastoral equivalents, with artisans especially evident. Landlordism was also considerably more muted in the tillage farm system which was much more difficult to regulate than the grazier system. Accordingly, estate owners in tillage areas tended to be marginalised into a rent-collecting, intermarrying superstructure. As a result, settlement in tillage areas exhibited more continuity than in pastoral areas. Tillage towns were bustling places, unlike pastoral ones where the intermittent cattle fair was the prime lifeline.

However, the most salient point about the commercialisation of the tillage economy was the spectacular increase in the number of agricultural labourers. Many of these were accommodated as cottiers, labourers who were given a cabin and a potato garden (up to one acre) in return for their labour. The farmer supplied dung for the garden, and the potato was an ideal precursor to the subsequent cereal crop. Expansion in the tilled area was achieved by expanding the number of cottiers. This created a cottier necklace around the perimeter of the tillage farms, the social dichotomy mirrored in the micro-segregation. Bell described the process in 1804: 'The master never fed a labourer of this description [cottier]. It was on the contrary a chief object with him to keep such a person as far away from his dwelling as possible. He therefore allowed him to occupy, at some remote corner of his farm, a miserable hut, a mere shell, formed of mud or sods, without loft, apartment or partition and sometimes without any other covering than that of straws or without any other chimney than the door. In one corner of this hovel lodged his cow, while in the opposite corner were his wife and children and himself.'[13] On large farms (over thirty hectares) the dependent cottier houses could run to double figures. The cottier necklace was the main form of settlement for agricultural labourers, but one could also find straggles of cabins along roads or lanes (equidistant between two farms), in dishevelled crossroads clusters, in shanties on the edge of towns and villages, or piling up in the back lanes.

Irish society therefore evolved from a seventeenth-century colonial status where social differences among native occupiers was limited, to a situation where the farmer/labourer split became decisive, especially in the more developed regions.

However, as well as great poverty, tillage areas also sustained agriculturally based industries which invigorated the towns in the late eighteenth century—mills, breweries, malthouses, distilleries. After the bounties for transport of flour to the Dublin market were instituted in 1758, large scale flour milling expanded in the 1760s and the 1770s, with mid- and south Kilkenny (valleys of the Kings river and the Nore) acting as an innovative area in technology and intensification. As a result, Dublin's grain hinterland shifted south, allowing south Meath and north Kildare to revert to pastoralism. Breweries, distilleries and malthouses also sprang up in response to a vibrant local agricultural economy. By 1796, Wexford town alone had 210 malthouses and in 1797 the town employed one hundred small ships in carrying malt to Dublin.[14]

Taken together, the tillage, dairying and fattening zones comprised the large farm world of eighteenth- and early nineteenth-century Ireland. Jones Hughes has plotted 7,200 farms of 100 pounds plus rating (in the Griffith Valuation) and their distribution pattern shows the crucial components in the emergence of modern Ireland.[15] In the post-famine period, selective emigration bled the agricultural labourer class dry and tenant proprietorship led to the legislative euthanasia of the landlord class; only the big farmer endured. One should therefore stress the strong elements of stability and continuity represented by these large farmers; there are very suggestive parallels between their 1850 distribution and that of the late medieval towerhouses. There may also be much stronger familial and therefore cultural, social and political continuity than has hitherto been suspected, as has been recently demonstrated for County Wexford.[16] However, a deceptively homogeneous landscape often concealed the social cleavages of Ireland, due to a Gaelic cultural tradition which did not lay a heavy emphasis on conspicuous consumption. The hurrying traveller, passing rapidly through the roadside raggle-taggle of miserable cabins, was overwhelmed by images of poverty; he failed to notice the discreet, but comfortable, world of the strong farmers, embedded in the centre of their farms, and insulated from the perimeter of poverty around them. The seat behind the coachman was therefore a biased one in pre-famine Ireland. It is in this broad sense, perhaps, that one should interpret the concept of the 'Hidden Ireland.' Corkery's twin insistence on approaching it only from the evidence of Gaelic poetry and on locating it largely in west Munster is misleading. The real 'Hidden Ireland' of the eighteenth century was not incarnated in the *cos-mhuintir*, the proliferating poverty-stricken base of the social pyramid, nor in the flamboyant but restricted world of the Munster middlemen; the custodians of tradition were the comfortable, Catholic, strong farm class (a Norman-Gaelic hybrid) of south Leinster and east Munster, who provided stability and continuity.[17]

Archetype Three: Small Farming

The large farm world can be contrasted with that dominated by small-scale family farms, the area that best approximates the 'peasant' model promulgated by Evans. Even then the small farm or peasant world explored by Evans and his followers was of limited extent in pre-famine Ireland. This small farm zone had two main components, the drumlin belt and the ragged fringe stretching from west Donegal to west Cork along the peninsular reaches of Atlantic Ireland. It is imperative to note that this small farm world was a spatially restricted one. It was never the dominant archetype, even at the height of its extent on the eve of the famine. Contrary to Evans' postulated continuities, large swathes of this small farm world were essentially new phenomena, a response to the surging demographic profile of Ireland between 1600 and 1840, which saw its population soar from one to eight and a half million. This explosion necessitated massive reclamation, intense subdivision and expansion into previously unsettled areas, aided by the potato's propensity to flourish even in wet, thin, nutrient-poor soils. In this sense, much of the drumlin and Atlantic region was only heavily settled as an outreach product of unrestrained population growth. Some of the classic small farm communities can trace their origins to the eighteenth century. Rann na Feirste, in Evans' favoured Rosses, was first permanently settled in 1750. Only the potato, the rundale village and hand tool cultivation allowed these areas to be won for farming people. In a settlement sense, much of the west of Ireland was but newly settled, an adventitious and desperate veneer born out of unprecedented demographic circumstances.

The demographic setting was one of continuously expanding population, initiated in the seventeenth century, but accelerating in the second half of the eighteenth century and first half of the nineteenth century. In the relatively sealed social system of the west of Ireland such growth was absorbed locally, despite the inherent danger of overloading the carrying capacity of the environment. The development of the rundale system can be seen as a safety valve in this high pressure demographic regime. The massive labour input required to cultivate the poor quality land of the outfield was only feasible in a period of population growth. Co-operative management, agreed land use and a joint labour system for certain tasks were a sophisticated ecological adjustment to using a fragile environment, where technology and capital were limited but labour was unrestricted. Hand tool cultivation (spade and sickle) was universal and the garden-like cultivation technique of *iomairí* (lazy beds) was used universally.

The use of the spade was also essential in this reclamation. The spade was a flexible and efficient tool; its use considerably increased yields over and above those gained from horse-ploughing. It allowed steep, irregular or inaccessible slopes to be cultivated, and was extremely well adapted to local conditions as studies of regional variety in spade type have shown. The considerable energy costs necessitated by spade cultivation of marginal land were absorbed by population growth. In a sense, then, as Dodgshon has shown in similiar circumstances in Highland Scotland, increased population became its own resource and a form of self exploitation was practised in creating the extraordinary lazybed landscapes of the west of Ireland.[18]

The instrument of colonisation was the potato, whose tolerance of wet and acidic conditions alone made possible the fruitful tilling of these areas. The potato was an excellent reclamation agent and it paved the way for further crops. Asenath Nicholson described the scene near Roundstone in 1845, emphasising the role of the potato:

> The poor peasants, men, women and children were gathering seaweed, loading their horses, asses and backs with it, to manure the wretched little patches of potatoes sown among the rocks. 'Three hundred and sixty two days a year we have the potato', said a young man to me bitterly 'the blackguard of a Raleigh who brought them here entailed a curse upon the labourer that had broke his heart. Because the landholder sees we can live and work hard on them, he grinds us down in our ways and he despises us because we are ignorant and ragged'.[19]

Rundale villages or clachans are not the degraded relics of an archaic, aboriginal settlement form, practising primitive agriculture in 'refuge areas'. They are instead a sophisticated solution to specific ecological, environmental and social problems, which maximised the carrying capacity of a meagre environment in an expanding demographic regime. They are well-judged adaptations to marginal situations. Indeed, the rundale villages acted as a type of mobile pioneer fringe; the spade and the spud conquered the contours as the limits of cultivation rose from ca. 500 feet to ca. 900 feet between 1650 and 1840. Given the extent of marginal land in Ireland (even in 1840 an estimated 30% of the land source was uncultivated) and given the efficiency of the rundale villages as a means of colonising such land, the marginality of the distribution becomes immediately intelligible. It also explains why they were so absent from good land, where such a system was unnecessary.

While much of the settlement in these marginal west coast lands is late, one must recognise that pockets of older settlements existed there. A useful distinction can be drawn between the 'old' and the 'new' west. The old west consisted of those parts of the Atlantic seaboard which had known continuous intensive settlement prior to the eighteenth century, areas like Corca Dhuibhne, the head of Galway Bay and the Burren in County Clare. Finally, one should also note that the west of Ireland had undoubtedly known previous settlement spasms but these had been shortlived, as they had breached environmental equilibria, initiated ecological regression and were eventually abandoned. One such surge was in the neolithic (best known from the Ceide fields project); another was in the early Christian period. The potato and rundale village phase of settlement was ultimately pathological and fell victim to the fragile ecological base with its limited recuperative potential. The essential point is that the 'new' west did not in any meaningful terms have a continuous settlement history from the prehistoric period onwards. On this reading, much of the west of Ireland landscape represents ecological catastrophe on a large scale.

Archetype Four: Proto-Industrialisation

Beef and butter were two of the great Irish exports of the eighteenth century. Linen was the third. The growth of the Ulster linen industry to be among the world's leading half dozen industries by 1800 was based on a number of factors.[20] Ulster landlords in the late seventeenth century became aware that their agricultural production suffered edaphic, climatic and locational disadvantages; they were therefore keen to encourage their tenants to diversify their production so as to keep rentals buoyant. Ulster, unlike Scotland, for example, could grow its own flax and thereby integrate linen production in a controlled fashion. Landlords and central government encouraged the rapid development of an efficient marketing system, which allowed independent farmer-weavers to flourish. This lent flexibility and resilience to Irish production methods as opposed to the more urban-based, putting-out system prevalent elsewhere. Irish linens were cheaper to produce in a low labour cost environment and the link to Dublin-London financial services plus their custom-free status in Britain gave them a competitive advantage.

Linen production soared in these propitious circumstances, sustained by technological, infrastructural and organisational innovation. The end product was an immense proto-industrial system. As elsewhere in Europe, this was accommodated by subdivision of leaseholdings, intense population growth and the incorporation of women and children into the workforce. The Ulster countryside was festooned with myriad small farmer-weaver holdings, especially within the linen triangle of Belfast, Dungannon and Newry. In turn, this area created a prosperous aureole of agricultural production (oats, cattle, potatoes and turf) which also supplied yarn to the spinning zones. This aureole arched from north Connaught to north Leinster and fell within the broad Belfast hinterland.

Intensification of agricultural production via small, diligently laboured family farms triggered massive demographic growth. By 1770, there were 42,000 weavers in Ulster; by 1820 at the height of the proto-industrial phase, this had reached 70,000. In 1821, Ulster's population of two million was greater than the total population of Scotland. Population densities were very heavy: County Armagh had over 500 per square mile by 1841. Linen production was especially suited to inferior land such as the difficult drumlin country of south Ulster. This adaptation to poor land is illustrated by the inability of the linen industry to make any impression on the fertile fattening lands of north Leinster. The spread of the farmer-weaver had one other often disregarded side effect: it obliterated the large farmer in Ulster. By 1841 the average farm size in County Armagh was five acres and by 1850 only ten percent of the total number of large farms in Ireland were in that province. Yet, Ulster remained a province where the landlord influence was strong, especially in the east.

Thus, nineteenth-century Ulster ended up in the anomalous position of being a province of great estates but small farms. The success of the linen industry promoted commercialisation. A 1792 pamphleteer observed: 'We may justly say that the county of Armagh is a hotbed for cash for the industrious farmer and weaver'.[21] The industry therefore ensured the continued vitality of its towns, to which the brown linen markets were a major fillip. By 1800, Belfast's future glory was not yet adumbrated; only with the industrialisation of linen and with the rise of cotton production did Belfast centralise the Ulster economy around itself, and push back Dublin's hinterland.

Crawford's investigations have elucidated the complex internal geography of this proto-industrial macro-region.[22] In the period from 1780 to 1820 four distinct sub-regions can be identified within the linen-producing area. The quality of linen in these four regions varied widely. Only the fine product of the linen triangle was capable of adapting easily to factory production (and in particular to mill-spun yarn). The coarser linens of the other regions were rendered technologically obsolescent and were killed off by the influx of cheap industrial textiles from Belfast and the British cotton manufacturers.

This microcosmic approach satisfactorily explains how the Ulster linen industry in the 1780–1820 period could simultaneously industrialise and de-industrialise. Crawford's recent work has also demolished the influential thesis of Conrad Gill's *The Rise of the Irish Linen Industry* that in the 1760s the Ulster industry moved from a primitive cottage (proto-industrial) phase to a modern capitalist factory-based phase, and that the transition was signalled by the advent of the putting-out system. In fact, the independent farmer weaver working through the vibrant brown linen markets flourished right through the whole span of the century; no extensive putting-out system ever developed, except in highly specialised sectors like damask production. Crawford's conclusions explain why such a dense pattern of small farms persisted in south Ulster and especially in County Armagh. It also has devastating implications for some of the most quoted 'explanations' of the nature of political and social change in late eighteenth-century Ulster, especially the origins of the Orange Order, Defenders, and associated political developments.[23]

Archetype Five: The Cities

The most under-researched area in the study of the settlement/ society interface in the eighteenth century is the role of the large cities. This lacuna exists, despite their undoubted significance at a European level, their massive transformations in this period, and their pivotal role in restructuring their hinterlands. Demography alone is eloquent on the scale of the change. Between 1700 and 1800, Dublin grew from 62,000 to 180,000, Cork from 17,000 to 60,000, Limerick from 10,000 to 42,000, Waterford from 7,000 to 22,000, Kilkenny from 4,000 to 14,000, and Belfast from 4,000 to 20,000. These cities shared the great wave of energy and centralisation surging through the major Atlantic ports of Europe in the eighteenth century. At a national level the even distribution of towns and cities was unbalanced by the configuration of the country. The sodden heartland in the peat-filled midland basin could never sustain a major urban centre. Augmenting this eccentricity, the river Shannon, a potential unifying thread down the centre of the island, was robbed of its potency by its truncated navigation at the falls of Ardnacrusha. The capital of the country, therefore, was not located centrally in the island but at its eastern periphery. Dublin was ideally located to benefit from the increasing orientation of the Irish to the English economy, and this was crucial to the city's achievement in centralising the Irish economy around itself. Andrews' map of the main road in 1780, or Henry Drury Harness's 1836 map of trade flows, provide a powerful visual representation of Dublin's hegemony, the fat spider sitting at the centre of the national webs.[24]

These trends were reflected in the tripling of Dublin's population between 1700 and 1800.[25] This astonishing growth catapulted Dublin into being the second largest city of the British empire and the sixth largest European city. Growth was triggered by Dublin's economic control, by its ever widening hinterland articulated by a transportation system orientated around itself and by its unprecedented accumulation of functions. Dublin monopolised tertiary services (law, finance, education, publishing); it controlled foreign trade (especially its remunerative wholesale and re-distributive sectors); it was the centre of the court and administration; and it had a significant manufacturing base. Thus, Dublin was both national warehouse and national workshop, combining the functions of Glasgow and Edinburgh: only Copenhagen could rival its sheer range of functions. As the eighteenth century progressed, Dublin became, in Werner Sombart's terms, a classic city of consumption, both Court city and aristocratic social centre, dominated by a gentry absorbing rural rent increases in conspicuous consumption. Dublin was full of luxury craftsmen—gold and silversmiths, bookbinders, silk weavers, watchmakers, peruke makers—and servants (ten percent of the urban population in 1798).[26]

Building on these developments, Dublin produced a Georgian housing sector in the mid and late eighteenth century, of a size and quality unsurpassed elsewhere; this sector was planned and funded by the landed class, then at the height of their wealth, ambitions, and expectations. Its implementation, however, fell largely to smaller fry, each developing small areas, but within an overall structuring plan. The eighteenth-century self-image of the Dublin elite is reflected in the compelling arrogance of its major architectural statements—Trinity College, Parliament house, Customs House, Four Courts—inserted in an architectural discourse in a sophisticated Enlightenment idiom.

However, it is important not to allow the very real architectual and planning achievements of the eighteenth-century city to degenerate in dangerous stereotyping of 'Georgian' Dublin. In many respects, the elegant facades of Dublin were gorgeous but deceptive masks, obscuring the teeming life of the cramped courts and putrid alleys which lay behind them, especially in the unfashionable and unreconstructed Liberties, increasingly neglected and left high and dry west of the old city, as the new city spilled elegantly into a gracious gridiron on the reclaimed Liffey floodplains. With an ample water supply from the Poddle and cheap accommodation, the Liberties had hosted the workshops of the city and became the focus for an as yet poorly understood textile industry, the Liberties were already in sharp economic decline and were a byword for social problems (poverty, vagrancy, underemployment, disease, crime, overcrowding). The decline was accelerated by the migration of the textile industry in search of more salubrious locations and a combination-free labour force. Simultaneously, the segregation of rich and poor took on (as in the countryside) a spatial (rather than its previous vertical) character, with the richer inhabitants filtering out to the fashionable eastern squares and terraces. The economic stagnation of the Liberties was copperfastened by the eventual undermining of Dublin industry by the cheaper products of the British Industrial Revolution in the first half of the nineteenth century. Any image of the eighteenth century city which neglects this dark but dynamic tint is fundamentally flawed.

The received image of the eighteenth-century city being a Protestant one should also be discarded. Undoubtedly at the beginning of the century, Dublin was still a Protestant city, at both popular and higher levels. However, as it grew rapidly, its social composition became increasingly Catholic, an inevitable progression as its surrounding migrant field was mainly Catholic. Kildare, Wexford and Wicklow people moved into the Liberties, Meath and Louth people into the Smithfield area on the north side. As the century proceeded, Dublin's changing social composition underneath its stylish veneer was inevitably subversive. Dublin as a result became an urban political crucible, in which the new political mentalities of the period were forged, typified by the United Irishmen in the 1790s. It was no accident that they found the bulk of their activists in the Liberties.

This survey has suggested a context for study of settlement and society in eighteenth-century Ireland. We have now identified five leading regional archetypes in Ireland in a 'long' eighteenth century, albeit in a simplistic fashion and focusing primarily on the settlement/

society dialectic. These regional archetypes are merely conceptual scaffolding, not to be mistaken for the building itself; they should not be treated as reified abstractions and their intellectual shelf life should be short, as they are inevitably replaced by better products. However, even this limited survey establishes a number of conclusions. One, the older notion of a 'peasant' Ireland should be discarded as simplistic and deterministic: it should be replaced by a more sophisticated understanding of the intense social stratification of Irish life in this period and the associated regional dynamics which underpin this pronounced stratigraphy. Two, the concept of the 'two Irelands' should be decisively rejected. Irish society as a whole was decisively, indeed precociously, commercialised, as illustrated by the complex integration of the different economic regions. Three, it may be possible in the future to pinpoint dates which mark major transition phases in settlement transformation. Some like 1815 are well known; others (1695?, 1720?, 1740?, 1770?) remain to be clarified and their regional relevance explored. Four, detailed work like Crawford's on Ulster and Dickson's on the Cork region is required to provide precise spatial and temporal specifications of those regions. In particular, we need to understand more fully the under-researched zone from north Kerry to Mayo, and to fill the gaping research hole in the midlands, especially in the transitional counties of Offaly, Longford and Westmeath. Five, nationwide generalisations should be assessed for their validity in each of these contrasting regions.

As we head towards 1992 and a more European vision, our work may expand to a broader perspective. We should now begin to move outside the English language world in search of appropriate comparative material. By contemporary standards, Britain and America were exceptional societies in the eighteenth century: if we compare Ireland only with them, Irish developments will always appear aberrant. Contextualised in a wider European frame, Ireland appears as a reasonably typical Ancien Regime society. Such a European perspective might help in transcending an obsession with distinctive 'Irish' or 'Celtic' settlement types. With obvious exceptions like the round tower, the pub-cum-shop and the handball alley, very little of Ireland's settlement framework is unique. Additionally, an emphasis on sub-national frameworks may help us to deconstruct the nationwide generalisations so beloved (and so frequently misleading) of some historians and many cultural commentators. A focus on a common European heritage and settlement tradition can help us to nurture a less anxious, less divisive and more enabling view of the island which we share. Jones Hughes correctly reminded us that 'it is the territorial synthesis, not the individual landscape components that possess unique qualities'.[27] This is the exciting challenge facing the current generation of historical geographers.

CHAPTER 5

A Sense of Place: Landscape and Locality in the Work of the Rhyming Weavers

by

Ivan Herbison

Throughout the period from 1750 to 1850, the century during which the weaver poets of Antrim and Down produced the greater part of their work, Ulster remained a predominantly rural society.[1] The population continued to increase until the Great Famine of 1846–48 reversed this trend, ushering in a period of rural depopulation. The Rhyming Weavers were born into this agricultural environment; many continued to maintain smallholdings to supplement their income from weaving. Given this context, one could be forgiven for assuming that traditional themes of life in the countryside, of landscape and locality, of nature and environment would feature prominently in the work of these poets. However, there is no coherent or well-defined tradition of landscape poetry to be found in the Rhyming Weavers. Few of them seem to have analysed their experience of rural life and landscape as comprehensively as one might have expected from poets who were acknowledged and proclaimed as bards of their native townlands. What one does find in the work of the most prominent, such as James Orr of Ballycarry and David Herbison of Dunclug, is a deep attachment to the notion of community and a sense of local identity.

Yet this sense of place which is so evident in their work is merely one aspect of a much more complex and ambivalent relationship to the land. There is a danger of exaggerating the extent to which the Rhyming Weavers identified themselves with their localities, or of misrepresenting the concept of local identity as a wholly positive allegiance. In reality there was a constant tension in the lives and writings of the weaver poets between the sense of place and the experience of displacement. They were not immune to the forces of economic and social change which were transforming Ulster from an agrarian to an industrial society, nor could they avoid the effects of the political transformation which led to the decline and eventual collapse of the radical dissenting tradition.

The experience of displacement manifested itself in several ways. The most obvious was the process of urbanisation, which had a profound impact on the lives of several rural bards. The case histories of two, Andrew McKenzie of Dunover and Thomas Beggs of Ballyclare, will serve to illustrate the fate of many of their contemporaries.

Andrew McKenzie was born near the village of Dunover, County Down in 1780. He was the second son of a smallholder who worked hard to provide his family with a modest education. According to the poet John Fullarton, 'in his fourteenth year McKenzie was apprenticed to the trade of linen-weaving. . . . He followed this branch of occupation for many years, and his best and happiest days were passed on the loom'.[2] Like so many of his fellow-weavers, he developed a passionate interest in poetry, which offered an escape from the tedium of work. In the Preface to his first volume, he wrote: 'I found poetry a sweet walk for the imagination'. In the same Preface he also comments on the constraints of his economic situation, referring to himself as one 'whose feelings have been too frequently wrung by the hard hand of poverty' (p.8). Despite many hardships he continued to write poetry and became a regular contributor to the *Belfast Newsletter*. Encouraged by the Ballymena printer and bookseller George Dugan, his first collection, *Poems and Songs on Different Subjects*, appeared in 1810. According to David Herbison, this publication earned him the not inconsiderable sum of 200 pounds, with which he built a cottage, 'Mount Gaelus', named after his pseudonym as a contributor to the *Belfast Newsletter*, and also acquired a fishing boat.[3] In the midst of this apparent security two disasters were to underline the precarious condition of human happiness. His fishing boat was wrecked and McKenzie barely escaped drowning. Then, as a consequence of a dispute over his lease, he was evicted from his cottage. He was forced to seek employment in Belfast and held a succession of poorly paid jobs. Despite these trying circumstances he continued to write poetry, but was unable to publish another collection, *The Masonic Chaplet and Other Poems*, until 1832, 22 years after his first volume. Unfortunately it failed to revive his fortunes. Fullarton paints a distressing picture of his final years:

> His eyes were somewhat sunk, mild and tranquil; and possessed of little fire or determination. He bore all the appearance of a man of seventy, although then sixteen years under that age, his voice was slow, subdued, and broken.[4]

McKenzie died a pauper in 1839, and was buried in Shankill graveyard. A fellow poet, William McComb, erected a headstone to his memory.

Not surprisingly, McKenzie's use of landscape reflects his experience. He has a nostalgic regard for his native countryside, made the more poignant by his sense of irrevocable loss. Nowhere are these feelings more eloquently expressed than in his poem 'Gannaway Burn':

> The spot whare the earliest May-flowers I gathered,
> On memory's vista I mark wi' delight:
> The bank whare I watched till the nestlings were feathered
> An' wept when I found they had a' ta'en their flight:
> That pool where the quick fleeting minnows pursuing,
> I waded, nor wist how the time glided by;
> That nook where I lingered the green rushes pu'ing,
> Till gloaming' had spread her dark veil o'er the sky. . ..
>
> The dark grove o' pine which its margin o'ershaded,
> Fond memory will cherish while life warms by breast;
> There often ere sorrow my bosom invaded,
> I strayed wi' blithe comrades, in innocence blest.
> But that grove is laid low, an' my comrades so cheery,
> Are gane to that country whence nane can return:
> While some who survive wander heartless an' weary,
> Like me, far awa' frae the Gannaway Burn!

The experience of Thomas Beggs in many respects parallels that of McKenzie, and confirms the pattern of misery which could so easily befall a rural poet driven to the city out of economic necessity. Beggs, born at Glenwherry, County Antrim, in 1789, was the son of a farm labourer. As a boy he went to sea for a brief period and was shipwrecked off Rathlin Island, an experience which diminished somewhat the attractions of the seafaring life. He then sought employment in the bleachworks of Richard Bell at Ballyclare. During his time there he published his first volume, *Miscellaneous Pieces in Verse* (1819). He was promised a more rewarding position in Belfast but it failed to materialise. During an unsettled period Beggs undertook a walking tour of North Antrim and did not find regular employment again until 1825, when he obtained a position in a bleachworks in Belfast. Once again he lost his job and, unable to support his family, was forced to return to his mother's home. He was constantly in and out of work during the 1840s. He died at the age of 58 in the typhus epidemic of 1847.[5]

Another important cause of displacement was emigration. There were many poets amongst the great exodus of emigrants from Ireland during the nineteenth century. James McHenry of Larne (1785–1845), John Smyth of Ballymena (1783–1854), and Henry McD Flecher of Moneyrea (1827–c.1909) all left for America.[6] David Herbison of Dunclug emigrated to Quebec in 1827 but was shipwrecked and returned home to Ballymena. Yet his three brothers and all but one of his children joined the exodus.[7]

It is evident from these brief biographical sketches that for most rural poets displacement and dispossession were the experiences which formed their attitudes to concepts of place, landscape and identity. John Hewitt's assertion that 'a poet of the folk was emphatically a poet of a place'[8] needs careful qualification. That sense of place so conspicuously valued by Hewitt cannot be taken for granted. When it is successfully achieved, as in the case of Orr and Herbison, we must attempt an explanation and analysis.

James Orr of Ballycarry achieves a distinctive sense of place in his poetry with a comparatively restrained use of description. There are, admittedly, several encomia of his native Ballycarry, where he lived throughout his life, apart from a brief sojourn in America, where he had fled after the failure of the 1798 Rebellion.[9] Yet Orr's sense of place owes more to his use of language than to his use of landscape. His vigorous, unselfconscious use of the vernacular Ulster-Scots dialect in his work creates a vivid sense of locality. In his dialect poems style and subject-matter are perfectly matched. They speak of a whole community: the language, the landscape and the people are united in a single vision of their identity.

Orr's technique is well illustrated by a poem such as 'To the Potatoe'.

Waeworth the proud prelatic pack,
Wha Point an' Pratoes downa tak!
With them galore, an' whyles a plack
To mak' me frisky,
I'll fen, an' barley freely lack—
Except in whisky.

What wad poor deels on bogs an' braes,
Whase dear Cot-Tacks nae meal can raise;
Wha ne'er tase butter, beef or cheese,
Nor pit new clais on;
While a' they mak' can har'ly please
Some rack-rent messon. . . .

The weel-pair't peasants, kempin', set ye;
The weak wee boys, sho'el, weed, an' pat ye;
The auld guid men thy apples get ay
Seedlin's to raise;
An' on sow'n-seeves the lasses grate ye,
To starch their claes.
(*Collected Poems*, pp. 56–59)

This poem characteristically condenses the whole life of his community into a series of vivid scenes. The potato becomes a focus for his real subject, an invocation of rural life: planting, harvesting, loading carts, starching clothes, eating 'creesht scons' and champ. Orr's appeal is to shared experience. 'The Irish Cottier's Death and Burial' similarly depends for its success on its qualities of homeliness, its intimate domestic references, its characteristic ambivalence towards the customs of the wake:

Cou'd he whose limbs they decently hae stretch'd,
The Followers o' freets awake an' mark,
What wad he think o' them, he oft beseeched
To be mair wise than mind sic notions dark?
To bare the shelves o' plates they fa' to wark;
Before the looking-glass a claith they cast;
An' if a clock were here, nae ear might hark
Her still'd han's tell how hours and moments pass'd;
Ignorance bred sic pranks, an' custom gars them last.
(*Collected Poems*, p.263)

Orr's highly developed sense of place and sense of language may be seen as both his strength and his weakness. In addressing his own locality Orr cannot address a wider audience outside his own locality. There is a price to be paid for his faithfulness to the idea of community and shared experience.

The work of Thomas Beggs provides an interesting contrast to that of James Orr. Though Beggs was capable of writing strong dialect verse, as in 'The Auld Wife's Address to her Spinning Wheel', he is nevertheless defensive about his use of Ulster Scots, and evidently feels the need to justify himself against the accusation of literary imitation:

> Should the reader of the following effusions suppose, that in some parts the Author has imitated the Scottish Dialect, he would wish to correct the idea by alleging that he has written in his own style — in the language of his native glen — not constrained but spontaneous as the lispings of our first speech.[10]

Beggs' removal to Belfast and the subsequent periods of unsettlement and unemployment meant that he lacked that strong sense of local identity which was the basis of Orr's poetry. So Beggs looks for a substitute landscape to replace the locality which he conspicuously lacks. He finds one in the only landscape fully accessible to him, that of poetic convention. In his eyes Rathlin Island is transformed into a mysterious place of romantic wildness, where the lone bard meditates on the sea:

> The crimson flush of eve had shed,
> O'er heath-cowl'd Carey's wizard head,
> The grey goat bounded o'er the waste,
> To shun the traveller's path in haste;
> On pinions fleet of hoary blue,
> In ether far the heron flew —
> The wind was hushed — the clouds away,
> And nature looked as glad and gay
> As if an angel's smile had been
> With all its brightness o'er the scene;
> When from that desert, dark and wild,
> A lonely, musing, minstrel child
> Stood gazing on the Celtic sea,
> As if spell-bound so rapt was he;
> And dreaming in poetic vein,
> Saw paradise in bloom again.
>
> (*The Poetical Works of Thomas Beggs*, pp.99–100)

Here Beggs is seeking a reversion to the landscape of Eden, and attempts to find security in some prelapsarian poetic paradise. His desire for escapism is understandable, given the circumstances of his own experience as a rural poet deprived of his native landscape by urbanisation and economic imperative. Beggs' use of the pastoral can thus be seen as an expression of and a response to displacement.

The experience of David Herbison, The Bard of Dunclug, complements that of Orr and Beggs. Like Orr, he spent nearly all his life in one place, and thus possesses a strong sense of local identity. Like Beggs, he found it more and more difficult to express that identity. The displacement experienced by Herbison was of cultural and linguistic nature. Questions of cultural identity are raised in his early works as he attempts to discover a distinctive voice. His first two volumes, *The Fate of M'Quillan and O'Neill's Daughter* (1841) and *Midnight Musings* (1848), are exploratory works in which he tries his hand at a number of poetic styles. Not surprisingly, these volumes reveal a sometimes confused eclecticism rather than a comfortable sense of belonging. Herbison's poem 'The Rowantree' resembles Beggs' 'Rathlin'. It is a naive attempt to transplant an English topographical poem to a local setting. The following extract demonstrates the unconvincing result:

Now oh now old Killyfleugh!
Breaks upon the enraptured view;
Lying on the green hill side,
Robbed of all its power and pride,
See it sinking in decay,
All its splendour is away.
On its melancholy walls
Every night the owlet calls.
And the bat in safety sleeps,
Where the mantling ivy keeps
Free from winter's withering power
Fragments of the ancient tower.
(*SW*, p.14)

Nevertheless, one particular strand of influence has special significance: the Scottish identity. For poets such as David Herbison, the only firmly estabished example of a regional literature was that of Scotland.[11] So it is hardly surprising to discover a strong Scottish influence, particularly that of Sir Walter Scott, in his early works. Other influences include Allan Ramsay (1686–1758) and James Hogg (1770–1835).[12] Moreover, though Ramsay, Burns and Hogg were regional writers, Regionalism as a literary movement owed more to the example of Scott.

Scott had come to prominence at the beginning of the nineteenth century as a collector of ballads.[13] In novels such as *Waverley* (1814), *Old Mortality* (1816) and *Heart of Midlothian* (1818) he drew upon a rich Scottish historical background. His work did much to create a taste for the regional setting. In his elegy on the death of Sir Walter Scott, David Herbison praises his devotion to Scottish landscape and history:

For scarce in Scotland lies a glen
That has escaped the Poet's pen. . .

Their father's wrongs he brought to light,
And mourned the fall of Squire and Knight;
And wept when maiden suffered wrong,
And sung her praise in deathless song.
In distant climes, his verses show
The bloody deed done in Glencoe,
Where Scotland's blood bedewed the plain,
And left on English hands a stain.

('Verses written on hearing of the death of Sir Walter Scott', *The Fate of M'Quillan and O'Neill's Daughter*, pp.49–52)

The title poem of Herbison's first collection, 'The Fate of M'Quillan and O'Neill's Daughter', is an historical ballad which recounts a legend of Dunluce Castle. It is a story of Squire and Knight, of a maiden wronged, and of bloody deeds. Like Scott's work, it exploits the attractions of setting and period, but Herbison is much better at creating a sense of place than he is at sustaining the narrative or depicting a sense of historical distance.

Keen and cold blows the o'er the lofty Knocklayd,
And the Bush water rolls o'er the wide-spreading plain;
But of wind or of water I'll ne'er be afraid.
When hastening away Evelina to gain.

I'll cross the broad ford ere the twilight be gone,
Leave the green spreading Aura behind me afar;
Every danger I'll brave on the mountains alone,
Though elements round them rage wildly in war.

For the Lord of Dunane has requested the maid,
And with pleasure her father agrees to his will:

But I swear by the sun that oft burnished my blade,
She'll stray with no traitor o'er Carbery Hill.

('The Fate of M'Quillan and O'Neill's Daughter', *SW*, pp.4–7)

By contrast, historical ballads do not feature so prominently in Herbison's second volume, *Midnight Musings*. Here the influence of Burns is more prominent. Herbison had made a visit to Burns' grave in the mid 1840s, and admired his achievement as a regional poet.

Warmed with a spark of Nature's fire,
How gloriously he swept the lyre!
Sang — and his country needs no more —
Her fame is spread the wide world o'er!
For her he wak'd his witching lyre
With wild and energetic fire.
('Lines composed at the grave of Burns', *SW*, p.44)

Following the example of Burns, Herbison wrote confidently in his own dialect in poems such as 'The Auld Wife's Lament for her Teapot' (*SW*, p.45), 'The Poet to his Auld Hat' (*SW*, pp.45–46), 'Michael Queen to his Auld Shoes' (*SW*, pp. 47–48), 'M'William' (*SW*, pp. 54–55) and 'The Auld Dotard's Bride' (SW, p.57). Yet for many years Herbison was virtually forced to abandon the medium of dialect verse because of the strength of the prejudice against non-standard forms. Literary journals and newspapers were reluctant to publish in dialect. Even his friend and fellow poet John Fullarton contemptuously dismissed Herbisons's 'Scotch rhymes'.[14] His work was undoubtedly impoverished by this linguistic displacement.

However, one cannot speak of David Herbison's regional identity solely in terms of the Scottish model. Though by language and cultural tradition Herbison was an Ulster Scot, he was also an Irishman, and consciousness of his Irish identity finds expression in his work. His poetry is seldom directly political, but that does not mean that it is devoid of a political viewpoint. The clearest indication of the controversial nature of some of his early work is the decision of his editors, in the changed climate of the 1880s, to suppress his poem, 'The Irish Boy', because of its political sentiments.[15]

O Erin, sweet Erin, thy fame is extending!
May want ne'er appear on thy wave-beaten shore.
Undaunted thy sons are for freedom contending,

Enraptured they meet, her blest smile to restore.
United together they'll brave every danger—
They'll keep the hills free from the blood-thirsty ranger—
They'll ne'er turn away from the weary-worn stranger—
He's still a loved guest at the Irishman's door.

(*The Fate of M'Quilland and O'Neill's Daughter*, pp.94–99)

The famine of 1846–48 roused his indignation and also sharpened his political awareness.

Wre we sink in ruin's wave
Let us show that we are brave —
Trample on each tyrant knave
Brands us with iniquity;
By the foes we have defied,
By the death which Emmet died,
We will drain life's dearest tide,
But we shall have liberty!

('Song: O'er green Erin's flowery plains', *SW*, p.78)

Herbison's sympathy for the radical dissenting tradition more often took a lyrical rather than a political form. He continued to write about the 1798 Rebellion in terms of its impact on individuals. His poems of exile seek to portray a sense of loss and alienation.[16] Even in 1877, Herbison was still writing about the events of 1798.

I now am left an exile here
Of friends bereft who loved me dear;
Nor have I hope that e'er I'll see
Their smile bring life's joys back to me.

But ah! I fear my wish is vain,
I still must bear the Exile's chain;
And only in my dreams I'll see
Her beauty where I'll never be.

But ah we failed to break the chain
Which long has held our Isle in pain. . ..
My latest prayer in life shall be
That Erin ne'er may discord see.

('The Ulster Exile 1798', *SW*, pp. 292–93)

Herbison remained (in some respects, at least) a radical dissenter, and continued to feel a certain kinship with the idealism of the United Irishmen. But during his long life this feeling of Irishness was transmuted from a political consciousness to an emotional, or even a sentimental attachment. Separated from the mainstream of Ulster-Scots politics, he identified with the figure of the exile in his poetry.

In Herbison's later volumes, such as *The Snow-Wreath* (1868) and *The Children of the Year* (1876), there is an attempt to resolve the problems of identity. Unable to keep in equilibrium his Ulster-Scots and Irish identities, he attempts to find a common ground. In choosing to write about the landscape and people of his local district Herbison is seeking to create an intimate personal identification with his own 'country'. This is a more limited sense of identity, but one which offers him both emotional security and an acknowledged position. As the Bard of Dunclug, David Herbison is the voice of his countryside and community. His familiarity with his subject matter, and his ability to capture the character of his rural landscape give his verse a particularly intimate quality:

The lapwing flutters round about,
To wile us from her bield—
Lights at our feet, and cries peweet,
Then flies far o'er the field.
And gladly from the auld cow's back
The magpie steals the hair,
To clothe her nest, where she may rest,
Beyond the school-boy's snare.
('Summer Time', *SW*, p.87)

In his nature poetry, and his descriptions of landscape, as well as in elegies for local worthies, election poems, poetical advertisements, acknowledgements of personal gifts, and even occasional poems for the backs of cheques he recreates the close relationship between poet and community.[17] More problematic identities are resolved by becoming the Bard of his 'ain native toun', who delights in presenting a portrait of Ballymena and its people.

Since I was a boy in my ain native toun,
There's naething but bigging and pu'ing wa's doun;
The streets are grown wider, the houses are high,
And half o' the windows peer into the sky;
Their doors wad let in ony cart from the street,

Their owners ne'er think o' a shoe for their feet,
They a' maun hae boots ere they venture abroad;
Their claething appears to an auld body odd;
How changed from the times when our forefathers lay
In houses weel streekit wi' heather and strae!
Happy hames, happy hearts, we had ilka place roun',
When I was a boy in my ain native toun.
('My Ain Native Toun', *SW*, p. 305)

Yet even here, in a poem with such an intimate sense of place as 'My Ain Native Toun' there is a degree of ambivalence. Its original title was 'An Auld Body's Notions o' the Improvements in Ballymena'; the narrator remains at a distance from his subject:

The castle is gane, and its garden destroyed,
Nae langer about it our Easter's enjoyed;
Its banks and its braes are a' weedy and fogg'd,
And felled is the tree whare the sodger was flogg'd:
There's naething I see has the same hue it had
When I was a boy in the arms o' my dad,
Except the wee house whare the poet was born,
It still braves the blast o' the wild wintry morn,
Was't no' for it now, as I saunter alang,
I wad scarce know the place whare I first sung my sang;
Its chimneys and windows and scraw-covered croun
Are a' that see o' my auld native toun.
('My Ain Native Toun', *SW*, pp. 305–306)

The poem is a chronicle of change rather than a celebration of the sense of place. In the Ballymena of the mid-nineteenth century described by Herbison the steam loom has replaced the hand loom, and skilled weavers have been turned into factory workers. This was an aspect of contemporary life with which Herbison's narrator cannot identify. He remains an 'auld body', proudly and stubbornly aloof from the changes transforming his community, and clinging desperately to a vain hope that 'Times wad revive in my ain native toun'. In exploring his sense of place, the Bard of Dunclug had renounced all identities beyond that of his local community. Even so, he could not avoid the sense of displacement experienced by so many of the Rhyming Weavers.

The three weaver poets, Orr, Beggs and Herbison have each attempted to define their sense of place in a different way. Orr's poetry uses dialect in a particularly forceful manner; his work is rooted in the homely details of rural life. Beggs seeks to escape from the grim realities of unemployment and urban deprivation through the invocation of a pastoral idyll. Herbison attempts to resolve the insecurities and uncertainties of political and social change by the affirmation of a purely local allegiance to his ain native toun. But for all of them a sense of place provides the context for their achievement.[18]

CHAPTER 6

The Lonely Rebellion of William Drennan

by

Adrian Rice

I

For almost two centuries, the Belfast doctor William Drennan has been widely regarded as the poet of the United Irishmen, due mainly to his famous ballads entitled 'Erin' (1795) and 'The Wake of William Orr' (1797). To what extent, however, does this mean that he was the patriot-poet of the 1798 Rebellion? To many this question may seem puzzling, perhaps even pointless. They may know of Drennan's reputation as a radical within the political arena of eighteenth century Ireland; they may be aware of his involvement in the formation of the United Irishmen Society in 1791; they may also know of his position as the pen-man of that Society, who had indeed been responsible for the vast majority of the pamphlets and addresses of the movement up until 1794. And even Drennan's behaviour following his trial for sedition in 1794 and his subsequent lack of involvement in United Irishmen affairs, may not be sufficient for them to doubt Drennan's reputation as the patriot-poet of '98.

However, after much research into this area, I have come to the conclusion that there can be no easy acceptance of Drennan as the laureate of the '98 Rebellion. Two intriguing discoveries made in the course of my investigation highlight this point.

The first discovery was made in the Ulster Museum. The Museum has given evidence of Drennan's poetic service to the United Irishmen cause of 1798 by displaying two lines from a poem written to commemorate one of the most famous leaders of the '98 Rebellion, Henry Joy McCracken, and attributing these lines to Drennan's hand.[1] The implication is that Drennan clearly supported the men of '98. The lines in question are as follows:

> At Donegore he [Henry Joy] proudly rode and wore a suit of green
> And brave though vain at Antrim town his sword flashed lightning keen . . .

However, upon investigation, nowhere amongst Drennan's published or unpublished writings could any reference whatsoever to the above lines be found. Neither could one find the same metre in any of Drennan's other poems. On consulting a collection of Irish ballads, bound under the title *At the Sign of the Harp*, my growing doubts about the authenticity of the lines finally proved to be well-grounded. Most of these ballads date from the late 1800s, but their subjects and themes centre on local historical events, with a fair percentage of them celebrating the '98 Rebellion. Among them is a poem entitled 'The Belfast Mountains – A Story of '98'. This is the poem the Museum attributed to Drennan. However, the author is clearly a certain P.J. McCall. Upon consulting other collections of P.J. McCall's work, for example selected ballads and poems, a similiar metre to that of 'The Belfast Mountains' is found to be in constant use. This oversight on the part of the Museum is especially revealing, since it illustrates that popular opinion can sometimes obscure historical fact.

A second and more important discovery focuses upon a fascinating series of letters, both private and public, and newspaper editorials found among Drennan's unpublished manuscript material, which together constitute a debate about the claims or counter-claims surrounding Drennan's status as the patriot-poet of 1798. These documents relate to the years 1891 and 1897. Those of 1891 are written against the background of the nationalist celebrations taking place in Ireland on the centenary of the inauguration of the United Irishmen. Those of 1897 are set against the backdrop of nationalist celebrations on the eve of the centenary of the United Irishmen Rebellion itself.

In a newspaper editorial (*Northern Whig*) dated October 19, 1891, and headed 'The Centenary of the United Irishmen – Parnellite celebration in Belfast',[2] a certain Mr Robert Johnston is given as the 'president of the local branch of the Independent Union, the new Parnellite organisation'. Mr Johnston and Dr John Swanick Drennan, one of Drennan's own sons, and himself a far from mediocre Irish poet of the nineteenth century, are the main protagonists of the 1891 debate. Mr Johnston's organisation was clearly formed in support of the great Irish Nationalist leader, Charles Stewart Parnell, who, along with Michael Davitt, had managed to unite nationalists of all persuasions, from moderate home-rulers to extreme republicans under the banner of the Irish National Land League (1879).[3] From the information provided in the rest of the editorial it would seem that the organisation was Catholic, and Fenian, and verging on the extreme Republican side. Their celebration was on October 18, and involved a company of about two hundred having a dinner in Central Hall, Rosemary Street, Belfast, a meeting which ended with various toasts being drunk, all to loud applause. One of the toasts was to 'Our Protestant Fellow-countrymen', but the best received seems to have been that to 'The Memory of the Dead', which was hailed as 'the most glorious toast that any Irish Nationalist could be called upon to respond to'. Names toasted here included some of the martyrs of the United Irishmen, such as Henry Joy McCracken, Rev James Porter, and William Orr, though poignantly, the greatest toast was to Parnell who had been buried merely one week previously. He is called 'the greatest of Irish patriots'. The toasts are not the only interesting thing worth noting, as it is revealed that on the same day the organisation had made 'pilgrimages' to the graves of men who had taken 'an active part in the United Irishmen movement'. One of the graves visited was that of Dr. William Drennan, in Clifton Street, Belfast, and it is this occurrence which sparks off the ensuing debate.

John S. Drennan wrote a letter on October 20 to the editors of both *The Northern Whig* and *The Ulster Echo*, in which he states that while being gratified by every indication of respect for his father's memory, he must nevertheless protest strongly' against any attempt to identify his (father's) name and opinions with those of the present so-called Nationalists and Nationalism . . .'.[4] He acknowledges his father's involvement with the United Irishmen but stresses that 'he had ceased his connection with the society before it had made separation from England its ultimate object, and invoked foreign aid to attain it'. He proceeds to say that the end of the eighteenth century had seen the great bulk of Irish people the 'subjects of social degradation and territorial despotism. But now how completely altered is the state of affairs.' He bases this last assumption on what he judges to have been the prolonged efforts made by the British Parliament in the nineteenth century 'to remove or rectify the agrarian, educational and administrative evils of this country'. In the light of such efforts comes the major thrust of the son's argument:

> Thus, then, there is not a doubt in my mind that my father, had he been now alive, would have been, like myself, a Unionist: and in confirmation of that belief I may cite his own words, uttered at a town meeting of Belfast in 1817 (quoted in preface to Berwick's '*Historical Collections*', page xiv):

> Dr. Drennan 'begged leave to assert that in the event of
> a full, free, and frequent representation of the people
> in Parliament for the whole empire, he would be reconciled
> to the Union. He would, not unwillingly, merge his country
> in a fair and faithful representation of these realms'.

Having played this quotation as his trump card, the son finishes his letter by stating that he has 'been guarding the memory of [his] father from possible misapprehension or misstatement'.

For his stance, and before the Parnellites had a chance to reply, J.S. Drennan received both private and public support. A relative, Mr. Duffin, wrote to him on October 21, congratulating him for protecting his father's name and saying that 'these miserable exemplars of modern patriotism have no right to claim fellowship with such men as your father and you do well to riposte them on his behalf'.

The public support came on the same day, in editorials in *The Ulster Echo* and *The Northern Whig*, both of which contrasted the merits of the United Irishmen and the modern Nationalists, taking very much J.S. Drennan's line that the latter should not claim any connection with their more illustrious predecessors. *The Ulster Echo* editorial voices disgust that 'the sham patriots of today – the apostles of plunder, terrorism, and outrage – should claim to be the heirs-at-law of the illustrious men who fought and sacrificed. . . for a principle and not for self'. And the 'sham patriots' are further slammed in a reference to Drennan senior himself: 'It was an insult to the memory of the pure patriot for the representatives of the decadent and dishonest patriotism of this pettifogging or Nationalist era to go on a pilgrimage to his grave'. *The Ulster Echo* clearly rejoices in J.S. Drennan's letter defending his father and asserted that 'the sons of the United Irishmen were loyal now, because everything, and more than everything, for which their fathers contended and even rebelled, is now enjoyed under the British Constitution and Imperial rule'. Because of this assertion the paper believes that Drennan senior, who was 'a man of honour as well as principle', would have acknowledged Britain's reforming efforts and would have been a 'staunch Unionist' had he lived in the 1890s. J.S. Drennan's letter was 'unanswerable confirmation of this statement'.

The Northern Whig also supports the hypothesis that Drennan senior would have been a Unionist in the late nineteenth century, believing that Drennan's speech in 1817 was spoken 'like a patriotic and sensible Irishman, a patriotic and sensible Ulsterman'. J.S. Drennan's letter was 'a rebuke to the Irish Nationalists of today'.

J.S. Drennan therefore gained credence for his views from these private and public sources, even if they were from a Unionist relative and two Unionist-influenced newspapers. But an opposing view quickly emerged when Robert Johnston responded to J.S. Drennan's letter by writing on behalf of the Parnellites to *The Ulster Echo* on October 22. Johnston insists that William Drennan struggled for Irish nationality, and argues that by way of his political poetry, coupled with his manifestoes to the United Irishmen, Drennan showed himself as a 'revolutionist of the most advanced type and total separation from England was the idea taught by him. . .'. He stresses that his association was merely honouring Drennan as an Irish patriot, and is annoyed that anyone should imply that Drennan 'had abandoned the cause of the United Irishmen after having brought them to the point of insurrection': a truth, if real, that Johnston would have been ashamed to own. He finishes the letter by saying that Drennan's reputation 'will only suffer at the hands of the son', while Parnellites will remember the ideas of Drennan as taught in the following lines of his poem entitled 'Erin':

> The cause it is good, and the men they are true,
> And the green shall outlive both the orange and blue.

Overall the letter is sarcastic in tone, and is insensitive, as when Johnston suggests that William Drennan's name is really only revered in Ireland because of his separatist doctrine, without which his 'existence would have been as totally forgotten as that of his son will be when he has passed away and has carried with him all his Unionist principles'. This is bitter, considering that J.S. Drennan was a man in the eighty-second year of his life.

J.S. Drennan appears to have been given the last word in the debate of 1891. He wrote a reply to Johnston, published in *The Northern Whig* on October 23, restating his initial motives in raising the controversy as being 'to give a correct conception of my father, Dr. William Drennan's political opinions and conduct', which had seemed to him in danger of misapprehension. He gets his own digs in at Johnston by criticising his 'incoherent bluster and unmannerly insinuations', and finishes by reiterating his belief that his father 'never advocated insurrectionary movements'.

If J.S. Drennan had felt duty-bound to protect, as he viewed it, his father's reputation as a patriotic liberal in 1891, then his mantle was assumed by Drennan's grand-daughter, Mrs Maria Duffin, in 1897. She finds it necessary to make similiar statements regarding Drennan's precise brand of nationalism/patriotism in the face of two written approaches made to her on the eve of the centenary of the United Irishmen Rebellion of 1798. These approaches came from the 'Dr. Drennan '98 Club', and the 'Dr. Drennan Centenary Club', both probably titles for the same organisation.

First, Mr. W.D. Harbinson writes to Mrs Duffin on February 5, 1897 on behalf of the 'Dr. Drennan '98 Club', giving his address as '*The Northern Star*, 12 High Street, Belfast', *The Northern Star* being a nationalist influenced periodical. His purpose is to ask Mrs Duffin for some information as to where a likeness of 'the only singer of the '98 movement might be procured', because the '98 Club 'are very anxious to obtain a portrait of the author of the famous *Letters of Orellana*. Mrs Duffin's response is brief and un-co-operative, and she takes pains to point out to Harbinson that though he speaks 'of Dr. Drennan as the only singer of '98', as far as she knew 'he never wrote a line on the subject and with the rebellion itself he was never in sympathy'. She finishes, saying, 'He was always an ardent patriot and an advocate of equal rights to all Irishmen, but to associate his name with the rebellion of '98 would be a simple misrepresentation of facts'.

The second approach to Mrs Duffin is made some ten months later, this time by a Mr. Michael Doran, who gives his credentials as being the Secretary of the 'Dr. Drennan Centenary Club', and gives his address as '130a Divis Street, Belfast', a Catholic and nationalist area of the city. He too requires a description of Dr. Drennan to facilitate a painting of him for the Club's Centenary Banner. Mrs Duffin's answer to Doran is longer than that provided for Harbinson, but is as equally un-co-operative. Echoing J.S. Drennan's sentiments, she says that 'while feeling very grateful for any appreciation of [Drennan] as an Irishman and sincere lover of his country, who devoted his talents to her service', she nevertheless does not 'wish his name to be associated with the rebellion of 1798'. Her reasons for this opinion are given in an astute manner, and they are worthy of quotation in full.

Speaking of Drennan and the Rebellion of 1798 she says:

> With it he was never in sympathy and was not in the confidence of the leaders, having withdrawn from any active part in the counsels of the United Irishmen, when he saw to what end the more advanced spirits were tending.
>
> He was an ardent advocate of Catholic Emancipation, constitutional freedom and privileges for all Irishmen, but, I believe his

> ideas of a resort to other than constitutional means, were, like those of many thoughtful men of that time, greatly altered by the excesses and result of the French Revolution, the commencement of which they had regarded with sympathy and hope.
>
> Dr. Drennan was at first opposed to the Union, but afterwards modified his view of it.

Mrs. Duffin then quotes Drennan's words at a town meeting in Belfast in 1817, the same trump card that J.S. Drennan had played in the 1891 debate, and the records of the 1897 exchange come to a close on this note.

II

The argument thus presented could totally baffle the uninitiated and impartial observer of the complex nature of Irish history. What have been seen above are the views of two opposing camps within nineteenth-century Irish politics – the Presbyterian liberal unionists, and the Catholic republican nationalists – who both, nevertheless, claim Drennan as their type of Irish patriot-poet. From the argument outlined there are clearly two ways, at least, of looking at what constitutes an Irish patriot poet. Robert Johnston and the Parnellites seem to suggest that unless Drennan was, in fact, the poet of the '98 Rebellion, then his claim to Irish patriot-poet status is nullified. On the other hand, J.S. Drennan and the Duffin family clearly believe that there is no contradiction in anyone's being an Irish patriot-poet despite not being the poet of the '98 Rebellion. One side sees Drennan as a revolutionist and insurrectionist: the other views him as an antirevolutionist, though an 'ardent patriot', and 'a sincere lover of his country'. Which side is correct? As with many political arguments the fact is that each side has elements of both truth and error woven into its opinions.

Although it is rather bemusing to think of an Irish nationalist poet quickly becoming a 'staunch Unionist', it must be said that it is not so highly improbable at all, given the unique political circumstances in the late eighteenth and early to mid-nineteenth centuries in Ireland. The whole argument needs to be seen primarily against the background of the history of the Ulster Presbyterians in this period. They appear to go full circle, from being fervent Irish nationalists and separatists, to being staunchly patriotic servants of the Crown. In recent years historians such as Maureen Wall, Marianne Elliott, and, most recently, Peter Brooke,[5] have provided valuable information in an attempt to explain this seemingly unfathomable shift in Ulster Presbyterian Nationalism to post-1800 Unionism. But, the initiator of such interest in this field is A.T.Q. Stewart whose M.A. thesis, entitled 'The Transformation of Presbyterian radicalism in the north of Ireland from 1790–1825', and his subsequent book, entitled *The Narrow Ground*, provide the reader with a thorough exposition of the phenomenon.

In his book, Stewart faces what he terms 'one of the most puzzling questions in Irish history. Why did the northern Presbyterians, who had been nationalists and radicals in 1798, so quickly become unionists and conservatives thereafter?'[6] He proceeds to give three basic reasons in an examination of the whole pattern which demonstrates that the antithesis is less sharp than appears at first sight. He states, firstly, that it is erroneous to imagine that the whole of the Presbyterian body held radical opinions in the hectic years between 1790 and 1800. Indeed, it is a fact that

> Throughout the whole period the majority of ministers in the General Synod of Ulster was conservative, suspicious of Catholic political designs and critical of Presbyterians who became infected with French revolutionary ideals. The records of the Synod mention the insurrection only to deplore it, and to censure the levelling and republican principles which brought it about.[7]

He further emphasizes the existence of this stratification of political views within the whole body, even amongst the differing sects, such as Old Light, New Light, and Seceders. It is maintained that the radical element merely came to the fore in the 1790s, thus temporarily overshadowing the Conservative side, which, however, has so swamped the radical element ever since that today the radical tradition of Ulster Presbyterianism is almost obliterated from memory. Stewart concludes his first point by also showing that from a territorial point of view the United Irishmen and their supporters were in a minority, despite all allusions to the contrary.

Stewart's second main point – and it is here that he mentions the importance of Drennan's correspondence as part proof – stresses that because the central aim of the United Irish political programme was to unite Catholic and Protestant to achieve political power, it is logical to think that the Protestants in the movement had jettisoned their attitudes of distrust towards Catholics. However, Stewart argues that such was not, in fact, the case. And, equally, traditional suspicion of Protestant planters still existed amongst the Catholic radicals of the United Irishmen. Both these factors had a crucial effect on the demise of the movement after 1798. In fact, they constitute the grounds of Stewart's third point, that these areas of distrust, despite rhetoric to the contrary, reflected a real disunity, along traditional religious and sectarian lines, which characterised the United Irish rebellion itself. It was a disunity which led to scenes of sectarian massacre, particularly in Wexford, that mocked the very appellation 'United Irishmen'.

III

It is against such an historical backdrop that Drennan produced his famous patriotic poetry. It is true, as Patrick Curley maintains, that Drennan's poetry both represents a 'rational, radical, realistic and Protestant' effort within a difficult political and cultural period situated between the eras of tradition and revolution, Augustanism and Romanticism, and merits consideration as the 'crowning example' of an 'eighteenth century Protestant libertarian protest'[8]. Also, Drennan's lifework does indeed symbolise the 'radicalism and reaction that lies at the heart of Ulster Presbyterianism'.[9] Such conclusions may be reached by any serious reader of Drennan's poetry. However, Curley does well to ascertain the hitherto unexplored importance of the religious undercurrent to Drennan's political poetry, a discovery which leads Curley to claim that, 'There can be little question that Drennan's active Presbyterianism finally fashioned his aspirations and gained a precedence over all his ambitions'.[10] I would basically agree with such a conclusion, though not without certain crucial qualifications which emerge from a full examination both of Drennan's political poetry and, most importantly, of his hitherto neglected poetry relating to various personal, social and religious issues. For example, Curley's phrase 'active Presbyterianism' presumes that a united presbyterian polity existed in eighteenth-century Ireland, whereas we have already seen that this is not the case. That Irish Presbyterians of the period were divided into the two main rival camps of Old Light and New Light – reformed orthodoxy versus the liberalism and individualism of the Age of Reason – meant membership of either wing could dictate one's support for or against a political event as relevant to the poetry of Drennan as the 1798 Rebellion. Accepting that such important differences existed within the Irish Presbyterianism of Drennan's era, proper stress needs to be given to an accurate assessment of the religious principles which permeate Drennan's poetical responses to political event.

The literary critic and poet, Ted Hughes, has said:

> Poetic imagination is determined finally by the state of negotiation – in a person or in a people – between man and his idea of the Creator. This is natural enough, and everything else is naturally enough subordinate to it. How things are between man and his idea of the Divinity determines everything in his life, the quality and connectedness of every feeling and thought, and the meaning of every action.[11]

Drennan's 'idea of the Creator' cannot simply be brought under a theological umbrella term like 'Presbyterianism'. Rather, it must be recognised that his 'idea of the Creator' is expressed from within a dissenting, non-subscribing Unitarian Presbyterian framework. His muse is predominantly moral, and specifically New Light, constituting the final groundplan for his chief poetical statements.

The religious undercurrent to Drennan's patriotic verse is significantly different to that contained in the bulk of Irish nationalist poetry, written mainly by patriots of a Catholic persuasion. The religious symbolism which pervades much Catholic Irish patriot verse (from Drennan's era to the present-day) is the blood sacrifice motif. By this I refer to the tendency of many Catholic Irish patriot-poets to elevate those who suffer and die for the 'cause' to the station of Christ-like martyrdom. This equation – patriot-hero = Christ the Redeemer – is seen in its most extreme in the messianic swansongs of Patrick Pearse. Add to this religious invocation of blood sacrifice a popular conviction that God will help the 'Gael' in the battle against the oppressor, and we have the two basic tenets of the religious bedrock to Catholic Irish patriotic verse.

By contrast, the New Light liberalism of Drennan's religious concerns lend a more egalitarian complexion to his patriotic poetry. Although in 'The Wake of William Orr' (1797),[12] Drennan draws a certain parallel between the 'murdered brother' and Christ "Countrymen, UNITE", he cried, And died for what our Saviour died' – he (paradoxically) goes on to lament the often tragic results of the volatile mixture of such religious symbolism and nationalistic fervour:

> Monstrous and unhappy sight!
> Brothers' blood will not unite;
> Holy oil and holy water
> Mix, and fill the world with slaughter.

The truly distinctive religious slant which he then incorporates into the same poem is drawn from two New Testament exhortations not commonly heard in Irish patriotic poetry – the commands to love one's neighbour, and forgive one's enemies. Drennan suggests that the only thing worse than the 'foreign weight' of Britain, is the 'domestic hate' separating Irishman from Irishman. In this way the poem becomes an urgent, and refreshing, call for dialogue as opposed to violence:

> God of mercy! God of peace!
> Make this mad confusion cease;
> O'er the mental chaos move,
> Through it SPEAK the light of love.

A similiar plea for reconciliation forms the core of Drennan's equally famous ballad, 'Erin' (1795). Here again, the triumph over internal Irish divisions is seen as important as, perhaps more important, than the expulsion of the colonial power:

> Drive the demon of bigotry home to his den,
> And where Britain made brutes now let Erin make men.
> Let my sons like the leaves of the shamrock unite,
> A partition of sects from one footstalk of right,
> Give each his full share of the earth and the sky,
> Nor fatten the slave where the serpent would die.
>
> Alas! for poor Erin that some are still seen,
> Who would dye the grass red from their hatred to green;
> Yet, oh! when you're up and they're down, let them live,
> Then yield them that mercy which they would not give.
> Arm of Erin be strong! but be gentle as brave!
> And uplifted to strike, be still ready to save!
> Let no feeling of vengeance presume to defile
> The cause of, or men of, the Emerald Isle.

Drennan's deeply held religious principles must not be underestimated in the debate regarding his patriotism. I would contend, for instance, that the underlying religious restraint in his political verse goes a long way to explaining his absence from the fighting in 1798. However, the strength of Drennan's religious opinions was certainly underestimated by a Mr. Archdale, who published an article[13] in *Faulkner's Journal*, dated June 27, 1793, in which he accused the members of the Society of United Irishmen of being 'despisers of all religion'. Drennan was sufficiently incensed to reply personally, on July 1, in the following manner:

> Sir,
> Having seen an unqualify'd and indiscriminate censure of yours in Faulkner's Journal, on the whole Society of United Irishmen as despisers of all Religion, and finding myself necessarily included as being a member of that Society, I am convinced that you will do me the justice to except me from those on whom you meant to bestow such an appellation.
>
> I am Sir, . . .
> W.D.

Though Drennan's sensitivity is somewhat amusing, it is also very revealing, in that he is at pains to defend himself from the irreligious charge, but not the rest of the Society.

Given the extent to which Drennan's religious convictions permeate his political poems, it is only appropriate that a hymn (originally included as a footnote to a 'Monthly Retrospect of Politics', in the *Belfast Monthly Magazine* of August 1813) should present a summation of his views of the political events of his era a summation, which is, incidentally, not dissimiliar to the previously cited verdict of Maria Duffin. In the opening verse of 'Let all the creatures of this earth', Drennan, in true liberal and Enlightenment tradition, portrays Nature's joyful acclamation of the primacy of man. However, in the second half of the hymn he indicates that, for him, something had happened to spoil man's noble position:

> So Nature spoke, with voice benign,
> When, from her blackest cave,
> Bigotry yell'd, 'A share be mine,
> From cradle to the grave!'
>
> The Sun of Reason then began,
> To set, eclips'd in blood;
> And He, alone, can rescue man,
> Who first pronounced him GOOD.

As with many others in the Enlightenment age, Drennan believed that Man had great potential for universal improvement. However, such meliorism was deflated when bigotry, the opposite of charity and brotherliness, queered the pitch. The high hopes propagated by the Age of Reason came crashing to the ground. This fall was symbolised for Drennan, internationally, in the bloody development of the French Revolution, and locally, in the circumstances surrounding the United Irish Rebellion of 1798. The last two lines of the hymn point Drennan's final recourse to his religious beliefs to sustain him with hope for the future in the midst of social and political uncertainty.

IV

Certainly Drennan was a convinced Irish radical, but one who, as far as possible, rose above the sectarian nature of Ulster Presbyterian/ Irish Catholic politics, to leave behind an example of a much more noble, moral, philanthropic patriotism than that generally espoused by adherents of both traditions. It is a patriotism that must not only be seen in the important context of the largely unacknowledged influence of Drennan's religious beliefs, but also in relation to a term coined by Joseph Leerssen in a book published in Amsterdam, and entitled *Mere Irish and Fior-Ghael: Studies in the idea of Irish Nationality, its development and literary expression prior to the nineteenth century* (1986). The term is 'love of the fatherland' a form of patriotism which Leerssen claims motivated Irish patriots of Grattan's generation, the same generation as Drennan. Leerssen describes such a patriotism as being 'one of public virtue and accountability, of opposition against corrupt power-politics and against neglect of the public good for private interest'.[14] It was a kind of political philanthropy which was generated by a person's desire to contribute to the public benefit, to fulfill one's duty as a citizen by actively aiding the improvement of Society. Leerssen illustrates his theme by quoting Bishop Berkeley, in his *Maxims Concerning Patriotism* (1750): 'A patriot is one who heartily wisheth the public prosperity, and doth not only wish, but also study and endeavour to promote it'.

Leerssen continues:

> . . . love of the fatherland counted since Roman days, and especially in Roman-inspired political thought, as one of those virtues which the Patriots (Irish Patriots of Grattan's era) sought to advance – not, indeed, as a principle governing a political attitude, but as a general, moral virtue among other virtues like 'veneration of one's parents', 'loyalty to the King', 'chastity in women', etc.

> Love of the fatherland, as an ideal, a virtue, was as ubiquitous and as little politicized as a religious belief in a supreme being.

Drennan was heavily influenced by his classical education, and what may be termed his classical patriotism is very much in line with Leerssen's 'love of the fatherland' theory. For example, note the remarkable similarity between Leerssen's comments and remarks made by Drennan at a meeting in Belfast in 1816:

> Religion should not be confined to a single day in the week. Nor ought public spirit, (a religion from the first, the second best), to be confined to a single day [St Patrick's Day] in the year. Public spirit is an active duty. It should be in a state of constant requisition, pervading life, like our duty to parents, to wives and children. It is a duty, that in reality embraces them all, coalesces with them all, invigorates them all. It rounds the whole character . . . and were it more common abroad -. . . then we might say to our country welcome home again! Ireland is herself once more.[15]

Furthermore, an examination not just of Drennan's political verse but his entire poetic oeuvre, highlights the relevance of Leerssen's concept to Drennan's particular strain of patriotism. For instance, throughout his poetry Drennan's admiration for the moral man or woman, the person who fulfilled diligently and honestly his or her varied functions as a citizen, knows no bounds. The roll call, as it were, of the social qualities which Drennan believes are noteworthy can be stated in his own words which form part of an epitaph written 'In Memory of Adair Crawford, MDFRS':

> . . . and he lived to enlarge the limits of human knowledge,
> And to complete the circle of social duty:
> An obedient son,
> An affectionate brother,
> An endearing husband,
> A fond father,
> An independent citizen,
> And a steady friend.

For Drennan, these were the attributes of a true patriot. And it is surely significant that Adair Crawford could well serve as a role-model for the type of patriotic citizen born of Leerssen's 'love of the fatherland' concept. Moreover, this is a crucial point, for it helps to explain both Drennan's brand of patriotism and his absence from the '98 Rebellion.

Given that he held this very noble (if somewhat idealistic) view of what constituted a patriot, I believe that his gentlemanly standards went unsatisfied when applied to the increasingly conspiratorial dealings of the United Irishmen. Indeed, looking back (in 1802) Drennan informs his sister:

> I always liked the persons of our leaders [and] Democrats much less than their professed principles. [I] thought I saw in most of them aristocracy in a shabby coat, aristocratic self-sufficiency, aristocratic vengeance, aristocratic intolerance, under a maratism of manners and of language . . . I have seen the numbers of a description of character, which the best political principles could not sweeten. . ..[16]

For Drennan, a patriot's moral walk had to match his political talk. Further support for this point is seen in the following extract, in which Drennan again expresses sentiments akin to Leerssen's theory:

> I think men are disappointed in Patriots, and come at length to believe, that there is no such thing as public spirit, chiefly from their own faults; by too hasty and premature confidence in men of splendid talents, without taking a view of the whole character, and particularly, without watching the connexion between the moral man and the political man. No man is a good citizen, if he is not a good son, a good father, a good brother, a good friend, a good husband.[17]

Drennan places a similiar stress upon the interdependence of the moral and the political, in a letter written towards the end of 1796. Here, he alludes to his lack of involvement with the United Irishmen in the run-up to the Rebellion: 'I am of no late Association nor shall I, because it brings on a responsibility moral as well as political for what has been done, for what is doing or for what may be done, which may be more than I chuse to bear'.[18]

Throughout the 1790s, Drennan never wavered in his support for the United Irishmen's ideological quarrel. However, he became increasingly distrustful of its patriot leaders, and their proposed means of redress – physical rebellion. On January 14, 1797, he writes:

> I speak as one who is ignorant of what is going on, but who does not like the notion of being egged on by the initiated to serve as an

> instrument in the work, for I am not yet so thoroughly persuaded of its virtue, its real patriotism, or its practicability as to say like the Spartans when the Athenians disputed with them for precedence in rank on the field of battle, 'Place us wherever you think proper; there we shall endeavour to behave like brave men!'[19]

Drennan's reference to classical warfare in the latter half of this quotation is most pertinent to his attitude towards rebellion. Indeed, it could be argued that the poet, despite his moral and religious beliefs, would have marched to rebellion over strict points of honour and principle, with a noble, gentlemanly army of classical patriots: but to march alongside the precursors of our present-day hooded volunteers would have been anathema to his heroic sensibilities. To use Berkeley's execrable pun, Drennan distinguished between patriotism and pat-riotism.

Of course, it may be said that all this leaves Drennan open to a charge of extreme naivety. Though he might have believed himself to be a Tyrtaeus inspiring a classical army to honourable victory, the reality was very different. Chauvinistic elements within several of his famous ballads most probably fermented rebellion amongst many beleaguered Irishmen living in the real (and often sectarian) world of late eighteenth-century Ireland. Although Drennan could stir the disaffected by trafficking in nationalist stereotypes, they could never perceive his efforts to sublimate such symbols within a more illustrious Graeco-Roman context; nor could they have appreciated the restraining influence of Drennan's moral and theological convictions. What is more, the same people would have raucously derided Drennan's own description of his patriotic ballads as an attempt to 'write party songs without the rancour of party'.[20] Irish traditional/tribal divisions do not permit patriot poets the luxury of such ivory towers.

Drennan was certainly well aware that the advocates of revolution viewed him with much suspicion, given his equivocation between patriot balladeer and reluctant rebel. His correspondence bears witness to the fact that he wrestled with this dilemma throughout the 1790s. For example, as early as 1792, he writes: 'do I not hurt myself in the eyes of sanguine friends and act in a cowardly manner by not subjecting myself to any danger which I did not hesitate to subject other people to.'[21]

And in a subsequent letter he struggles to reconcile his involvement in the formation of the United Irishmen, with his dissociation from the kind of revolutionary exploits which culminated in 1798:

> The People here look on me as a solitary nine-pin standing by chance when the other eight are bowled down . . .I think, on the whole of my past life, I have done my country some service, tho' they don't know it. I have helped by all that I wrote to elevate and give a certain turn of public enthusiasm to the national mind. I have been an Inventor in some things which have grown into great good or great evil, but I can answer to my conscience for the Intention. I think I hear some one say, the Man who invented the Balloon had not the courage to ascend in it. Perhaps so.

Inevitably, though, the poet realised that it was his classical veneration of the fatherland, coupled with his religious concerns, which compelled his estrangement from the barbarous excesses of the Hibernian sansculotte:

> There is a degeneracy from pure principle into vindicative passions, which is every day more apparent; but it is passions of such a kind that act upon the greatest number and instigate to the greatest exertions. The hatred that Grattan has to the Chancellor is a more stirring principle than his philanthropy, or even his patriotism, and a Christian forgiveness of injuries will scarcely be well received by the bastilled inhabitants of Ireland.

For all his scruples Drennan, needless to say, found little comfort from the forces of conservatism, amongst whom were numbered many of his own Church. For instance, writing to his sister in 1796, he exclaims: 'Could you conceive that a clergyman refused to go into a seat at Church when his companion told him that your brother was there – yet this is absolute fact'. And despite his attempts to distance himself from the Terror of rebellion, he was branded by the reactionary press as 'a Pharisee instigated by a Devil'.

Although it became increasingly obvious to Drennan that he had taken up residence in a kind of political no man's land, he was resolute in his conviction that he had 'acted right [sic]'; for 'midst the two tempestuous parties 'of the country, he had' not shifted from solid ground'. Perhaps his most telling comments in this regard, however, occur in a letter to his sister in 1796, where he formulates the painful paradox of his splendid isolation:

> . . . I have few if any friends, partly owing . . . to my being a sort of aristocratical Democrat, which sort of character must prove very disagreeable in the wear, as it exiles a man from the confidence,

> and companionship of both parties, the great vulgar think him mean, and the small think him proud.

The oxymoronic quality of the phrase 'aristocratical Democrat' perfectly epitomises the ambivalent nature of Drennan's politics. On the one hand, his tirades against the lethargy of the common Irishry appear to betray a lofty fastidiousness characteristic of the landed gentry:

> My country! shall I mourn, or bless,
> Thy tame and wretched happiness?
> . . .
> True! thou are blest, in Nature's plan,
> Nothing seems wanting here, but – MAN;
> Man – to subdue, not serve the soil,
> To win, and wear its golden spoil;
> Man – conscious of an earth his own,
> No savage biped, torpid, prone;
> Living, to dog his brother brute,
> And hung'ring for a lazy root,
> Food for a soft, contented slave;
> Not for the hardy and the brave.[22]

And on the other hand, when he rages against aristocratic tyranny and privilege he seems to echo the opinion of the native Jacquerie:

> Titles and arms the varnish'd silk may bear,
> Within – 'tis nought but pestilential air.[23]

Certainly Drennan's commitment to democracy was never in question – consider, for example, his consistent demands for Parliamentary Reform and Catholic Emancipation. Even so, how could he square such convictions with the incongruity of the term 'aristocratical'? Perhaps Yeats provides us with the solution to this conundrum when he asserts that 'All who have any old tradition, have something of aristocracy . . .'[24] a dictum which Drennan himself might have penned, so accurately does it reflect his own disposition. For Drennan, the claims of 'old tradition' were enshrined within his peculiar strain of classical patriotism. Unfortunately, however, this was not the sort of banner around which the discontented masses could rally, since, as W.B. Stanford points out, 'in Ireland a political creed needs cultural and historical roots if it is to win and hold the imagination of the people'.[25] Ultimately Drennan's 'love of the fatherland' model was too elite and esoteric to accommodate the die-hard dogmas of the Orange and Green – those bred on the King William or Cuchulain mythologies. It seems likely that it was the realisation of this fact which forced the poet to adopt a position of radical neutrality in the revolutionary cauldron of 1798.

CHAPTER 7

Samuel Ferguson: A Tourist in Antrim

by

Eve Patten

It may seem ironic that a writer born and bred in Antrim is introduced as a 'tourist' in his home region, or, in his own words as 'A stranger in the land that give him birth'. What I intend to highlight by means of this apparent contradiction is Ferguson's position as a writer whose loyalities to a native place were countered by an affiliation to an adoptive society. Ferguson never lost touch with his roots or waned in his interest in the north east, but at times his perspective on Antrim tends towards that of the imperious outsider, promoting a sense of distance and denying identification. This was, I think, no accident, but part of a self-conscious manoeuvre which needs to be seen in a wider social context. Ferguson's depiction of Antrim is informed by conventions which systematically manipulated the concept of regional Ireland, and drew from the Irish landscape images which registered particular social values associated not with Donegore, the writer's birthplace, but with Dublin. And at the outset, the term 'landscape' must alert us to certain preconditions. Raymond Williams refuses to let the word pass without the reminder that 'A working country is hardly ever a landscape. The very idea of a landscape implies separation and observation.'[1] With his move to the capital in 1834, Ferguson had certainly effected a separation. But in what manner did he turn around to observe the countryside which he left behind? I want to explore the possibility that his deracination from Antrim and his subsequent integration into a Dublin intelligentsia formed elements of an antithesis, in which rural, regional Ireland was drawn into the confines of a self-enabling urban myth.

We might begin by considering Ireland in the late eighteenth and early nineteenth centuries as a country which had become accustomed to living under observation. The utilitarian face of enlightenment revealed itself in this periphery of the kingdom in the numerous land assessors, amateur and professional, who applied their minds to the problem of the Irish terrain in this period: agricultural surveyors pondered the physical capabilities of the soil, land economists calculated its resources and potential, pipe-dreamers laboured to produce convincing proposals for draining the Irish bogs. And if the Irish land was to be rationalised, it also needed to be charted efficiently. In the 1830s, the Royal Engineers of the Ordnance Survey Commission were at their most industrious, and their most conspicuous, posting their theodolites on the highest points of each county and establishing these as triangulation stations from which the land could be measured, defined, and converted into the regulation six-inch map.

Whether we analyse the Ordnance Survey project on a purely practical level, in terms of its significance for legal and fiscal administration, or on an ideological basis, as a symbolic extension of control from Dublin to the outlying counties, the same result emerges: the pervasive sense that rural Ireland could be contained on paper within a centralised bureaucratic system. For the young Samuel Ferguson, unofficially co-opted to assist the Topographical Department of the Commission, this aspect of the Survey perhaps represented its most influential dimension. The ethos of the Commission undoubtedly increased the confidence of the capital in its own ability to select and determine the appearance of the regions. But was such an authority limited to a trigonometrical sphere? The painters, the antiquarians, and the writers who frequented the Dublin headquarters of the Survey were subject to a parallel responsibility, for if this process of definition could be worked in mathematical formulae, could it not also be achieved through an artistic system of rural manipulation?

Some preliminary answers to that question lie in what may be seen as the aesthetic counterpart to the ultilitarian reading of the land. The scenic relief of the country offered an equivalent space within which the concept of Ireland as a recreational resort could be formulated, or, to put it bluntly, invented. Landscape, in this sense, was very much the prerogative of the urban middle-class tourist. When the Napoleonic wars made it difficult to travel overseas in the tradition of the Grand Tour, those with leisure time on their hands began to look to the domestic circuit, transferring to the landscape of Ireland conventions of late eighteenth century European tourism developed abroad, and a new generation of well-informed travellers sought out the countryside, equipped with preconceived ideas about how it should be approached, and what impressions it should give. From Thomas West's Lake District, they borrowed the notion of 'stations' – predetermined high points at which the tourist was obliged to stop and admire a particular vista according to the terms stipulated by the guide book. From Burke and Wordsworth they grasped transportable definitions of the Romantic Sublime, and from the classical landscape painters, Claude Lorraine and Salvatore Rosa, they took disciplines of form and perspective. Above all they indulged in one of the most prevalent cults of the age, the picturesque.

The picturesque now strikes us as a rather clichéd chapter in the history of taste. Its foremost advocate, the artist and writer William Gilpin, established a version of landscape appreciation which valued the terrain only in terms of its representational potential: quite simply, how well could it appear in a picture? Certain picturesque qualities, ruins and rivers, were prioritised; non-picturesque items such as agricultural workings or modern buildings were obliterated in favour of a romantic ideal. The land became subject to the composing eye of the viewer – artist or tourist – who selected and regulated the scene. 'We must recollect' Gilpin advised 'that nature is most defective in composition and must be a little assisted. Her ideas are too vast for picturesque use, without the restraint of rules'.[2] If nature presented a smooth mountain slope, its surface was to be roughened or 'chiselled' into interesting picturesque crags and hollows. Trees and banks might be removed, waterfalls and ruins highlighted, storm clouds added, and perhaps a solitary figure introduced into the foreground, to act as an internal tour guide, there for no other reason than to indicate towards the scene in rapt admiration. From the professional painter to the amateur sketcher to the tourist who imitated their methods, picturesque convention offered a formula for the individual to compose and constrain the landscape as he or she wished.

As a popular, commercially viable cult, the picturesque was the style adopted to illustrate a proliferation of guide-books on Ireland in the 1820s and 1830s. Ferguson's close friend, the painter and antiquarian George Petrie, was contracted by several publishers to produce, as they insisted, 'such scenes as unite picturesque beauty with interesting locality'.[3] Lithographs, etchings and aquatints not only accompanied a written text but came to take priority over verbal description in the representation of the landscape. Both on his own and in conjunction with fellow artists Henry O'Neill and Andrew Nichol, Petrie set about depicting parts of Antrim, publishing, in 1820 a *Guide to the North Antrim Coast* and in 1830 *Ten Views of Picturesque Scenery in the North and North West of Ireland*, reproducing many times perfect vignettes of Dunluce Castle, the Carrick-a-rede Rope Bridge, or the Giant's Causeway.

The tone of Petrie's art was irrepressibly melancholic, and his antiquarian obsessions are worth noting at this point as these frequently conditioned his artistic style. In his work, and particularly in his non-contracted paintings, he concentrated on scenes which conveyed a sense of Ireland's derelict native heritage; his love was for round towers and crumbling churches pictured against a setting sun, perhaps with a decrepit pilgrim or two, and a few sheep grazing in the foreground. The sense of nostalgia for a lost rural past, and the emblems of a mystic Celticism which he evoked in his art informed his commercial work too, making it a valuable tourist commodity. Through such representation, the Irish landscape became a package deal – an artifact which was accessible and controlled, but still exotic and atmospheric. Wordsworth echoed many other visitors in describing Ireland as 'a romantic itinerary, a succession of picturesque scenes with priority given to ruined monasteries'.[4] A rural terrain could thus be conveyed through regular, standard images, regardless of its economic or social identity, and regardless of its agricultural development.

Ferguson, who was a devoted disciple of Petrie as an antiquarian, also seems to have been influenced by him artistically. It was Petrie who in the first instance gave the young writer instruction in drawing. Ferguson was a fairly talented though unimaginative landscape artist, (the Linen Hall library, Belfast possesses some of his sketches and watercolours), and Petrie would occasionally give him tips and advice in exchange for snippets of Ferguson's antiquarian research on various localities. Through an aesthetic version of Ireland like that provided by Petrie, Ferguson encountered a specific set of artistic conventions, and these in turn may be seen to shape his written representation of landscape. The stylistic transfer from one medium to another is by no means surprising in any nineteenth century writer, but in Ferguson's case, the particular stress on picturesque detail suggests an indulgence in artistic mannerism which was deliberately and ostentatiously self-conscious. Here, for example, in an 1835 historical romance, he describes the terrain of the Antrim hills. This is the tale of the chieftain Corby McGillmore and his nomadic tribe, who in their secret encampment somewhere behind Cave Hill, are quietly enjoying the last few years of pagan, semi-barbarian life before Christianity and civilisation catch up with them. Ferguson's use of picturesque detail provides the backdrop to this wild, precarious, doomed existence.

> The ground below, thrown into grotesque undulation by which time had thus overlaid it with the ruins of the broken mountain, was clad with the tenderest verdure on all its slopes and hollows,

> where the long influence of the elements had wrapped the chaos underneath in a covering of vegetable mould, till the craggy mounds and riven abysses were smoothed into one continuous surface, . . . the green hollows and fantastic hillocks took more sweeping and picturesque outlines at each new succession of the series.

This reliance on a formulaic literary landscaping serves to reduce the object to a passive stereotype dominated by the ordering eye of the observer: the land loses its autonomy, and becomes subject to fashionable artistic doctrine. In an earlier tale the relationship between Petrie's antiquarian picturesque and Ferguson's fictional world seems even closer. *The Black Monday of the Glens* tells of a love affair between Phelim, a 'papist smuggler', and Letty, a virtuous farmer's daughter of solid Protestant planter stock. Despite having rescued Letty from drowning Phelim is not considered a suitable candidate for her hand in marriage. His religion, his occupation, and his suggested alcoholic indulgence (in addition to the fact that he believes in fairies) do little to improve his prospects. So the two lovers arrange to meet for a clandestine ceremony at which they will pledge themselves to each other for ever. Ferguson's choice of venue for this fateful encounter is the church of Layde – a ruin near Cushendall which, some years previously, he had visited, sketched, and discussed with Petrie. In the moonlight the couple meet.

> The winding beach brought them close under the ruins of Layde church, and climbing up the grassy slope, Phelim and Letty found themselves standing by the roofless walls that had once been the sanctuary of the saints. There on consecrated ground, under the grey ash tree which has rooted itself in the bare isle, Heaven, their hearts their only witness, they plighted their troth, come weal or woe.

The translation of archaeological detail into a picturesque backdrop for the union illuminates the manner in which antiquarianism, art and land were compounded by Ferguson into a fictional system of representation equivalent to the composition of a Petrie painting. These simple, superstitious and quaint folk from the Antrim Glens became inextricable from a landscape romantically conceived and picturesquely depicted.

Landscape no longer existed independently, then, but was created by a separate and standardised authority, And what the visual artist introduced, the tourist consolidated upon. With reference to the conventions of tourist travel mentioned earlier, a pattern emerges in Ferguson's writing in which the viewing protagonist finds a 'station' from which the surrounding area may be surveyed, described, and, to use Gilpin's word, 'appropriated'. There are numerous examples of this in both his poetry and fiction, but the instance to which I shall draw attention is from his 1833 historical romance, *The Return of Claneboy*, which tells the story of Yellow Hugh O'Neill, returning to Antrim to recover the territory held by the earl of Ulster. O'Neill's claim to the land is by birthright, but his knowledge of the terrain is scant, and so he travels into Antrim with a guide, an Erenach, who acts rather like one of Petrie's foregrounded indicating figures. The two men climb Slemish mountain, and in mid-story, Ferguson switches into the register of the tour-guide:

> Slemish is one great joint of that spine of mountain that runs between the vale of Glenwhirry on one side, and that of Broughshane on the other, heaved over its fellows so high, and so abruptly, that to the eye of one standing on its highest point, the platform of its summit is alone visible, like a green island underfoot, floating a thousand feet above the middle of the County Antrim, for from that point neither base nor side can be seen, but all around, from Louth upon the south, to the hills of the Causeway upon the north, and from the mountains of Argyleshire and Galloway upon the east to the western highlands of Derry and Tyrone, everything lies under view as on a map.

Here, the tourist idiom in the provision of a panoramic vista and a 'station' is backed up by a topographical dimension: 'Stand by my side, good Louglin' says O'Neill, 'and tell me how all these lakes and mountains around us are named, for I here seen loughs and countries that I never dreamed of till now'. Simultaneously it represents an act of territorial appropriation, and echoes the cartographical project of the Ordnance Survey, at its height in Antrim at around this time, with Slemish as one of its triangulation points.

Ferguson's literary engagement with practices drawn from landscape art and tourist writing lead us to consider what he wished the county of Antrim to signify to a Dublin audience familiar with those conventions. In a series of articles published in the *Dublin University Magazine* in 1836, entitled 'Attractions of Ireland', he takes the reader on an imaginary picturesque tour of the country, making clear from the outset that distinctions will be drawn between the Ireland which is regional, rural, and romantic, and the Ireland which is urban and progressive. Dublin is established as the civilised metropolis, a world apart from the primitive periphery: '. . . the man who takes delight in speculating on the peculiarities of national manners, and on the tendencies of national mind' he argues 'will find in Dublin the least part of his entertainment; for here we are as little Irish as we can; and our manners are characteristic only where we fail in coming up to the British standard'.

This hints at one of Ferguson's major obsessions: the attempt to maintain Dublin as a credible capital city, on a par if not with London, then at least with Edinburgh, sophisticated in taste and advanced in intellect. In setting up the regions of Ireland as antithetical to the progressive centre, he could emphasise that centrality, and imply the existence of a social stability which the Act of Union and the political upheavals of the late 1820s and early 1830s had threatened to erode. The cult of the picturesque which his writing negotiates was an affectation serving to prove that the city was secure enough to sustain a literate and moneyed bourgeoisie. Against the backdrop of a rural Ireland which was romantic but in ruins, the viewer of the picturesque scene implies, albeit silently, the presence of an authoritative urban alter ego. Just as England had defined itself as civilised in contrast with Spenser's wild Irish barbarians, Dublin required this internal counterproposition, and the undeveloped regions were thus brought under the jurisdiction, administrative and aesthetic, of a dominant central value-system.

Antrim is exploited in a particular way by Ferguson as tourist. If he saw County Wicklow as a suburban retreat parallel to the English Lake District, then he saw Antrim and specifically the Glens, as Dublin's answer to the Scottish highlands. After all, the region had a ready-made Scottish population. If the traveller ventures this far north, says Ferguson, 'Scotch language, Scotch looks, Scotch habits will strike him wherever he turns'. The sparse population of the Glens accommodated a version of the same shadowy and almost supernatural creatures which crop up in the novels of Walter Scott when the reader needs a reminder of a disappearing Celtic world. 'This light-limbed glensman is, to all intents and purposes' claimed Ferguson, 'a Highlander. Highland scenery surrounds his hut; the walls echo to the noise of waterfalls and mountain torrents; clouds rest halfway between his garden and his sheepwalk, and for nine months out of twelve he is, in strict truth, a child of the mist'. So the glensman is already half myth, and herein lies his value to the observer steeped in enlightenment materialism. Ferguson's 'child of the mist' represents a culture made even more precious by the fact of its own imminent extinction: '..they are a doomed race' he continues, 'the engineer has planted his theodolite against them, and the road-maker, who is following with his pick and shovel, will 'ere long level all distinctions as well of language and habits as of hill and plain'.

Contrived vignettes of the rural condition were the means by which an urban mentality could appropriate what was unknown within a terrain, and reduce it to something recognisable and functional, filtered through conventional perspectives. Picturesque versions of the landscape contained their own internal contradiction, pointing backwards to the values of the seeing eye, presupposing a distinguished urban sophistication. Similarly, the terminology in which Ferguson frames and manipulates his native county is aimed at self-exposure. The Glens thus become 'a little rustic Arcadia', and the weaver poets are patronised as spirited but misguided bucolic versifiers whose best efforts are generally in bad taste, and whose regular meetings are occasions for 'rough humour. . . absurdity and coarseness'. While Dublin thrives as a centre of civic excellence, intellectual prowess, and European urbanity, Antrim is reduced to a portrait of a charming but fossilised region towards which the capital could feel suitably patronising, and suitably superior.

Ferguson's response to Antrim and to the Irish landscape in general, is by no means unique; rather it typifies an early nineteenth century habit of viewing which selected and evaluated the countryside in a highly self-conscious manner. Nor did such representations in Ferguson's early prose writings exclude the sympathetic interest in Antrim, and indeed Ulster in general, which characterises his later poetry. His contributions to the picturesque map-making of his native county – panoramic, nostalgic, and detached – reveal, however, the needs peculiar to the urban side of his personality. His involvement with the Ordnance Survey Commission, with topography, antiquarianism and landscape painting, hastened his retreat to the position of 'separation and observation' with which this essay opened, but these factors were the props with which he sought to stabilise the early years of his career. Ferguson's version of Antrim as a picturesque idyll was therefore a projection of personal insecurity, and in turn, an attempted resolution in art of wider public pressures experienced within the society to which he aspired, and the city which had become his home.

CHAPTER 8

No Rootless Colonists: Samuel Ferguson and John Hewitt

by

Gréagóir Ó Dúill

I

Samuel Ferguson was born in High Street, Belfast, in 1810. He grew up in Glenwherry, a few miles west of Garron Point, and is buried – despite the offer of a place in Saint Patrick's Cathedral, Dublin – in the graveyard associated with his family at Donegore, a few miles further west again. Like Hewitt he was a Belfast-born lover of the Glens of Antrim and this region provides him with the locale and indeed the theme of much of his best work in both poetry and prose. Ferguson was the most significant east Ulster poet in the two hundred years from Séamus Dall Mac Cuarta to Louis MacNeice, indeed the most significant Ulster poet of the period with, perhaps, the exception of William Allingham.[1] John Hewitt had a close knowledge of Ferguson's life and work, much of it gained in the course of his research for an M.A. in Queen's University on nineteenth-century Ulster poetry. Hewitt disagreed with Ferguson on many artistic and other points, but the degree of basic similarity between the two is considerable. Both were happily but childlessly married to wives from more privileged backgrounds. Ferguson and Hewitt both came of families in which an appreciation of poetry is evidenced. Ferguson's mother, Agnes Knox, read much contemporary poetry to her family, even the terrible Shelley, while Hewitt had a grandmother who carried poems in her garter and 'remembering that satin pouch of poems,/ I clasp her bony hand'.[2]

Late in life, in an essay published in 1983, the enduringly leftist Hewitt faulted the verse of the Irish Literary Revival.

> All this original verse was filled with fairies, tramps of both sexes, tinkers, turfcutters, mothers crooning cradle-sings, cabins in misty

> glens or by lonely shores. This was now the accepted fashion; it had had its tentative beginnings in Ferguson's 'Fairy Thorn' . . . So from these voluble city dwellers there was not a word about where they lived and the people they lived among until [1917].[3]

One must ask in reply how many lines of poetry of social realism based in the cities Hewitt wrote despite the fact that it was the fashion of his youth and the duty of his ideology. Ferguson's 'Fairy Thorn' was not as immediately successful a poem, in its day, as his 'Forging of the Anchor', a poem celebrating Belfast's nascent shipbuilding tradition, which was singled out by Christopher North of *Blackwood's* for high praise precisely because it was a realistic poem with industrial theme, imagery and language. North contrasted it with what he regarded as the weakly pastoral and irrelevent concerns and language shown in Tennyson's *Poems*.[4]

Nevertheless Hewitt conceded in that late essay that Ferguson was 'the most nationally important poet to have been born in Belfast' – his use of adverbial qualification here may be double-edged. Earlier, in 1953, he had argued that in his translations from the Irish and in his bardic poetry, Ferguson

> occupies a pivotal place in the literary history not only of our region but of the whole country . . . [he] could turn a comely stanza in the vernacular when he pleased . . . But, for us, perhaps his chief value lies in that he recognised his personal position as an Irishman of Ulster Planter stock.[5]

He went on to quote the verse in Ferguson's 'Mesgedra' which includes the phrase which describes them both, 'no rootless colonist', and ends by describing Ferguson as one of the greatest writers born in Ireland. In an essay published at the end of the Second World War Hewitt admitted the importance (just as much to the planter as to the Gael) of the inheritance of the legendry of the pre-Plantation Irish, which had been revived through the scholarship of Ulstermen of planter stock such as Ferguson, Petrie, Sigerson, as well as of Germans such as Kuno Meyer and Englishmen such as Robin Flower.[6]

This argument of the central importance of the transmission of cultural inheritance is equally explicit in Ferguson's work, and he, too, even more explicitly than Hewitt, insisted that it was not a process monopolised or even best served by the Catholic nationalist majority, and still less by the representatives of the majority's political creed, but that it should be seen as a field in which the Protestant and Ascendancy scholar excelled, a field for international co-operation rather than for narrow nationalism.

However, in 1958 Hewitt found fault with Ferguson's artistic understanding. Ferguson, he says, works 'with Homer behind him, bent to the task of forging great banging and resounding couplets to recreate his antique narrative'. The relentless stride of the verse would knock the breath out of any reader, while the hyphenated epithets blur his imagination's eye. Congal, the epic of which Ferguson was most proud, failed, and the failure was one of touch, not tact, said Hewitt. He rejected the feasibility of one of Ferguson's main aims when he said that there can be no hybrid begot of English and Gaelic metres, and contrasted the efforts of such experimentalists with those of MacDiarmid and other Scots, struggling to preserve and regularise an historic language, that Scots so close to the east Ulster country dialect. To Hewitt, you either preserved a language, as the Scots appeared to be doing, or you failed to do that, as the Irish did.[7] To Ferguson, it was possible and desirable to cope with an inevitable language shift by transferring as much as possible of the spirit and culture of the dying Irish language into English.

Partly because of the length of the period over which Ferguson wrote and published, more than half a century from 1830 to the mid-eighties, partly because of the changes in his utterance in that period, and because he shifted his focus and artistic method more than once, Ferguson has tended to be misunderstood. Young Ireland hijacked him for their own politico-cultural purposes, and so too, over forty years later, did his young friend, to whom he was a mentor, W.B. Yeats. Ferguson was regarded by the political nationalists as one of their own, in cultural matters, although not of the elect in matters of religion and constitutional loyalty; he was, nevertheless, a true cultural patriot the effect of whose work would be to add to the cohesion and force of the demand for Irish independence and unification.

With Ferguson cast in this light it was difficult for Hewitt to see him whole, free from the associations which his most vociferous supporters attached to him. Moreover, Ferguson appears as precisely one of those Conservative east Ulster minor gentry who wrote poetry in standard or Hiberno-English, who moved comfortably from Presbyterianism not to a radical deism but to the established church, who played to the gentry and their publishers in Edinburgh, London and Dublin even more than to the new middle class. The Gaelicism of Ferguson's concerns did not recommend his work to Hewitt, who did not realise how thin the evidence was for the myth sedulously fostered by Ferguson and then, in her two-decker biography, by his widow, that he came of the gentry; for Hewitt was in the throes of his own campaign, insisting on the artistic and historical imporance of the rhyming weavers, a campaign as political as it was scholarly or critical. His campaign, and a certain lack of sympathy for bardic and antique themes, prevented him from examining the work of the best of these Irish gentlemen poets with an impartial critical sympathy. Nevertheless, in several important respects, Hewitt's comments on Ferguson are more illuminating that those of any other critic. Hewitt came to Ferguson's work with the knowledge that it derived from the mind-set of east Ulster in the first thirty years of the last century, a mind-set with which he empathised and which he studied closely. Thus Hewitt had advantages in the understanding of Ferguson which no other critics have had, advantages which balanced out his lack of sympathy for what he mistakenly regarded as Ferguson's positions on class and national politics.

II

John Hewitt made a special study of the poetic tradition of County Antrim. He argued in *Rhyming Weavers* (1974) that the strength of religious education and practice of the Presbyterian people led to intensive choir practice. A taboo on the use of the sacred words of hymns outside their proper context of divine service meant that choir practice often became the occasion for impromptu composition or doggerel, or indeed for light pointed verse about local events for singing to the hymn tunes. Hewitt saw evidence that these verses were marked by a developed sense of rhythm to fit the metre of the hymns and of repetition, assonance and alliteration to aid choir singing. The choir often sang under the leadership of a precentor.[8] Ferguson himself noted the practice in 1836. Each member of the choir could be asked in turn to provide an original couplet, and the verses so supplied were neither poetical in spirit nor elegant in diction, 'but a collection of them would be found to embody a good deal of rough humour'. These meetings, whether hymn-based or merely for entertainment, were known, Ferguson says, as 'singings'.[9] Hewitt saw that a characteristic of the popular verse of Antrim and Down poets of Scottish stock was 'a dense idiom, the rhymes . . . approximate, vowel-rhymes or assonances, more usually'.[10] Ferguson shared in this aural concentration and Bulmer Hobson, a Belfast republican leader, thought that some of his dramatic verse, particularly 'Deirdre', anticipated the potential and techniques of radio drama.[11] More recently, Brendan Kennelly has similarly stressed how oral

Ferguson's skills were and how aural the appeal remains of even his later poetry.[12] Hugh Kenner asked of 'The Fairy Thorn': 'Has anything like it been heard in English before?' but did not share Patrick Rafroidi's mistake of thinking that the haunting density of consonance and assonance came from the Irish language poetic tradition. Kenner knew they came from music. It is one of the ironies of Ferguson's reputation that the influence of Presbyterian hymn singing, identified as such by Hewitt, should be commonly thought to derive from Irish language poetry. Even George Russell, himself of Ulster nonconformist background and affected by Methodist hymns, made that assumption about Ferguson. Hewitt saw clearly that Ferguson was, and saw himself to be, a poet of the north-east regional culture, who reviewed a volume of folk poetry, sent collections to 'the dominant poet of mid-Antrim' David Herbison, and had close kin, probably sisters, who were listed as subscribers supporting the publication of other collections of local County Antrim poetry.[13]

Ferguson's paternal family belonged to the congregation of Donegore which had to choose between two of the most famous and contrasting Ulster Presbyterian divines of the first half of the nineteenth century. Both the Reverends Montgomery and Cooke were considered to fill a vacancy which occurred in 1808.[14] For the ten years from his eighth to his eighteenth year the congregation was ministered to by Henry Cooke. Hewitt has analysed the period closely. He argued that Cooke drove the more liberal and tolerant section of the Presbyterians from positions of power and influence in the north-east, that he tied the evangelicals to the landowners of the Tory party, moved the Presbyterian Church closer to the established Church of Ireland and identified Catholicism with nationalism.[15] Cooke and Montgomery reacted very differently to the French Revolution of 1830, and Ferguson followed Cooke in this matter, as in others.[16]

Ferguson took unto himself in an imaginative identification the heritage of a community which lived with a medieval graveyard, Donegore, and ancient fort, Rathmore Moylinney. The culture was heavy with recent memories of the hosting of the Presbyterian rebels on Donegore Hill the night before the Battle of Antrim in 1798[17] and the retreat of the broken insurgents, including their leader Henry Joy McCracken, through Glenwherry.[18] The strange violence of much of Ferguson's verse may be because he grew up in an area with bloody associations, both distant and very recent. Ferguson's enthusiasm for his area, its traditions and its history, is to be seen in much of his work, indeed in much of his best work. In this respect, as in others, Ferguson, as a provincial poet, was typical not of his own period but of the period before he was born, the later eighteenth century when loco-descriptive poetry increased in popularity.[19] Hewitt's strong sense of place, which has in turn influenced the Ulster poets of this generation, found a precedent and a strengthening in Ferguson as well as in the rhyming weavers.

Ferguson's romantic identification with the de-standardised folk culture of east Ulster led rapidly to an identification with the even more de-standardised Gaelic culture. His first identification, like Hewitt's, was with the people from whom he came, and their culture, and that identification was one of the few constants of his long creative life, which shows a number of shifts in political and cultural stance. In his second identification, with the Gaelic culture, Ferguson drew close to the people he regarded it as his birthright to lead and to govern. Unlike most other Protestant or Presbyterian men of letters of his period he did not recognise the Catholic majority as a threat because, in east Antrim and in Belfast as he grew up, their numbers and political organisation and economic strenth were so small that they were no threat. By the time the idea of the Catholics as a threat had grown in Belfast, at the period of Emancipation, Ferguson was already liberated from the fears which prevented most of his co-religionists from making an identification with what was, historically at least, the majority Irish culture – the Gaelic culture. The accident of his birthplace, the unimaginability of any threat from the Catholics there and his early removal to Edinburgh and London gave Ferguson the opportunity of identifying with the Gaelic culture. John Hewitt stopped short of making that second identification and remained a regionalist.[20] The two men shared an openness of mind to the world and to the majority of the Irish people, a concern for cultural integrity in its literary and linguistic expression. They developed differently and one reason was that a hundred years separated their birth dates, a hundred years in which socio-economic and political change created their own partition.

III

Nevertheless, the similarities between Ferguson and Hewitt are great. Ferguson may be regarded as an Ulster regionalist in a higher proportion of his work than is normally thought. This is true of his prose, such as his historical romances, for example 'The Return of Clandeboye' set in his own area in the Middle Ages, 'Shane O'Neill's Last Amour' set in Lough Neagh and east Tyrone in the 1560s, 'The Wet Wooing' set in the Antrim Plateau and coast in 1798 and, best of all, 'Corby McGilmore' set on the slopes of the Cave Hill, again in the

Middle Ages. These form part of an imaginative history of east Ulster, consciously undertaken and seriously researched. In poetry, 'The Forging of the Anchor' celebrated the great growth of Belfast's ship-building at the beginning of the 1830s; 'The Ballad of Willy Gilliland' celebrates a covenanting gentleman who escaped from persecution in south-west Scotland to Ireland but found the soldiery of Carrickfergus prepared to continue the harassment: they kill his hound and take his horse. Ferguson often concentrated on the way in which he and the east Ulster people came of Scottish stock a few score years before he wrote, and he insisted that Ulstermen should recognise their Scottish ancestry, and that the Scots, in turn, were descended from the Irish. Hewitt, too, in considering his position in Coventry, recognised that he came of stock which left that area.

Ferguson's regional east Ulster poetry includes a poem that remembers a Kilroot landlord, Dobbs, who took a boat out against the American privateer, Jones, in his descent on Carrickfergus; another relates the flight of lovers, a planter and a Gaelic girl from the slaughter of the Gobbins in 1642. There are popular pieces in the north-east dialect, 'Willy and Pate, a County Down pastoral', which is an Orange allegory, and 'The Loyal Orangeman' which seems to mix satire and seriousness, fond understanding and impatience. Ferguson also wrote a number of verse-letters or letters containing verse in the east Ulster dialect. One of his best poems, 'The Fairy Thorn', is set in the north-east, and shows the girls dancing a Highland reel, not an Irish one. As time passed he wrote longer poems, set in the remote past, peopled not with planters but with Gaels. A recurrent theme of this poetry is that Ulster is different. It is less dominated by priests and is kinder to poets. It is under attack from the other provinces, and is heavily out-numbered. It suffers from enemies within, and the real Ulster is that which can be seen from the summit of Slemish. The future lies in love and marriage across the divisions of religion and race. Ferguson was a didactic poet, as Hewitt himself tended to be. His later poetry can be read as unionist Ulster particularism in Gaelic code. He intended that the creation of an English-language literature based on Irish-language literature and a consciously Irish sentiment would assist in the unity of these islands. He knew that the number of people who understood what he was doing was very few in number, but, like Hewitt, he was satisfied to write for those few, 'for his own kind . . . across a roaring hill'. Ferguson's balancing act, to at least the same degree as Hewitt's, was a deliberate part of a political programme, as much as of an artistic one.

Hewitt shared much the same ambivalences. Alienated from the present, both men sought the past. The past was their professional concern, Hewitt as a museum curator and Ferguson as the deputy keeper of the newly founded Public Record Office of Ireland.[21] Each chose the past as the field for the exercise of his poetic art: in Ferguson's case, the remote past, and in Hewitt's case the recent past. Unlike Ferguson, Hewitt had little sense of security and this blocked his access to the rich well of the older past, of tradition. When he tried to meet the continuing Irish culture, and turned aside to watch Cuchullin's chariot, or the socialist tradition, or the pre-Plantation Scottish connection, Hewitt's encounter shows how fortunate Ferguson was.

> He'd imagined a highway of heroes
> and stepped aside on the grass
> to let Cuchullain's chariot through
> and the Starry Ploughmen pass;
> but he met the Travelling Gunman
> instead of the Gallowglass

So Hewitt in 'Local Poet' 'mourns for his mannerly verses/ That had left so much unsaid'. Ulster had become a more violent place, one more difficult to love in, and for all her people, and her mismatch with the rest of Ireland had become more pronounced than in Ferguson's time. In 'The Scar' Hewitt tells us that he was inextricably linked to his nation (his word) by the accident of his great-grandmother's charity to a famine-fevered man from the west. He returned disease for her gift of bread. The same ambivalence appears in 'An Irishman in Coventry' where he identifies his nation by the whisky-tinctured breath and the jigging dances, stirring the old rage and pity in his heart. In 'Rite', Hewitt says 'I am of the Irishry, by nurture and by birth' but his descriptive term is curiously antique. In 'The Municipal Gallery Revisited October 1954', Hewitt stumbled into history unawares, but found the stone and metal men disarmed. The images included George Russell, and he relates to him as his only fellow countryman, although Russell was taken from the north shortly after his birth, and was later glad of that. He sees O'Leary, fresh out of the saga of Fenianism, and a socialist orator. But the sculptors' names are not given, and the very sculptures are unfinished and badly cared for. History had only one hour of triumph, an hour which wrung a nation out of bitterness. He wonders if the sculptures, the nation-state or the nation itself will endure, 'for see, before me, threatening, immense,/ the creeping haircracks of indifference'. The museum curator, mid-century socialist and cultural regionalist merge in acid analysis of Ireland. Hewitt consistently applies the term 'nation' with the stereotypical meaning given it by the nationalists, a meaning which, to Hewitt, peripheralised if it did not exclude the Ulster Protestant people. The nation being alien, he was thrust back on the region. Political boundaries do not match the realities of his identification: 'the landscape does not alter;/ we had already entered these mountains an hour ago' ('The Frontier'). He knows that 'the story should have ended,/ the island now a nation, its people one' but the planters in 'The Mainland' have a race memory of the mainland that keeps them from identifying wholly with their new country.

Ferguson also saw the less attractive features of the majority in his own day, and did not hesitate to castigate them, but the historical Gaelic culture balanced out that repulsion, and permitted Ferguson to make a fuller indentification with the Irish nation. In his day, he was able (as Hewitt was not) to ignore for a while the link between Irish cultural identity and the arguments for, and violence associated with, the question of home rule or independence. Ferguson, too, regarded the politics of interfering with existing political boundaries as foolish. He thought that a strong Ireland could exist as a proud partner in the United Kingdom, at the head of the Empire, with Dublin at least the cultural equal of Edinburgh. Ferguson was a regionalist too, not only for the region of (east) Ulster but also for the region of Ireland in the community of these islands.

Hewitt and Ferguson shared, as their main concern, a desire to identify, describe, analyse and explain the identity of their community. Both were practical men, as their chosen careers show: As he tells us in 'An Irishman in Coventry', Hewitt disliked the 'glittering fables/ which gave us martyrs when we wanted men'. Before becoming head of Ireland's national archives at the age of fifty-seven and immersing himself in the detail of archivism, conservation and cultural administration, Ferguson concentrated in his professional career as a barrister on the north-east circuit on cases involving engineering, architecture and handcrafts. Both men concerned themselves with the past of their community and with the pre-Plantation culture, with 'all the buried men in Ulster clay' ('Once Alien Here'). By a concentration on nature and on simpler ways of living, and by a loyalty to the tradition and to an age-old cultural inheritance, both men sought to heal a wound in their community, and to increase understanding between the communities in Ulster and between Ulster and the rest of Ireland. Hewitt argued that we should dig below and past religion, and go with the sunburnt comrades carrying a picture into the temple; Ferguson empathised with the bards and druids in their rearguard action against intolerant, divisive Christianity. The identification was at the level of the mind, not of basic sympathy. Hewitt, for all his sympathy with the political left and with the people of the Glens of Antrim, said (in 'O Country People'): 'You are coarse to my senses, to my washed skin' and realised that 'even a lifetime among you would leave me strange,/ for I could not change enough, and you will not change'. Ferguson apologised for the rude manners to be found in some of the songs and poems for which he supplied verse translations into English. He bowdlerised others, and his failure to versify the main parts of the great Ulster saga, the Táin, may have been because it offended his sense of the socially admissible.

Hewitt was of the left, Ferguson was of the right, but their concentrations fell to a large extent outside the simplifications of the left/ right or the orange/green debate. Their careers suffered as a result of this independence, Ferguson failing to reach a judgeship, Hewitt losing his career prize, directorship of the Ulster Museum. Ferguson had a greater degree of formal loyalty, and could never write, as Hewitt did, in 'The King's Horses' that the cavalry wakening him by passing his London hotel in the early morning were 'going about the King's business, never mine'. His poems on the Battle of the Boyne and on the Resurrection show how much he valued his independence, how he fought to avoid being crowded or pushed. Of King William III, he wrote in 'The Crossing': 'I shall proceed carefully, keeping clear of the neat white heels' – but he still will cross the Boyne with him. With Christ, Hewitt can face any circumstance 'if I hold to the stubborn truth/ that he was killed, and most of us ran away' ('The Revenant'). Each a man of his century, Hewitt was more alone, more in doubt of the eternals.

Both poets celebrated the function of the poet or bard or file, and found reinforcement for their function in Gaelic poetry. Ferguson used a broad and knowledgeable focus while Hewitt concentrated on the figure of Oisin, so closely associated with his adopted area of the Glens of Antrim. His consciousness of Oisin strengthened both Hewitt's art and his realisation that tradition and art enrich the whole community. Coming home in the dark from Lubitavish 'a great white horse with lifted knees,/ came stepping past us, and we knew/ his rider was no tinker's son./ This (from 'Ossian's Grave') is early Yeats, and so much of early Yeats is Ferguson. Hewitt repossessed the word

Fenians from its debased contemporary currency in his celebration of Oisin, who was, he said in 'Homestead', his 'symbol',

> warrior and bard returning again and again
> to find the Fenians forgotten and unforgotten
> rising when bidden on the young men's lips . . .
> tougher than parchment or the string of beads . . .
> [Oisin] makes a show of genuflection, but in his heart
> still rises to the rhythms his Fenians knew.

He makes his own obeisance to Oisin in 'Rite; Lubitavish, Glenaan':

> And yesterday as I came down
> where Oisin's grave-stones stand,
> The holly-branch with berries hung
> Thrust upright in my hand.

To Ferguson, too, these ancient poets are a symbol and an example not only of the power of the poet, of an anti-clerical artistic caste and a culture independent of priest-ridden pietism, but also of cultural inheritance.

Both Ferguson and Hewitt were bilingual in the broad sense in that they talked standard Ulster-accented English and were at ease with the strong country dialect of east Ulster, so close to the broad Scots. They both used this bilingualism in verse, Ferguson by composing in dialect, Hewitt by including dialect words, phrases, rhymes and rhythms. His facility with a dialect then in considerable use in Scotland and in east Ulster provided Ferguson with the logic to use the Hiberno-English dialect as a medium for his translations from Irish. In this choice, Ferguson made one of his most significant contributions to Irish culture. But it was a cul-de-sac, given that Hiberno-English is even weaker than Irish, and one must be glad that Hewitt never found an Ulster Kiltartanesque style. Nevertheless, Hewitt remained more language conscious than most people of his background in Belfast, and many of his poems, particularly those set in the Donegal Gaeltacht areas, express this consciousness. The natives in 'Minotaur', for example, locate Hewitt and his party 'by speech, although we lacked/ the lilting Irish phrase, as Irish too'.

Ferguson and Hewitt both worked on a binary basis, with inbuilt artistic conflicts and creative tensions which enriched their art and increased their commitment to it. In his search for truth, Ferguson never managed to learn conversational Irish, and all his translations were with the help of more gifted or more fortunate people. The binary system of thought meant that Hewitt failed in his duty as a socialist poet of the forties to present us with a satisfactory Marxist form of poetry of the northeast, to give us those city poems of work and struggle, for lack of which he had faulted Ferguson. A constant fluid ambivalence is behind everything the two men did, creating the poetic tension inherent in their achievement. Ferguson expressed his ambivalence early in his career in his 'Dialogue between the Heart and Head of an Irish Protestant' in which one is rational, the other romantic, one just and hard, the other soft and flexible, one unionist and the other nationally inclined. Hewitt did not express the problem so clearly, but we can see the same theme of ambivalence appear in many of his poems and in his desire to step over into the other, kindly world of the Glens.

Ferguson was intensely loyal and unionist; some of his early attitudes were bitterly sectarian. Perhaps a shadow of this appears in Hewitt's cutting reference to 'the mumble and the gabble of the Mass'. Some of Ferguson's mature work is a coded incitement to particularism in Protestant Ulster a generation before the first Home Rule Bill. He felt strongly that the establishment ignored his literary efforts, and delayed publication of his first collection for fear it would harm his career. Yet he defended a young Catholic charged with treason-felony in 1848, formed a Protestant Repeal Association, remained in friendly correspondence with exiled Young Ireland leaders McGee and Mitchel. His reputation was dying in his own lifetime when a returned political exile, O'Leary, brought his work to the attention of the young I.R.B. man, W.B. Yeats, who championed the older poet on grounds of, for the purposes of, extreme cultural nationalism. Thus, Ferguson's work did not become enduringly popular in his own natural home constituency, east Ulster, as it moved towards the Ulster Covenant and the more uncompromising stance of the twentieth century and turned against the Gaelic revival. Professor Dowden of Trinity and of the Irish Unionist Alliance thought that Ferguson's unionism sat ill with his writings of Gaelic martial ardour, and this has frequently been said since. While the nationalists monopolised and misread Ferguson, the official view in this century was that his efforts cut across the national aim of the revival of the Irish language. Later, Roger McHugh, Professor of English in the other University College in Dublin, thought that Hewitt was being foolish and naive or even subversive in his attempts to form a movement of Ulster regionalist artistic activity. The Unionists ignored Hewitt's poetic aims, robbed him of his career prize.

Both Ferguson and Hewitt were in the middle each seeking space for his roots. Both were squeezed. Each of these foremost poets of planter stock sought roots in what we may call Gaelic Ireland, to express their striving. Both were left largely unfulfilled. Yet perhaps both had a considerable impact on the literary consciousness, Ferguson on the literary revival, Hewitt on the sudden flowering of Ulster poetry in the sixties. Hewitt and Ferguson were forerunners of two different literary movements which added greatly to the culture of Ireland, and to the literature of the English language.

CHAPTER 9

Natural History, Science and Irish Culture

by

John Wilson Foster

I

The Belfast Naturalists' Field Club (BNFC) was started in 1863 in response to classes in Belfast in geology given by J. Beete Jukes, and in geology, zoology and botany by Ralph Tate (both eminent British natural scientists), under the auspices of the Department of Science and Art set up by Westminster in 1853. The classes were hugely popular (nearly four hundred people took Jukes' course), and Tate's first series of lectures, which involved field work, prompted some Belfastmen to try to keep up the momentum Jukes and Tate had gained.

Local initiation and organisation of these courses came from the Belfast Natural History and Philosophical Society (BNHPS). This remarkably resilient body had come into being in 1821; it was then known as the Belfast Natural History Society and was formed for 'the cultivation of Zoology, Botany, and Mineralogy in all their branches, more especially the investigation of the Natural History and Antiquities of Ireland'. In 1842 the word 'Philosophical' was added to the title (thereby permitting lectures in physics, chemistry, engineering and psychology to be given) and natural history faded from prominence; hence the need for a specialised natural history society. The BNFC satisfied this need while responding to developments in field work in Britain. The BNHPS and BNFC, however, have always had many members in common.

The BNFC was only one of a dizzying number of satellite societies circling the BNHPS, all using its Museum in College Square North, open in 1831 – the first museum in Ireland built by voluntary subscription. Arthur Deane in his centenary history of the BNHPS (1924) – an essential document for the Irish cultural historian –

rescued these societies from oblivion: the Literary Society (begun in 1801), the Historic Society, the Phrenological Society, the Botanical Society, the Rhetoric Society, the Photographic Society, the Statistical and Social Inquiry Society, the Harmonic Society, the Ulster Fisheries and Biological Association, the Library Association, the Ladies' Institute, the Astronomical Society, the Architectural and Engineering Association, the Ulster Medical Society, as well as the several semi-autonomous sections of the BNHPS proper.

In the winter papers were read to the BNFC by members – papers on natural history were concurrently being delivered, of course, at meetings of the BNHPS. In the summer there were excursions: the Club's first field meeting was at Islandmagee on April 6th 1863, to visit the Lias beds near Barney's Point; the second outing was to Lough Neagh, the third to Castle Espie. There is a well-known photograph of an outing at the Giant's Causeway, June 11th 1868.

As well as occasioning serious amateur natural history collecting, some thought of these excursions as ways of improving and expanding the mind, and strengthening the constitution (young people were encouraged to join with these in mind); it was all quite Victorian and Protestant. And perhaps these outings were something of an early 'singles' scene. In the 1868 photograph, there is a generous sprinkling of women present. As in the English and Scottish field naturalists' clubs, 'ladies' were admitted to the BNFC, 'whose presence', W.T. Chew told the *Northern Whig* (quoted by Campbell), 'doubles the enjoyment both of rambles and scientific investigations'. The more learned socities in the U.K. excluded or ignored women up until the late 19th century, because, as Allen remarks, 'science was a man's business and the club a kind of intellectual stag-party where a male rattled his antlers'. In Deane's biographies of eminent members of the BNHPS active between 1821 and 1921, there are no women subjects. Deane lists 1,117 members of the BNHPS for the same century – I count 33 women among them. Yet the BNFC had a fairly good record in this regard, and women were freely admitted. One eminent female member of the BNFC (she joined in 1891) was Madame Christen, niece of William Thompson and a geologist specialising in glaciers. As well as being a keen botanist, she was a member of the School of Art Board and Secretary of the Belfast Art Society, showing a versatility common to the time and that I find quite astonishing. She died in 1923.

We oughtn't to be surprised at the situation of the sexes. Nor should we be surprised that the BNFC, like the other studious societies, was a preponderantly middle-class affair. Medical men, academic men, and Protestant clergymen were to the fore in the BNFC, but these professionals took their place, in numbers and influence, behind Belfast businessmen, especially members of shipowning families and more especially linen-manufacturing families. (The Pattersons, a natural history dynasty that included Robert Lloyd Praeger, ran a mill-furnishing company; families were important in Belfast's intellectual scene last century, notably the Pattersons, Workmans and MacAdamses.) There were fifteen founding office-bearers in the BNFC in 1863: eight were businessmen or sons of manufacturers. At the top, the BNFC reflected the make-up of class and economic power in Belfast.

The staggering proliferation of studious societies, many with newsletters, proceedings, lectures, reflects the weight of commerce in the city and reminds us, more generally, of that connection between economic and intellectual activity that many of us in the humanities overlook, or have been taught to overlook, and more particularly, of the importance of collaboration and access to publication in the dissemination of knowledge, and the capacity of those in business and the professions to erect and maintain, as a species of power, the infrastructure of that knowledge. (An economic profile of the Southern Protestant Revivalists early this century – disregarding their anti-commercial bias – might be revealing.)

And sons of affluence could make time for concentrated avocational study; William Thompson, for example, was the eldest son of a Belfast linen merchant; at twenty-one, upon completion of his apprenticeship, he made a four-month Grand Tour and after a six-year stint in the family business, he retired at the age of twenty-seven and devoted himself to natural history. (But since he went on to publish almost a hundred papers and described over nine hundred additional species to the Irish fauna, and all before the age of forty-seven when he died, 'retired' is not quite the right word.) Deane's biographical observation on John Brown (1850–1911) proves that Thompson wasn't unique: 'At the age of 35 he retired from active participation in business [linen manufacturing] in order to devote himself to scientific and educational pursuits'. He became a distinguished physicist, Fellow of the Royal Society, inventor of an electric automobile, President of the Irish Roads Improvements Association, President of the BNHPS, member of the BNFC, newspaper columnist, governor of the Academical Institution, member of the Ulster Reform Club.

Class statistics of the BNFC and other clubs reflected social reality but not necessarily, at least where the BNFC was concerned, the will of the club. Campbell claimed in 1938 that the BNFC welcomed representatives of all classes to its ranks. And certainly there was the example of Robert Bell who joined the BNFC in 1893. Primarily a geologist, he discovered a mineral new to the British Isles, and several new to Ireland. He was also an archaeologist and palaeontologist. The grant of a Civil List pension to him in 1930 in recognition of his scientific work was the more remarkable since he was, like most of his fellow Club-members, an amateur who, in his case, was a riveter in Harland & Wolff's shipyard, putting in a hard week's work. Praeger uses Bell's case to justify a reference to 'the democratic Field Club of Belfast'.

To its ranks, the BNFC welcomed 'all creeds, all shades of political opinion and united them in a common brotherhood', according to Campbell. Presumably it was important that the shades of political opinion not be expressed. And social reality dictated that the major creeds in the North of Ireland were not equally represented. The BNFC and many contemporary societies of artistic, intellectual or scientific nature were doubtless predominantly Protestant. To an outsider this might seem surprising, since by 1850 Roman Catholics represented a third of the city's population, but natives know the reality then of discrimination, relative power and economic inequality. The Catholic fraction had doubled since 1800 but most of the newcomers were rural and poor and unlikely candidates for the relatively privileged endeavours of natural history. But it is worth observing that a sizeable volume of Catholic energy may have gone into the attempts by followers of Gavan Duffy and others from the 1830s onwards to develop 'a distinct Roman Catholic political voice in Belfast', as Peter Brooke has it. So there was, perhaps, a measure of voluntary intellectual apartheid. Possibly, too, where the BNFC was concerned, the uneasy relationship between the Catholic Church and the study of Nature was a factor.

In any case, while it is proper to deplore any imbalance in class and sectarian representation in intellectual Belfast last century, it would be perverse to deplore, and wrong to neglect, the very real achievements – especially in the hard, applied and natural sciences – registered by its versatile, energetic, prominent, not to say dominant citizens.

In natural history, for example, Belfast had been home to three significant figures before the BNFC came into being and all associated with the BNHPS. Praeger called John Templeton (1766–1825) the 'most eminent naturalist that Ireland has produced'. Associate of the Linnaean Society, Templeton died before he could complete his *Flora Hibernica*, but his specimens were catalogued and depicted by the leading English botanists of the day, Sowerby, Hooker and others. *The Natural History of Ireland* (4 vols., 1849–56) by William Thompson is in my opinion one of the significant cultural artifacts of the Irish 19th century. Just as Templeton's work detailed from one region the nationwide botany of Hooker and others, so Thompson's work helped complete the ornithological map of the archipelago drawn in mid-century by Yarrell and by MacGillivray, leading ornithologists who cite Thompson routinely. Robert Patterson (1802–72), Fellow of the Royal Society, was one of the eight young men who formed the BNHPS (Patterson was 19). His text-books in zoology were standard (and accepted as such by the English Privy Council in Education) but he contributed widely to zoological journals and on his friend Thompson's death undertook to reconstruct from notes the fourth volume of *The Natural History of Ireland*.

Among the later Belfast naturalists, only Praeger rivalled in achievement and stature these three men, but the corporate accomplishment of the BNFC since 1863 has been impressive. The Club's *Proceedings, Guides* to Belfast and its hinterland published in 1874 and 1902 to honour and aide the visits of the British Association, and its 1886 handbook, *Systematic Lists Illustrative of the Flora, Fauna, Palaeontology, and Archaeology of the North of Ireland*, should be required reading for the Irish cultural historian. The BNFC was the senior corresponding society in Ireland for the BA and in that capacity made more than regional contribution to natural history.

II

A perusal of Allen's *The Naturalist in Britain* and Barber's *The Heyday of Natural History* is enough to show us that the BNFC and the BNHPS can be set firmly within the context of British intellectual history. The first field club was the Berwickshire Naturalists' Club, founded in 1831. According to Allen it was the hybrid of two quite different forms of social congregation. The first was the literary and philosophical societies which spread across the new industrial areas of England, 'from Manchester in 1781 to Newcastle in 1793, to Birmingham in 1800 and to Leeds in 1819'. And, we may add, to Belfast in 1821. The BNHPS, then, had the same industrial and manufacturing base as, and shared a certain class-exclusiveness with, its English affines.

These societies had replaced the older Gentlemen's Societies about the earliest of which the founder claimed: 'We deal in all arts and sciences and exclude nothing from our conversation but politics, which would throw us all into confusion and disorder'. Their apolitical form was inherited by the literary and philosophical societies, including the RNHPS, and indeed it may be the very success of the latter in being nonsectarian and apolitical in matter that has caused it to seem rather dull amidst the surrounding turmoil of Irish literature and politics and to be, perversely, neglected. We have all fed our hearts, perhaps, on brutalities instead.

The other kind of organisation, that mated with the literary and philosophical society to produce the field club, was the exclusively working-class botanical societies in Lancashire, Cheshire and Yorkshire, manned by factory operatives. If these existed in the North of Ireland I'm not aware of it. In any case, after the Berwickshire club came the Ayrshire club, then the Tyneside club in 1846, the Cotteswold club, then, as Allen puts it, 'a rash of these bodies', Belfast becoming infected in 1863. The typical membership of around 500 for the BNFC compares favourably with that of its British counterparts.

In the teaching of natural history, however, Ireland was not imitative but pioneering. At Belfast Academy, a Natural History Society, the first in the islands, was set up in 1828, though Allen tells us that as early as 1790 lessons in natural history were included in ordinary school courses in Ireland. And Ireland 'enjoyed' one of the first of the Victorian natural history crazes; 'limpet fever' gripped Bangor in the 1820s. By and large, serious natural history study lagged in the South of Ireland; the Natural History Society of Dublin began in 1838, the Dublin Naturalists' Field Club in 1885. (Praeger when he moved from Belfast to Dublin in 1893 found the Dublin club more professional, less amateur than the BNFC.) The Belfast, Dublin, Cork and Limerick field clubs formed a Union in 1894, held Triennial Conferences and went on joint excursions. The Union lasted, though, only until 1913 and the Cork and Limerick clubs died in the 1920s. Praeger thought the Union had accomplished its purpose, but it is hard not to posit socio-political strains as political rifts opened on the island.

Ross and Nash claim that natural history developed differently in Ireland than in Britain, but the five uniquely Irish characteristics they list await amplification and proof. What we can say is that natural history in Ulster had a decidedly regional development between Templeton and Praeger. This comes, quite literally, with the territory of field work, but I mean something more. Templeton declined Sir Joseph Banks' invitation to move permanently to Australia to do scientific work on a good salary and with a grant of land, and was not induced, in Praeger's words, 'to leave Ireland and his native Antrim'.

Like Templeton, Thompson, remarks Praeger, 'was content to work almost entirely in the North of Ireland'. Aware that this might endanger the legitimacy of his title, *The Natural History of Ireland*, Thompson in his Preface made a radically regionalist defence: 'The neighbourhood of Belfast, including the bay, may be considered too fully dwelt upon throughout this work; but what is alluded to in this locality should, unless mentioned as of a local nature, be viewed in the light of an epitome of the general habits or economy of the species'. But Belfast, in cultural fact, was the natural history capital of the island.

The BNFC, then, was in the 19th century a largely amateur detail of the total natural history picture in Britain and Ireland. It was also a detail of a cultural picture in the North of Ireland, a picture whose frame was provided by the BNHPS, that impressive intellectual consortium. That picture was enriched by the way societies overlapped in membership and matter, and also by those figures whose versatility reflected that of the BNHPS. Many of the natural historians worked in several of what would nowadays be regarded as separate disciplines – botany, zoology, geology, archaeology, palaeontology. Furthermore, they had interests beyond natural history. A skilled illustrator as well as botanist, Templeton was a liberal and philanthropist and strongly supported the Belfast Literary Society. Robert Patterson the elder read and memorised Shakespeare and became a published expert in the natural history of the plays; he wrote poems that were collected from anthologies after his death; all the while he was a successful businessman. Thompson was equally rounded. His interests shifted from business and shooting to zoology, landscape gardening, and the arts (he was president of the Fine Arts Society). He advanced the welfare of the handloom weaver poet, Francis Davis, dubbed The Belfastman; through Thompson's help, Davis became Librarian and Secretary to the Working Classes' Association and then assistant librarian in Queen's College.

These men saw no great gulf between the arts and sciences. In his 1904 profile and memoir of 19th century Belfast – another essential document for the Irish cultural historian – William Gray, President of the BNFC, claimed that members of the BNHPS 'endeavoured by every means in their power to utilise and extend their advantage for the purpose of promoting local artistic culture and popular scientific instruction'. From this distance, the scientific achievements outstrip the artistic, but the story Gray tells is of a genuine intellectual community of the kind we should expect to find in an industrial, commercial city. Several figures were one-man intellectual communities.

Henry MacCormac (1800–86) was one of these. Robert Shipboy MacAdam (1808–95) was another. Son of a Belfast hardware merchant, MacAdam was Honorary Secretary of the Academical Institution, member of the Belfast Literary Society, founding member and later President of the BNHPS, Honorary Secretary of the Harmonic Society. It was claimed he knew thirteen languages; he published *An Introduction to the Irish Language* and was a leading member of the Ulster Gaelic Society. He founded, financed, and edited for nine years the *Ulster Journal of Archaeology*. He established and ran a foundry in Townshend Street and designed a water turbine, an example of which was in operation until 1974. He had the finest collection of medical manuscripts on the island. Aodn Mac Póilin tells me that MacAdam was the first systematic collector of folklore in Ireland.

Northern science was no small beer and far outshone Ulster literature. Thomas Andrews, George Dickie, Joseph David Everett, John Frederick Hodges and E.A. Letts were among the most eminent. Then there was Alexander Mitchell, the blind engineer. He was born in Dublin but came to Belfast when a boy. He invented a way of building durable lighthouses in deep water in shifting sands that was subsequently used around the British coast, and he and his son installed the prototype themselves, at night, at sea. Seamus Heaney has expressed admiration for the rural blacksmith who beats real iron out: these Northern engineers did it in a big way. And Wyville Thomson, the zoologist, who did his best work when he lived in Belfast between 1854 and 1870, among other things directed the scientific staff on board the *Challenger* expedition. This, after traversing 69,000 miles of the Pacific and Atlantic oceans between 1872 and 1876, finally ended the American pre-eminence in scientific exploration established by the U.S. Exploring Expedition of 1829.

The North of Ireland, then, was in the 19th century a region of scientific and natural scientific achievement, much of it by zealous amateurs. The alliance between science, art, education, business and industry was the chief feature of the Victorian Belfast intellectual scene. Instead of seeing industry as a brake on intellectual advance, Gray sees it as having been created by that advance. 'The material prosperity of Belfast', he claimed, 'was the direct outcome of that intellectual activity that characterised the early years of the nineteenth century, when our chief educational institutions were founded, which were in advance of similar institutions in many of the chief cities of the United Kingdom. There is an obvious and direct connection between the educational results of the Royal Academical Institution and our chief shipbuilding yards and other important manufacturing establishments'. This could be dismissed only by those ignorant of the history of science and education in the North of Ireland. 'Belfast', Gray goes on, 'was one of the foremost towns of the United Kingdom to recognise the necessity for popular education, and the value of a knowledge of science and art in relation to productive industries'.

III

There was a downside, of course: too much proselytising religion, too little humour; too much organisation, too little impulse; too much Protestant anal-retentiveness (probably explaining all that collecting and cataloguing in Victorian natural history). There would have been an element of Gradgrindery, and Belfast, to a lesser degree than Preston, could have modelled for Coketown in Dickens' *Hard Times*. But Dickens was, for his own triumphant purposes, squinting at Preston and deliberately failing to admit the necessity of statistics for social reform, the desirability of an educational curriculum more suitable to a northern, industrial working class than what had obtained (Collins is illuminating on this score), the justified concern of utilitarians with an absolute increase in human happiness, and the real achievements of Victorian natural history. Victorian Belfast was implicated in all of this, and I confess to finding Gray's connections between science, art, education, industry and commerce refreshing, because I was schooled to regard most of what he discusses simply as evidence of invincible Philistinism. Yet this is not the case: rather, the history of intellectual Belfast has been driven underground and Northern attainments in these fields have been culturally sequestered. Why?

One reason is the influence in Britain of Matthew Arnold's notion of what constituted true culture. His reservations about science encouraged that dissociation of sensibility C.P. Snow called the Two Cultures, and when 'the arts' appropriated culture, Ulster as a primarily scientific culture became one of the culturally dispossessed. Arnold's strictures on religious Dissent didn't help matters in the industrial North of England or of Ireland.

Dickens' idea of culture in *Hard Times* coincidentally includes Arnold's imminent idea of Celticism, itself imported from Renan then re-expatriated by Yeats, double-fastening Ulster's cultural dispossession. Yeats multiplied Arnold's Celtic note into a symphony in which industry, business, science, rationalism, religious Dissent, the middle class, formal education and democracy in sum, the bulk of

Ulster Protestant culture – were given no important instruments to play. Yet now, despite the splendour of Irish literature, I find the idea of culture promulgated by the Irish Revival thin and unrealistic. The Republic (and even Northern Ireland) semi-officially inherited the Revival idea of culture. But in any case, as Dorinda Outram points out (in *The Irish Review*, No.1 and elsewhere), nationalism, Catholicism, and the failure of Enlightenment values also explain the short shrift science has been given in the South of Ireland. Michael Viney (in *The Irish Review*, No.1) goes farther afield in explanation. The Irish View of Nature, as he calls it, in his account (adapting Keith Thomas) was shaped by the paucity of towns, the absence of industrialism, little continuity from benign Anglo-Irish views of Nature, the collapse of faith in Nature after the Famine, and the minor role of Dissenters, Quakers and Evangelicals. The North, of course, had the Protestantism (and the industrialism) aplenty. Outram believes it noteworthy that the Catholic Church shows scant interest in any form of natural theology. All this indirectly explains the interest in natural history in early 19th century Belfast, and in James L. Drummond, brother of William Hamilton Drummond the poet, Ulster had its own natural theologian. In *Letters to a Young Naturalist* (London 1831), Drummond (founder member of the BNHPS) continued a tradition begun by Derham, Burnet and Ray and, as late as 1802, by William Paley in his *Natural Theology or Evidences of the Existence and Attributes of the Deity*. This was the tradition of trying to deepen the understanding of God through a detailed appreciation of the marvels of Nature. Such rational devotion aided the advance of natural history, though when the time came it prevented those like Drummond who saw adaptation as evidence of purpose and design from seing it as evidence of natural selection. Yet the versatile Drummond (and *Letters* is fascinating missionary zoology) had a deep educational commitment to natural history. Even when natural theology subsided, it left as a benign residue the independent subject of natural history, itself spawning independent scientific disciplines. The conservatism or Cosmic Toryism (as Basil Willey called it) of natural theology gave way to the progressive and secular whiggery of Thompson, Patterson and the BNFC.

Yet even in the North of Ireland, an intellectual, science-based culture withered this century. After the attainment of majority (i.e. Protestant) rule in Northern Ireland, an anti-intellectual, truly Philistine Unionism emerged, which by back-formation seems to have invalidated and made suspect its ampler Victorian predecessor. The community Gray celebrates disintegrated and left Ulster looking cultureless. Meanwhile, the fortunes of science in the South of Ireland remained, and remain, low: we read this as complaint in Herries Davies, in Neil Holman, in Sean Lysaght (*The Irish Review*, No.7) and most recently in Roy Johnston, who in *The Irish Review* (No 8) has called justifiably for the rehabilitation of science in Irish culture. The book put out by the Royal Irish Academy in 1985, *Some People and Places in Irish Science and Technology* (to which Holman provided a Preface), was an attempt to redress a very real grievance.

A larger sense of culture – without invidious cultural comparison – and commemorating and encouraging all our cultural productions and enabling regional and islandwide pride in our science – is, I'm sure, a prerequisite to amicable relations in Ireland. It is being offered to us, in any case, from without. There is a move afoot, in the U.S.A. and the U.K., through the efforts of such writers and scientists as Stephen Jay Gould, James Gleick, Stephen Hawking and Oliver Sacks, to reverse the trend this century and put science back into general culture. Simultaneousely there is a sudden rise of interest in natural history, for obvious reasons: it is the future that needs to be mapped if we are to survive. But the old maps of the Irish naturalists and the Belfast Naturalists' Field Club are still useful and we need to turn to them.

CHAPTER 10

An Irish Naturalist: Robert Lloyd Praeger

by
Timothy Collins

To those who know something of Irish natural history, the name of Robert Lloyd Praeger conjures up an image of a veritable giant among men striding across the Victorian landscape, noting its flora and fauna and writing about it later. This is actually not far from the truth, as in his prime Praeger stood well over six feet in height and was solidly built, weighting seventeen stone.

It has been said that Praeger was very much a product of his time. This is a dangerous oversimplification, as a study of his life and his writings shows he was a man of many parts with many apparent contradictions. An engineer by qualification, a librarian by profession and a naturalist by inclination, it was initially as a geologist and later as a botanist that Praeger made his mark on turn-of-the-century Ireland. Today, though, he is best remembered for his many books and articles extolling the virtues of tramping through the Irish countryside. Praeger was influenced by the landscape into which he was born, but he in turn influenced others to become more aware of their surroundings through his activities in the field and more importantly, through his writings.

Born August 25, 1865 in Holywood, Co. Down, Robert Lloyd Praeger was the second son of Willem Emil Praeger and Maria Patterson, daughter of Robert Patterson, a well-known mid-nineteenth-century naturalist. Robert Lloyd Praeger had four brothers and one sister. Very little is known of his family life, except what has been written by himself and his sister Sophia Rosamond, who was a gifted sculptress and writer of children's stories and rhymes. His father, a Dutch Presbyterian who emigrated to Belfast from The Hague in 1860, ran a thriving linen exporting business with a brother in The Hague as partner. They appear to have been well-off, as Belfast at that time was a thriving centre of commerce, and industriousness brought its own visible rewards. As Praeger himself said in mild criticism later, when moving from Belfast to Dublin to take up his appointment as Assistant Librarian at the National Library: 'The Dublin which I entered in 1893 was a pleasant and placid place, as vaguely concerned with the squibs and crackers of Ireland's representatives at Westminster as it was with the earnest money-worship of Belfast'.

Without a doubt Praeger inherited an interest in natural history from his mother, who encouraged him in every way. Her family was well-known for its contributions to natural history. Praeger's grandfather Robert Patterson wrote many books, among them *The Natural History of Insects mentioned in Shakespeare's Plays* (1838), *Introduction to Zoology* (1846) and his well-known *First Steps in Zoology* (1849) which became a standard text for schools. A founder-member of the Belfast Naturalists' Field Club, he lived just long enough – 1872 – to give Praeger some of his first lessons in that subject. Many years later Praeger still vividly remembered his grandfather: 'After seventy-five years I can still see him – a man of middle height, and rather formal manner, pursuing his country rambles on Saturday afternoons in black frock-coat and top hat, and pointing out to us delighted children ladybirds and tree creepers and 'devil's coach-horses' and strange chrysalises'.

Some of Praeger's early experiments in science incurred parental wrath, such as boiling the head of a very dead dog in his mother's best saucepan to obtain the skull, or collecting the corpses of dead cats to see if they would swell up and explode, as a schoolfriend had reliably informed him would happen! Other projects were a little more productive, such as a study of the leafing of some sycamore trees in the garden of 'The Croft', the Praeger family home:

> There was one of a row of these trees which each Spring came into leaf ten days or so ahead of the others. With the aid of the gardener, I procured in Autumn some cuttings of it and of its neighbour on either side, and planted them in the single bed that constituted my garden. They grew, and great was my joy to find that the precocious one maintained its reputation for early rising (I was an enthusiastic early riser myself), and each April fairly outstripped its competitors. In years a little later I grew the same trees from seed, to find that the baby trees also showed the same sequence in development. That made me think that after all there might be something in statements by Darwin and other revolutionaries of the day, who were looked on but coldly by certain Presbyterian friends in County Down.

In common with his brothers, Praeger received primary school education at a private school in Holywood run by a Rev. Dr Macalister, a Unitarian minister, before going on to the Royal Belfast Academical Institution, better known then as 'the Inst'. Praeger then entered Queen's College Belfast (as it was then known) in 1882, graduating with degrees in Arts and Engineering.

For one who was so obviously interested in natural history, it seems strange that he did not pursue a course at university that might have satisfied his thirst for knowledge in the natural sciences. Basically the universities of the time were at fault. His abhorrence of professionally taught courses stemmed from this rejection of botany as it was then taught at 'Inst'. This antipathy led him to avoid studying natural history at Queen's College, because the course there did not include any field work or laboratory work whatsoever. All his life Praeger was a believer in going out and learning about something by observation and deduction, rather than by having it taught by repetition for later regurgitation in examinations.

His interest in the natural sciences, which was developed in childhood, survived into adulthood in spite of 'educational' difficulties, largely because of his close connections with the Belfast Naturalists' Field Club. A large part of the Field Club's activities consisted of excursions during the summer months to places of interest to amateur naturalists, and fortnightly conversazioni during the winter months at which topics of interest were discussed, and specimens collected were exhibited. In *The Way that I Went* Praeger traces his own scientific education rather self-effacingly:

> My scientific life began in the field, and has continued there. When I was promoted from a small private school to the 'Inst' in Belfast I knew a good deal about local plants – where they grow, when they flowered, what their roots and seeds were like as well as their blossoms: and I eagerly joined the small group of boys who attended a bi-weekly botanical class. But when I found that botany consisted in drawing a series of adnate parallelograms and entering in the blank spaces such terms as 'mono-chlamydeous' and 'gamosepalous' I fled in terror, and later at college I did not venture again to approach my favourite subject as seen through the eyes of a teacher of Victoria's glorious days. Indeed, Queen's College, as it was then, was a rather forbidding and comfortless place. The professors for the most part arrived five minutes before lecture-time, talked for an hour, and departed again to the fastnesses of University Street or the Lisburn Road. There were no laboratories or practical work

except in chemistry – and for medical students, of course, anatomy. In each of the three Colleges that constituted the Queen's (later the Royal) University there was a chair of Natural History. This is too wide a field for any man, and it is not surprising that some of the subjects were treated in a rather perfunctory manner . . . But all the time I was fast learning geology and zoology and botany of another kind through the Belfast Naturalists' Field Club . . . It was an association of enthusiastic amateurs, remarkably well versed in local geology and biology, eager to impart knowledge: and under this stimulating influence I probed wonderingly into the fairyland of nature. Experience gained on the field excursions stood me in good stead. I remembered a viva voce in geology in Dublin at the old Royal Univesity in Earlsfort Terrace. 'Can you name that rock?' 'Granite'. 'Can you say what part of Ireland it comes from?' 'Dublin' (the wall in front of the building was of granite, and I had noticed in passing how it differed from the Mourne rock, the only granite I knew). 'Quite right: now point out the constituent minerals' I could have done this at six years old. 'Do you see any other mineral there?' Horrors! What was there besides quartz, felspar and mica? 'Tourmaline' I said at a venture. 'Right: now show me the tourmaline' I chose an almost microscopic black speck, which might be anything, so far as I knew. 'Yes – but you might have selected a larger crystal, like that. Now show me another'. Not difficult, once one knew! Then presently, 'Have you any ideas about this fossil?' '*Gryphaea incurva*, a mollusc from the Lower Lias, allied to the oyster' – I could have named almost any Irish Liassic shell, thanks to Field Club excursions to Barney's Point, and the friendly instruction of Swanston, Stewart and Bulla. Full marks. A bit of Old Red conglomerate was equally easy, for had I not played about the caves at Cushendun, and read Miller's *Old Red Sandstone*? So the Field Club did for me what R.O. Cunningham's lectures might have failed to do. All the same, I have felt continually the want of the laboratory training in the natural sciences which I never got: that is a bad handicap in modern scientific work of whatever kind: but it was not to be had in Belfast fifty years ago, and as I always preferred the field as a laboratory, I have continued to have a wonderfully good time without it.

Praeger's membership of the Belfast Naturalists' Field Club dates from 1877 when his uncle Robert Patterson proposed him for membership at the age of eleven. Many of the friends Praeger made in the BNFC were, like himself, amateurs who pursued their interests in their spare time. These were people like S.A. Stewart, founder-member, trunk maker, botanist and geologist; William Swanston, linen manufacturer and geologist; F.J. Bigger, solicitor and archaeologist; Joseph Wright, grocer and specialist in the Foraminifera; Wm. Gray, Corkman, Inspector under the Office of Works, 'and in science jack-of-all-trades'; Charles Bulla, commercial traveller and palaeontologist; S.M. Malcolmson, physician and microscopist; Robert Bell, shipyard worker with Harland & Wolff and geologist; A.W. Stelfox, mollusc specialist; Canon Lett, botanist; W.J. Knowles, insurance agent and voracious collector of prehistoric artifacts; and, of course, R.J. Welch, 'photographer and fanatical crusader in the interests of Irish natural history'. With this group, people who knew all there was to known about the local flora, fauna and antiquities, Praeger was literally able to forage all over ULster, picking up the field lore that is not found in any book, but is passed on from generation to generation. His excellent organisational abilities meant that Praeger soon became essential to the smooth running of BNFC activities. On excursions he was everywhere with his whistle, hastening stragglers and ensuring strict adherence to timetables. Through BNFC outings Praeger cooperated with W.H. Phillips in his work on native ferns and their varities resulting in the publication of *The Ferns of Ulster* in 1887 and assisted S.A. Stewart with the fieldwork for the *Flora of the North-east of Ireland* in 1888.

As secretary to a committee set up specifically for the purpose, Praeger took part in a study of the gravel beds and raised beaches near Larne, the stratigraphic dating of which was in contention. The 'Larne Gravels Controversy' was amicably ended when Praeger, working with William Swanston, Joseph Wright, William Gray, Praeger's uncle, William Patterson and of course S.A. Stewart, was able to show by the distribution of flint tools that man was present during the whole period of deposition of the gravels. In going back over the findings, present-day archaeologists are of the opinion that this may not be exactly correct, but at least learned arguments based on fieldwork were common among BNFC members.

As a result of his work on the Larne gravel beds and the estuarine clays of Belfast Lough, Praeger became involved in the Broighter Gold Ornaments Trial, along with his friend and fellow Field Club member George Coffey, as witness for the Crown. At the time, the trial drew a lot of attention in the press and even today is a tale worth telling.

In 1896 a man ploughing a field near Limavady, County Derry turned up a collection of objects made of pure gold. The ploughman parted with them to his employer for a small sum who sold them for

600 to Robert Day, a wealthy collector from Cork, who subsequently sold them to the British Museum. It was only when the British Museum went public with its acquisition of the collection, that the Royal Irish Academy learned of the discovery. Through the State Solicitor, the Academy claimed the collection as treasure trove and immediately began legal proceedings to have the collection returned. The law of treasure trove states roughly that, if precious objects are found under circumstances which point to their having been lost or abandoned, then it is a case of 'finder's keepers', but if there is evidence that they were concealed or deposited with the intention of ultimate recovery, then the Crown claims them on behalf of the unknown next of kin.

The British Museum countered the Royal Irish Academy's claim by refusing to return the objects on the grounds that they were not treasure trove and backed their refusal by asserting that, at the time of deposition of the articles, the waters of Lough Foyle flowed over the lands in question. Consequently, the Museum felt that the objects could not have been deposited there with a view to recovery, and may even have been cast overboard from a boat as a votive offering. The British Museum's contention was that the objects were therefore abandoned.

Praeger and Coffey were asked by the State Solicitor to demonstrate, if possible, that the site where the collection had been ploughed up was actually dry land at the time of their deposit. The collection, which consisted primarily of a richly ornamented Celtic collar, a little boat with beautifully detailed oars, mast and rigging of Mediterranean origin, some bowls, a torc, a necklace and other assorted jewellery, all dated from about the beginning of the Christian era. After visiting various sites, Praeger and Coffey found what they were looking for in excavations conducted near Portstewart. Analysis of core samples showed 'black layers' of charcoal and ash as well as other organic waste matter and implements, which could not have been submerged, as seawater would have destroyed such layers. All of the samples were taken from undisturbed Neolithic land surfaces of proven age, so Praeger and Coffey were able to satisfy the court that the field where the collection was found had been part of an earlier geological uplifting which had occurred many thousands of years previously.

The case was finally heard in June 1903, Mr Justice Farwell presiding. There was an imposing array of counsel. The British Museum defence was led by R.B. Haldane (afterwards Lord Chancellor and 1st Viscount) who brought in evidence from many quarters. J.L.

Myers, then Lecturer in Classical Archaeology at Oxford, and A.J. Evans, Keeper of the Ashmolean Museum, were among those called to give evidence which dealt with the practice of votive offerings from the time of Xerxes onwards, in places as diverse as Finland and the Malay archipelago. Frazer's *Golden Bough* was quoted, and Mananaan MacLir was dragged in as an Irish sea god. For the Academy, counsel was led by the Attorney General for Ireland, Sir R.B. Finlay, the Solicitor Genral, Sir Edward Carson (afterwards Lord Carson, the father of Ulster Unionism); and Henry Sutton (afterwards Sir Henry, Judge in the King's Bench Division).

The judge got restive over the wealth of folklore and legend which was turned up in the examination and cross-examination, and protested as much more than once. His judgement is worth quoting, and I give Praeger's abbreviated version of it:

> I must express my opinion that the Court has been occupied for a considerable time in listening to fanciful suggestions more suited to the poem of a Celtic bard than the prose of an English Law Report. The defendants' suggestion is that the articles were thrown into the sea, which they suggest then covered the spot in question, as a votive offering by some Irish sea king or chief to some Irish sea god at some period between 300 B.C. and A.D. 100, and for this purpose they ask the Court to infer the existence of the sea on the spot in question, the existence of an Irish sea god, the existence of a custom to make votive offerings in Ireland during the period suggested, and the existence of kings or chiefs who would be likely to make such votive offerings. The whole of their evidence (if I may so describe it) on these points is of the vaguest description... It was perhaps natural that the defendants should grasp at theories which, in justice to them, I may say were not invented for the purpose of the defence; but it is really little short of extravagant to ask the Court to assume the existence of a votive offering of a sort hitherto unknown, in a land where such offerings are hitherto unknown, in a sea not known to have existed for 2000 years, and possible for 4000 years, to a sea god by a chieftain both equally unknown, and to prefer this to the commonplace but natural inference that these articles were a hoard hidden for safety in a land disturbed by frequent raids, and forgotten by reason of the death or slavery of the depositor . . . The result is that I will make a declaration that the articles in question are treasure trove, belonging to His Majesty by reason of the Prerogative Royal, and order the delivery up of the same accordingly.

The jubilation which must have been felt by all with such a result is apparent, as Praeger finishes his account by telling us of the sequel: 'And so we won by two goals (or more) to nil. I was present at the closing scene, when, at a meeting of the Royal Irish Academy on 11th November 1903, these beautiful objects were placed on the table, and George Coffey narrated their adventures. Since then they have occupied a place of honour in the Academy's unique collection of Irish prehistoric gold in the National Museum'.

After graduating in 1886, Praeger worked under L. Livingston Macassey, at that time Chief Engineer to the Belfast City and District Water Commissioners and one of the leading civil engineers in Ulster. In 1886 Macassey was involved in the major excavations relating to the construction of the Alexandra Dock and the floating dock off the Spencer Basin in Belfast harbour. It was here, as site engineer, that Praeger successfully completed major work on the estuarine clays being exposed, along with detailed lists of the fossil shells being found. In effect, his interest in natural history grew to such an extent that he actually turned down a site engineer's post in the Stonyford Water Scheme and began to look for something more rewarding.

From 1888 to 1891, apart from occasional engineering contracts, Praeger's work in Quaternary geology took up much of his time. Also, his work on the flora of the north-east continued, with regular notes appearing in print. His botanical work was made possible primarily through unfailing attendance at the outings organised by the Belfast Naturalists' Field Club, of which he was by now a committee member.

In the summer of 1891 his old friend, the Rev. Canon John Grainger of Broughshane, County Antrim, decided to present his extensive collection of fossils and archaeological specimens to the city of Belfast, with the stipulation that Robert Lloyd Praeger supervise its removal. Canon Grainger was in poor health at this time, and died before the end of the year. However, this is an indication that Praeger was at a loose end, for he took up residence with Canon Grainger at Broughshane in August of that year 'receiving sundry sums as fees', until the completion of the transfer, the following year. It was no easy task, for Canon Grainger was a collector of specimens and objects from all parts of the world. A specialist in Pleistocene fossils, he filled his house with archaeological, geological, botanical and zoological specimens which were more often than not unlocalised and unlabelled. Praeger later recalled some of the problems encountered in listing a collection that ranged from '. . . a fair sized dolmen to New

Zealand weapons, fling flakes, stuffed birds, beads, crystals, and microscopic shells'.

The following year, 1892, Praeger embarked on an ambitious project. Together with his friend George Carpenter (who was now in Dublin working as an assistant in the National Museum), he founded *The Irish Naturalist.* This journal appeared in response to a growing need for a forum to discuss matters of interest to Irish naturalists. Larger societies like the Royal Zoological Society of Ireland and the Belfast Natural History and Philosophical Society began publishing their Minutes in its pages, although the journal was primarily aimed at the amateur and was mostly concerned with the affairs of the many amateur naturalists' field clubs which had sprung up around the country, drawing people from all walks of life together.

Things were beginning to move more rapidly for Praeger during the spring of 1893. He spent some time in London with F.J. Hanbury, helping him in the completion of his monumental work the *Monograph of the British Hieracia.* While on a visit to Dublin later, he met R.F. Scharff. Scharff told Praeger that there was a post vacant in the National Library which had opened its doors only in 1878, and that he should apply. Much to his surprise, Praeger was successful, although unqualified for the post, and was appointed an Assistant Librarian in the autumn of 1893. He freely admits that, up to this, he was inclined to regard a library '. . . as a dusty kind of mausoleum rather than a factory. It was a place where were entombed the dead thoughts and dead words of dead people'. These views soon changed, for he took a deep and lasting interest in his work. Probably because the qualities that make a good botanist are similar to those which make a good librarian, Praeger went on to have a long and successful career in Librarianship, ultimately reaching the pinnacle of the profession in Ireland. 'My colleagues at the National Library – who were friends also, which does not necessarily follow – were men of varied attainments. Our chief was T.W. Lyster, 'a frolicsome and gentle Wordsworthian', as J.M. Hone has styled him, whose passion for expounding the best in English literature opened new fields to us all. There was W.K. Magee ('John Eglinton'), shy, reserved, and lovable, who wrote essays sparkling as precious stones – and equally rare; and R.I. Best, intent on Irish studies, and now a distinguished Celtic palaeographer'.

Of course, it was more than just the job that attracted Praeger to Dublin in 1893. By 1891 he had been elected a member of the Royal Irish Academy and regularly attended its meetings. The editing and publishing of the new journal *The Irish Naturalist* was being done in Dublin, and his botanical work was taking him farther and farther afield; so a move to Dublin seemed the logical thing.

As mentioned earlier, Praeger had very definite views about which was the preferred city to live in from the point of view of scientific learning.

> Dublin was a much greater centre of scientific activity, on a much more professional foundation, as was to be expected in the metropolis of a still undivided country. The difference in the scientific atmosphere of the two places was very marked. In Belfast the Field Club was an imporant local organization, a centre of scientific life. It had no sister-society except the already long-established Natural History and Philosophical Society, with its more formal and indoor functions: for natural science in the Queen's College (the future Queen's University) was concentrated in a single professorship, with practical work and field work quite undeveloped. In Dublin on the other hand the Field Club movement had begun only in 1886 and the Club was still in its boyhood, overshadowed as it was by the activities of the Royal Irish Academy, Royal Dublin Society, Royal Society of Antiquaries, and Dublin Microscopical Club, and practical biological teaching available in Trinity College and College of Science.

Praeger speaks the truth when he says later: 'when I left the north in 1893 I exchanged the Belfast Club and Ulster for the Dublin Club and Leinster, Connaught and Munster'. His work on natural history continued unabated, and he was elected Secretary of the Dublin Naturalists' Field Club almost as soon as he arrived from Belfast. On an individual level he continued to make sure that the results of fieldwork were published either in the pages of *The Irish Naturalist* or in book form. In 1893 he published the *Flora of County Armagh* in nine parts in the *Irish Naturalist*. Stewart and Corry in their *Flora of North-east Ireland* had excluded Armagh and typically, Praeger felt he should rectify the oversight. *A Bibliography of Irish Glacial and Post-glacial Geology* was published in 1896 as a special appendix to the *Proceedings of the Belfast Naturalists' Field Club* and in 1897 his first book *Open Air Studies in Botany* was published. By the turn of the century he had published two further books, *The North of Ireland Illustrated* in 1899 and the *Official Guide to County Down and the Mourne Mountains* in 1900 for the Belfast and County Down Railway Company.

Besides having over two hundred short articles and notes in various journals to his credit, Praeger also published *Irish Topographical Botany* as a special volume of the *Proceedings of the Royal Irish Academy*. This huge volume, which is still a useful work of reference for botanists today, was the result of 'botanising' literally every county of Ireland personally. The knowledge gained from tramping the whole island of Ireland was immense, and gave Praeger an insight into the interaction of species which could not have been gained from books. With seemingly limitless energy he applied himself to other scientific endeavours, taking part in the deep-sea dredging expeditions off the south and west coasts on board the 'Flying Falcon' in the late 1880s and the Rockall expedition on board the 'Granuaile' in 1896. With W.J. Sollas he studied the causes of bog-flows and their possible prediction. With R.J. Ussher and R.F. Scharff he examined the major cave systems of Ireland, and with R.A.S. Macalister he worked on the archaeology of the major Bronze Age sites of this country.

In other areas he was equally active. Under the auspices of the Royal Irish Academy Praeger set up the Fauna and Flora Committee to supervise fieldwork all over Ireland. This committee is still in existence, providing funds to researchers to ensure their work is completed.

As a further step towards marshalling interested naturalists into a group with a common aim, Praeger organised, through the pages of *The Irish Naturalist*, the first Irish Field Club Union conference which was held in Galway in 1895. About one hundred naturalists attended the week-long conference which, besides representatives of the Irish field clubs, included delegates from British societies like the North Staffordshire Naturalists' Field Club, the Wolverhampton Naturalists' Field Club, the Conchological Society of Great Britain and Ireland and the Nottingham Naturalists' Society. During the week excursions were made to the Aran Islands and various localities in the Burren of County Clare and in Connemara. These excursions by large, well-organised groups of naturalists proved extremely successful in extending the knowledge of the fauna and flora, as the results showed. It was further agreed at Galway that triennial conferences should be held, and meetings consequently followed in Kenmare (1898), Dublin (1901), Sligo (1904), Cork (1907) and Rosapenna (1910). The well-prepared, detailed and illustrated programmes which were circulated by Praeger beforehand show vividly the careful organisation which went into them. On the field trips Praeger was everywhere with his whistle, dragooning the mixed crowd of naturalists from one place to another, dragging along the stragglers and moving on the serious collectors whose intense application to particular problems endangered the timetable. It was also a remarkable fact that, although the conferences invariably took place in July, the reports and detailed results were published without fail by Praeger in the September issue of *The Irish Naturalist* following the conference. After the Rosapenna conference the Irish Field Club Union gradually faded out as it was considered that its original objective to bring Irish naturalists into contact with each other for joint investigations, had been accomplished. The 50th Anniversary celebrations of the Belfast Naturalists' Field Club in 1913 replaced the triennial conference of that year, and by 1916 war and social unrest made excursions difficult.

How Praeger managed to meet his future wife with his free time so completely taken up might be a mystery to some. Yet he did, and in unusual circumstances. In the autumn of 1901 Praeger went over to Schleswig Holstein for a holiday after seeing *Irish Topographical Botany* through the press. It was there that he met Hedwig, daughter of the artist Christian Carl Magnussen. Difficulties of communication apparently proved no hindrance. Praeger could not speak a work of German (about the only thing he didn't excel at was languages) and Hedwig, or Hedi as she was known, could only speak what he called 'schoolgirl English'. Nevertheless, from the beginning she learned to share his interest in natural history and also to share his love for the beautiful scenery of Ireland. In fact she accompanied him on all his wanderings and, up to her death in 1952, they were inseparable. Her organisational ability was second only to Praeger's, and her invaluable assistance ensured the smooth running of every excursion or survey.

In 1905, Praeger embarked on another ambitious group project, a biological survey of Lambay, an island off Dublin, for the owner Cecil Baring (of the merchant banking family). The results of this survey were so fruitful that it was decided to do a similar survey on a much larger scale of Clare Island and the surrounding district of west Mayo. This survey still stands as the largest ever undertaken in the British Isles and, to my mind, is the crowning achievement of Irish naturalists. The original aim of this survey was to study the dispersal of animals and plants across open sea in order to throw light on the problems of passage, subsequent differentiation and specialization of species. Later the history, archaeology, language and folklore of the area were also studied. Under the guidance of a free-lance committee, professional naturalists from the National Museum, the universities and the relevant government departments as well as amateur naturalists from all the Irish field clubs, and members of both the Royal Irish Academy and the Royal Dublin Society, travelled in groups to the island, which was already well-known to Praeger:

> My first experience of it began weirdly. Noting that its botany was curiously unknown, my wife and I crossed over from Roonah Quay in the post-boat on an evening in July 1903. It was dead calm, with an oily roll coming in from the west. All the hills around were smothered in a white mist, which over the island formed an ernormous arch, solid enough seemingly to walk on, and descending nearly to sea-level. We lurched slowly across in an ominous stillness, and darkness descended before it was due, as we groped our way to the little quay. Next morning, when he wished to get away to explore the island, all was dense mist and heavy rain, still without wind, and all day we fretted in our little cottage, unable to move. Late in the day the rain ceased, and a strange red glow, coming from the north-west, spread through the thinning fog. We hurried out to the north point of the island, and there, just sinking into the ocean, was a blood-red sun, lighting up dense inky clouds which brooded low over the black jagged teeth of Achill Head, rising from a black sea tinged with crimson. It was a scene fitted for Dante's *Inferno*, and if a flight of demons or of angels had passed across in the strange atmosphere it would have seemed quite appropriate, and no cause for wonder.

From 1909 to 1911 parties of workers numbering anything from six to 16 were sent to the island at monthly intervals and a large number of individual specialists arrived separately, so that there was no month of the year during which observations of some kind were not carried out.

The results were startling. The main object of the survey, that is, the detailed biological study of a chosen area, and its analysis with the view to throwing light on the questions of species dispersal, was more than adequately fulfilled. Over the three year period more than 180 workers took part. The opportunity of working on such an amazing survey brought volunteers from England, Scotland, Germany, Denmark and Switzerland, as well as most of Ireland's leading field naturalists. Indeed, the experience gained was to stand most of them in good stead later in other expeditions.

The results began to appear in print in 1911, in the *Proceedings of the Royal Irish Academy*, culminating in 1915 with 68 lengthy reports. Again, the speed with which they were got to press is yet another example of Praeger's ability to get things done. In all some 3,219 species of plants were listed, 585 of which were new to Ireland, 55 previously unrecorded in the British Isles, and 11 new to science – mostly algae and fungi. The total fauna listed comprised 5,269 species, 1,253 of which were new to Ireland, 343 previously unrecorded in the British Isles, and 109 new to science. It was a great achievement, and one of which Praeger must have been proud.

The completion of the Clare Island Survey in 1915 saw a slackening in Praeger's activities. He was now fifty years old and, although he was to produce much more work and initiate new schemes, he never again attempted anything on the same scale. It is possible that the strain of organising such large endeavours was beginning to tell, making them less appealing. It is on record as an unusual event at this time, when, after a long day's 'botanizing' on the Garron plateau in County Antrim, he remarked in the evening that he 'felt somewhat tired'. Travel anywhere was becoming an expensive luxury, and, coupled with the war which was looming in Europe, the naturalist's way of life was going into decline. Anyway, the universities had finally begun to include practical field work in their curricula, leading to the rise of the professional naturalist. It may have been, too, that the hysteria which accompanied the advent of the 1914–18 war, and led to the removal of people like Prince Louis Battenberg from his post as First Sea Lord of the Admiralty (the family later changed their name to Mountbatten to appease patriotic feelings), may have driven him in on himself. After all, Praeger had a foreign-sounding name (Praeger is derived from Prager, meaning a native of Prague) and a German wife. In fact, in the ensuing 'witch hunt', it was only after the strongest representations were made on their behalf to the government that they were not interned for the duration of the war. R.F. Scharff, Praeger's old friend who had been responsible for his coming to Dublin, and who had been indispensable during the Clare Island Survey, narrowly escaped the same fate, because he was of German parentage. Whatever the reasons, the two major botanical research projects of the last part of Praeger's life, on the Sedums and Sempervivums for the Royal Horticultural Society, were solitary tasks.

Availing of the fledgeling Free State government's offer of full pensions for those who wished to retire in 1922, Praeger left the National Library and embarked on the first of his many trips on the Continent. It is a curious fact that it was only now, at the age of fifty-seven that Praeger began to travel widely abroad. His botanical work brought him, in his own words, 'from Bergen to Florence and from

Edinburgh to Sofia'. His ability to see new places with an open mind, without preconceived ideas, led to a refreshing style of writing when he began publishing the narratives of his field trips as essays and reminiscences. These *belles lettres* show us his love of life and appreciation of it in a way that his scientific achievements never do. Praeger's lengthy visits to the Canary Islands, an area of special interest were, on his own admission, the most interesting and delightful that he and his wife ever spent abroad. Because civilisation existed only along the coast, where hotels had been built to cater for the increasing flow of tourists, Praeger and his wife slept by preference in open fields or on sea sands and avoided the 'civilised' areas except for food. Many of the adventures he had at this time were recounted in various journals such as *The Cornhill Magazine* and *The Irish Statesman*. Some were gathered together later and published in book form under the title *Beyond Soundings*.

His travels abroad merely confirmed what he already knew, namely, that Ireland is a very lovely country. Indeed, as he said:

> There is only one thing wrong with it, and that is that the people that are in it have not the common-sense to live in peace with one another and with their neighbours. Past events and political theory are allowed to bulk much too large in our mental make-up, and the result is dissatisfaction, unrest, and occasionally shocking violence. That 'frontier', which is a festering sore in Ireland's present economy, was the noble gift of an English Government – but Ireland brought it on herself. 'Well, now', said a Connemara man to me, 'politics is the devil itself': and in this country that is only too true. If St. Patrick had banished from Ireland politics, instead of snakes, he would have conferred a far greater boon, and this lovely land would have had peace and charity, as well as faith and hope.

Although he lived through some of the most stirring years in the history of this island, Praeger was completely apolitical. He saw no reason to divide an island that was, to him, one ecological entity. Likewise, he bore no ill will towards anyone whose politics differed from his own.

During the 1930s and 1940s Praeger was looked on as the Grand Old Man of natural history in Ireland. Honours were heaped on him from many quarters. At various times he was elected President of the Belfast Naturalists' Field Club, the Dublin Naturalists' Field Club, the Royal Irish Academy, the Royal Zoological Society of Ireland, the Royal Horticultural and Arboricultural Society of Ireland and the British Ecological Society, among others. Because he remained so active and interested in any project he became involved in he was also a founder member and (almost inevitably) First President of the Geographical Society of Ireland, the Library Association of Ireland and An Taisce: Ireland's National Trust. The continued quality of his fieldwork can be assessed from his publications and also from the fact that he twice received the Veitch Gold Medal of the Royal Horticultural Society, the Gold Medal of the Belfast Naturalists' Field Club, was elected an Associate of the Linnean Society, Honorary Life Member of the Botanical Society of the British Isles and had honorary doctorates conferred on him by the three Irish universities then in existence (Queen's Univesity Belfast, National University of Ireland and Trinity College Dublin).

It has to be admitted that all of this recognition late in life meant very little to Praeger. In his twilight years he became more contemplative, ensuring that as much as possible of the knowledge he had acquired should be written down. *The Botanist in Ireland* published in 1934 sets down in detail the results of more than fifty years botanical research, and was his last major work on the Irish flora. *The Way that I Went*, published in 1937, is Praeger's best-known book and made his name a household word. Praeger described it as 'a kind of thank-offering, however crude, for seven decades of robust physical health in which to walk and climb and swim and sail throughout or around the island in which I was born, to the benefit alike of body and soul . . . disguised as an account of the beautiful land in which I have spent my septuagesimal holiday'.

In 1946 Praeger wrote a paper entitled 'Things left undone' in which he set down for future naturalists, areas where resarch needed to be done. Not that he was finished with writing or anything like that, as his rate of publication hardly slowed. *The Way that I Went* had gone into a second edition in 1939 and a third, revised edition appeared in 1947. *A Populous Solitude*, published in 1941, contains more short stories and anecdotal material. *Some Irish Naturalists* (1949) is a biographical reference book and is essentially a listing of Praeger's friends, 'men and women to whom the contemplative and gentle life appealed – love of the beautiful in whatever manifestation, a wide tolerance, a reverence for life that shrank from the wanton destruction of even the lowliest creature, a shrinking from "the strife for triumph more than truth", a belief that happiness is not be to measured by mere worldly success'.

The Natural History of Ireland, published in 1950, is yet another useful work of reference. Praeger's last book, *The Irish Landscape*, was published posthumously in 1953, some months after his death at his sister's house in Craigavad, Co. Down. Like all his books, it is still very much in demand today, as his style of writing is extremely lucid. Indeed, had television been as widely available as it is today I feel sure that Praeger would have been extremely successful as a presenter of documentaries, as he was always interesting, always interested.

As a lover of the landscape and all its constituent parts, Praeger was always moved when he saw others express similar feelings. For instance, he recounts in *A Populous Solitude* meeting a 'returned American' in a remote area over-looking Lough Foyle:

> Over cigarettes we got into talk, chiefly at first about the technique of the turf-cutting; the 'breast slean' he had 'heard tell of' but had never seen used. Further talk disclosed that he had been fifteen years in Pittsburg. He must have been a useful hand in the steel works there, for he was a 'son of Anak', with a bared forearm that would delight a sculptor (or an anatomist!).
>
> I yielded to temptation, looking at the very poor holding he had to work on here, and asked him: 'What brought you back after all these years to a poor holding like this? Over in the States you must have been making good money'. I can see him answer me yet. He drew himself up to his full six feet, looked along the hilly coast before us, clear from Aghla to Melmore, filled his lungs and breathed it out: 'Man, the peace of it!'.

CHAPTER 11

The Achievement of Estyn Evans

by

R. H. Buchanan

The theme of the 1990 John Hewitt Summer School, 'Turning to the Landscape', is highly appropriate to the subject of this brief memoir on the life and work of Emyr Estyn Evans, first Professor of Geography at Queen's University, Belfast and first Director of the University's Institute of Irish Studies. Like John Hewitt, his contemporary and professional colleague, Estyn Evans had a love of landscape and an especial affection for Hewitt's County Antrim, from Fair Head to Garron Point and Glenarm.

For Estyn, the fascination of landscape lay in the duality of its creation, fashioned in the beginning by natural processes and then fine-tuned by the work of man, extending over many generations. In a short essay, *Ulster: The Common Ground* (1984), written towards the end of his long life, he encapsulated his work in a few phrases: 'My theme is the common people and the land itself, the land that they've helped to make . . . I'm convinced that we've got to look to the land to understand the nature of its products, material and spiritual'. As a record of the past, he believed the landscape can often provide evidence more objective than the written document, less fallible than people's memories. Within the landscape can be found the hard facts of history, a history of ordinary people, of individual lives lived within and yet beyond the institutional framework of law and politics, of economic and social systems which form the subject-matter of conventional histories. In the land and in its landscapes lie the roots of a history and a folk culture that is common to us all, the 'common ground' from which we grow. That was the past he sought to interpret, a past that extended far beyond the span of documentary history, into the millennia when man first came to Ireland. The study of the past he valued for its own sake, but he was equally concerned with understanding the past as a key to the present and to the future. 'Without understanding the past' he wrote in the introduction to his first book on Ireland, *Irish Heritage*, 'how can we hope to plan for the future?' Teaching us the better to understand ourselves, through the study of our landscape and our folk culture, was perhaps Estyn's main achievement for the people of Ulster.

Before developing that point more fully, let me first outline some biographical details, dwelling first on his early life and career. Emyr Estyn Evans was born in May 1905, one of a family of four sons and one daughter. His father was a Minister of the Presbyterian Church in Wales, a man who in his early life had worked in the mines of the South Wales Coalfield. The Rev. Evans had little formal schooling, but he had a love for scholarship and an intellectual curiosity and drive which had an abiding influence on his youngest son; and though Estyn himself had little time for formal religious practice, he had a prodigious knowledge of the Bible and a special love for the Book of Psalms. I think his feeling for words came in part from this deep knowledge of the King James version of the Bible and partly from the rich vocabulary of the country people of the Welsh borderlands among whom he spent his childhood. The poet, A.E. Housman was part of that verbal tradition, and he was one of Estyn's favourites, not least because for him Housman recaptured the scenes and images of the Shropshire of his school days, its landscape and its countryside.

The experiences of a country childhood had a major influence on Estyn's later life. His knowledge of flowers and trees, of birds and animals, came from the fields and laneways in which he played as a child, and from walks in the wooded valleys of his father's parish in Montgomeryshire. He had a keen eye for detail, so sharp indeed that he could spot man-made flint tools on a shingle beach where others would pass them by. Above all he enjoyed the company of country people, and had a profound respect for country skills, the work of arable farmer and stockman, and the craftsman in wood, metal and stone. It was in keeping with his background that the academic historian whose work he most admired was Marc Bloch, who 'wrote his classic books as a farmer who could plough, who knew the feel of the land and the smell of hay and manure'. His own writing derives much of its directness and character from the same 'hands-on' experience, and from the keen observation of a gifted artist, whose sketches of tools and implements reveal an intimate knowledge of their manufacture and use.

From the Welsh borderland Estyn moved on to Aberystwyth, where he studied geography and anthropology under H.J. Fleure, one of the foremost human geographers of his generation. Fleure's influence was profound; trained originally as a natural scientist, he had an holistic view of man's place in the natural world, seeing the evolution of human culture as a constant process of interaction between human inventiveness and the resources available in specific environments. Fleure's philosophy and teaching provided Estyn with the framework for his own intellectual development; and Fleure's backing and influence provided him with the opportunity for his first appointment – a research studentship at Oxford under the classical scholar Sir John Myers, abandoned with great reluctance with the onset of tuberculosis. Convalescence was followed by an editorial post with the *Encyclopedia Britannica*. He used to say that he was an expert on every subject beginning with the letters A to C, but before reaching D he left to take up a lectureship at Queen's University, Belfast in 1928. He was only 23, yet he was asked to establish geography as an academic discipline within the University. Soon after, he married a fellow student from Aberystwyth, a remarkable woman who bore him four sons, nurtured his talent and provided both intellectual stimulus and sound common sense. Without Gwynneth I doubt if Estyn could have accomplished so much, for she provided companionship and a warm domestic environment readily shared with friends, colleages and students. Many of us have the fondest memories of the welcome we received at their homes, and the steady stream of visitors from many countries and backgrounds – including such literary figures as Louis MacNeice and W.R. Rodgers.

Estyn worked at Queen's for over forty years, establishing his own Department of Geography and helping to found two others, Archaeology and Social Anthropology. He also became the first Director of the University's Institute of Irish Studies, a research institute established to promote postgraduate research on Ireland in any academic discipline. Through these teaching roles he influenced a generation of students, from his first honours graduates in geography in the 1930s to the last class he taught in the early 1970s. None who came in contact with him during those years can forget his lectures, for their breadth of vision, their originality and depth. As a lecturer he was unforgettable, a tall, spare figure slightly stooped about the shoulders and with all the tricks and props of the consummate performer – the misplaced chalk, the untidy sheaf of notes, the slides that never were quite in focus. But there was another side to his lecturing style: a beautifully modulated voice and a sly sense of humour which could puncture most effectively any sign of academic pomposity and pretension. Superficially Estyn appeared as a somewhat remote and reserved figure, but this was a cloak to hide an essential shyness. For those who got to know him, and especially students who attended the Department's annual field trips, he was a quite different person: warm, supportive, encouraging yet never paternalistic – he encouraged students to learn from their own mistakes; above all, he was a stimulating and humorous companion who enjoyed talk and music. Those student field trips, held each year in Ireland, were the real catalysts which brought staff and students together in an atmosphere which made Estyn's department one of the happiest and most close-knit at Queen's. They were real family gatherings, for Gwynneth, the children and the dogs usually came too, along with any visitors who happened to stop by. The relationships developed on field trips help to explain the affection in which Estyn was held by his students; his personality ensured that the messages of his teaching were so widely accepted and promoted by those who became teachers in the schools of the Province and beyond. Through them, local studies of landscape and local history were taught in Northern Ireland long before such work was formally recognised in the schools' curriculum as 'cultural heritage'.

Estyn's primary achievement was the establishment of the several academic departments already mentioned, but outside the University his influence extended into many areas of public life. For example, he was the author of a document, *The Ulster Countryside*, published in 1947 on behalf of the Northern Ireland Government's Planning Advisory Board. This was a policy document, a blue-print for action on rural planning and landscape conservation based on Estyn's own deep knowledge of the regions and landscapes of Ulster, gained through field work. For an academic of that time, this was an unusual venture into the public domain, but it reflected Estyn's abiding concern that the results of academic research should be made available to a wider public, and if appropriate, stimulate action by government or other bodies. In his advocacy of the need to conserve landscape and wildlife by designating national parks and nature reserves, Estyn was way ahead of local politicians: it took another twenty years before the policy he advocated was incorporated in the Amenity Lands Act, passed in 1965.

Another area in which he was active was the preservation of the Province's rich legacy of ancient monuments. When he came to Ulster as a young man in the late 1920s, his primary interest was Ireland's prehistoric cultures and the impact of man in the shaping of the landscape, especially during the neolithic and bronze ages. But in the Ireland of that time there was no systematic record of field monuments, and few sites had been excavated with any degree of scientific precision. Along with his colleague Oliver Davies, he had to undertake the basic field work himself, helped by friends from the Belfast Naturalists' Field Club. By bus, train and bicycle they travelled throughout Ulster, surveying and excavating. They re-established the *Ulster Journal of Archaeology* as a vehicle for publishing their work, and in 1940 with D.A. Chart, they published *A Preliminary Survey of Ancient Monuments of Northern Ireland*, a remarkably accurate and wide-ranging inventory of sites throughout the six counties. This stimulated new legislation for the protection and care of the Province's ancient monuments, the establishment of the government's Archaeological Survey in 1949 and of the Ancient Monuments Advisory Councils which Estyn was later to chair for many years.

The third area of public service is perhaps his most significant achievement and certainly one for which he will be long remembered: the foundation of the Ulster Folk & Transport Museum. Estyn's work on folklife was initially a by-product of his field-work in archaeology, and through it he met many people, visited their houses and watched them at work in the fields and farmyards. Visits to Donegal in the mid-thirties provided a particular inspiration, and in 1939 he published two papers which have since become classics: 'Donegal Survivals', which dealt with the traditional houses and farm implements of a small community near Errigal: and 'Some Survivals of the Irish Openfield System', which described for the first time the system of land tenure and farming known as rundale, formerly widely practised in Ireland and which he believed to derive from earlier systems of prehistoric land-use. In 1941 with the help and encouragement of Harry Tempest of Dundalgan Press in Dundalk, he published his *Irish Heritage*, a book he described as 'an adventure into ill-charted seas . . . the study of a working example of peasant culture, based on traditions of immemorial antiquity and thus of the greatest scientific interest'. Fifteen years later he developed this theme more fully in *Irish Folk Ways*, a work more systematic and better documented than its predecessor, and better known since it appeared under the imprint of the London publisher, Routledge and Kegan Paul.

The success of *Irish Heritage* and *Irish Folkways* established Estyn's international reputation for folklife research, and encouraged him to pursue his ambition to establish a folk museum, similar to those in Scandinavia. The task required patience, tact and diplomatic skills; and the support of a heterogeneous group of civil servants, politicians, teachers and businessmen, their only bond a deep respect for

Estyn and for the work he was attempting to do. Among those whose support was crucial was the late E.T. Green, father of Professor Rodney Green who succeeded Estyn as Director of the Institute of Irish Studies in 1970; and G.B. Newe of Cushendall, then Secretary of the N.I. Council of Social Services and Honorary Secretary of the Committee on Ulster Folklife and Traditions, the pressure group whose work led to the establishment of the Museum in 1958. Its first directors, George Thompson and Alan Gailey, were both graduates of the Department of Geography at Queen's, and with Estyn as a trustee and later as Chairman, the Museum has become one of the foremost institutions of its kind. Estyn watched its growth with pleasure and not a little pride. It is perhaps his finest legacy to the people of the Province, for through its exhibits and galleries the Museum conveys a sense of dignity in the achievements of ordinary people and their role in the making of the Ulster countryside.

In outlining the public achievements of Estyn Evans – in teaching, public service, and in the development of the Folk Museum – less emphasis has been laid on the scholarship upon which his work was based, and from which he derived his international reputation as geographer, archaeologist and ethnologist. It is not appropriate to dwell on these now, but I will refer back briefly to his work on landscape, the theme of this conference. For Estyn, landscape encapsulated a trilogy of habitat, heritage and history, whose interconnections give each place on earth its own unique personality. 'The whole story of human culture is indissolubly bound up with the landscape with which it has both influenced and been influenced by'; 'Irish peasant life', he wrote, 'is inseparable from the country which helped to mould it', and this belief he domonstrated in two works. The first, *The Personality of Ireland*, was published first in 1973, and in a more attractive edition by Blackstaff in 1981; and the second, *Mourne Country*, was published by Dundalgan Press in 1951. In writing about the Mournes his aim was simple: 'to trace in the intimacy of a small and well-loved region the physical components and human responses which make up the Irish countryside'. It was written in the Mournes, with all the senses, eye, ear and nose, fully engaged to capture the essence of the place:

> I have written much of it at a little window on the seaward slope of Slieve Donard, where I had only to lift my eyes to see the hill and watch the coloured seasons climbing from the golden whins to the glowing heather and the snows. I have come to know Mourne intimately, to learn that its stony soils respond best to the toil of the

mis-named lazy-bed, to experience the hazards of carrying wet wrack on the back over slippery rocks, and to build walls of granite in the vain hope of keeping the mountain sheep out of my garden.

Mourne Country has been described by a leading academic geographer as 'probably the best regional study in the language', yet essentially it is concerned with the activities of ordinary people, with the farmers and fishermen, granite workers and craftsmen whose work over many generations had shaped the land. His chapter headings reflect this emphasis: Field and Farm, The Wrack Harvest, Luggers and Long Lines, The Stone Men, Pedlars and Smugglers, House and Hearth. In writing on these humble topics he averred his belief that 'The crafts of arable farming, of animal husbandry and the home industries have done more to shape our instincts and thoughts than the tramplings of armies or the wranglings of kings which fill the documents from which history is written'. Not everyone agreed. Some of Estyn's contemporaries, trained in the conventions of documentary history, were critical of his methods and attached little importance to archaeological and landscape evidence, even when it related to historical periods. John Hewitt had some reservations, too, not so much about the role of ordinary people in making history – in that respect he was very close to Estyn – but in what he saw as an undue emphasis on material culture, on artifacts and implements and houses, as opposed to things of the spirit, expressed in ballads, poetry, speech. Hewitt makes this point in a poem he wrote for Estyn on the publication of *Irish Heritage*. I suspect it may not be known to many people here, and I read it by courtesy of Gwynneth Evans who owns the manuscript. The poem, entitled 'On the Choice of a Title', seems to me a fitting tribute to the life and work of a remarkable man who did so much to reveal the richness of their heritage to the people of this Province.

An earnest scholar skilled to weigh
from evidence of shard and bone
why creatures of a cruder day
left laboured rituals in stone,
took note of nimble peasant hands
and what they wrought at, page by page,
till bound in bulk the record stands
entitled Irish Heritage.

Tho what he wrote was rescued well
from progress and its daft machine

that nearer tolls the craftsman's knell
to me that title still must mean
the coiling tangle of desire
that threshed across this misty stage
with breaking hearts or wits on fire
that is the Irish heritage.

The coarse buffoon with bawdy laugh
who moulds the mob with crafty hand;
the randy squire whose epitaph
is scrawled across a beggared land:
the poet's talk, the tenor song,
the cattledealer's storm of rage
when sober daylight proves him wrong:-
this is the Irish heritage.

The stubborn martyr to a cause;
the rebel's final eloquence;
the waster wheedling your applause
and, after, pocketting your pence;
the man who faces death or kills
with only threadbare words for wage;
the dreamer walking in the hills.
This is the Irish heritage.

CHAPTER 12

Dinnseanchas and Modern Gaelic Poetry

by

Caoimhín Mac Giolla Léith

I would like to begin by explaining that by 'modern gaelic poetry' I mean the body of poetry produced since the closing decades of the last century in the Celtic languages which are still spoken and written by a minority in Ireland and Scotland. 'Irish' is, of course, the term generally used to describe the language spoken by an ever-decreasing number of native speakers in the various Gaeltacht areas, mostly on the west coast of Ireland, and by a considerable number of native English speakers for whom it is a second language.[1] The term 'Gaelic' has for some acquired an unfortunate suggestion of tweeness and condescension and perhaps a faint whiff of the visiting or returned Yank, and stands in urgent need of rehabilitation. It is, however, the term used in Scotland to refer to the language spoken by a significant number of native speakers in the Western Highlands and Islands and a small number of Scottish learners.[2]

Irish and Scottish Gaelic are usually thought of nowadays as separate languages but they share a common linguistic and literary inheritance. Thus, professional poets in Gaelic Ireland and Scotland wrote in the same literary register down to the seventeenth century and this common language was, for instance, the language in which John Carswell, Superintendent of Argyll and Bishop of the Isles, wrote his translation of *The Book of Common Order* which in 1567 was the first book ever published in Gaelic. The fortunes of Scottish and Irish Gaelic in the years since the turbulent seventeenth century have been similarly troubled but there are also, inevitably, certain differences between the sociolinguistic histories of the two diverging languages. This essay is an attempt to cast some light on these similarities and differences by a reading of a number of contemporary Irish and Scottish Gaelic 'poems of place'. I shall, therefore, sketch a necessarily brief history of the nature and role of *dinnseanchas* in early Gaelic literature before proceeding to discuss some reflexes of and responses to this tradition in poems by the most highly acclaimed of the Modern Scottish Gaelic poets, Somhairle MacGill-Eain (Sorley MacLean), and by two Irish poets, Nuala Ní Dhomhnaill and Liam Ó Muirthile.

The term *dinnseanchas* is a compound comprising two elements, *dinn* and *seanchas*. *Dinn*(*dind*), which is cognate with Old Norse *tindr*, may originally have meant 'a spike or a point'. In early Irish, however, it is usually taken to mean 'a mountain, hill or hillock'. By extension it acquired the meaning 'landmark, eminent or notable place'. The second element is *seanchas* (*senchas*). The usual translations of *seanchas* as 'lore, history tradition or traditions' give little indication of the semantic range of the term or of its centrality to the intellectual life of early Gaelic society. The professional learned classes of early Christian Ireland, as D.A. Binchy has remarked, were the custodians of its *seanchas* and their duties included the conservation of 'the genealogies of the powerful families, the tribal lore, the stories of conquest or migration. . .(and) the traditional laws, the customs of the tribe'.[3] Putting the two elements together we may translate *dinnseanchas* as the 'traditional, legendary lore of notable places' or, more prosaically, as 'topography'. However, as one recent commentator on the *dinnseanchas*, Charles Bowen, has suggested

> we must try to imagine a science of geography based on *senchas*, in which there is no clear distinction between the general principles of topography or direction-finding and the intimate knowledge of particular places . . . Seen from this point of view, a modern road-map transmits knowledge of a kind that primitive Celts would have found inconceivably abstract. Places would have been known to them as people were: by face, name, and history. The last two would have been closely linked, for, as the *Dindshenchas* illustrates again and again, *the name of every place was assumed to be an expression of its history*. (my emphasis)[4]

As reference has been made both to *dinnseanchas* in general and to '*the Dinnseanchas*' some clarification may be necessary. Onomastic lore, or traditions concerning individual placenames, and aetiological legends, or stories purporting to explain the origins of places or peoples, abound in early Gaelic literature. Indeed, they are frequently woven into the fabric of longer narratives in such quantity that they obscure the primary narrative almost entirely. Thus the modern reader may find irritatingly obtrusive what he or she may feel should be incidental and subordinate. This is not peculiar to Gaelic literature, but it is a very prominent feature of it. As Bowen remarks, 'The Irish considered every form of literature a fitting vehicle for antiquarian lore and onomastic lore seems to have been among the most popular'.[5]

Readers of the most famous of the early sagas, for instance, *Táin Bó Cuailnge* ('The Cattle Raid of Cooley'), will recall the various disruptions or diversions of the narrative in order to explain the origins of a placename. The explanation of Ardee or *Áth Fhir Diad*, 'The Ford of Ferdia', so-called because it is the place where Cú Chulainn fought and slew his foster-brother, is just one of many such incidences to be found in the early sagas. The tale most thoroughly saturated by *dinnsenchas* is probably the twelfth-century *Acallamh na Senórach*, commonly called 'The Colloquy of the Ancients'. This takes the form of a *Rahmenerzälung* or frame-tale in which Caílte mac Rónáin and Oisín, son of Fionn mac Cumhaill tell stories of the adventures and exploits of Fionn's warrior band to St. Patrick and his scribe as they make a circuit of Ireland. Many of these tales are onomastic and are told in response to Patrick's enquiries as to the circumstances in which the particular place they are visiting acquired its name.

Dinnseanchas then is endemic in Early Gaelic literature. When Bowen and Celtic scholars in general refer to the *Dinnseanchas*, however, they are referring to a corpus of Middle Irish toponymic literature known as *Dinnshenchas Erenn* which has been preserved mainly in three forms, one collection of poems and two of prose-and-verse units. This material was probably compiled in the twelfth century and comprises in all about 200 poems and 200 prose pieces. The fact that many of the most important of the late medieval Gaelic manuscript miscellanies include this text – *The Book of Leinster*, *The Yellow Book of Lecan* and *The Book of Ballymote*, for example – may give some indication of its popularity. In the fullest version of the *Dinnseanchas* the material is arranged in the form of 'articles' consisting of a prose piece ostensibly 'explaining' the derivation of a particular placename followed by one or more poems on the same name. There a number of ways in which a given placename might be accounted for. As Bowen puts it

> A survey of the *Dindshenchas* suggests that tradition supplied the authors with two principal means of accounting for placenames. When the sense of the name suggested a story, such as *Ard Lemnachta* ('New-milk Height') or *Loch Cenn*, ('The Lake of Heads') a story could be discovered, adapted or invented. When

> this technique was impracticable, an eponym could be borrowed or coined.[6]

The attitude of the authors of *the Dinnseanchas* to eponyms might fairly be described as latitudinarian. While there are many placenames for which an eponym is clearly appropriate there are many others which equally clearly require alternative derivations. The authors of *the Dinnseanchas*, moreover, are as likely to provide the 'wrong' eponym as the 'right' one and display considerable ingenuity in the invention of entirely spurious 'legendary personages'. Thus, as Bowen points out, '*Slige Midluachair*, for instance, must have sounded to any speaker of Irish something like 'Mid-Marsh road', or 'Road in the midst of the rushes'. It was explained, however, as the 'discovery' of a fictitious Midluachair mac Damairne.[7] In a number of cases such as this, quite obvious if banal derivations were discarded in favour of more exotic 'eponymous' explanations.

The third, and most *recherché*, technique favoured by the toponymists who contributed to the *dinnseanchas* tradition, was that of lexical fission. The early Irish learnéd classes show an almost pathological need to explain the meaning and origin of words by chopping them into little pieces. This habit in all likelihood derives ultimately from the *Etymologies* of Isadore, the early seventh-century Bishop of Seville, but the Irish made it very much their own. As one Celticist has commented 'Early Irish scholars married paronomasia (i.e. punning) and folk etymology, with medieval scientific etymology, and developed it into a fine art'.[8] That the vast bulk of these etymologies were entirely spurious seemed not to bother them unduly. Still less did it worry them that they were often able to produce a number of equally improbable, and mutually contradictory, etymologies for the same placename. Thus, the first entry in the printed version of '*The Prose Dindshenchas*' in Gaelic and Latin offers the following derivations of 'Tara', *Temair* in Early Irish, as translated by Whitley Stokes:

> *Te-mair* then. . .is the múr (rampart) of *Tea* daughter of Lugaid son of Ith, when she wedded Geide the Loud-Voiced. 'Tis in his reign that every one in Erin deemed the other's voice as sweet as the strings of lutes would be, because of the greatness of the peace and friendship each man had for the other in Ireland. Therefore, then, is that rampart more venerable than every rampart, because these are Erin's first free covenants, the covenants of the daughter of Lugaid with Geide the Loud-Voiced. . .

> Or, Te-mair, that is Teipe-mur that is the rampart of *Tephe* daughter of Bachter king of Spain. 'Tis she that lived with Canthon son of Cathmenn king of Britain, till she died with him. . .(And) after her death. . . a rampart was built around her to wit, Teipe-múr. Now Tea Eremon's wife saw that, to wit, the rampart of Tephis. . . And afterwards she designed [on the hill of Tara] a rampart like the rampart of Tephis, and therein she was buried. Hence it is called Temair. . .

> Or thus: *Temair*: Authors affirm that the name of this town we call *Temoria* in Latin is derived from the Greek word *Oewpēw* which in Latin is interpreted *conspicio*, and every conspicuous and eminent place, whether on a plain or in a house or wherever it may be, may be called by this word *Temair* . . . This town, therefore, claims what is common to many [i.e. the name *Temair*] and, as it now surpasses all [other] Irish towns, aptly possesses their common name, for its ruler even to this day obtains the sovereignty of the whole island of the Scots [i.e. Ireland – 'totius insolae Scotorum'].[9]

Both common sense and modern Celtic scholarship hold that this is pure invention although it must be admitted that a reasonable alternative has yet to be suggested. All of the techniques used in *the Dinnseanchas* to elucidate placenames may be used implausibly and, as Bowen remarks, they 'usually are'.

> Even where error is not demonstrable, we have scant ground for supposing that the onomastic information they offer is accurate. Toponymic legends belong to the tradition of etiology, not historiography, and the essence of etiology *is the attempt to confront a past which is unknown and reduce it to knowability* (my emphasis)[10]

Dinnseanchas in early medieval Ireland, then, may be described, as Baumgarten, following E.R. Curtius, has described etymology in general in the same period, as 'a category of thought and of literary creation',[11] and a particularly fecund one at that.

But many centuries separate us from the medieval period and one might well ask what relevance, if any, this has to contemporary Irish thought and literature? The following two prose extracts, from John Montague and Ciarán Carson respectively, which may be more familiar to readers of contemporary Irish literature than much of the material discussed so far, provide an initial response to this question:

> Take the name Knockmany. One could explain it as 'Cnoc Maine', the hill of the Manaig or Menapii, a tribe of the Belgae who travelled as far as Lough Erne; after all they gave their name to the adjoining county of Fermanagh. But the local translation of the name is Ania's Cove, and Ania or Áine or Ano is the Danaan Mother goddess, whose name is found in the river Boyne, the Boan or Good Mother . . .[12]
>
> Belfast is a corruption of the Irish *Béal Feirste. Béal* is easy. It means a mouth or the mouth of a river, an opening; an approach . . . But it is this feirste in which meaning founders, this genitive of *fearsad*, the Irish for . . .
>
> The Rev. Dineen glosses it as a shaft; a spindle; the ulna of the arm; a club; the spindle of an axle; a bar or bank of sand at low water; a deep narrow channel on a strand at low tide; a pit or pool of water, a verse, a poem. . .
>
> But let us take the simple approach, and imagine that *fearsad* is a sandbank, formed by the confluence of the river of that name – the Farset – and the Lagan. So Belfast is the *approach to the sandbank*, or the *mouth of the Farset*; or the *approach to the ford* . . .[13]

Both poets are clearly and acutely aware that, as Montague puts it, 'the least Irish placename can net a world with its associations'. Montague's *The Rough Field* is inter alia an attempt to recuperate and reclaim the landscape of Tyrone for Irish poetry in English, to decipher and translate that 'manuscript we had lost the skill to read' while Ciarán Carson has already devoted two remarkable collections to his own bewildered attempt to come to terms with the changing map of Belfast. These projects involve the claiming of a landscape, one rural, one urban, through the process of naming it.

The attempt by the medieval authors of *the Dinnseanchas* 'to confront a past which is unknown and reduce it to knowability' is echoed by these contemporary attempts to confront a present which is troubling and uncertain and construe it as poetry. That both poets should focus on the evocative polysemy of placenames (as indeed have other Irish writers in recent times, most notably Brian Friel in *Translations* and Seamus Heaney, especially in his earlier volumes) comes as no surprise to Terry Eagleton. In fact for Eagleton it appears to be almost part of the national character. In a review of *The Penguin Book of Contemporary Irish Poetry* (London 1990) he remarks, with a certain wistfulness, that

> Thematically (Irish poets) brood upon place and parish in a way impossible for the contemporary British. You just can't feel about

> Dorking or Dunstable as you can about Kinsale or Killala. Irish placenames are spots in time as well as space, palimpsests in which a whole disrupted history lies waiting to be deciphered.[14]

While it may not be entirely frivolous to wonder how the homiletic value of this observation would be affected if instead we compared, say, Glastonbury or Gloucester with Kilbehenny and Kinnegad, Eagleton's comments could apply with equal, if not greater, validity to the work of the Scottish poet Sorley MacLean.

MacLean was born almost eighty years ago in Osgaig, a small township on the predominantly Free Presbyterian, Gaelic-speaking island of Raasay off the east coast of Skye. His output has never been extensive and recognition of his achievement came late in life. Although his first book, Dàin do Eimhir agus Dàin Eile, ('Poems to Eimhir and Other Poems') published in 1943, has been aptly described by Douglas Sealy as 'an eruption. . .which permanently altered the landscape of Gaelic literature'[15] he has published only sporadically since and his work was not made widely available until 1970 with the publication of *Four Points of a Saltire*, a compendium of contemporary Scottish Gaelic poetry with English translations.

Denis Donoghue has said of MacLean that 'remorse is his true vocation' and he has indeed mined a rich seam of melancholy. *Poems to Eimhir* counterpoints the tragedy of unrequited and ill-fated love with the political crisis of Europe in the nineteen-thirties. Yet informing, and to some degree motivating, the poet's response both to the tragedy of his personal history and the tragedy of contemporary European history-in-the-making is his engagement with the communal history of his native place and, as he himself has said, 'always the steady unbearable decline of Gaelic'.

MacLean is a poet in sure and supreme possession of the history of his native place, but it is a history of loss, disruption and dispossession. His is a profoundly rooted poetry. When, for instance, some years ago he responded to an invitation by the editors of the journal *Chapman* to contribute an exposition of his 'relationship with the Muse' MacLean's account of why he was a poet began with a lengthy discussion of his family and ancestors. That place holds equal importance with people is indicated by the inclusion in a recent volume of critical essays on his work of an eight-page register of placenames which appear in the poems.

Nowhere are these more numinous than in the poem 'Hallaig', which has been described by Seamus Heaney as 'a rich and strange ode to melancholy' and 'a kind of condensed symbolist epic'.[16] 'Hallaig' is the name of a deserted township in the south-east of Raasay which was cleared after 1846. The boarded windows of a derelict cottage provide the image of the opening stanza which frames the poem. Paradoxically, the poet's *vision* (and by extension the reader's) is impeded right at the beginning of what is in essence a modern *aisling* or 'vision-poem'.

Tha bùird is tàirnean air an uinneig troimh 'm faca mi an Aird an Iar 's tha mo ghaol aig Allt Hallaig 'na craoibh bheithe, 's bha i riamh	The window is nailed and boarded through which I saw the West and my love is at the Burn of Hallaig a birch tree, and she has always been
eadar an t-Inbhir 's Poll a' Bhainne thall 's abhos mu Bhaile-Chùirn: tha i 'na beithe, 'na calltuinn, 'na caorunn dhíreach sheang ùir.	between Inver and Milk Hollow, here and there about Baile-Chùirn: she is a birch, a hazel, a straight, slender young rowan.
Ann an Screapadal mo chinnidh, far robh Tarmad 's Eachunn Mór, tha 'n nigheanan 's am mic 'nan coille ag gabhail suas ri taobh an lóin.	In Screapadal of my people, where Norman and Big Hector were, their daughters and sons are a wood going up beside the stream.
Uaibhreach a nochd na coilich ghiuthais ag gairm air mullach Cnoc an Rà, dìreach an druim ris a' ghealaich – chan iadsan coille mo ghràidh.	Proud tonight the pine cocks crowing on the top of Cnoc an Rà, straight their backs in the moonlight- they are not the wood I love.
Fuirichidh mi ris a' bheithe gus an tig i mach an Càrn. gus am bi am bearradh uile o Bheinn na Lice f' a sgàil . . .	I will wait for the birch wood until it comes up by the Cairn, until the whole ridge from Beinn na Lice will be under its shade . . .[17]

While the poem is both haunting and haunted the poet's gaze westwards quickly shakes off any intimations of the generalized reverie of a Celtic Twilight by grounding itself in the specifics of the Raasay placenames. The invocation of these names firmly plots, maps and encloses a territory, the native landscape of MacLean's people. 'Norman and Big Hector', and the locus of his loss: 'between Inver and Milk Hollow' and, later, 'between the Leac and Fearns' and 'From the Burn of Fearns to the raised beach'. Even his diction subtly intimates tragic loss. His love is *thall's abhos mu Bhaile-Chùirn*, 'here and there about Baile-Chùirn', a phrase which, as John MacInnes has noted, is used in seventeenth-century Gaelic poetry with clear overtones of tragedy, loss and grief.[18] First the poet's symbolic beloved, then his people, become trees, and the sensuousness of his description of the woods of Hallaig signals his reluctant love of their desolate beauty, a beauty bought at great cost. He distinguishes between the raucous crowing of the *arriviste* pinewoods, planted in the 1870s, on the one hand, and the native birches, hazels and rowans he loves, on the other. Yet we know, as he himself knows, that his forlorn hope that, like some Gaelic Birnam Wood, they will spread and somehow repossess the land from which his people were disinherited, is unfounded.

Séamus Heaney has characterized the 'bardic dignity' he associates with MacLean as 'the effect of a proud self-abnegation, as much a submission as a claim to heritage'.[19] While Heaney may be overstating the case it is, nevertheless, clear that Maclean has willingly shouldered the burden of his cultural, literary and linguistic inheritance from an early age. This is not so true of any modern Gaelic poet in Ireland for a number of reasons.

One of the principal differences between modern Irish and Scottish Gaelic poetry is the fact that almost all of the Scots are native, autochthonous speakers of Gaelic whereas most of the Irish are not. This distinction between native and non-native speaker is not intended to establish some sort of élite or hierarchy of poets writing in Irish. Nor is it made in order to lay a deterministic dead hand on writing in the language. Nevertheless, the particular, not to say peculiar, sociolinguistic circumstances of modern writing in Irish are in some way written into the poetic DNA and inevitably condition the poet's response both to the Gaelic past and not-so-Gaelic present.

Nuala Ní Dhomhnaill is the best-known contemporary poet writing in Irish. She is also the poet with the most keenly felt sense of place and she has rooted her poetic imagination firmly in the traditions and folklore of the Kerry Gaeltacht where both of her parents' families are from, and where she spent a significant part of her childhood. While her poetry is in a very real sense of the Gaeltacht, however, the fact that she was born in Lancashire and spent much of her childhood in Co. Limerick, and most of her adult life in Cork, Dublin and in Turkey, where she lived for a number of years, is not irrelevant to a consideration of her poetry. The poem 'I mBaile an tSlibhe', has commonly been read, as Gearóid Denvir reads it, as 'a revelation of self. . .an account from within..on both the personal and communal levels'[20] or in Heaney's terms 'a submission rather than a claim to heritage'. The poem might, however, just as easily be read as a self-conscious arrogation of Ní Dhomhnaill's position in the continuum of the Gaelic literary tradition, through an assertion of her Gaeltacht credentials.[21]

I mBaile an tSléibhe
tá Cathair Léith
is laistíos dó
tigh mhuintir Dhuinnshléibhe;
as san chuaigh an file Seán
'on Oileán
is uaidh sin tháinig an ghruaig rua
is bua na filíochta
anuas chugam
trí cheithre ghlún

In Baile an tSléibhe
is Cathair Léith
and below it
the house of the Dunleavies;
from here the poet Seán
went into the Great Blasket
and from here the red hair
and gift of poetry
came down to me
through four generations . . .[22]

Here the invocation of a litany of placenames situates the poet firmly in the landscape and evokes a pervasive sense of familiarity and belonging. Nowhere is this more evident than in the reference to the departure of her collateral ancestor, the poet Seán Ó Duinnshléibhe, 'on Oileán.' In English this is correctly translated as 'into the Great Blasket' but in the Irish of the Dingle peninsula it means literally 'to the island', further specification being unnecessary for the native. Yet in the second stanza we find a reference to the pervasive scent of 'lus anainne nó camn meall/mar a thugtar air sa dúiche/timpeall' ('pineapple mayweed or camomile/as it is commonly known in the surrounding/countryside'); while the local term is obviously preferred, the 'book term' is what most immediately suggests itself to the poet. The third stanza closes the poem with a list of local legends which equally smacks more of the amateur folklorist than of the local seancha!. Most intriguing of all, however, is Ní Dhomhnaill's claiming of the gift of poetry through direct descent when one considers the common Munster saying, with which she is undoubtedly familiar, that 'when poetry passes to the women in a family, it is gone from the men forever'.[23]

Liam Ó Muirthile is an almost exact contemporary of Ní Domhnaill's. A native English speaker from Cork city Ó Muirthile is one of a generation of young Cork-based poets who in the late sixties and early seventies followed the advice of the elder statesman of poetry in Irish at the time, Seán Ó Ríordáin in forging strong links with the West Kerry Gaeltacht. But while Ó Muirthile has written a number of poems which directly engage with the western landscape he seems more recently to have turned away from the Gaeltacht as an imaginative resource. In a suite of poems on the gradual refurbishment of a newly-acquired cottage in rural (English-speaking) West Cork he has attempted to reclaim for poetry in Irish some of the territory abandoned a generation earlier by Ó Ríordáin. 'Tobar' ('A Well') is a poem which owes something to Séamus Heaney, in which an almost sacramental purification precedes the ritualistic claiming of a landscape through the process of naming it. In the closing stanzas, having successfully unblocked an old, disused well (the faint presence of Derek Mahon may also be detected in these poems), the poet addresses a landscape which is neither that of his urban upbringing nor the deeply mythologised Gaeltacht.

Daingním na clocha rabhanálta a roghnaigh an té a bhí romham is á dhíonadh le leacacha dom is ea 'tharlaím ar a mheon Táim fe dhraíocht aige, bainim slat ghlas den bhfuinseoig is deirim ortha na fola os a chionn im chaomhnóir	I carefully replace the round stones chosen long since by another and fall into the rhythm of his mind. Entranced, I cut a green ash wand and recite the charm for bleeding as if at his insistence.
I Reifidím i bhfásach Sín thug Maois le hómós Masá is Miribeá ar an áit gur steall an charraig le n-ól. Athbhaistimse mo pholl in Achadh 'Mhíl le hais Abhainn na Seangan Tobar an Mhonabhair' a thug croí nua dhom is taoscán den síocháin.	In Rephidim, in the wilderness of Sin, Moses humbly named the rocks from which the precious water was released Massah and Meribah. I rename my well at Aughaveel, here by the Shangaun's banks, *Tobar an Mhonabhair*. It has given me new heart and a cooling draught of peace.[24]

In a fusion of popular piety and Biblical invocation Ó Muirthile augments, with his own newly minted Tobar an Mhonabhair' ('The Murmuring Well'), the local placenames 'Achadh 'Mhíl' and 'Abhainn na Seangan'. David Lloyd has criticized certain 'poems of place' in Heaney's *Wintering Out* for their dissembling ahistoricity and 'foreclosed surety of the subject's relation to place, mediated by a language which seeks to naturalize its appropriative function'.[25] Yet for all that Anahorish and Aughaveel are Gaelic placenames equally adrift in English no such naturalization seems to be available to the Irish language poet. The placenames in 'Tobar' are shards of a lost Gaelic tradition into which Ó Muirthile has consciously chosen to incorporate himself by writing in Irish. The explicit personalization in this poem of a landscape the Gaelic poet has so recently planted is thus merely one more, intensely private, and therefore luminously transient, episode in a constant and continuing process of dispossession and reclamation.

The notion that Irish literature in English is haunted if not hamstrung by 'the silence of the old language' has become such a critical commonplace in recent years that some might question its universal applicability to contemporary Irish writing.[26] An obvious, if rarely articulated, corollary of this argument would be that the contemporary writer of Irish is untroubled by such a radical discontinuity of linguistic and literary tradition. The evidence of these poems by Ní Dhomhnaill and Ó Muirthile, however, suggests that this is not the case.

In Thomas Kinsella's essay 'The Divided Mind', arguably the best known treatment of this topic by a contemporary writer, he describes his own predicament as follows:

> I recognize that I stand on one side of a great rift, and can feel the discontinuity in myself. It is a matter of people *and places* as well as writing – of coming from a broken and uprooted family, of being drawn to those who share my origins and finding that we cannot share our lives (my emphasis).[27]

Yet Kinsella recognizes that this sense of loss and disruption, an important element of which is an estrangement from place and a consequent defamiliarization of placenames, is the common lot of contemporary writers in both languages. According to Kinsella, literature in Irish before the nineteenth century 'has an air of continuity and shared history which is precisely what is missing from Irish literature, in English or Irish, in the nineteenth century and today'. While this statement may need to be emended somewhat to account for the various disjunctures in Gaelic literature in the medieval and early modern period, his assertion 'that silence on the whole, is the real condition of Irish literature in the nineteenth century' cannot be dismissed lightly, certainly in relation to Gaelic literature. It is precisely this silence which motivates the self-consciousness of the appropriations and invocations of place in contemporary Irish literature in both languages.

While nobody would argue for a golden age of Scottish Gaelic writing in the nineteeth century, the maintenance of certain linguistic domains, such as the religious domain, lost to Irish during the same period, made for a less deafeningly 'silent' century. I would argue that this may provide some insight into the relative 'rootedness' of Sorley MacLean's verse. Yet even so MacLean is unusual if not unique among modern Scottish Gaelic poets in his appeal and access to the comforting validation of a 'native place'. The one consoling certainty of 'the dispossessed', that of a fundamentally unproblematicized provenance, of ultimately 'belonging', would appear to be as unavailable to those few poets of a subsequent generation who choose to write in Gaelic as they are to their Irish contemporaries.

CHAPTER 13

No Dusty Pioneer: A Personal Recollection of John Hewitt

by

Roy McFadden

Whatever the mythologisers may seek to make of him, there is the poet's honest account of himself in the poetry. In *Conacre*, first published privately in 1943, John Hewitt wrote:

> I nod assent, no dusty pioneer
> complaining that the road has come too near,
> but one who needs the comfortable pace
> of safe tradition.

As we struggled with buckets of water from the well at Tiveragh, he paused to declare 'The tap is a great invention', and uttered his barking half-laugh of derision whch was characteristic of him at that time. For all his love of Cushendall and its environs, he was essentially a townsman who looked for 'the punctual packet and the telephone that I may not be lonely when alone'.

Our friendship extended throughout the Forties and Fifties, and was renewed after his return from England in 1972. That friendship was close in its early years, for, in spite of an age-difference of fourteen years or so, we had much in common. Both politically of the Left, we shared a preference for decentralised government, welcoming what was small, modest and intimate. Both of us had a feeling for place and tradition, while at the same time we shared a common anger against the corruption of place and tradition by those in authority at municipal and governmental level. However, there were degrees of difference in our commitments and aversions. Where I, in my early twenties, was belligerently anti-militarist, he stood back. For some time after he had begun his romance with Ulster Regionalism, I continued with a romantic Irishness. And in his last years, when, as I saw it, he was bemused by tardy recognition and haphazard acclaim, we differed over his acceptance of institutional honours.

In 1947 Hewitt declared that for him 'now at forty life begins/ with the Catholic church and forgiveness of sins'. He began to attend services at All Souls church in Elmwood Avenue, Belfast (which is Unitarian) and exhorted his friends to join him: not, as I understood the invitation, in a conversion to Christianity, but rather to share his broadening horizons and the experience of brotherly love. The minister, Arthur Agnew, a well-known figure in leftwing circles, perhaps attracted him with his forthright sermons. It was indeed at one of Dr Agnew's Sunday-afternon meetings, shortly after the declaration of war, where I heard John Hewitt declare 'Some are for a fight to a finish; some are of military age'.

It was in the same year, 1947, that I published my third collection, with the Hewittean title 'The Heart's Townland', dedicated to John Hewitt and John Boyd. One of the poems, which he liked, was called 'Calendar'. It included some lines addressed to himself.

> Once you were symbol of the arrogant mind,
> Cold hand that blighted miracle at birth,
> Philosopher of all the noisy blind
> Who flouted those who swore they saw the sun.
> It might have been so once; but though you still
> Assume opinions with your hat and coat
> You have an eye to greet the miracle
> In all well-rooted things . . .

My mother knew John Hewitt while I was still at school. They encountered each other at meetings of the Adult School, at W.E.A. lectures, and at various fringe gatherings, political and cultural, in the late Thirties. They also attended symphony concerts in the Wellington Hall in Belfast; and my mother observed Ruby Hewitt, dark-eyed and haggard, being supported out after the concert, overcome by the music.

At that time Hewitt had a reputation for outspokenness and brusqueness amounting sometimes to rudeness. He was a well-known figure on the Cavehill Road bus, aggressively reading 'The Daily Herald' with its red rooster clamant at the top of the title-page.

In 'Conacre' Hewitt gives us a self-portrait:

> Reckon from my face
> and its smooth lazy cheeks, the close set eyes,

the tight shut mouth aggressive that belies
the hand that scarce dare push a latchless gate,
and you will gauge me hero in debate
who funks decisions nor will shift his hams
save to applause for savage epigrams
which skim a laugh and leave mistrust behind
that one so harsh insists he still is kind.

To my later embarrassment, my mother showed him some of my juvenile verses, one of which had appeared in *The Sunday Referee*, to which the young Dylan Thomas (relatively young: he was 19; I was 13) had also contributed. However, Hewitt's first letter to me, dated 31 August 1943, put relations on a man-to-man basis. 'My dear McFadden', it began. A year later, writing to thank me for having proposed him for nomination as chairman of the Belfast PEN Centre, he added: 'I have often felt that we ought to know each other better. Serious workers in any craft have the responsibility of solidarity. Especially in this Sahara of the arts. I go on a few weeks' vacation tomorrow. When I come back I'd be very pleased if you came to see me perhaps to discover a wider ground of agreement than you at present think possible. I hope I may send you a card fixing date and time'.

I accepted his invitation, and presented myself at 18 Mount Charles, where I met his wife Ruby (later to become Roberta) and eyed the walls of books meticulously arranged in order of author, subject and date, and firmly indexed in his mind. John Luke's painting, 'The Road to the West', had place of honour over the fireplace; and I remember a cock-eyed Virgin by Colin Middleton on one of the other walls, and also a brace of oils mysteriously signed 'Jon', which John said were by the world's worst painter.

The flat was on the top floor. The livingroom was large, with a good view of Mount Charles from the windows, and I was reminded that the young Forrest Reid had enjoyed the same prospect from the house next door. Mount Charles was still something of a private road, with gate pillars at each end and its own green; and it was within short walking-distance from Hewitt's place of work at the Museum and Art Gallery on the Stranmillis Road. With a choice of two trams from the city centre, he made a point of rejecting the upper-class Malone Road tram in favour of the Stranmillis one. Workers of the world, unite; you have nothing to choose but your trams.

I became a frequent visitor, sometimes informally and alone, sometimes at formal gatherings. During the war-years several writers in the Forces were directed to Mount Charles. Rayner Heppenstall, John Manifold, Emmanuel Litvinoff, Hamish Henderson. Others, stationed in Omagh for a while, regrettably did not board the Stranmillis tram: Sidney Keyes, for one, a fellow Routledge poet, subsequently killed in Tunisia at the age of twenty.

Among the painters, I recall Alicia Boyle wearing red stockings; John Luke, ascetic-looking and down-to-earth; Colin Middleton, curly and puckish; Paul Nietsche, an elderly Buffalo Bill, who dismissed the young painters as 'A Storm in a Water Glass'; Markey Robinson and Rowel Friers, both observers with caustic tongues; William McClughan, a Hewitt protege, never the first to speak.

Of local poets, occasional visitors were W.R. Rodgers, then between the devil and the BBC, Patrick Maybin, James Mackinlay and Freda Laughton. From the other jurisdiction I recall Robert Farren standing up to read one of his poems. Afterwards, Hewitt impressed on me the difference of intonation between Irish and English poets. 'Spender throws it away', he said. But I had been more affected by the poet's *standing* to read, a gesture which I found courteously formal.

Howard Sergeant, editor of the long-running poetry magazine *Outposts*, and later a judge of numerous verse competitions, sat to read. After his departure, Hewitt said: 'Howard has no small talk'. That was said in his chuckling confidential voice, in contrast to the savage laugh which often acclaimed some telling remark to his taste.

'Johnny'. Ruby would glance up at the ceiling-light, and then at him. 'Sorry', he would say, hanging his head. Ruby worked long and hard at that laugh; and, in the end, she subdued it.

In later years, the Hewitts entertained E.M. Forster, H.O. Meredith, my wife and myself to dinner, which was followed by a gathering including the not-yet-known Philip Larkin, whose capacity for conversation was crippled by a stutter. Shortly after Dylan Thomas's death, John Betjeman was a guest, and I recall the crimson satin lining to the jacket of an otherwise nondescript suit: and how, round-eyed and baby-mouthed, he joined in my admiration for Thomas's gift for reading poetry aloud. The actor Michael MacLiammoir distinguished himself by upstaging Corale Carmichael and seducing her audience away from her.

MacNeice read at the museum, but I don't remember him at 18 Mount Charles. He would have stayed with George and Mercy McCann in Botanic Avenue, and his preferred meeting-places were licensed premises, which Hewitt did not frequent.

We were both members of the Belfast Centre of International

PEN, and regularly attended the Saturday-afternoon meetings in the Union Hotel at the back of the City Hall. We shared ambivalent feelings towards PEN. Each of us had a high regard for the hardworking secretary, May Morton, herself a work of art as well as a prize-winning poet. But we did not discover among the members any great degree of commitment to writing as a troublesome art, and the meetings were usually tepid. Was it Hewitt or myself, or someone else, who declared that the initials P.E.N. stood for Phoneys, Eccentrics and Neurotics?

However, right up to his death, Hewitt recalled with affection the International PEN Congress in Dublin in 1953. I drove John and Ruby down – up, he insisted – to Dublin. In fact, we stayed at Howth; and I acted as chauffeur to a great variety of receptions, cocktail parties, dinners, debates and social gatherings. John gorged on cocktail sausages at the German embassy, playing truant from his vegetarian diet; and I bought Ruby a long vampish cigarette-holder to enhance her gestures. I recall some late-night drinking with Benedict Kiely, and a still later visit to his house, where he presented Hewitt with the manuscript of his novel *The Cards of the Gambler* as a gift to the Belfast Public Library. In those less knowing times authors did not always look for a price for a manuscript. Hewitt continued in that tradition by bequeathing his manuscripts, letters, books and paintings to the local universities.

We encountered the not-yet-famous Brendan Behan in the street. He was, he said, on his way back from the Gaeltacht, where they had been trying to seduce him from his native language. Twelve years later I was astonished to read his account of our meeting, which I had forgotten, in his book *Confessions of an Irish Rebel.*

We were both impressed by a production of *The Playboy of the Western World* at the Abbey. During the interval a small Indonesian woman joined us and delighted John by announcing that the play had great significance for young emerging nationalities seeking to break ties with the colonial fatherland. That remained one of Hewitt's favourite stories, which he would tell on occasions, nodding wisely behind the smoke from his pipe.

We did a broadcast from Radio Eireann, under the tutelage of Monk Gibbon. The lift was out of order, and as we walked upstairs to the studio Monk Gibbon – a new boy there, in spite of his age and reputation– protested that he got blamed when anything broke down. He remembered, and rebuked me for it, that, years before, I had given an appreciation on the BBC – a reassessment– of his compilation of AE's writings in *The Living Torch*, without once mentioning his name as the compiler. I remember these trifles, but not the substance of our broadcast.

One of the most pleasant interludes in a busy week was a visit to Geoffrey Taylor, whom I met for the first time. Both Hewitt and Rodgers knew him well, and had reason to be grateful to him. Already an admirer from afar of his poetry-editorship of *The Bell*, I found him to be modest and charming. No one exists today in this country with his breadth and tolerance, and indeed his authority, capable of an equal appreciation of the old and the new. He wrote a foreword to Hewitt's first collection, and gave a title to Maurice James Craig's volume. 'Watch your syntax, Jack', he wrote in a letter to Hewitt. I used to greet Hewitt with those words, to his mild irritation.

Before we left Dublin, we walked the length of O'Connell Street with Peadar O'Donnell. Every fifty yards or so he was hailed by a passer-by, whom Peadar was able to name on each occasion, and, as often as not, ask after a relative or friend.

After he became editor of *The Bell* Peadar made occasional forays to Belfast, promising an Ulster number. We were summoned to the Union Hotel on one occasion – W.R. Rodgers, John Hewitt, Sam Bell and myself – where Peadar presided in the coffee room over a crate of Guinness for us and a pot of coffee for himself. He always called John Jack, as indeed I did until Ruby weaned me off the habit. Peadar had heard that I had decided, with my co-editor, not to continue with *Rann*, and he made a generous offer of financial support and circulation facilities from *The Bell*. But I explained that tiredness, not need of cash or an increased circulation, had convinced us that five years had been a brave innings; that enough was enough.

Peadar was a great talker. His store of anecdotes was like the herbal tobacco Hewitt introduced me to; with every pipeful the pouch swelled full again. Hewitt too was a conversationalist; but, while he enjoyed anecdotes and literary gossip spliced with mild malice, he preferred to talk to a theme. It was with that preference in mind that he proposed that a group of writers should meet for a meal every first or fourth Sunday and address a pre-arranged topic. But inevitably the conversation degenerated into chat, and one anecdote borrowed another. My main recollection of those evenings is of Joe Tomelty's performances, and of Hewitt's uninhabited laughter. (And an associated memory of Joe Tomelty, at a party at 18 Mount Charles, singing *The Bard of Armagh*, while a BBC Controller tried to persuade his reluctant wife to collect her senses and recover her coat).

The teachings of C.G. Jung dominated the Hewitt household during the Forties. In a letter written in 1945, complimenting me on my second book, *Flowers for a Lady*, – 'Quite honestly no recent book of verse by any of the younger moderns has so delighted me or interested me so immediately. Indeed most of what I want to say is in the sonnet I enclose: the verses occurred tonight after I had spent most of the evening reading and thinking about your book' – he concludes: 'Ruby joins me in her enthusiasm. Together we have agreed that in Jung's phraseology you are a fine 'feeling' poet – you know the quartering – sensation/feeling/intellect/intuition. I am satisfied that I can praise you objectively, as I am a 'sensation' type'.

After an evening at Mount Charles, when Jungian allusions pervaded the room like the persistent aroma of herbal tobacco, the Yeats scholar, Oliver Edwards – whose projected book on Yeats was constantly overtaken by others – later, at home, undressing for bed, invented a rival guru and paraded around the bedroom, sock in hand, intoning 'Alt. Alt. Alt'.

Ruby interpreted her dreams, so she said, as she went along. John interrupted her account of one revealing dream apparently relating to his most unusual tipsy homecoming, saying jocularly but firmly: 'Message for Today: Keep your dreams to yourself'.

Hewitt was troubled not so much by Jungian dreams as by the fear of sleep itself. Each night as he settled in bed he became afraid that he would die if he closed his eyes. The fear persisted until, in exasperation, he told himself 'All right; die'. After that defiant surrender, the dread of death left him and he was able to sleep.

For a number of years before they elected to go to England, where Coventry offered an exciting job of restoring the municipal art gallery after the wartime bombings, the Hewitts had a small house at Tiveragh, outside Cushendall. It had originally been the gatelodge to Glenville House, which by then had become a convent school. I spent several weekends in Cushendall, when I walked the poet's 'twisty roads' and met some of the people celebrated in his poems. Hewitt proudly displayed a large leather briefcase which he had had specially made to allow him to bring books from Belfast, that he might not be lonely when alone. Books on British birds and wildflowers were within convenient reach. Of one of those visits, I wrote in 1946:

Staying with the poet and his wife
In their small fat house beside the glens.
I learned the virtue of those milder moods,
Shaped by knowledgeable innocence,
Where thought and aspiration dwell in peace:

The strange necessity of being kind,
Punctilious even, among violence:
Of keeping house within a well-built mind.

I imagine that the concept of Ulster Regionalism began with and was nurtured by Hewitt's affection for the glen country. The idea was first advanced in 'The Bitter Gourd', an essay published in the third number of *Lagan* in 1945. The Ulster writer, Hewitt says, 'must be a rooted man, must carry the native tang of his idiom like the native dust on his sleeve; otherwise he is an airy internationalist, thistle-down, a twig in a stream'.

The poems in *The Heart's Townland* showed the influence of Hewitt's thought and something of his style. Each of us responded to the other's endeavours. In the early Fifties John wrote a radio play about Colmcille called *The Angry Dove*. I wrote one about Cuchulain called *The Angry Hound*. In the Eighties, he responded to my clutch of poems about my antecedents with 120 sonnets about his forebears.

When we were the only resident poets here, it was his custom to introduce me as The Younger Poet or The Other Poet; and I think he valued me not only as a friend but also as a lieutenant in an Ulster Regionalist crusade. When I finally cooled and backed away, I suppose he felt disappointment and perhaps resentment. But the principal contemporary influences on my thought, loyalties and even style, were the writings of Herbert Read and his apostles; and while I never identified myself with the neo-romantic movement in general or with the New Apocalypse group in particular, I did contribute to the same magazines and anthologies, and shared the same publisher, so that whatever rubbed off was not immediately reconcilable with the verses of Porter of County Down, Orr of Ballycarry, or Herbison of Dunclug.

I suspected that the Ulster Regionalist idea could be used to provide a cultural mask for political unionism or a kind of local counter-nationalism. I was also troubled by Hewitt's use of the word 'Ulster', which he did not clearly define. Denis Ireland, when referring to the six counties and not the nine, always meticulously said 'North-east Ulster'. In a late conversation Hewitt confessed that his concept of Ulster had omitted that part of it on the west of the Bann. In truth, the Hewitt region did not extend beyond the familiar home counties of Antrim and Down.

We gave an unscripted broadcast on the BBC on our differing views on Regionalism; but we pulled our punches and talked round our differences. In the street, after the broadcast, we laughed at the non-event, and John said that he was frightened to go home.

Some time later, I wrote a lighthearted poem called 'Postscript to Ulster Regionalism', which amused him; for, however serious his concern, he rarely lacked a sense of humour. In 1974 I vetoed its inclusion in the *Faber Book of Irish Verse.*

Hewitt was not published in volume form until 1948, at the age of 41. He was by no means averse to publication; indeed he impressed on me the importance of having one's work printed, in the hope that some of it might survive. From time to time he published at his own expense pamphlets of his poems, including *Conacre* (1943), *Compass* (1944), *Those Swans Remember* (1956), *Prologue to an Evening at Whitefriars* (1970), *An Ulster Reckoning* (1971). *The Lint Pulling* (1948) must surely be a collector's piece.

'Och, Hewitt's a lazy fellow', Michael McLaverty used to say. However, Hewitt persisted in his fashion, writing doggedly, in virtual isolation from a reading public. Ruby protected his privacy; and, while John wrote in the kitchen, she would entertain persons from Porlock in the livingroom until he emerged; or, on occasions, firmly turn them away. She had, she told my wife, been obliged to wean him away from his mother; and in many instances she behaved like a substitute mother, tigerish in his defence against slights and imagined slights; and I believe that she instigated the move to England some years after John's failure to obtain the Number One job at the Museum and Art Gallery. Where John was wounded, Ruby was resentful.

At one of the gatherings at Mount Charles, when Mercy Hunter sang her celebrated Chinese song, which went ping, ping, ping, ping, pong, Ruby followed her on the guitar, and sang in her pleasant voice:

> Some say he's black, but I say he's bonny.
> The fairest of them all:
> My handsome, winsome Johnny.

After she died, John said to me, with the simplicity of a child: 'I've no one to tell things to'.

After W.R. Rodgers' death, Hewitt confided that he had been jealous of the success of *Awake! and other poems* (1941); but that he had overcome his resentment with the realisation that he had his own style, whatever the fashion of the day preferred. 'I owe his thought much thanks, but not his style', he wrote of Rodgers in the original version of *Freehold*, in a passage entitled 'Roll Call', which he omitted from the final version as published. The reference in full is:

that still man I have praised, whose hanging pipe
and tweedy gestures cover up the press
and hurtling force of his bold images
that crash his words together till they break
with harsh new light that strikes us wide awake;
I owe his thought much thanks but not his style.

Immediately following, is his portrait of myself aged 24:

next the grave lad with disconcerting smile,
the countrytown solicitor whose verse
touches new riches, as the drifting years
kindle his vision to a friendly blaze:
we marvel one so young can be so wise.

As we grow older we become accustomed to seeing myths sprout around the memory of the departed. One such myth is that John Hewitt was 'driven out of Northern Ireland'. I was there; and I participated in a semi-professional capacity in what actually happened.

In 1953 the directorship of the Belfast Museum and Art Gallery became vacant, and Hewitt, as assistant director, applied for the top post. The voting in the appointing committee resulted in a tie and the chairman used his casting vote in favour of another applicant on the grounds that he had better over-all qualifications for the job. It was generally thought among Hewitt's supporters that his radical views had told against him. ('Roots are all very well', Ruby said, 'until they rise up and strangle you').

Hewitt approached me after the appointment had been made, and lamented the well-intentioned support of a non-unionist councillor, which, he thought, had militated against him. He was, however, concerned to obtain the number two position, and he asked me to arrange for a shorthand-writer to attend the next meeting of the council to record any further references to him. However, nothing was said at the meeting, and Hewitt was appointed deputy. In fact, he became Director of Art, and was virtually his own master in the department which interested him most. He spent four years in that post before going to England to a more prestigious appointment.

Any Number Two must feel aggrieved at failing to obtain the Number One job; and, with Hewitt's personal identification with a locality of which the Museum and Art Gallery was some sort of symbol, he was perhaps more disappointed than another unsuccessful candidate might have been. One is bound to say, however, that the magnitude of his disappointment, as recorded by him, suggests a previous existence singularly free from misfortune.

In any event, he accepted the alternative appointment, and, so far as I could judge, he appeared to be happy in his work during the succeeding four years. It may be that Ruby felt rancour, and encouraged him to move when the opportunity offered. It is of some significance that after his return to Belfast fifteen years later, he accepted the freedom of the city from a unionist mayor on behalf of his former employer, the City Council. I alone thought it inappropriate to attend the proceedings. 'I remain boringly consistent', I said.

To describe Hewitt's departure as some sort of expulsion is nonsense. If in fact at the end he did feel that he was shaking the local dust from his shoes, the local ash from his sleeve, it cannot be said that he left in a hurry or suffered materially as a consequence.

Hewitt's acceptance of honours during his final decade must be set against the decades when he soldiered on with his verse, almost totally disregarded. The lean years no doubt whetted his appetite for recognition, and he readily accepted the role of father figure offered by a younger generation. 'I get on well with the younger poets', he wrote, 'whatever they may say of me behind my back'. Behind their backs, he confessed to a dislike of their poetry. 'They're all dull', he asserted. And: 'I always thought that poetry was supposed to be about the condition of man'.

During his last years he was affected by an old man's vanity. He allowed himself to be taken around public houses and shown off as the Grand Old Man; and when some illiterate lout pulled his beard and mocked him, Hewitt continued to smile benignly without complaint. When I heard the story, I thought of him in his prime barking at an obseqious head-waiter: 'For Christ sake, man, get up off your knees'.

His personality changed with age. 'The tight shut mouth' had become tighter and too knowing for the savage epigram; the beard and the jockey cap solemnly asserted the role of poet; and his natural caution in speaking out – 'Never tell anyone more than he needs to know' – became closer and warier. But sometimes when we met privately he would throw caution, if not to the winds, then to a local breeze perhaps, and talk without reserve to someone who was not in contention.

Some who did not enjoy my special position of former Other Poet, and the occasional candour to which that status entitled me, saw only the caution and inhibition, or retreat. At the showing of the archival film, one of his oldest acquaintances exclaimed in my ear: 'Why did he leave us?'; and he did not mean the move to England.

John Hewitt was a hardheaded poet with a sentimental core. Among the abrasive language of his early and middle years, one of his pet words was 'nice'. 'Och, he's nice', he would say; or 'Which is nice'. He would smile and touch his moustache as if he enjoyed being nice on occasions. He needed affection, but often lacked the confidence to encourage it and the capacity to sustain and cope with it. He endorsed progressive thought and unpopular causes, but he did not offer dedication. And the solidarity which he had commended in his early letter was not always available when it conflicted with his own interests. In spite of his consistent output over the years, he did not permit poetry to distort orderly living. Any expression of political convictions was on a take-it-or-leave-it basis; he did not seek to convert.

Although, as he told me, he was considered to be a Robinson (his mother's side of the family) I believe that he had only one hero throughout his long life, and that was his father: against whom he constantly measured himself, and, rightly or wrongly, concluded that his father was the greater man.

Towards the end, with the poems published and his standing established, he said to me, perhaps sentimentally, perhaps with the wisdom of hindsight: 'Having children is best'. Talking of death and its aftermath, I said that once round was enough. He nodded. But, he said, after a time he would like to open one eye to see what was going on, and then go to sleep again.

During the last years I tried to look behind the increasingly public persona to the need, not so much for acclaim (though that existed) as for companionship. I sensed, as I am sure others did, a final loneliness for which we had little or no remedy. 'I've no one to tell things to' might be an epitaph for his concluding years, when, with Ruby gone, public recognition had come too late for her approbation.

CHAPTER 14

The Note of Exile: Michael McLaverty's Rathlin Island

by

Sophia Hillan King

I

The history of Rathlin Island has been, at times, a violent and bloody one, its cliffs and hollows more than once filled with the cries of the wounded, bereaved and sacrificed, as invader upon invader put the islanders to the sword. Throughout these times, Rathlin has been a rare repository of legend and folk-tale, as mermaids and men rose from the sea to live for a time with the island people. Deirdre, returning from Kintyre with Naoise, her lover, is said to have landed at Carrig Uisneach, just east of Ballycastle; Fiona of the White Shoulder, eldest of the enchanted children of Lir, arranged that she and her weary swan-siblings should meet, when parted by gale and storm, at Carricknarone, a rock on the north side of Rathlin; and Robert the Bruce is thought to have noted the tenacity and patience of the humble spider, in a cave beneath a cliff on the eastern shore.[1]

It is rare that reference to this colourful, turbulent history is made in Michael McLaverty's stories of patient island people; but his tales of young boys and old folk are rich with implied knowledge of the island's topography, history and mythology. McLaverty wears his learning lightly, but carries the reader with him, so that Rathlin becomes familiar terrain, and the reader cannot help but feel McLaverty's sadness at the island's decline. In turning for inspiration to the landscape of Rathlin, McLaverty makes clear his affection, respect, and, ever, his sense of loss. This melancholy is evident even in his earliest writings about the island, as here, in the 1937 story, 'Leavetaking':

> Colm got up to go and Maggie sent him out for a cabbage leaf, as she had some fresh butter for his mother. The garden was dark

> with rain and the black soil squelched up between his toes. Shining puddles lay in the furrows and rain freckled the cabbage leaves; when he broke off a leaf it creaked like new leather and the drops rattled off it like pebbles. He stood up and looked towards the north and thought of the swans flying through the wet mists of the mountains and their black feet alighting in the cold water of a Scottish lough.
> ... Passing by an empty house he whistled loudly; frightened rabbits thudded out of danger and the dog raced after them. As he drew near home he began to run. He halted when he reached the door. The square of light in the window and the noise of this mother talking brought his courage back. And looking round now at the ships' lights far out at sea, he thought again of the dusty green bottle on the mantelpiece and the swans pushing into the shelter of rushes in the night-grey waters of a lonely lough.[2]

Already, McLaverty has struck his characteristic note. There are the sounds, the sights, even the smell and the feel of the natural world; there is the small boy half-fearful, half-entranced by that world as he finds it; and there, above all, is what McLaverty himself loved to call, 'the note of exile'. It is precisely that note of exile which makes his writing about Rathlin Island so particularly vivid, and often poignant. The 'square of light' in his mother's window welcomes and reassures the boy, Colm, it is true; but the story, 'Leavetaking' (later incorporated into the first novel, *Call My Brother Back*, 1939), concerns the boy's last day on Rathlin Island before leaving home to go to boarding school. In a sense he is caught half-way between the square of light in the window, which tomorrow will be a nostalgic memory, and the equally evocative lights of the ships at sea, emblems of departure. Colm is about to be sent into exile, and, somewhere, he knows it.

Although 'Leavetaking' does not represent McLaverty's very first writing about the island, I mention it at the outset because of its striking of this characteristic note of regret, almost of grief at the passing of a kind of prelapsarian purity. This note is sounded all through McLaverty's early writing, from 1932 until the early 1940s: it is in this period that he concerns himself with the fate of children, mostly boys, living through childhood's joys, or, more often, its vicissitudes. Childhood, as is always clear in his writing of this period, can often be difficult, but it is the best time, even though, in the midst of joy and exhilaration, shades of the prison house begin to close. This is not to suggest that these early stories are gloomy, for they are not, but they are shaded always with an awareness of the darker side of human existence.

For McLaverty, Rathlin represents a powerful objective correlative for this feeling. Its rugged beauty, and the sound principles and spartan lifestyle of its inhabitants, are, he knows, out of tune with the rest of the world. He knows Rathlin to be in decline, even in the early stories of the 'Thirties. Increasingly he displays this in the work, as he moves away from the stories of innocent children to explorations of the ways of life of the old, or the dispossessed. Again, these are often inhabitants of Rathlin. It is hardly too much to say that McLaverty does not trust in a theme until he has once tried it out in a Rathlin setting.

II

In 1978, an American, David Wilkinson, descendant of Rathlin people, wrote to McLaverty about his connection with the island, and McLaverty's reply indicates very clearly the mixture of pride and desolation inherent in his attitude to the place:

> I'm not a native of Rathlin though I know it and its people very well. I spent two months on it every summer for about twelve succeeding years. It made a great impression on me when I was young and later when I was writing about it, scenes and incidents came to my mind with great vividity. It was part of me and still is: in my mind I often travel the roads, the paths through the hills, and the paths along the edges of the lakes. My brother goes every year but I haven't been back for a long time . . .
>
> The island is a beautiful one but, sad to say, the young are leaving it and the old are heading for the graveyard. My last visit there was a sad one: the people I stayed with were all dead and the house in ruins. It depressed me.[3]

He echoes almost to the letter the sentiments expressed by Colm's Uncle Robert, in 'Leavetaking': 'And you'll be going away soon. It's sad to see so many young people leavin' the island and none comin' back. There'll soon be nothin' on the island only rabbits – with nobody marryin', the ould dyin', and the young goin' away'.

If, then, a kind of doom-laden, ambivalent affection lies at the heart of McLaverty's attitude to Rathlin Island, is there no place for enjoyment of its beauty, of its remoteness, of the fact that it is apart from the concerns of the world? There is: for McLaverty does genuinely exult in his personal Eden, even while he sees the serpent approach.

An interesting example of his ambivalence is seen in the original version of a famous 1934 story, 'The Wild Duck's Nest'.[4]

Rathlin comes to life, though even in the midst of delight there is 'sin': a boy's disturbance of the birds' nest. Persuaded by John Middleton Murry (to whom, as editor of *Adelphi*, he had submitted it) to alter the ending, so that the boy is absolved from guilt, it is interesting to note that the story remains an exploration of wrongdoing in Paradise, and the boy does not escape his agonising purgatory, sitting miserably and in despair for a long time in school before he can return to the scene of the crime.[5]

In fact, disaster, loss and grief are never far away, even in the lightest-seeming of the stories. An even earlier story, 'The Grey Goat', published in 1933, tells of the days before a much-loved goat is to be sold, despite the fact that she is the children's pet.[6] It is a delightful story, full of bright mischief on the part of the children, but McLaverty is conscious always of the reality of the situation: the children's parents cannot pay the rates, and therefore have no choice but to sell the goat. In fact, she is not, in the end, sold; but only because the 'fat, red-faced' mainland woman who is the only potential purchaser, rejects the goat as a 'poor, thin, island crayture'. The goat is reprieved, and the story ends there, but it is hard to see how the rates were paid, since there is clearly no ready solution to the family's financial problem. Equally, there is no guarantee that the goat might not be sold another day, should things become worse. Life on Rathlin is precarious, and there is no room for childish sentimentality over pets: the father does not relent because of his children's feeling for her, but because he feels that 'It's likin' the goat for nothin' these people want, and them knowin' we don't like the trouble of boatin' her back . . .'. It is a small gesture against the hard world which rejects island animals and island ways, but there is no suggestion that it is a victory, or, indeed, that is is any more than a stay of execution for the goat.

The 1936 story, 'The Prophet', is an interesting one, because in it there is the now familiar picture of the boy working through a personal crisis, but a new and significant element is present. Brendan's misery at the death of his beloved grandfather is at the root of his problem. Missing him, he wants and needs confirmation that he resembles the old man in some way, and he wishes that the resemblance could lie in inheritance of the grandfather's gift for weather prophecy. Consequently, he puts himself in a position where he must foretell the weather on a given day, or risk every child's greatest fear – ridicule and contempt from his peers. His desperate attempts to feel as his grandfather must have done are both comic and touching, and the reader senses the bitter disappointment of a fine day when Brendan has foretold rain – 'bucketfuls and bucketfuls of it':

> That night he prayed for a long time, prayed to God and to his Granda to bring on the rain, and in bed he thought he felt whatever Granda felt. At one time he was sure he felt the rain at the window, but it was only the fuchsia leaves brushing against the pane. He lay for awhile thinking of wet days with the rain sizzling in the lake, the hens hunched up under the cart, the ducks suttering in the shughs, and Prince running across the kitchen floor with wet paws. And from such thoughts sleep came.
>
> In the morning he awoke and lay listening, listening for the sound of rain. But outside the birds sang and in the window a large fly buzzed. He raised himself on his elbows and stared around. A blue sky was framed in the window. The sun was shining and a leafy shadow of the fuchsia bush trembled on the white-washed bedroom wall. The birds' songs came clearer now to his keener wakefulness. He looked at his sleeping brother. Then he lay back on his pillow, and dripping drearily into his mind came thoughts of his companions jeering and shouting – The Prophet! The Prophet![7]

By the mid-'Thirties, McLaverty was already beginning to think of the island from the point of view of more than its children. The world of the old, or those alone on the island, began increasingly to exercise him.

In 'Stone', published with 'The White Mare' in *The Capuchin Annual* in 1939, the need to compete, to hold off the jibes and taunts of the other men, leads the lonely, embittered, childless Jamesy Heaney to plan a revenge and a method of preserving his name beyond death. Living with a dog and old goat, 'shrunken with cold', in a 'wild draughty place . . . far from the villagers', he plans to invest his carefully-saved money in stone to make a monument which will be greater than the finest now standing, the McBride stone. He plans to have it out with the others:

> He held his breath, as if to calm his mind, to allow it to gather the sweet breeze of thought and unfold its joys to him. Stone is lasting: all life ends in death but stone lives on. It was more lasting than all their childen. They needn't chaff him any more about his name

> dying with neither chick nor child to lave behind him! They needn't mock him any longer! There they were as usual the three of them – Joseph McDonnell, John Joe McQuilkin, and Johnny John Beg. He'd have it out with them this evening.[8]

They receive his great thought, that only stone is lasting, with derision and contempt, especially when he uses as his prime example the hill of Cnoc-na-Screilan, Hill of the Screaming. It was here that women and children of the island witnessed in 1642 the bloody massacre of their menfolk, before they themselves were hurled over the edge of the cliff. Jamesy laughs at them, and goes home, hugging to himself his secret plans for his monumental tribute to himself. A terrible storm blows up, and Jamesy fears, not that he will die, but that he will die before he has made his arrangements for the stone. McLaverty shows us the land after the storm, 'clear and cold', 'scoured clean', 'filled with the noise of the sea'. Even the uprooting of his one scraggy tree does not trouble Jamesy deeply, for his faith is now only in stone. However, his desolation is complete when, in the evening, after a day of clearing up after the storm, he goes up to the graveyard, and finds where the great McBride monument stood, only emptiness: 'a great vacancy held the sky'. And as he takes his terrified way homeward, the only sound to be heard is that of the children, who 'screamed in delight as they gathered the sticks washed up on the stormy shore'.

III

During the early and middle 'Thirties, it had never been McLaverty's intention to publish anything other than his short stories. By the end of the decade, however, at the behest of various publishers to whom he had sent his work, he had written a novel. He recalls that it did not require a great deal of effort, saying of the novel, eventually published in 1939 as *Call My Brother Back*, that 'it wrote itself'.[9] He built it around the short story mentioned earlier, 'Leavetaking', which became the third chapter of the first section of the novel, dealing with Colm's boyhood on Rathlin. The second section, based in the city of Belfast, describes the involvement of Colm's brother in the IRA, his death at their hands, and its effect on the family as a whole.

In a sense, they are two different stories, or novellas, loosely connected by the picaresque figures of Colm and his two brothers, Alec and Jamesy. Yet the boys who live on the island are quite different from the characters they become in the city. Perhaps this is deliberate, suggesting the change wrought upon people by a move away from the country; but they are almost different boys. Our concern here is with the island part of the novel only, the point needs to be emphasised, because, once again, there is the feeling that the Rathlin existence is the true, the noble one, and that all else is a substitute, and a poor one at that. John Wilson Foster, writing in 1971, makes a similar point:

> A striking feature of the social world from which McLaverty draws his inspiration and his fictional settings is the way in which the individual, his family, and his community are bound together by interlocking bonds and restraints. Also striking is the way in which these bonds and restraints form a ritual nexus with the land the individual and his family have lived on for generations. Actions and events as a result reverberate: to separate a man from his kin is to separate him from his forbears and from his land, for blood and the land intimately connect . . . It is blood as a genealogical force and as community spirit. It is denied at a very high cost: the most serious taboo which can be violated is the almost sacred relationship between a man and his land and kin. A man separated from land and kin will try desperately to return and will even . . . die in the attempt.[10]

Foster makes his case clearly, though he is not, in fact, discussing *Call My Brother Back* but later novels, set outside Rathlin, and still intimately concerned with the unbreakable connections of man and land. My understanding of McLaverty's writings on Rathlin is slightly different: more than any other place in his work, it pulls and draws those who know it or have lived on it; but, once left, it cannot be repossessed. It is not simply an island; it is almost another world – consciously rural and unsophisticated, but also hard, pristine and, ultimately, unassailable. It is most certainly not to be possessed by those who fail to conform to its unwritten rules, and it is to this theme that McLaverty returns in his later Rathlin novel, *Truth in the Night*. In *Call My Brother Back*, even more than in 'Leavetaking', the reader is aware of the valedictory note, and of the islanders' realisation of their eventual fate:

> Daniel told of his grandfather that had great Latin verses in his head, learnt in a school that had no seats, or maps on the wall, or coloured books like the childen have nowadays. 'There were three schools in the island in his day; three schools, and now there's only one with forty wee childer in it.'

> 'Emigration was the cause of that!'put in Paddy John Beg. 'Look at the many ould wrecks of houses there are strewn about the place. Nobody spins now and Johnny McQuaid had to make hen-roosts out of his loom. It bates all that the land could rear three families in them days where now it can hardly rear one.'
>
> 'The people's not the same as they used to be; there's a softness in them,' Daniel said quietly.
>
> 'We'll soon have nothin' in the island at all only wild goats and rabbits,' answered Paddy. 'All the young are goin' away, the ould people are dyin' and there's nobody marrying'. . . 'Tis a pity Colm's goin' from you shortly; that's the third you have away'.[11]

It is interesting to note that the speech deploring the lack of marriage and children on the island is here given to one of the old men who are contemporaries of Colm's father, Daniel; in 'Leavetaking', it was spoken by Colm's Uncle Robert. Nonetheless, 'Leavetaking', now Chapter Three of Part One, remains central to the novel, because it contains the essential valedictory note.

There is one other very vivid chapter in the Rathlin section of the novel, Chapter Six, where McLaverty describes the wreck of a ship, and the scavenging that goes on as it lies on the beach. McLaverty may grieve for his lost island, but he is under no illusions about it; and while the early short stories celebrate the innocence of the island children, this chapter in *Call My Brother Back* displays the pragmatic ruthlessness of which the islanders are capable. One of the organisers of the systematic and chilling stripping of the boat is Colm's brother Alec, now the head of the family since the death of their father, Daniel. Always a distant, half-realised character, determined to leave the island himself, he is not especially concerned about the fate of his younger siblings, except in his stern and uncompromising discipline. This is an interesting chapter, for its tone veers between disapproval and an amused approbation; but in the end, the author does not condemn, for the scavenging has its own value, as a means of survival.

Critics at the time of its first publication felt that the episodic nature of the second half of *Call my Brother Back* contrasted unfavourably with the first part, described by McLaverty in his letter to David Wilkinson, quoted earlier, as 'a lyrical evocation of [Rathlin] as I knew it when young'. Interestingly, although McLaverty was ultimately willing that the novel be reprinted, as it eventually was, he had severe doubts, resting partly on the fear that his novel, with its descriptions of murder and street fighting in the 'Twenties, might incite the young to violence, and partly on the regret that his description of the shipwreck had been unfair to the people of Rathlin. To the Manager of Mercier Press, in Cork, he wrote in November 1964:

> A short while ago I sent you a copy of my first novel *Call My Brother Back* for your consideration. On thinking it over I find that the chapter on the shipwreck in Part I is false and untrue to the decent people of Rathlin Island and for that reason I do not wish the book to be re-issued. Much of Part II is also out-of-date and belongs to bitter history. Would you please return the book to me.[12]

In the event, Figgis published it in 1970, and Poolbeg brought it out again in 1979, with reprints since that time.

One other novel of the island remained to be written, but it would not appear until 1951, and its tone would be very different, because the intervening years changed irrevocably the author's outlook on life and, more particularly, on the kind of books he would write. McLaverty's writing of the 'Forties is dominated by a darker vision, an increasing concern for those who, in Thoreau's phrase, quoted by Corkery, and assimilated by McLaverty, 'live lives of quiet desperation'. By 1951, when *Truth in the Night* was published, the time for lyrical evocation of childhood memories had gone.

Truth in the Night tells the story of Martin Gallagher, jaded after a number of years working in Belfast, and glad to return to his island home, and Vera Reilly, the widow of an island man, Tom Reilly. Vera has been left, since Tom's untimely death, with a daughter, Mary; a kind and intelligent mother-in-law for whom Vera does not care; and an unsympathetic brother-in-law. Unlike other stories of the island, this has discord on almost every page, and Vera is at the heart of it, ever discontented and restless. She is the representative of the outside world, as she hankers in her discontented way for the city, and she disturbs the balance of the whole island. Her dissatisfaction with the island is placed in relief by the real and dignified grief of an old man, Michael John Craig, who must leave the island and go to live with his married daughter in Belfast. Certainly Vera is not fitted to make her life there. Restless, uncomfortable, and sarcastic, she seems a totally unattractive character, deliberately holing her dead husband's model schooner before an important race, entirely through spite; telling the orphan boy whom Martin has adopted that he is a bastard, and causing thereby the boy's broken-hearted departure; and, ultimately, by neglecting the needs of her own child, causing the death of that child, of her unborn child by Martin, and herself.

Before she dies, she repents, the truth of the title revealed to her in the last long night of her life:

> '. . . Ah, Martin, I've had a long night and I sensed that this would happen. I didn't deserve to have her. I wasn't good to her . . . I turned her against all that her father loved. And now I am having my reward . . . I was spoiled. I lived for what was to come, and in my foolishness didn't know that this was it. No, Martin, we must live each day as best we can and not wait for the great days to come. The days are here, but we do not live them because they're not the kind we want. We cry out against them, and before long the years are upon us and we are still preparing to live . . . To live for the future is to live for the fog . . .'[13]

In a sense, the whole novel waits for that revelation, and this, I feel, puts a strain on the writing and the characters. Vera, like some of the characters in the preceding novel, *The Three Brothers* (1948), is one dimensional, and so, to a lesser extent, are the two young people: Mary, her daughter, and Jamesy Rainey, Martin's adopted boy. Yet, in the earlier stories of Rathlin, these children would have had tales woven about them. Jamesy, indeed, bears a resemblance to the young orphan in the 1939 story, 'Look At The Boats' (originally named 'The Sea'), who is adopted by an old couple, seems content with them, becomes all in all to them, and then cannot deny the irresistible call of the sea, thus leaving the old man desolate.[14]

It is a frustrating fact that in *Truth in the Night* (as in *The Three Brothers*) the reader comes time and again on such possibilities for McLaverty's unique style of short story, deliberately stifled in the cause of a selfish character's ultimate enlightenment. It seems, too, that the writing is most free, most itself, when the author is echoing the spirit of an earlier short story, such as 'The Schooner' or 'Look at the Boats', or involved in the very real tragedy of the old man Craig's uprooting.

The real story might be said to lie with Craig and his enforced exile to the city – in itself a kind of amalgam of the first two novels, *Call My Brother Back* and *Lost Fields* (1941) – and in the island family who have lost in Vera's first husband, a loved son, but hope to keep near them his daughter. This deeper theme celebrates the resilience of the island people, thrown into relief, though not ultimately disturbed, by the disruptive and alien force represented by the venomous Vera. It is difficult to understand why McLaverty made Vera, the misfit, his central character, rather than some member of the steady island community, unless it is that the same moral imperative which compelled McLaverty to renounce the short story in the late 1940s and concentrate on the moral novel, in the style of the later Mauriac, caused him also to bring the unlikely figure of a Mauriac malcontente to his island paradise. Like Alec in *Call My Brother Back*, Vera is a one-dimensional figure, apparently created for the specific purpose of demonstrating the manner in which life ought not to be lived. Neither seems to shake off the burden of this moral symbolism in order to emerge as a living being.

IV

McLaverty published nothing more about Rathlin, although, interestingly, he returned to the theme of the old man uprooted from his home, in a short story, actually called 'Uprooted', which he published in the *Dublin Magazine* in 1956. The theme of the wilfully damaged boat recurs in the last novel, *The Brightening Day*, published in 1965.

Two fragments exist, however. Both are tantalisingly incomplete, but pleasantly free from the pall of gloom felt so heavily at the end of *Truth in the Night*, and which seems so far from McLaverty's fundamental vision of Rathlin. One, dated July 20th 1963, is entitled 'The Island School' and contains two drafts of the opening of a story about an old Rathlin problem—the difficulty of keeping young people on it. It has the authentic McLaverty note, recognisable from the early stories, acknowledging the enormous problems of the island but glad to be alive on it, and missing nothing of its extraordinary beauty.

The second fragment is a plan for another Rathlin novel, which seems never to have been written. It is headed simply, 'Synopsis'. Two thoughts occur on reading it: firstly, that it might have become a novel of the kind McLaverty had stopped writing after *Call My Brother Back:* and, secondly, that even if its parts had not been gathered in to the novel form, many of them might have been short stories. What is present in the synopsis, and in the fragment of the island story, is the unmistakeable note, the elegiac note of exile. Had the novel been written, the perfection of the remembered days of childhood might have been punctuated by the intrusion of the outside world, and the memories, like Colm's in *Call My Brother Back*, perfectly preserved in the mind for ever.

For when, in 1939, 'Leavetaking' became Chapter Three of *Call My Brother Back*, leading towards the career of moral novelist a man born to write short stories, the wording of the story's end was slightly, but significantly, changed:

> He whistled as he passed an empty house, and when rabbits thudded out of danger his heart thumped wildly. Passing by Cnoc-na-Screilan (the hill of the screaming) he blessed himself and ran the rest of the way home. Outside the house he stood to quieten his breathing. The square of light in the window and the noise of his mother talking brought his courage back. Below on the shore the sea grumbled and far off a handful of ships' lights were twinkling. He sighed as he turned into the house.[15]

It is not the addition of Cnoc-na-Screilan, the scene of the massacre, that changes the passage, though it adds a chilling reminder of Rathlin's violent history; it is, rather, Colm's sigh before he goes to spend his last night as a child on Rathlin that strikes the telling note. More than the welcoming square of light in the window, more than the ships' lights far out at sea, it is that sigh, the whispered elegy for the life of childhood, soon to be memory, soon to be consigned to the unattainable past, that most characterises McLaverty's vision of Rathlin Island.

CHAPTER 15

History and Poetry: Derek Mahon and Tom Paulin

by

Peter McDonald

Any serious reading of the poetry produced by writers from the North of Ireland over the past twenty years soon has to encounter the various imperatives of 'history'; indeed, a great deal of what we understand by 'Contemporary Northern Irish Poetry' is in some part at least a contribution to an all too pressing historical discussion, one conducted in the contexts, not just of memory and tradition, but of real bullets and continuing deaths. The very simplicity and obviousness of all this has tempted critics to see the role of poets in such a situation as similarly straightforward as reflective, prescriptive, or disengaged from the different arguments of force. Yet poetry's place in relation to 'history' is not susceptible to rules of this sort, and good poetry tends to prove them futile, just as bad poetry takes them for its yardstick of orthodoxy. For all that, it is important to make sense out of the points of contact between poetry and history in recent Northern Irish writing, and to see the variousness of the writer's approaches to this attractive and powerful, yet also sometimes creatively dangerous, artistic crux.

One overwhelmingly influential artistic meeting with the past is of course to be found in the work of Seamus Heaney, whose development in this respect, especially in his volume *North* (1975) has been seen widely as a paradigmatic one, that is, a development of historical understanding bearing direct and valuable relevance to widespread experience in the present. What has sometime been forgotten is that Heaney's uses for history are not the same as those of other poets from the same place and generation; nor are they necessarily the most advanced and challenging of poetic dealings with history, binding in some way on the approach – the 'historical' approach – we take to understanding the continuing conflict in Northern Ireland. The two poets at the centre of this essay, Derek Mahon and Tom Paulin, represent two further efforts to engage the imaginatiion in the process of understanding history; they differ widely from each other, and widely too from the paradigm represented by Heaney. To say that these two poets ought to be pigeonholed under 'Protestant' as opposed to the Heaneyesque 'Catholic' imagination is to play by rules other than those that govern poetry; however, they are both from a Northern Irish Protestant background, and neither is identified with the predominantly rural conditioning so important in Heaney's metaphorical thinking on issues of place and belonging. Mahon, the elder poet, has reached levels of artistic success at least comparable with Heaney; Paulin has perhaps yet to do so; but both poets represent different, and extremely valuable, examples of the ways in which poetry touches and survives the stuff of history. In a critical context in which the imaginative archaeology of Heaney becomes fully and bindingly paradigmatic, these approaches tend to receive less than justice.

Derek Mahon's poety seems at first to have escaped the pressures of history altogether, insofar as these are seen as particular and pressing contingencies of events upon the individual life. The poems have always gravitated towards a cold and unpeopled area, one that exists before, or after, what we recognise as history. At the same time, the poems also come from a clearly recognisable point and persona – one notable form in which Mahon succeeds being the verse-letter – and exercise a technical accomplishment and descriptive fidelity that are themselves parts of a warm and living enterprise. Mahon's poetry is urgent in its concerns, but is never pitched at the level of emergency: for Tom Paulin, from a younger generation, poetry has been infected by the emergencies of the time, and is unapologetically a part of the discourse by which it is surrounded and threatened. In this essay I will compare certain aspects of both poets' work in an attempt to bring into focus their different dealings with the things they perceive as history, and pursue some of the implications which this aspect of their work might have in complicating the overall view of the relationship between history and poetry in contemporary Northern Irish writing.

One very important point of reference tends to be that of 'community'. The term has its sociological uses, but is sometimes open to considerable distortion in the context of political argument, even more so in that of the criticism of poetry. Yet it is also a notion of some relevance to Mahon and Paulin, in very different ways. Again, the problematic understanding of the term for both of these poets might suggest a contrast with the approachable and comprehensible sense of community upon which much of Heaney's most influential work depends: neither Mahon nor Paulin can have access to the certainties of 'belonging' that served Heaney as an artistic resource. It is perhaps no surprise to find different influences at work: where Heaney has been able to use Patrick Kavanagh's work as a kind of touchstone of community, Mahon and Paulin have needed figures like Samuel Beckett or Louis MacNeice to help mark out their own imaginative territory, writers who offer, not a discovery, but a fundemental suspicion of the notions of 'place' and 'belonging'. While the absolute zero of metaphysical loneliness is at one, Beckettian, end of the spectrum of Mahon's imagination, his work is vitalized by a feeling for the lives away from which this impulse drives it; in this sense, his writing balances Beckett against the more gregarious (on the surface at least) imaginative drive of MacNeice. This kind of label-sticking is of some importance when we come to consider Mahon in the context of his Northern Ireland. In the early poetry, the issues involved can sometimes look comparatively straightforward – 'The Spring Vacation' (originally 'In Belfast') plays some clever tricks with the notion of 'belonging; to anywhere:[1]

> Walking among my own this windy morning
> In a tide of sunlight between shower and shower
> I resume my old conspiracy with the wet
> Stone and the unwieldy images of the squinting heart.
> Once more, as before, I remember not to forget.

The poem is indeed one of public 'conspiracy', but it is a conspiracy with the reader against certain perceived imperatives of place and situation. It is characteristic of Mahon that, 'Walking among my own' or not, it is the 'wet/Stone' that is at the foreground of his attention, the material, mineral, reality outfacing the human scenes played before it. The poet goes on to acknowledge the coldness of this particular comfort:

> We could all be saved by keeping one eye on the hill
> At the top of every street, for there it is,
> Eternally, if irrelevantly, visible —

Of course, this is a very watchful poem, but one in which perspectives are twisted or forced, 'the squinting heart', 'Eternally, if irrelevantly, visible', or even, as if it were of any use, 'the cold gaze of a sanctimonious God'. Seeing straight is, for Mahon, essentially a metaphysical accomplishment, or at best one which has no relation to the 'interest' or 'pity' of human concerns, 'The things that happen in the kitchen-houses/And echoing back-streets of this desperate city'. Mahon's perspective is often in this sense inhuman in its rigour, and 'The Spring Vacation' follows its model, MacNeice's 'Belfast' (1931) in pushing a line of vision into, through and beyond the sufferings of a known community: both poems set the human against, or into, the mineral, the cold absolutes of 'basalt' or 'wet/Stone'. Yet for Mahon, as for MacNeice, this rather stern conclusion is far from the whole story.

In one of his later poems, 'A Refusal to Mourn', Mahon re-approaches the kind of human surroundings which 'The Spring Vacation' saw through. The rigour of the earlier poem is still there, but is tempered by being more fully understood; if the perspective has on one side become still clearer and more unrelentingly absolute, on the other its human focus has become more surely realised:[2]

All day there was silence
In the bright house. The clock
Ticked on the kitchen shelf,
Cinders moved in the grate,
And a warm briar gurgled
When the old man talked to himself;

The old man's world in the poem is itself made up largely of the inanimate, from the stanza just quoted to 'the photographs of his dead/Wife and their six children'. Mahon uses the poem to move from this particular surrounding towards other last things, where the animate faces, accommodates and finally becomes the inanimate:

In time the astringent rain
Of those parts will clean
The words from his gravestone
In the crowded cemetry
That overlooks the sea
And his name be mud once again

And his boilers lie like tombs
In the mud of the sea bed
Till the next ice age comes
And the earth he inherited
Is gone like Neanderthal Man
And no records remain.

It is worth taking note of the site where this imaginative journey past the history of humanity takes place, 'the crowded cemetry/That overlooks the sea', the landscape of other Mahon poems (like 'My Wicked Uncle'), and that of the imaginative geography of MacNeice, where the thickly populated country overlooks a grey and inhospitable sea (poems such as 'Carrickfergus' are set here). It is a Northern Irish scene, of course, and the stark contrasts it represents, of a living community on the edge of an ungovernable perspective, are of primary importance, first for MacNeice, then for Mahon, and subsequently for Paulin. In Mahon's 'My Wicked Uncle', the last scene is both 'real' – that is, faithful to what is actually there – and 'literary', that is, made possible by MacNeice's imaginative charging of a particular land and sea-scape:[3]

> He was buried on a blustery day above the sea,
> The young Presbyterian minister
> Tangled and wind-swept in the sea air.
> I saw sheep huddled in the long wet grass
> Of the golf-course, and the empty freighters
> Sailing for ever down Belfast Lough
> In a fine rain, their sirens going,
> As the gradual graph of my uncle's life
> And times dipped precipitately
> Into the black earth of Carnmoney Cemetery.

When Paulin chooses to single out MacNeice's 'House on a Cliff' for special praise, he is also returning to a central literary image which has provided his own work with crucial co-ordinates. Indeed, if we are to follow Paulin, the understanding of this image need not be, or in fact must not be, only a literary understanding; rather, it opens up areas of political analysis and self-knowledge. 'House on a Cliff', which MacNeice wrote in 1955, is one of the poet's later, complex return journeys to the contradictions of a remembered place:[4]

> Indoors the tang of a tiny oil-lamp. Outdoors
> The winking signal on the waste of sea.
> Indoors the sound of the wind. Outdoors the wind.
> Indoors the locked heart and the lost key.
>
> Outdoors the chill, the void, the siren. Indoors
> The strong man pained to find his red blood cools,
> While the blind clock grows louder, faster. Outdoors
> The silent moon, the garrulous tides she rules.

> Indoors ancestral curse-cum-blessing. Outdoors
> The empty bowl of heaven, the empty deep.
> Indoors a purposeful man who talks at cross
> Purposes, to himself, in a broken sleep.

Paulin's reading of this poem is suggestive, and shows how closely MacNeice's images are linked for him to the problematic idea of 'community' in the North. Praising the poem's 'terrible stoic isolation', Paulin speaks of 'a mysterious openness within or beyond [its] mirror-like reflections of a dead closed universe', and continues:

> If this is one man facing his lonely mortality on the far extremity of an unnamed place, the 'ancestral curse-cum-blessing', the cross purposes and broken sleep, suggest that the house is Ireland.[. . .] If this poem fits that baffled and contradictory term 'Irish', it also has an asocial, even a derelict, quality which makes it difficult to place. It subverts any comfortable notion of belonging, and this is true of all MacNeice's poetry.[5]

Paulin's reading of 'House on a Cliff' raises notions which trouble and stimulate his own poetry: extremity, loneliness, the asocial and derelict, an impossible imperative of 'belonging' to something which, under scrutiny, ceases to exist. It is worth noticing, however, how much all of these terms recall the world inhabited by Mahon, as in his poem 'Entropy':[6]

> We are holing up here
> in the difficult places –
> in caves, terminal moraines
> and abandoned farmhouses,
> the wires cut, the old car
> disposing itself for death
> among the inscrutable,
> earth-inheriting dandelions.

Mahon's transposition of the situation into terms of the inanimate is characteristic, his imagination finding an extremity answering that of his subject. It would not be unreasonable, however, to read 'Entropy' in terms of 'belonging' in 'the far extremity of an unnamed place'. Paulin is ready in his poetry to name his places, but the imaginative dilemma they represent is substantially the same. In his poem 'Desertmartin' the asocial and derelict takes named form:[7]

At noon, in the dead centre of a faith,
Between Draperstown and Magherafelt,
This bitter village shows the flag
In a baked absolute September light.
Here the Word has withered to a few
Parched certainties, and the charred stubble
Tightens like a black belt, a crop of Bibles.

This 'far extremity' is up for specifically political analysis in the poem, yet, like MacNeice's house on a cliff, the process of disentangling inside from outside in the perspective may not turn out to be all that easy. Even Paulin's poems of denunciation are engaged with the problem of 'belonging', the 'comfortable notion' which MacNeice subverted for good, just as Mahon's apocalyptic projections beyond human history, in their way, question the notion of 'community'. The diverging paths of Mahon and Paulin are of great interest. Where Mahon has examined the seemingly empty spaces in the imagination, the gaps in which the very notion of 'self' has become problematic, as 'places where a thought might grow', Paulin, especially in his volumes *Liberty Tree* (1983) and *Fivemiletown* (1988), has attempted to take up the theme of Protestant 'identity' and lay bare its arcane symbolic complexities. It is the difference between a *via negativa* and a direct route; but it turns, crucially, on the significance of history.

The easy reaction to Mahon's work, if we are looking for historical 'engagement', is to dismiss it as somehow beside the point, an irresponsible aestheticism that always looks the other way. Poetry, however, can no more answer the charge of irresponsibility than that of responsibility for disaster; Mahon's poem, 'Knut Hamsun in Old Age' faces that harsh fact squarely:[8]

Yes, I shook hands with Hitler; knew disgrace.
But time heals everything; I rose again.
Now I can look my butcher in the face.
Besides, did I not once, as a young man,
Cure myself of incipient tuberculosis
Inhaling four sub-zero nights and days
Perched on the screaming roof of a freight train?

The trauma of that freezing 'cure' might stand as a symbol for Mahon's own imaginative journey into the cold; there is no loss of sharpness in the actual observation of evil ('Now I can look my butcher in the face' sends shock-waves through the poem) but there is an equal, clear-eyed perspective, a distance which is at once desperate and level-headed. This kind of extremity must perforce set itself outside society, but it can also serve as a means of understanding the society from which it is distanced: Hamsun makes himself an outsider, but is thereby able to see inside and outside at the same time. Two other Mahon poems visit the isolated community from inside and outside at once: 'Nostalgias', a seven-line piece, aligns the inanimate, and its material links back to aboriginal substance, with a small community clinging to some guarantee of identity:[9]

> The chair squeaks in a high wind,
> Rain falls from its branches.
> The kettle yearns for the
> Mountain, the soap for the sea.
> In a tiny stone church
> On the desolate headland
> A lost tribe is singing 'Abide With Me'.

This last image is taken up and elaborated in 'Songs of Praise',[10] transposed now into the middle-class gentility which has provided Tom Paulin with much of his satirical register. Here the lost tribe of 'the outlying parts', on best behaviour, 'Lift up their hymn-books and their hearts/ To please the outside-broadcast cameras'. The theme of 'Nostalgias', which is ultimately that of belonging, is examined again, and again Mahon's canvas stretches to include more than the incidental figures of humanity:

> Never look back, they said; but they were wrong.
> The zinc wave-dazzle after a night of rain,
> A washed-out sky humming with stars, the mist
> And echoing fog-horns of the soul, belong
> To our lost lives. We must be born again,
> As the gable-ends of the seaside towns insist;

The easy religious cliché of being 'born again' points towards the 'lost lives' in the midst of which, and possibly thanks to which, the self seems to exist. The inside, the community of 'proud parishioners of the outlying parts', face, or rather might face, the outside, the lost lives of everything which, by being outside the community, helps that community to define itself. Mahon's readers are therefore obliged

> to look back constantly
> On that harsh landscape and its procreant sea,

> Bitter and curative, as tonight we did,
> Listening to our own nearly-voices chime
> In the parochial lives we might have led,
> Praising a stony god who died before our time.

This outside view asks the viewer to identify with what is happening inside, and to understand it as somehow 'our own'. This is partly to demand a revision of the simple idea of self, to ask that the self should be born again, and then again. It is no surprise that this 'bitter and curative' process should take place in sight of 'that harsh landscape and its procreant sea', the characteristic setting for Mahon's extreme perspectives.

What is probably Mahon's best-known poem, 'A Disused Shed in Co. Wexford', is essentially a sustained meditation on 'lost lives' and a muted insistence on the self's having to be 'born again' in order to live them. The poem's fungi shut away in 'the grim/ Dominion of stale air and rank moisture' stand between the inanimate and the human as symbols for both:[11]

> Magi, moonmen,
> Powdery prisoners of the old regime,
> Web-throated, stalked like triffids, racked by drought
> And insomnia, only the ghost of a scream
> At the flash-bulb firing squad we wake them with
> Shows there is life yet in their feverish forms.

The language is that of suffering and efficient brutality; Mahon's exclamation in the last stanza – 'Lost people of Treblinka and Pompeii' – makes explicit a parallel which has already been felt beneath the surface. The discovery of fungi in a disused shed carries the symbolic weight of all the 'lost lives' that make up history, and that 'lift frail heads in gravity and good faith' into the present:

> They are begging us, you see, in their wordless way,
> To do something, to speak on their behalf,
> Or at least not to close the door again.

This is a plea on behalf of history as well as a testimony to history's destructive cruelty. It is, however, history in a fuller sense than that of the politically significant only; its significance is that of the forgotten as well as the momentous. The poem is a vindication of Mahon's determinedly cold, detached perspectives, his distance which clarifies and makes more urgent. A stance which may appear abstract in its concerns enables the poet to see more than the close-ups of 'commitment' would make possible.

Tom Paulin has written interestingly on Mahon's 'Disused Shed', in terms which suggest some of the underlying concerns of his own work. In fact, Paulin seems to regard Mahon's poem as embodying a kind of solution to the many problems presented by 'politics' or 'history' in poetry:

> Such poems issue from that condition of supremely unillusioned quietism – the wisest of passivities – which is usually the product of bitter historical experience and which is temperamentally different from disillusion. To be politically disillusioned is often to be cynical; to be politically apathetic is usually to be ignorant, but to possess no illusions is to understand a spiritual reality which is religious in its negativity.[12]

This is more than just an analysis of Mahon's poem, pointing us towards certain elements of Paulin's own poetry, and revealing something of the embattled, threatened nature of his imagination. It is significant that Paulin should feel able to speak of 'a spiritual reality which is religious in its negativity' at the end of a process of political 'unillusions'. The path from 'bitter historical experience' towards this state is Paulin's equivalent to Mahon's metaphysical *via negativa*, and is an aspect of his poetry which tends to be ignored. Indeed, critics have treated Paulin badly, on the whole, letting his work provoke adversarial, affronted or mocking responses. There are several reasons for this: partly, Paulin has disguised the design of his poetry by the urgency of the 'bitter historical experience' which he has chosen as his starting-point. Critics otherwise attuned to certain oblique angles of approach in other Irish poets can be misled by Paulin's directness into thinking him single-minded, or even crude, in the direction of his work. This is a mistake, but it is one which has perhaps begun to influence the way in which Paulin sees his own poetry, and has in part suggested certain strategies in his more recent work, in particular *Fivemiletown* (1988). Paulin has not yet reached in his writing that 'condition of supremely unillusioned quietism' he perceives in Mahon, but the gravitational pull of such a condition, along with its religious overtones, is still to be felt in much of his poetry, and even his most urgent and concretely located work is under its influence.

For Paulin, one vital way of stripping the self of its illusions is the practice of criticism, and the wholesale debunking of the bourgeois concept of 'pure' literature untouched by the contingencies of its contexts. He puts this crisply in the *Faber Book of Political Verse* (1986):

> In the Western democracies it is still possible for many readers, students and teachers of literature to share the view that poems exist in a timeless vacuum or a soundproof museum, and that poets are gifted with an ability to hold themselves above history, rather like skylarks or weather-satellites. However, in some societies – particularly totalitarian ones – history is a more or less inescapable condition.[13]

Yet, as any reader of Paulin's criticism knows, this is far from the 'all literature is politics by proxy' arguments of some literary historians or theorists. For Paulin, literature becomes more powerful when it confronts history, and it does not then sink to the level of an illustration of something larger than itself. The problem, as he sees it, lies in the societies with whom the condition of 'history' seems to be abstract, or easily escapable. Paulin's attention moves towards the extreme condition in which 'history' threatens to engulf the poet's voice altogether, the totalitarian societies in which delusions of 'freedom' are harder to maintain. The state of Northern Ireland is, for Paulin's purposes, just such a society, a place of extremities where history has to be encountered and faced down. Despite the tactics of Paulin's work since *Liberty Tree* (1983), it would still be a mistake to assume that the poet has chosen his preferred version of 'history' and decided to follow where it leads. On the contrary, Paulin's work, with its near-visionary ideal of 'freedom' and frequent invocations of 'the Word' (sometimes allowing these to become artistic liabilities) has always been pulled towards a more socially-based and humane victory over 'history's' attempts at determinism.

One way in which Paulin sets out to overcome the more narrowing and limiting interpretations of history is by using history itself as a tool. The volume *Liberty Tree* is an exercise in making history part of a contemporary, explicitly political, argument. In the poem 'Father of History', Paulin sets up his new curriculum:[14]

> Folded like bark, like cinnamon things,
> I traced them to the Linen Hall stacks –
> Munro, Hope, Porter and McCracken;
> like sweet yams buried deep, these rebel minds

endure posterity without a monument,
their names a covered sheugh, remnants, some brackish signs.

The special qualities of this hitherto-hidden history, these particular 'lost lives' that have been forgotten, are as foreign to the spiritual waste land that is Paulin's Ulster as cinnamon or yams, and it is these which the poet insists upon. The dissenting Radical tradition is in *Liberty Tree* a crucial tool for analysing the shortcomings of the present-day Protestant community. It is important to remember that what Paulin is actually doing is making an imaginative appropriation of history, creating symbols from history. As for the application of his symbols, Paulin has ideas of audience, but these are not perhaps as clear as they might be, and seem sometimes to cause the poet himself confusion. Once again, the question of perspective intrudes, of the writer's being inside or outside his subject. *Liberty Tree* strikes an uneasy balance, with Paulin's register of vocabulary stretching from the most abstract and theoretical to what he hears as the Ulster vernacular; on the whole, this results in more failures than successes for the poetry, and fails to reconcile inside with outside. Yet behind the sometimes rather academic veneer, Paulin is still capable of an eerie immediacy and sensitivity which comes much closer to experience in Northern Ireland than any amount of vernacular experiment. In 'Martello'[15], he asks:

Can you *describe* history I'd like to know?
Isn't it a fiction that pretends to be fact
like *A Journal of the Plague Year*?
And the answer that snaps back at me
Is a winter's afternoon in Dungannon,
the gothic barracks where the policemen
were signing out their weapons in a stained register,
a thick turbid light and that brisk smell of fear
as I described the accident and felt guilty
guilty for no reason, or cause, I could think of.

Even though it is a good idea for poets to avoid in general answering their own questions, the passage reveals something more than Paulin's critics will admit: far from wheeling out a packaged and essentially prescriptive commodity called 'history', the poet refuses to define history as either fiction or fact, opting instead for the concrete – to re-use an overused literary adage, it is as though history should not 'mean' but 'be'. The poetry, in Paulin's hands, creates a police-state, a condition of total interrogation which seems to assume and enforce guilt on the part of the individual. To be 'guilty/ guilty for no reason, or cause' is to experience the original sin of dissent from an orthodoxy which has sought to define and incorporate 'history' as an instrument of repression. As often in Paulin's poetry, Calvinistic religious shadows merge into those of political realities, of history happening.

The truism that in Ireland, as in Europe in the past, religion is politics and politics religion, applies to Paulin's vision. For a writer who gives his explicit allegiance to the values of Enlightenment republicanism, Paulin is much preoccupied with the hermetic imagery of harsh, dark beliefs, the arcane flip-side of Presbyterianism which is a stylised version of the history of community, grounded in the themes and imagery of the Old Testament. Indeed, it is worth looking briefly at the ways in which Paulin has in the past spoken about the Ulster Protestant 'identity' which his work continues to examine. In an interview with John Haffenden published in 1981, for example, there is a frustrated, almost baffled tone, mixed with that of the history lesson:

> But what I find at the moment is a real sense of how fundamentally ridiculous and contradictory it is to be an Ulster Protestant. It's a culture which could have dignity, and it had it once – I mean that strain of radical Presbyterian, free-thinking Presbyterianism, which more or less went underground after 1798. I pretty well despise official Protestant culture, and can't now understand how people can simultaneously wave the Union Jack and yet hate the English, as many Protestants do.[16]

The concerns of *Liberty Tree* are taking shape here, the search into a particular facet of Irish history for a way of 'understanding' a culture which, seen as too far debased for the poet to share, has to be despised; history offers a way back to the community which Paulin has disowned. This process, at work in the earnest dialect-peddling of the *Liberty Tree* poems, goes further in the introduction to Paulin's stimulating collection of essays, *Ireland and the English Crisis* (1984) where he writes of 'the experience of growing up inside an Ulster Protestant community':

> That community possesses very little in the way of an indigenous cultural tradition of its own and in its more reflective moments tends to identify with 'the British way of life'. Although the dis-

> senting tradition in Ulster created a distinctive and notable culture in the closing decades of the eighteenth century, that tradition went underground after the Act of Union and has still not been given the attention it deserves. This is largely because most Unionists have a highly selective historical memory and cling desperately to a raft constructed of two dates 1690 and 1912. The result is an unusually fragmented culture and a snarl of superficial or negative attitudes. A provincialism of the most disabling kind.[17]

Maybe we ought to distinguish the 'highly selective historical memory' of the debased community mentioned here from the highly selective historical imagination of the poet, clinging desperately to one date, 1798, and proposing a kind of Ulster dissociation of sensibility at the end of the eighteenth century. At any rate, it is this 'provincialism' which Paulin's writing tackles: the questions which remain unsettled are whether he is trying to change or to condemn it, whether he addresses himself to the dissociated culture or holds it up to an outside audience for ridicule.

That dangerous word, 'community' is close to the heart of Paulin's concerns in *Fivemiletown*, in which there is a Protestant community which, broadly speaking, coheres and has 'identity'; this community has its totems, its sign-systems, its conception of history, all of which can be cracked; it is also, of course, on the verge of historical crisis. A short poem, 'The Red Handshake', sees Paulin confronting the thing itself, or rather unearthing it:[18]

> Maybe if I could scrape the earth
> from off that ridge where the Third Force
> melted out of *The Tain* one Antrim night,
> I'd find a man called Bowden Beggs
> wrapped in black plastic, like a growbag,
> and breathing 'Mind, it can get no worse'?

What happens here is that Paulin begins to inhabit the Heaney version of history, one which accepts some of John Hewitt's historical metaphors for its own purposes. This is the Planter all right, but he isn't planted all that deeply in the Antrim soil; the very name, Bowden Beggs, is both a kind of stage-Ulster and itself the earth, Boden; where Heaney has to dig, Paulin need only scrape, finding the threatened, resilient, slightly absurd character.[19] And how ironic is the alignment of the Third Force with *The Tain*? Whatever its ironies, the poem seems to collaborate with the *cliché* of the Protestant

Ulsterman as both tenuously rooted and somehow cheap and nasty, vulgarised, wilfully blinded to realities. This is the handshake which Paulin has to understand in *Fivemiletown*, and there can be no doubt of the strenuousness of his poetic attempts to do so, but the basic assumptions remain open to question: is Paisleyite Third Force Protestantism a key to unlocking the 'identity' of Paulin's community, or is it just one aspect of something far more complex and diverse? Both Fivemiletown and the satirical play *The Hillsborough Script* see Ulster Protestants as having been driven into a corner by events, or, to use Paulin's image, forced up to an open window. 'The Defenestration of Hillsborough' puts this starkly:[20]

> Here we are on a window ledge
> with the idea of race.
>
> All our victories
> were defeats really
>
> and the tea chests in that room
> aren't packed with books.

Like much of Paulin's verse, this is pared to the bone, maybe enacting in poetic terms the tired old *cliché* of the laconic, sometimes wilfully inarticulate Ulsterman. The poem's final point is similarly rough and clear — 'This means we have a choice:/ Either to jump or get pushed'. Even allowing for the appearance of Woodrow Wilson, Lutheran engravings and Tomas Masaryk in the poem, its bluntness leaves little room for doubt as to its direction: the loyalist mind, presented with a *fait accompli* as its political future from London and Dublin, has either to leap into new thinking or be forced there. Paulin differs from British and Irish politicians in wishing to see this act as something different from obeisance or humiliation; one metaphor he uses freely throughout *Fivemiletown* is that of sexual disruption and parting, the salvaging of self-respect at the end of destructive relationships. In 'Waftage: An Irregular Ode', a lover who has bought 'this tin/ of panties coloured/ like the Union jack' is given his marching orders:[21]

> 'Please don't come slouching
> near my bed again'.
> So, real cool, I growled
> 'Lady, no way you'll walk

right over me'.
Dead on. I chucked her then.

One side pushes, the other defiantly jumps: yet the defenestration goes ahead in any case, and the punishment is final.

In Louis MacNeice's *The Strings Are False* there is a memory of being a young boy in an English prep-school, an Ulster Protestant among the English:

> On the Twelfth of July Powys came into my dormitory and said: 'What is all this they do in your country today? Isn't it all mumbo-jumbo?' Remembering my father and Home Rule and the bony elbows of Miss Craig and the black file of mill-girls and the wickedness of Carson and the dull dank days between sodden haycocks and foghorns, I said Yes it was. And I felt uplifted. [. . .] But Powys went out of the dormitory and Mr Cameron came in, his underlip jutting and his eyes enraged. 'What were you saying to Mr Powys?' Oh this division of allegiance! That the Twelfth of July was mumbo-jumbo was true, and my father thought so too, but the moment Mr Cameron appeared I felt rather guilty and cheap. Because I had been showing off to Powys and because Mr Cameron being after all Irish I felt I had betrayed him.[22]

MacNeice's awareness of the importance of audience began early, but it all seems curiously relevant to the position in which Tom Paulin has found himself: simple truth-telling suffers in translation from one side of the Irish Sea to the other, where it can be telling the British what they want to hear rather than telling one's countrymen what they should already know. Paulin has asserted that 'the Irish writer who publishes in Britain has a neo-colonial identity', identifying the 'central question' for such a writer as 'whom am I writing for?' and once described V.S. Naipaul as writing 'for nothing and nowhere', being 'simply against certain ghastly elsewheres', warning that 'Otherness is a specialising feature, a distinguishing mark, but it can reduce the writer to an entertainer, a media clown';[23] his own otherness has special dangers for Paulin, and, perhaps, special temptations.

Both Derek Mahon and Tom Paulin raise in their poetry the issue touched in *Little Gidding* by T.S. Eliot, who asserts that 'History may be servitude, History may be freedom';[24] *making* history into one thing or the other is an imaginative as well as a political act, and it is poetry's responsibility, not to the dead only, but to its proper constituency, the living

CHAPTER 16

Against Piety: A Reading of John Hewitt's Poetry

by

Gerald Dawe

I

> *co'lony* n. 1. Settlement or settlers in new country forming community fully or partly subject to mother State; their territory; people of one nationality or occupation in a city, esp. if living more or less in isolation or in a special quarter . . . 2. (Gk Hist.) independent city founded by emigrants; (Rom.Hist.) garrison settlement (usu. of veteran soldiers) in conquered territory.

I will not deal in any extensive way here with John Hewitt's poetry or indeed with the various motives and interpretations surrounding his changing views about regionalism and so forth. Instead I want to consider the intersection, if you like, between the two phrases 'roots' and 'horizons' as they present themselves to me in a highly selective reading of John Hewitt's work.

My connection with John Hewitt was mostly through correspondence, although I did meet him in the early 1970s and his encouragement then was very important to me. I met him later at the occasional poetry reading in Belfast but my understanding of John Hewitt has mostly been through his books, rather than via his personality. His was a presence formed in precise letters; not through regular contact. So I am intending now to explain to myself, publicly as it were, John Hewitt, a poet engaged by particular public and historical issues, the most central of which was his artistic and intellectual bearing on what being a writer might involve for someone, like myself, whose background was (is?) Protestant Belfast.

So these are two of my main concerns today: the public face of Hewitt's poetry and the 'Protestant' dimension of that. I had found, ironically, that my title came first when I was asked to participate in the Summer School. For I had already been thinking of John Hewitt and of how he seems to stand as a rather remote, isolated figure as regards both contemporary Irish and other literatures in English.

While he had anticipated many of the developments which have taken place in Irish poetry over the last twenty years, there always seemed to be about the man, as much as the poetry, a distance and reserve not solely temperamental in character. He rebuked the easy pieties of populist fashion and shadowed the cultural self-confidence of other Irish writers with an almost Victorian doubting. I felt that this distance had something specifically to do with his own sense of himself as a poet, reinforced by a curiously ambiguous expectation of, and reception for, the fact that he was, in some manner of speaking, a 'Protestant' writer from the 'Black North'; a strange fish, in other words.

Now I know I may well be accused here of raising a hare while letting myself sit, to mix a typically mannered expression sometimes used in the Republic of Ireland where I have lived, worked and been a fully paid-up and taxed citizen for the past fifteen years. What is a Protestant Writer, after all? By what peculiar gestures, accents, manicure, or space between his eyes, is this species known to man? I will pass this by and concentrate upon some of the features – the themes, attitudes, turn of voice – in John Hewitt's work which make me think that there are relationships between these two terms, 'Protestant' and 'Writer', which run parallel to, but by no means perfectly in line with, the terms of our conference: 'roots' and 'horizons'.

For in my own experience as a poet, I have been amazed by the complex and complicated tensions which link that background in Protestant Belfast (roots) with the world outside (horizons). Between these two poles of attraction and/or rejection, various images and caricatures, often absurd, sometimes funny, occasionally infuriating, intervene.

With John Hewitt the relationship was remarkably clear, stable and accessible. It was based, I think, upon his belief in a rational, reasonable world on which could be superimposed the dialectical decorum of art, both literary and visual, and maintained against the distortions and divisions of history itself.

> *John Hewitt*: 'You have been asking whether we think our poetic role is analogous to Yeat's frequent public stand. Well I, for example, have written poems which are relevant to the political situation. Yet they are quoted in *The Irish Times* but not in the *Belfast Telegraph*. I am not speaking to my people. They are public utter-

> ances but they are taken up by a more distant audience than that for which they were intended.
> *Timothy Kearney*: Is that an inescapable thing?
> *John Hewitt*: Yes, it is an inescapable thing. But linked with it is the important fact of the total lack of literary interest amongst unionists of the north, the lack of any fixed literary tradition.[1]

This ordering of Hewitt's 'public utterances' is sharply focussed in a recent paper by Edna Longley called 'Including the North'. The poetry, writes Ms. Longley, can be viewed from three angles: as cultural retrieval, defence and encounter based on local history and local artistic expression; as cultural self-criticism; and as an historical consciousness registering not only 'seventeenth and eighteenth century events, but the First World War, the Easter Rising, the Second World War and other twentieth century shocks and changes . . .' deeply implicated in the poetry – to a further depth in poems written after 1968.[2]

It is to the substance of and attitude to these three areas of Hewitt's writing that other critics will need to turn for an adequate account of his achievement, influence and example. I can merely gesture in that direction today by raising what I hope are constructive questions.

II

One can, for example, turn to Hewitt's pioneering 1945 article, 'The Bitter Gourd: Some Problems of the Ulster Writer', to see how he linked the issues of 'roots' to the effect of boundless horizons. The Ulster writer, you recall Hewitt stating, 'must be a *rooted* man, must carry the native tang of his idiom like the native dust on his sleeve; otherwise he is an airy internationalist, thistledown, a twig in a stream'. And later he returns to this 'question of rootedness', as he calls it himself.

> I do not mean that a writer ought to live and die in the house of his fathers. What I do mean is that he ought to feel that he belongs to a recognisable focus in place and time. How he assures himself of that feeling is is own affair. But I believe he must have it. And with it, he must have *ancestors*. Not just of the blood, but of the emotions, of the quality and slant of the mind.[3]

Now I find this passage highly revealing of Hewitt's 'emotions, of the quality and slant' of his own mind, particularly when we align these statements with the central literary parallel which he draws in 'The Bitter Gourd' – New England and Robert Frost.

As a poet, Frost's 'rural portraits are not alien to us', writes Hewitt, his 'avoidance of ornament and rhetoric is kin to our logic, whose unhurried and sinewy wisdom is sympathetic to our highest moods'. Against this 'rooted man', we can place a poem of Hewitt's, taken from what I think is Hewitt's best individual book, *The Rain Dance* (1978). The poem is 'On Reading Wallace Stevens' *Collected Poems* after Many Years':

> Put this artificer of *chiaroscuro*
> on the high shelf with all those phrase-bound poets,
> padded with pedant's resonance, ballooned
> with bouncing echoes of their paladins.
>
> Give me, instead, the crisp neat-witted fellows,
> sharp and laconic, making one word do,
> the clipped couplet, the pointing syllables,
> the clean-beaked sentence, the exact look.

Clearly Stevens, another New England man, is not rooted enough but enters the world as 'an airy internationalist'. I think this poem and what it implies is closely related to Hewitt's earlier statements about the Ulster writer being someone 'who must be a *rooted* man' because that decision in itself is a gesture of appropriation, of domestication, of asserting one's self in one place, of becoming, as it were, a naturalised citizen. It has other implications, as well. Whereas 'this artificer' Wallace Stevens is up to his eye-teeth wth literariness ('a twig in the stream') floating along impossible horizons, the neat-witted fellows have their feet squarely on the ground. In *The Rain Dance* there are several poems singing such fellows' praises, as in 'William Conor, R.H.A. 1881–1968' and particularly the following lines from the opening stanza;

> So, Conor, take our thanks for what you've done
> not through those harsh abstractions whose despair
> of finding teeming earth forever fair
> strip to a disc what we would face as sun,
> nor lost in lonely fantasies which run
> through secret labyrinths and mazes where
> the dream-drenched man must find but few to share

the tortured forms his agonies have won.
Not these for you, but your kindly skill, . . .

There is, though, in these phrases 'lonely fantasies' and 'secret labyrinths' a closing off of possibility, a distinctive circumspection, that I want to come back to towards the end of this talk.

We have, in Hewitt's example of New England and the reference to Robert Frost in preference to Stevens, an interesting background to Hewitt's own view of himself as a rooted writer. For, as Robert Lowell remarked about Frost, 'somehow [Frost] put life into a dead tradition' and in a way I think this was what Hewitt set himself to do in Ulster.

Indeed, like Robert Frost, John Hewitt's poetry has itself become a cultural fact, involving one of the central themes of our life on this island as much as of our literature, and when Hewitt quotes Frost's 'The Gift Outright' he anticipates the last three lines of possibly his own most famous poem, 'The Colony':

We would be strangers in the Capitol;
This is our country also, no-where else;
and we shall not be outcast on the world.

Who is 'we'; which 'Capitol'?; what 'country'? In 'The Colony' and in many other poems John Hewitt has addressed that much abused concept, 'identity'. In 'Conacre', for instance, Hewitt writes:

This is my home and country. Later on
perhaps I'll find this nation is my own
but here and now it is enough to love
this faulted ledge . . .

and in that resolve, ('here and now it is enough to love'), the characteristic imaginative gesture in Hewitt's poetry is to be found: the roots. It is curious, though, to place alongside these lines of Hewitt's a passage from Seamus Heaney's 'Feelings into Words' (1974), roughly a quarter of a century after Hewitt's poem. In his lecture, Seamus Heaney takes up the notion of 'colony' in terms of the Roman *imperium*, a garrison settlement in conquered territory.

I mean that I felt it imperative to discover a field of force in which, without abandoning fidelity to the processes and experience of poetry as I have outlined them, it would be possible to encompass

> the perspectives of a humane reason and at the same time to grant the religious intensity of the violence its deplorable authenticity and complexity. And when I say religious, I am not thinking simply of the sectarian division. To some extent the enmity can be viewed as a struggle between the cults and devotees of a god and a goddess. There is an indigenous territorial numen, a tutelar of the whole island, call her Mother Ireland, Kathleen Ni Houlihan, the poor old woman, the Shan Van Vocht, whatever; and her sovereignty has been temporarily usurped or infringed by a new male cult whose founding fathers were Cromwell, William of Orange and Edward Carson, and whose godhead is incarnate in a rex or caesar resident in a palace in London. What we have is the tail-end of a struggle in a province between territorial piety and imperial power.
>
> Now I realize that this idiom is remote from the agnostic world of economic interest whose iron hand operates in the velvet glove of 'talks between elected representatives', and remote from the political manoeuvres of power-sharing; but is not remote from the psychology of the Irishmen and Ulstermen who do the killing, and not remote from the bankrupt psychology and mythologies implicit in the terms Irish Catholic and Ulster Protestant.[4]

The 'tail-end of a struggle in a province between territorial piety and imperial power' is one way of contextualising what John Hewitt has written. The irony is that Hewitt's ambiguous relationship to the 'imperial power' is founded *absolutely* upon 'territorial piety'. As he says in regard to 'The Colony' in 'No Rootless Colonist' (1972):

> I have not attempted to predicate by what means we may isolate the moment when a colony set among an older population ceases simply to be simply (sic) a colony and become something else, although I have not hesitated to take that 'something else' to be a valid *region* with the inalienable right to choose its place within a smaller or larger federation.

Hewitt's understanding of 'colony' looks almost more like its Greek root than the Roman: namely, an independent city founded by emigrants. And this is where the ideas of regionalism come in and the sense of ancestral voices and rootedness takes on a radical dimension; because in both his poetry and prose, behind the seemingly low-keyed, formal determination, there is a belligerent doggedness to Hewitt ('as native in my thoughts as any here') very much in keeping with the community from which he came. After all, it is the '*sullen* Irish limping to the hills' in 'Once Alien Here' (my italics). While in 'The Glens', Hewitt registers another old score in the disturbed northern mindfield: 'I fear their creed as *we* have always feared the lifted hand between the mind and truth' (my italics), later on revised for Alan Warner's edition of Hewitt's *Selected Poems* to: 'the lifted hand against unfettered thought'.

Hewitt sees an 'imperial power' closer to home than a 'palace in London', yet there is a kind of awkward, self-conscious strain, the literariness of the city man perhaps, in much that he has written about the countryside, and those who live in it (strictly speaking, the barbarians). We detect it in the following poem, 'The Rosses':

> The hospitable Irish
> come out to see who passes,
> bid you sit by the fire
> till it is time for mass.
>
> The room is bare, the bed
> is shabby in the corner,
> but the fine talk is ready
> and the wide hearth is warm.

The note of outsider-status feeding stereotypes here in what is, as Hewitt subtitled 'Scissors for a One-Armed tailor', *marginal* verses (1929–1954), should not be taken too much on face-value because underlying it a very real uncertainty characterises Hewitt's attitude and understanding of the 'hospitable Irish'. While we can, I suppose, overlook the jaunting-car, tear-or-twinkle-in-the-eye postcard view, the trouble is in that 'but' between the 'bed . . . shabby in the corner' and 'the fine talk': quaint, oral consolations. And there is too 'the time for mass'. It is probably more just to say that in keeping with a man of his temperament and middle-class, suburban baackground, Hewitt may simply have had, like many of us, difficulty engaging with the human realities of actual impoverished country life. As several of his important poems, like 'Conacre', show, the country, like 'The Irish', operated quite forceably in Hewitt's mind at an abstract, intellectual level, and as a compensatory outlet for sensual, visual release.

This somewhat abstract quality, though, the sense of strain and putting on airs, has I think created an obstacle for already unsympathetic literary critics 'placing' Hewitt in the canon of Irish poetry. For as most of us realise, the critical reception Hewitt has received as a poet in Britain, the Republic of Ireland, not to mention the U.S., has been less than his due. On the one hand he seems a more dowdy Edmund Blunden and hardly a suitable case for redbrick deconstruction. On the other hand, in the Republic, when on those rare occasions critical attention has actually travelled northwards, Hewitt stands as a reminder of the unassimilated Protestants. But perhaps in this sense, Hewitt could have been more forthright in his address to the Republic of today rather than the ideal aspirations and hopes of republicans of two and more centuries ago.

I am thinking here of his remarks in an interview with Ketzel Levine in 1985 where, referring back to his poem 'The Colony' as 'the best statement of my point of view', he talks about his struggle for fifty years to sort out his own identity:

> I think I have a pretty clear grasp of it now . . . I couldn't for instance, happily belong to a Gaelic-speaking Irish republic, because that's not my native tongue, and I don't want to separate it from Britain because the complete body, the corpus of my thought, has come from Britain. The ideas I cherish are British ideas . . . my intellectual ancestry goes back to the Levellers at the time of Cromwell. England had become a republic, and they believed that people should be levelled, should be equal.[5]

This, I fear, is a bit like having your seventeenth-century cake and eating it with your eyes closed three centuries later. What about applying the radical ideas, 'strong British roots' and all, to the actual Republic on one's doorstep? Hewitt is less than enamoured of the prospect: '. . . there were no Irish Levellers, no Irish Diggers. The Irish people, before my ancestors came here, were a tribe of cattle-rustlers, fighting each other and burning churches and what not. They wrote very nice songs and somewhat good poetry. I'd like to include them too in the general picture, but they're not the whole of the story.'

'They', of course, are not 'the whole of the story', but who ever is? There is the strongest whiff here of a defensiveness turned, under the informality of an interview, into fighting talk. And needless to say, this is very important in itself because it relates to one of the crucial issues John Hewitt represents. For his poetry is all about his attempts to find practicable resolutions to what history has given him by way of a home, a family's past and the 'natural' cultural world into which he was born. The word 'resolution' implies not only something determined upon as an act of faith, but also an assurance to keep going, no matter what, the need to bear witness. The first sense invokes the making of a Myth; the second involves personal integrity and an artistic single-mindedness. Both senses are revealed in how the poetry itself is made. Perhaps this does not amount to a Vision, but when one looks around at poetry in the English language today, one must ask: how many other poets have come as near as Hewitt to creating a vision for himself and for others to live by?

III

Taken as a whole, Hewitt's poetry provides us with a myth and one that is not circumscribed by the immediate experience of Irish history. Indeed, Hewitt's poetry can be viewed in a different light that reflects upon the actual homelessness of modern man. By saying this I am not suggesting that John Hewitt's poetry is allegorical in any conscious forthright manner but that in its constant focussing upon the present and in its romantic attachments to the past, in the description of certain places during certain times (The Glens of Antrim, Belfast, Coventry and Greece during various periods ranging from the early 1920s to today), and in the portraits he gives us of poets, craftsmen and his own descendants, Hewitt defines the tenuous grasp we effectively have on the 'real' world. His poetry actually argues that we must make the conscious effort to decide who and what we are (establishing 'roots') rather than accepting an identity imposed from without. The ambivalent attitude to the country people ('You are coarse to my senses/to my washed skin') and his acknowledgement of his own 'separateness' ('I found myself alone who had hoped for attention') are marks of a man at least unwilling to acquiesce in the domination of the past. He has, as it were, been pushed reluctantly to make his own way in the prodigal world. The reluctance is shown in Hewitt's antipathy towards artists such as Wallace Stevens whom, as I've already mentioned, he sees as making a virtue out of what is an unwelcome and possibly disabling state – having to find a language in which the writer can report back on his experiences to those who are willing to listen 'across a roaring hill'. Those experiences I see condensed in the relationship between Hewitt's myth-making and his sense of restraint in dealing with the ambition of his art. It is a restraint that can cause problems for the reader more accustomed to a provocative art, and lends itself, perhaps a little too readily, to quotation and paraphrase.

In the articles he wrote in 1953 for *The Bell* as 'Planter's Gothic: An Essay in Discursive Autobiography', writing under the name of John Howard, Hewitt traces his family's past and notes laconically that not having been baptised gave him 'a sense of liberation, spiritually I have felt myself to be my own man, the ultimate Protestant'. Perhaps taking his cue from this remark, John Montague in an article called 'Regionalism into Reconciliation: The Poetry of John Hewitt' (1964) referred to Hewitt as the 'first (and probably the last) *deliberately* Ulster, Protestant poet.'[6] But both the autobiographical gloss and Montague's description are a little misleading for it seems to me that Hewitt's poetry expresses the *contradiction* between a 'sense of liberation', be that spiritual or not (horizons), and the claims that a specific form of Protestant faith, Methodism, made upon him ('his roots').

For while the temper of Hewitt's poetry is often one of dissent, from the orthodoxies of his own past as much as that of 'a vainer faith/ and a more violent lineage' (the 'creed' he fears in 'The Glens'), there is always a counter-aesthetic which restrains him. It could be described best in Isaac Watts' terms: 'because I would neither indulge any bold metaphors, nor admit hard words, nor tempt the ignorant worshipper to sing without his understanding'. This is the reasonable liberal light by which we should read Hewitt's poetry. Donald Davie says in *A Gathered Church* (1978), from which source the Watts quotation comes, that the 'aesthetic and the moral perceptions have, built into them and near to the heart of them, the perceptions of license, of abandonment, of superfluity, foreseen, even invited, and yet in the end denied, fended off!'[7] For what better way is there to view one of the more significant features of Hewitt's poetry than to see in it the struggle against art's enticement, the lure of the imagination, distant horizons, the unknown – and the need to resist this in both poetic and political terms. Hewitt writes of this tension convincingly, implicitly, but rarely do we see such a personal stating of it as we do in one of his finest achievements, 'Sonnets for Roberta (1954)', with their calm, almost Shakespearean poise:

I have let you waste
the substance of your summer on my mood;
the image of the woman is defaced,
and some mere chattel-thing of cloth and wood
performs the household rite, while I, content,
mesh the fine words to net the turning thought,
or eke the hours out, gravely diligent,

> to drag to sight that which, when it is brought,
> is seldom worth the labour . . .

or in 'The Faded Leaf: a chapter of family history':

> I know that grave, the headstone; the text
> I am proud of, for its honesty:
> We all do fade as a leaf: no easy hope,
> no sanctimonious, pentecostal phrase,
> simply a natural image for the fact.
> I've written verses of the falling leaf.

As he wrote in *The Bell* (July 1952), discussing possible attitudes open to the writer in modern society, the one of 'rarefication' led to a 'withdrawal from the community, from the day-to-day, from the topic of the time, into memories of childhood, nostalgia, the pastoral, the slightly fantastic, the rather obscure, accompanying this, a deliberate modification of technique, a narrowing of focus, a magnification of detail, a meticulous searching for precision in phrase and image, an increased preciosity. This way so much is left out . . .'. And while he remarks later, 'I am not decrying all work in this mode', we can clearly sense his disapproval of such work since the assumed responsibility of art in the writer's community is neglected which results in 'increased preciosity' in the writing.

To balance then these different demands seems to be Hewitt's overriding concern and he has, I think, achieved this by concentrating his imaginative energies upon that theme I referred to earlier in relation to 'The Colony'. For Hewitt has founded a myth within which these conflicts between art and morality, imaginative release and self-restraint, roots and horizons are absorbed and transcended. This myth concerns his relationship as a Protestant or Dissenter to Ireland's past, the disputed territory of land that Hewitt metaphorically possesses through identifying with its natural beauty, the countrysides of a place 'irremediably home'. To what extent this myth has narrowed Hewitt's appeal as a poet or limited the imaginative scope of his work is open for debate. He has, however estranged from the other perceptions made of the common Irish inheritance, acknowledged the conflicting versions of history in this country and embodied these in his poetry. On occasion, Hewitt sees his own myth-making ironically, as in 'Away Match: June 1924', when recollections of his boyhood are checked: 'Idyllic the setting: the myth spoored from paper;/ our school-story values never were true'. But in the major poems like 'An Irishman in Coventry', 'The Scar', 'The Glens' and 'Clogh-Oir', Hewitt weds his personal life to 'all the past foregathered' and instructs us with that imaginative union.

Such poems, like much of his prose, has, as we know, encouraged critics to look at Hewitt's work solely in terms of regionalism. Hewitt has, indeed, at various stages drawn attention to this very issue. From the 1952 'Writing in Ulster' article published in *The Bell*, for instance, to his afterword in Judith C. Wilson's *Conor: 1881–1968*, Hewitt has discussed the viability of a regional culture and its provincial virtues but always bearing in mind the status of the creative artist, considering what other options may be open to him or her. Yet, it must be said, these options like 'exile' are of only abstract interest to Hewitt. In 'Conversations in Hungary, August, 1969' the poet finds that his country's past catches up with him as if it were his fate; his host asks

> You heard the bulletin?
> And added, with no pause for our reply;
> Riots in Northern Ireland yesterday:
> and they have sent the British Army in.

In this, one of Hewitt's more free-formed poems, the confidence of the lines, the conversational ease, are drawn up against the reality they allude to:

> we turned to history:
> the savage complications of our past;
> our luckless country where old wrongs outlast,
> in raging viruses of bigotry,
> their first infection.

and in the 'ironic zest' of his host, Hewitt poses the European experience of war as a backdrop to Ireland's violence, 'Between two factions, in religion's name':

> Your little isle, the English overran –
> our broad plain, Tartar, Hapsburg, Ottoman –
> revolts and wars uncounted – Budapest
> shows scarce one wall that's stood two hundred years.
> We build to fill the centuries' arrears.

Yet Hewitt neither despairs nor opts for the enlightened pain or wounds to which some critics 'attach a very high degree of spiritual prestige' (Lionel Trilling's phrase). Instead, as he says, 'he mourns for his mannerly verses/That had left so much unsaid' ('A Local Poet').

IV

Much is always left unsaid. Poets, as we know, can only ever write the kind of poems they alone write. In his contribution to the *Fortnight* Supplement on John Hewitt (July–August 1989), Terence Brown has accurately identified an area in John Hewitt's writing that was not sufficiently explored: '[Hewitt] established a certain range of tones and poetic manners early on and although his work accumulated impressively it did not seem to deepen or change in any fundamental way. But in [his poem] 'Man Fish and Bird' one senses another dimension to this poet's imagination, his shadow'.

It seemed as if that other dimension led to those 'secret labyrinths and mazes', of the 'dream-drenched man' which in his poem to William Conor, Hewitt dismissed as an indulgence, if you will: the perceptions of license and abandonment which Hewitt was chary of and mostly avoided in his poetry for a sharper, ~~more~~ publicly accessible verse. It is here too that John Hewitt strikes me as being an important, *the* important, bridge between poet and audience. With time I am sure the proper dimension of his work will be weighted by the necessary checks and balances of literary criticism. Be that as it may, Hewitt's legacy is in his poems, not in the polemical awareness he sought to find in response to the political questions the sorry state of Northern Ireland provoked. If this legacy did not include an opening-up to other literary traditions and horizons (European and otherwise) it has established a *moral* context for younger writers to honour. I think this is the personal presence that John Hewitt handed on and it is visible in the persistence and graciousness of Michael Longley as well as in the local researches of Frank Ormsby. Hewitt also rebukes those who would insist (or more cunningly, assume) that Protestants have in some way to prove their Irishness. The grim spectacle that unfolds of Aran-jumpered and cacophonous bodhran-players anxiously drowning their Identity-Crises is best left well enough alone.

For me, ultimately (and selfishly), John Hewitt's greatest, and simplest, contribution has been to reassert the viability of actually having 'roots' in a Belfast Protestant background that will not necessarily lead to the stranglehold of bigotry, or half-baked and ludicrously gentrified 'Anglo' self-images. A chip off the old block of Protestant 'inarticulateness' was not a tautology in terms but the kind of reality from which (given the desired artistic resources) poems and plays and novels could come, if not *should* come, since Hewitt always resisted the imperative view that poetry could be written to order.

John Hewitt also reminds us of the primacy of politics in a divided culture having the responsibility to 'solve' its problems. He was an activist in this sense. Literature cannot take up that burden but can offer itself instead as something which, to an exhausted and frustrated people, overcomes those problems momentarily and provides a kind of new idiom, an imaginative space. For when one thinks of the enormous problems faced by a writer like Nadine Gordimer in South Africa, or the decay and collapse of their language which German writers such as Gunther Grass and Heinrich Boll experienced in the years after the Second World War, it makes one wonder how, in the infinitely less oppressed, yet paramilitarised, atmosphere of Ireland today, we have not – the writers, readers and teachers of literature – had a greater influence on the predicted course of events in our own country over the last two decades. (Where is the Irish version of Charter 88, for instance; is there no need for one?). Perhaps, unlike John Hewitt, we are not speaking the same language any more; or our priorities have become estranged from one another. My own feeling, for what it is worth, is that things are changing, for the better, slowly and often all too painfully, that an opening out is taking place throughout the island. We should be engaged by these developments as much as by the old wounds.

Cultural debate such as that which John Hewitt to a large degree initiated can well anticipate or even inspire political action, as Yeats well knew. But it cannot substitute the terrible need that we face in Ireland for political action. It is well worth our writers reminding themselves of this fact when they talk about their work or allow their work to be spoken of in terms of risk, crisis and so on. Poetry in Ireland is mostly an accepted form of the tradition and most poets in Ireland voice ideas and beliefs totally at one with official cultural orthodoxies. Consequently, the forum that cultural discussion provides is always, and can only be, an alternative one, that must fail unless the civic space of political acts and responsibilities is made publicly available and accessible in institutional form. There is no way around this. What has happened over the last number of years in the North is that, in keeping with experience in England, this space has shrunk to little fragments. In Ireland these are fragments of different historical nations – English, Scottish and Irish, with other floating sects and religious residues like my own, French Huguenots. While elevated above these we have been asked to subscribe to one of the other stereotypical images of 'Ireland' or 'England' without any real purchase on what such images actually mean, in economic, social or cultural terms, to the people involved.

All this is, of course, sociological, and why should a poet or literary critic be concerned with it, when it will be thrown back in his or her face by the experts as unscientific or speculative? Yet we must remember that public prominence is often given to writers in Ireland (and Irish writers abroad) on the basis of these very contexts and not primarily on the nature and quality of their writing. Try talking to a foreign radio interviewer about poetic diction and see how far it will take you!

I think, however, it is necessary for us, on another level, to disengage the creative and critical preoccupation with an imagined place called 'Ulster' from, on the one hand, the necessary economic, legal and moral demands of justice, and, on the other, the experience of a people deemed by history to be oppressors, as the Protestants of this part of Ireland are cast worldwide. That task is the sack that Lundy reputedly carried out with his bag of matches. It has very little in common with the calculators of Identity Crises who purvey ready-made answers and anxieties, but it remained, I believe, an obsessive burden that John Hewitt sought, with enlightenment and modesty, to deliver his community from. In his witty contribution to a recent issue of *The Irish Review*, Bernard Crick has the following useful piece of advice:

> In Northern Ireland most people are, in fact, torn in two directions: 'torn', that is, while their political leaders will not recognise that people can, with dignity, face in two directions culturally at once, and refuse to invent political institutions to match. 'No man is an island': nor are nations as intermingled as ours. We have not been able to be one people, but nor can we ever be fully independent of each other, even politically. We are all inter-dependent. Irish, Scottish and Welsh intellectuals have long complained about Anglicisation. But there is less study or appreciation of how much whichever culture one starts with is itself so much a product of the others, and probably the richer for it. Not only intellectuals can live in, or in and out of, two or more cultures. The migrant poor have done it for centuries.[8]

I think such bi- or tri- location is the only decent way we can cope with the introverted divisions that are so deeply entrenched in northern society and their feedlines into and back out of the Republic and Britain. This means, or at least I am proposing it to mean, the creation of a new 'we', something along the lines of what the rigorous Neal Ascherson implies when, in *Games with Shadows* (1988), he states:

> The Irish Declaration of Independence begins: 'In the Name of God and of the dead generations . . .' Do not let the dead bind the living, for all the love and respect you have for them. That has been an Irish problem, and it remains the sickness of the English, so lost in the contemplation of 'heritage' and pageant spectacle that they have no sight of their own national condition. To use the word 'we' in Scotland is to refer to 'us now'; to we who exist now and not then. Nationalism is innovation, using selected fragments of the past to build a new house.[9]

Like John Hewitt's researches in trying to understand his own place and its connections with the rest of Ireland and Scotland, it is essential for us to learn this lesson from him, or else we will endlessly repeat ourselves in a language and manner no one outside such walls as these will really be interested enough to care about. It was with that selfless commitment in mind that John Hewitt wrote his poems and essays; against the grain a lot of the time and also, I think, against the wrong kind of piety. As he wrote in 'Ars Poetica':

> So, be the poet. Let him till his years
> follow the laws of language, feeling, thought,
> that out of his close labour there be wrought
> good sustenance for other hearts than his.
> If no one begs it, let him shed no tears,
> five or five thousand – none will come amiss.

CHAPTER 17

Assertors and Protesters: John Hewitt as Literary Historian

by

Patricia Craig

John Hewitt always had a strong sense of the riches in the Northern Irish literary tradition, not only in the work of mainstream writers like the novelist William Carleton and the poets Samuel Ferguson and William Allingham, but in all sorts of odd corners and byways. No one else, for example, was taking any interest in the dialect poets of the eighteenth and nineteenth centuries when Hewitt turned his attention to them and their work, first of all in his M.A. thesis written in 1951, and later in the collection *Rhyming Weavers* which he edited for the Blackstaff Press.

From about the middle of the eighteenth century, in Northern Ireland, weaver-poets and others were starting to turn out works (printed locally and sold by subscription) in a dialect akin to Lowland Scots. These working-class writers, of Planter stock, were cut off from their Irish-speaking compatriots, and they had no sense of being in competition with those authors to whom it came naturally to write in standard English. Their audience consisted of people like themselves, although it is true that their verse had an incidental appeal for the educated classes attuned to rural idiom through the poems of Robert Burns. The weavers, to begin with, at any rate, subscribed to an idea that they were well-adjusted socially, not resentful of their low status or inclined to grouse about living conditions:

> In Moneyslan his little hame is,
> A wattled cottage – an' his name is
> HUGH PORTER,

wrote one of them. However, by the end of the eighteenth century, with book clubs and reading societies established in many Presbyterian townlands, and then attacked by the yeomanry on account of their supposed radical bias, dialect verse was about to become a medium for social criticism – first in response to the prevailing republican spirit and the impending insurrection of 1798, and later in opposition to the effects of the industrial revolution. As late as 1848, John Hewitt reminds us, David Herbison of Dunclug has a poem about an 'auld wife' looking back with nostalgia to the small-scale, orderly industrial arrangements of the previous century:

> The days are past when folk like me
> Could earn their bread,
> My auld wheel now sits silently
> Aboon the bed.

Such verses, Hewitt says, 'if seldom of high literary value', 'remain . . . the best, and often the only record of important aspects of our social history' – and it is largely due to his efforts that they have come back into circulation, after having been unobtainable for many years.

Hewitt has a story about how, when he submitted his M.A. dissertation on Ulster poets between 1800 and 1870, one member of the examining board, being unable to find any trace of the authors under consideration in the university library, began to wonder if Hewitt had invented the lot of them – until a visit to the Linen Hall Library put him right. There, sure enough, he found what he was looking for: a lot of little books, stitched paper or in boards, with titles like *Poetical Attempts by Hugh Porter, a County of Down Weaver*, and *Midnight Musings: or, Thoughts from the Loom, by David Herbison*.

The weaver-poets' uprightness and sturdy independence of outlook were admired by John Hewitt, and it also pleased him that each was associated with a particular locality – Campbell of Ballynure, Herbison of Dunclug, and so on. One of the most prominent among them was James Orr of Ballycarry (1770–1816), who took part in the United Irish uprising of 1798, and wrote a poem, 'Donegore Hill', about this experience. In a very sarcastic tone indeed the poem denounces the behaviour of certain would-be rebels who did not acquit themselves at all well, when it came to the bit. Some of them preferred to skulk at home instead of taking up their pikes like men and marching on Antrim. Of those that started, a good many contrived to fall out along the way; while others, though they stuck it out as far as the field of battle, misliked the look of General Nugent's red-coats when they got there, and hastily removed themselves from the danger-zone:

The Camp's brak up. O'er braes, an' bogs,
The patriots seek their sections;
Arms, ammunition, bread-bags, brogues,
Lie skailed in a' directions;
Ane half, alas, wad fear'd to face
Auld fogies, faps or women;
Though strong, untried, they swore in pride,
'Moilie wad dunch the yeomen',
Some wiss'd for day.

Once they reached home, the good sense of these defectors was applauded by their wives:

'Guid God'. Is't you? fair fa'ye'.–
'Twas wise, though fools may ca't no' brave,
To rin or e'er they saw ye.'–

'Donegore Hill', which runs to 14 verses, gives an unusually robust and disabused account of the Battle of Antrim and a few of the events surrounding it, and makes salutary reading in comparison with all the popular songs and ballads of '98 which stress the idealism and heroism of the undertaking. Orr, who was on the spot, cut a better figure himself than the people in his poem, by all accounts, and his gibes are understandable: such wholesale skedaddling was not a suitable ingredient of the unimpeachable enterprise. Still, Northern heroes of '98 were not lacking, the most notable among them being Henry Joy McCracken, with whom Orr went on the run after the defeat at Antrim. Also on the run at the same time was James, or Jemmy, Hope, a weaver from Templepatrick (and one of John Hewitt's adopted ancestors), who had organized an adroit withdrawal of his troops in the face of Colonel Clavering, and escaped with his men to join McCracken at the rallying point on Donegore Hill. Jemmy Hope, political thinker and reluctant United Irishman, was one of John Hewitt's 'brave old pre-Marx Marxists of Ireland', to use the term he coined for these early socialists and radicals. In George A. Birmingham's novel *The Northern Iron*, which was published in 1903, Hope and the fictional Lord Dunseveric are presented as complementary symbols of courage and integrity, artisan and aristocrat standing respectively for whatever is best in the systems of republicanism and hereditary government.

In 1796, the embryo Linen Hall Library in Belfast had lost its librarian Thomas Russell in the government drive to root out radicals. Russell, transported to Dublin and subsequently banished, was out of action for the chief event of the era, the foolhardy Rebellion. Undeterred by the way things had fallen out for the '98 leaders, including his friend McCracken who was hanged in Belfast, Russell came secretly to Ireland as soon as he could, still advocating insurgency, and thereby added himself to the company of those who died for their beliefs. He was hanged at Downpatrick Gaol in 1803, after a failed attempt to rally the North in support of Robert Emmett's Dublin rising. One hundred and fifteen years later, the wife of a Presbyterian solicitor from Lisburn, Florence M. Wilson, recreated the events of the period in a dialect poem – very highly thought of by John Hewitt – putting her vivid words into the mouth of a stalwart Co. Down farmer, into whose townland, 'on a night of snow, rode a man from God-knows-where'. The Man from God–

knows-where turns out to be Thomas Russell, the ex-librarian, on one of his seditionist excursions, and the label has stuck to him ever since. This is how the poem ends:

> . . . Then he bowed his head to the swinging rope,
> Whiles I said, 'Please God' to his dying hope,
> And 'Amen' to his dying prayer,
> That the Wrong would cease, and the Right prevail
> For the man that they hanged at Downpatrick Gaol
> Was the MAN FROM GOD-KNOWS-WHERE'.

What we learn from Florence Wilson's poem is that Ulster Presbyterians, as late as 1918, had no wish to repudiate their republican past: it was, on the contrary, something to take pride in, since it represented a right action at a particular time, when circumstances suggested no other course consistent with integrity. This was the historical view. At the time in which the poem is set, some adaptation to altered circumstances was indicated, in particular the egregious circumstance of union with England, which came about in 1800–1801.

The weaver-poet James Orr, for example, never relinquished his hopes for a true democracy in Ireland, but after 1798, when he had witnessed the inadequacy of republicanism in action, he attached these hopes to a different system: reformist rather than revolutionary. Orr, as an ex-rebel, one-time contributor to the radical newspaper the *Northern Star* and ultimate pragmatist, exemplifies the attitudes prevailing one after the other among the Presbyterians of the North. At one moment, it seemed, republicanism was an impeccable doctrine; and the next it was not. It was impeccable while it thrived in opposition to misgovernment, but not when it started to resemble a disruptive force. What else? Anti-sectarianism, which involved deploring the treatment of Catholics, looked as though it might not weather an absence of democratic principles among Catholics themselves, when this absence became apparent at the height of the emancipation struggle. That, however, was not until the 1820s – and James Orr, up until his death in 1816, remained on the side of the emancipationists. So too did Dr William Drennan, another of John Hewitt's heroes, and another lifelong upholder of the principle of tolerance. (Hewitt was fond of quoting Dr Drennan's modest couplet about himself: 'Man of taste, more than talent, not learned, though of letters,/His creed without claws, and his faith without fetters'.)

Drennan, in a verse review for the *Belfast Monthly Magazine*, in 1811, of a long topographical poem, 'The Giant's Causeway', by the Revd William Hamilton Drummond, delivered this unabashed injunction to his readers – 'Avaunt his verses be they e'er so fine,/Who for the Catholics – REFUSED TO SIGN!' The cause of Dr Drennan's outrage was a past refusal by Drummond to add his name to a petition in support of Catholic Emancipation. Even at the height of the reformatory clamour in Belfast, there were Presbyterian ministers who considered too much tolerance a bad thing, leading, as it might well do, to the triumph of disaffection.

Contemplating the recent Act of Union puts the Revd Hamilton Drummond in a mood of rather obtuse satisfaction. In 'The Giant's Causeway' we read:

> No more fell faction hurls her flaming brand,
> But smiling concord waves her olive wand,
> From east to west see equal rights prevail,
> And Erin's seas are now Brittania's pale.
> One king, one sceptre, rules the sister isles
> In Union's flowery wreaths blithe Erin smiles . . .

So it goes on. It is no wonder that the author's complacency got up the nose of an old Irish separatist like Dr Drennan. Since Drummond valued the English connection so highly, we need not be surprised to find his historical references falling within the tradition of Unionist orthodoxy: 'Boyne foams with blood – a coward monarch flies,/War sheaths his gory blade – Rebellion dies'. As a comment on the Orange victory of 1690, this has less emotional appeal than the jubilant popular songs which commemorate the event. In expressing an aversion to 'rebellion', though, it was topical; such opinions kept being interpolated into the work of loyalist authors of the period. The Revd Samuel Burdy, for example, in his topographical poem of 1802, 'Ardglass; or, the Ruined Castles', suddenly breaks into a panegyric on Queen Elizabeth I, in which we find the downhearted observation: 'Yet all the glories that adorn'd her throne,/Ne'er moved the rebel bosom of Tyrone . . .'. It's likely that both authors had in mind a more recent rebellion than those actually cited. At this reactionary moment, armed insurrection held little appeal for anyone, and none at all for those of conservative or religious temperament.

John Hewitt, with his keen eye for oddities, had considerable affection for at least two works by the Revd Samuel Burdy, the rector of Kilclief parish in Co. Down. One of these, 'Ardglass', is a very long poem into which everything is crammed, historical allusion, orthodox sentiments, down-to-earth observations; there are long descriptive passages full of fancy phrases, 'flowery pastures', 'verdant hill', 'woody vale' and so forth, and it is rather startling, in the middle of this kind of thing, to come on something like the sudden criticism of eating habits on the Isle of Man which bursts out of Burdy:

> Herring's the food of Mona's greedy sons,
> Who eat them up as fast as butter'd buns.

The Revd Burdy was attached for a time to the literary circle surrounding Bishop Percy at Dromore (Percy, compiler of the famous *Reliques of Ancient British Poetry*, had come to Ireland in 1782) – however, he proceeded to make a fool of himself over Bishop Percy's daughter, of whom he wrote with disarming triteness:

> Such pleasing sweetness, such a graceful air,
> Such sense as seldom happens to the fair

and the bishop was not pleased. Burdy was excluded from the Dromore circle for a time. He remained unmarried.

So did the Revd Philip Skelton, subject of the other work by Burdy that attracted the attention of John Hewitt. Burdy's *Life of Skelton*, published in 1792, is a book to which Hewitt was for ever directing the attention of research students and others curious about conditions in the North of Ireland in the eighteenth century. Skelton, who died in 1787, was a very eccentric clergyman who lived for 55 years in remote parishes of Monaghan, Fermanagh, Tyrone and Donegal – so remote were they, indeed, that at one period the unfortunate cleric was obliged to make a seven-mile journey on horseback in order to find 'a person of common sense to converse with'. Skelton (his biographer tell us) was given to dramatic acts of charity, once whipping off his shirt in the roadway and tearing it in strips to bandage a burnt child. He twice sold his library 'to feed the poor', buying oatmeal with the proceeds and distributing it to supplement the usual famine diet of boiled weeds and blood stolen from cows. From the Burdy biography, we gain an impression of considerable straits in the Ulster countryside.

Skelton, along with other clergymen at the time, kept up a campaign against drunkenness, to very little effect. Food was hard to come by, but drink was plentiful, 'the private stills in the parish of Pettigo being at that time innumerable', as Burdy put it. (An English traveller, E. Wakefield, who visited Ulster towards the end of the eighteenth century, likewise found the mountains of the north-west positively crammed with illicit stills). Sermons like the one delivered by Skelton under the title, 'Wo to the Drunkard', did not halt the practice, any more than the later verses on behalf of the temperance movement which certain high-minded authors felt obliged to turn out – Dr Drennan's 'The Worm of the Still', for example, and a heart-rending effort about a child called Jacky, 'the hero of the spelling class', who met a bad end at the hands of a drunk. Skelton had better luck as an evangelist, gaining quite a few recruits for Protestantism among the Catholics in his parishes, including one Anne Devlin whose obdurate family 'strove by all harsh means to bring her back to popery'. We are reminded that the earliest printed book in the Irish language was a bible, to be used for prosletyzing purposes. Recanters, being comparatively rare, were especially prized by the faction that acquired them.

Among Skelton's interests were the habits of caterpillars and the state of his soul; he used to get people out of bed in the middle of the night to pray for his salvation, which probably did not make him popular with any neighbours he happened to have. He also suffered from what Burdy calls 'the hips' – an extreme form of hypochondria. Death was constantly on his mind – a person doing him a favour might expect to receive, as a token of gratitude, a piece of fine linen to be used as a winding-sheet. He feared that marriage would interfere with his calling, and therefore ate nothing but vegetables for two years, to keep his passions down; however, on holiday in the Mourne Mountains, he still had sufficient energy to run up the side of turf-stacks, Burdy tells us, 'like a cat, without stopping till he came to the top, which amazed everyone present'. He was always amazing people. At the age of fifty he claimed to be a virgin, and made an announcement to this effect at a social gathering, whereupon one outspoken old lady told him plainly that she did not believe him.

So – from Burdy, we get a picture of an agile, highly-strung celibate naturalist, of forceful character and firm faith, a sufferer from night fears, a scaler of turf-stacks, a dispenser of oatmeal and winding-sheets, always craving sensible conversation while Irish fecklessness found innumerable outlets around him. The combined peculiarities of author and subject – one artless, and the other exceptionally full-hearted – make this a most engaging work indeed. Another, equally engaging and well-known to John Hewitt, is what is probably the first historical novel to come out of Ireland – *O'Halloran, or, The Insurgent Chief*, by James McHenry. The date of this remarkable book is 1820, and it was written, according to the author's preface, to fulfil a condition laid down by a literary aunt, in her will: if he failed to produce a novel of Ulster life within three years, the clause went, her money would go elsewhere. So he got down to it promptly, and O'Halloran is the result.

Things never improved throughout the remainder of the nineteenth century, as far as realism in the Ulster historical novel is concerned. What do we have? A truly terrible piece of writing called *The Irish Legend of McDonnell and the Norman de Burgos*, by Archibald McSparran; Sir Samuel Keightley's *The Pikemen* – subtitled '*A Romance of the Ards of Down*' – which is notable for conveying the mood in the country just before the '98 Rebellion in the following phrase: 'All Down was up'; and W.G. Lyttle's *Betsy Gray; or, Hearts of Down*, a book very widely read in its day – the 1890s about a girl popularly supposed to have taken part in the Battle of Ballynahinch, fighting alongside her brother and sweetheart in the most dashing manner. It is a good story: never mind if the realistic view transforms this character into a camp follower at the rebels' base on Ednavady Hill. What's beyond dispute is that, in the aftermath of the battle, Betsy Gray, her brother George and William Boal were accosted by mounted yeomen and shot dead in the townland of Ballycreen. According to Lyttle, Willie Boal, Betsy's lover, was the first to die. The brave girl's hand is no sooner raised to remonstrate with the murderers of Willie Boal than it's lost to her for ever – 'smote off' is the expression resorted to. Things then get worse for Betsy:

He drew a pistol from his belt,
And shot poor Betsy in the eye;
She sank upon the heathery mound,
And died without a sob or sigh.

Handless and eyeless – it is not a dignified exit. John Hewitt was greatly entertained by innocent verse of this kind, and indeed of all other kinds – I think as much as anything he admired the aplomb of authors who had the gall to write atrociously, and let the results get into print. Throughout the nineteenth century we find a cult of death and gloom, which reached some kind of apex in the poems of a morbid pair who wrote under the pen-names of Rose and de Rupe. Of the 30 original poems in the collection they brought out in 1856, 15 end with a reference to death or God or eternity or the tomb. They are all called things like 'My Grave'; 'To a Dying Girl'; 'The Children's grave'; 'The Death-Bell'; 'The Traveller to Heaven'.

The ghastly couple cannot look up at the stars without exclaiming, 'They speak to me of loving hearts, long gone from earth – ah! where?' Even childhood is evoked in graveyard imagery: 'Where shadows broad and deep/At rest are laid'. A lot of poets, especially, it must be said, women poets, seem to have got hold of the idea that it was high-minded to dwell on death – as an antidote to 'the false glory/ This world hath', as one of them put it. 'Each step that guides me to the tomb,/Promises a happier bloom,' said another. One of these death-mongers went so far as to write a poem in praise of consumption: 'O blest disease! to man in mercy given,/To steal from earth, the favourite of heaven'. The whole miserable business persisted for a very long time: we even find the much later poetess Alice Milligan announcing at one point, 'I long to die; my soul is tired of earth' – an affected sentiment in anyone, indeed, but one especially inappropriate in the case of someone who went on living for eighty-seven years.

Sometimes, with death-poetry, the pseudo-philosophical tone is abandoned in favour of the frankly gothic and gruesome, as in the following gem from a book of Christmas Rhymes for 1846:

'Great God' she cried,
'Tis he who died'.
And, through the thickn'ing gloom,
In frenzy wild
From her gentle child
She fled from room to room;
And all that night,
In wild affright,
She rav'd of a baby's tomb.

Another of John Hewitt's literary curiosities of the mid-nineteenth century is a 1,506-line poem called 'The Knitting Needle' by a Mrs

Alicia Catherine Phillott. This work actually has considerable sociological interest. It was written to commemorate the establishment of a school of knitters at Ramoan, Co. Antrim, and later at Ballymoney, in the Famine year of 1846–47. 'During that season of distress,' says Mrs Phillott in her preface to the poem, 'fine and fancy knitting prevailed to a great extent in the North of Ireland . . . And I believe that . . . the poor were saved from starvation by these means'.

The poem is written in relentlessly self-perpetuating octosyllabic couplets:

> . . . And now does women's industry,
> Active and zealous, oft supply,
> For the much-prized, regretted root,
> The means to find a substitute.
>
> . . . Daughters of England'! Yours the power
> To help us in our adverse hour;
> To patronise our merchandise
> And purchase what our hand supplies, . . .
>
> . . . Ye who are blest with means to give,
> Remember, that they knit to LIVE; . . .

'Young active females', too, could be employed as weeders and stone-pickers to encourage the growth of crops, though this type of outdoor work was probably less abundant in emotional satisfactions. The girls bent over needle points of temper'd steel were reminded, by Mrs Phillott, that George III's queen Charlotte of Mecklenburgh was in the habit of knitting her own petticoats, a fact that may or may not have afforded consolation for long hours and small pay: '. . . little of the mountain air,/Blows on that simple cotter fair'.

Mrs Phillott is an evangelical author, and she lavishes praise on an intelligent girl among her knitters who's been converted from Roman Catholicism – 'God has talent rich bestowed,/To lead her up to Heaven's high road . . .' – while another knitter, born illegitimate, pays for her parents' transgression by being lumbered with defective brains – 'Unfit', Mrs Phillott pronounces, 'her understanding or her wit/For aught but simplest workmanship . . .'. The author's own properly-grounded Protestant faith in the goodness of God never falters, even in the face of prolonged exposure to social misery and death by starvation. It's by 'God's mercy', we may note, that the potato crop eventually thrives after three consecutive years of blight.

Once Mrs Phillott gets going, there is no stopping her – among her poems, for example, we find in one instance 41 pages in praise of the holy, holy, holy Lord.

When it comes to more substantial authors – Hewitt was among the first to point out the merits of William Allingham's 'Laurence Bloomfield in Ireland', over and above the more facile verse for which Allingham is better known; he also admired Ferguson's late-nineteenth-century monologues 'in the manner of Browning', one concerning the Phoenix Park murders of 1882, the other treating the same event from a different point of view. I remember Hewitt remarking on the continuity in Irish terrorism indicated by the following passage from the second of these monologues:

> . . . a single man,
> Risking no more than his particular life,
> With fairly even chances of escape,
> Might carry half a town's destruction packed
> In greatcoat pockets or a Gladstone bag;
> Or dowdy woman drop her petticoat
> And wreck a nation's palace, and walk off
> Slim and secure . . .

Another poet in whom Hewitt saw a good deal to admire is T.C. Irwin, born in Warrenpoint, Co. Down, in 1823, and eventually succumbing to madness in Dublin, threatening to shoot his next-door neighbour, the antiquary John O'Donovan, and issuing a series of advertisements relating to cats which, he claimed, had been stolen from the back drawing room of his home. Irwin's poetry, if you read it in bulk, seems to be set in a perpetual melancholy autumnal landscape – 'Every shrub on wall and ground,/ Droops in the damp grey light'. His scene-painting is in fact extremely effective and often lyrical, as in the final section of the otherwise whimsical 'May-Day revel'.

By the turn of the century the dismal, devotional note in popular Northern Irish verse had given way to an obsession with rural charm: the paraphernalia of country living had begun to be used to provide an easy stimulus for the imagination. The recurrent motifs – the heathery hill, the spinning wheel, the milk churn, the misty glen, the little green linnet, the black, black wind from Northern hills – were handled with varying degrees of expertise by many, many poets, all of them familiar to John Hewitt. Joseph Campbell is head and shoulders above all the rest of them, but one or two, like Alice Milligan and 'Ethna Carbery', turned out the odd memorable verse.

Hewitt, without stopping to think, could detail the Northern exponents of every Irish mode from mist to mysticism – as far as the latter was concerned, he took some interest in a writer called James H. Cousins, a working-class Belfast Protestant whose spiritual quest took him first to Dublin and then to India, where he lived for many years. Cousins became a theosophist, a vegetarian and a feminist, and developed an ardent literary manner to accommodate the high tone of his convictions. He does not seem to have been very full-blooded: 'What lost I to prefer/Soul's touch to body's cries . . .?' he asks rhetorically at one point in his poetry, mystical celibacy being one of the fashions of the day.

'Richard Rowley' the Belfast businessman who impersonated some of his own workers in his verses; W.F. Marshall the Tyrone poet well-known for a single effort written in a mood of comic dejection, 'Me An' My Da'; Alexander Irvine of the 'bogus-brogue'; Lynn Doyle of the intolerable facetiousness; innumerable minor poets like Helen Lanyon, Cahir Healey and Cathal O'Byrne, John Lyle Donaghy, R.D.N. Wilson, Padraig Gregory, Thomas Carnduff, the shipyard poet; May Morton; Siobhan Ni Luain . . . John Hewitt would have had something good to say about all of these, though of course, in literary terms, some are more deserving of commendation than others. He took a certain amount of pride in the distinctiveness of the Northern Irish literary tradition, and that, as far as he was concerned, meant cherishing its idiosyncratic authors, those like the famous Amanda McKittrick Ros who amused him greatly, along with others – I suppose Louis MacNeice is the most obvious example – who became absorbed into the mainstream of English literature. Hewitt was always ready to praise any author who had made an impact in one way or another – but he was at the same time very selective when it came to the question of those towards whom he felt a temperamental affinity.

In an essay entitled 'The Bitter Gourd', (1945) Hewitt made the statement that a writer must have ancestors – 'Not just of the blood, but of the emotions, of the quality and slant of mind' – and for his own part, he allied himself with people like the weaver-

poets of Down and Antrim, like James Hope, Dr Drennan, Mary Ann McCracken, and, outside Ireland altogether, with those like Blake, Paine, Cobbett, John Ball, the Diggers, the Levellers, the Chartists, William Morris – socialists, reformers, people of strong views, 'the assertors, the protesters', as he put it himself.

Among his own contemporaries, Hewitt had an especial regard for MacNeice and W.R. Rodgers, for Peadar O'Donnell, Michael

McLaverty, Sam Hanna Bell, John Boyd, Joseph Tomelty – and for the Armagh author of a single novel, published in 1948 – John O'Connor, whose *Come Day, Go Day* lets us in on some facets of spirited working-class life in the 1920s. John Hewitt had the entire history of Northern Irish literature at his fingertips; I have only indicated a fraction of the works that pleased him, for one reason or another. John Hewitt always stressed the fact that Northern Irish writing, by and large, embodies an egalitarian tradition – or at least, when it lapses into something else, keeps its sectarianism colourful rather than malevolent. As George Russell – AE – an Ulsterman from Lurgan, challenged his readers and Hewitt quoted: 'Name, if you can, a single Unionist writer of genius'.

CHAPTER 18

John Hewitt and his Womenfolk

by

Geraldine Watts

Out of the one hundred and seven autobiographical sonnets in John Hewitt's *Kites in Spring* (1980), admittedly dealing largely with his childhood, only one mentions his future wife, Roberta, and twelve others deal with women alone, not all relations. The vast majority of the sonnets deal with stories about himself and his male relatives. To Robert Hewitt, his father, John Hewitt dedicated one long poem,' The Lonely Heart' in *Freehold* (1986) while four poems record the father's death. Aunts are mentioned as the wives of uncles; some half-dozen poems mention Roberta Hewitt by name and the 'Sonnets for Roberta, 1954' (*The Rain Dance*, 1978) deal with their relationship in that critical year.

Not a lot to write about in an essay given over to John Hewitt's womenfolk, some might say. Indeed I am going to suggest in what follows some reasons for this absence of women and love poetry in Hewitt's work by first looking at his poem, 'Hesitant Memorial', from his last volume, *Freehold*. It is a very 'hesitant memorial' to an early love which, after a conventional courtship and engagement came to nothing and has left now only regret, mild curiosity and indifference about the death of the once beloved. Even after fifty years absence 'vague indifference' seems a bit bloodless. The woman is left at the hearthside and he is involved in the wider world of thought and action. Of course the expected marriage did not take place and there seems to have been a mutual feeling that what they felt for one another was not love but affection. The break 'incised no scar' so here is no romantic poet heart-broken by an early love gone wrong. What we have rather is the scientific analysis of his degree of feeling and an honest appraisal of the situation. In 'Below the Mournes in May' Hewitt wrote:

the nature poet
has no easy prosody for
class or property relationships
for the social dialectic.

perhaps he should have added 'for deep-felt emotion'. In 'Hesitant Memorial' there was no deep felt emotion so there was no need to look for a way of expressing it. The lack of feeling in this one poem is openly acknowledged. In 'Retreaded rhymes' he wrote:

Henceforth my slow wits I must only spend
to phrase affection or to mourn a friend;
to state the convolutions of my thought
in quiet verse deliberately wrought,
leaving the coloured crags' romantic line
for humbler acre fairly mapped as mine;
stranger to passion, never strongly moved
by those emotions use has not approved;

I will look later at those poems which do deal with deep feeling and see that while they may lack the 'coloured crag's romantic line' the 'humbler acre' is mapped with such care that it has become part of himself and cannot be viewed from outside like his early love affair. Similiarly, Hewitt's relationship with his family, particularly his father is an intense, lifelong preoccupation of the poet. As a child Hewitt loved and admired his father, as 'A Holy Place' (*Kites in Spring*) clearly shows:

I loved to watch him shave, his splayed thumb pressed
on chin upraised, to let the stropped steel skim
the fluffed froth off. I felt I could not rest
till, one day, I should share this rite with him;
such skill, such peril, such unerring grace.
This was my daily vigil none might share;
that morning bathroom was a holy place:
one celebrant, one breathless worshipper.

This finished, he'd begin a lesser rite
scrubbing my face, my neck, my hands, my knees,
wholly engaging me, in sheer delight
my stance entranced by some repeated spell
from Aesop, from Lamb's Shakespeare, Kingsley's Greece
Gould's Book of Moral Lessons, William Tell.

The poem captures beautifully the child's feeling for his father. The language is the language of religion as they share the rite of shaving, keeping vigil, one celebrant, one worshipper, and it is easy to see the loving but respectful attitude of the child with the father at once parent, teacher and priest. Many other poems in *Kites in Spring* testify to the relationship between father and son during childhood. Later he came to identify with him in looks and ways:

And in the looking glass
appear and disappear
my lonely father's face
the coarser face I wear,

as he wrote in 'My own and not my own' and in 'The Modelled Head'

When I turned it round to observe the profile
it brought my father's face at once to mind.

When I visited John Hewitt in Stockman's Lane, Belfast, the picture which held a central place on his wall was a drawing of his father. The adjective 'lonely' is the one he applies frequently to his father. 'The Lonely Heart' is the title of his longest poem to him and is one he uses often of himself. Of his father's achievements he wrote in *Freehold*

He wrought hard and unequivocally stood
for quality of life and brotherhood
without defiance, in all charity
towards those who in themselves were not yet free.

These were words which could equally well have been written of himself. A person to look up to, a teacher, a friend to love and admire and later to see himself in – these pictures of his father stand out clearly from the lines of the poetry and give him a central place in the poet's life.

John Hewitt's search for his own place and the identity of the Northern Irish dissenter may have coloured his attitude to his relations causing him to place greater emphasis on those whose name he bore. Of his grandfather Hewitt he wrote how he expanded the past for him as a child by telling him:

How in those Planter lands
our name is hearth rolled, Generation, place,
he gave you foothold in the human race.

None of his womenfolk could get close to him in this way.

Consider, for instance, his references to his mother. Although four poems deal specifically with his father's death in hospital we do not know how Mrs Hewitt died. In a poem entitled 'My widowed mother' he tells how she had to be taken to a mental home ten years after her husband's death. On the way to the home her description of a new built church as 'well-behaved' brings back to the poet what he had always admired in her–

> a shrewd remark, scant evidence at all
> her envied choice of words had gone astray
> which since my childhood held my wits enslaved.

The use of the word 'widow' twice in the poem and title states her position in John Hewitt's hierarchy of values – his father's wife first, then his mother.

In '*Kites in Spring*' he gives us a description of her

> a little woman, when I knew her, stout,
> as small but plumper than her sisters were,
> before she married, slight with hip length hair,
> feet firmly planted, stepping neatly out,
> propelled her nimble movement everywhere.
> Her features comely, her complexion fine,
> her ankles, when I glimpsed them, slim as mine,
> she chose her costumes, hats, gloves, scarves with care.

This is as much of a physical description as Hewitt gives of anyone. For their relationship we look to the poem 'E.H. 1877–1958'

> She was my harbour, larder and my lexicon
> I ran to her for shelter.
> She filled my plate with food
> I learnt my letters from the tins
> She lifted from the shelf
> These twenty letters hint my debt.

In other words, his mother provided the basic necessities for his life – she looked after him, fed him and taught him his letters. Without this basic security he could not have lived as 'a happy boy' and grown into the man he became. The bond between them was deep and long lasting although he never uses the word 'love' or describes their attachment in emotional terms. She was loved and valued as a basis for his whole life. But love is never accepted just at face value, as a blind emotion. Like all Hewitt's feelings it has to be explained in terms of rational usefulness – harbour, larder, lexicon – all useful things physically and mentally. His sister Eileen was 'half roads to mother' a companion and protector 'and with the years her uses multiplied': 'I loved her always, there ahead of me' he wrote, in the October sonnets, 'She loved her brother, equally would greet/When he announced it, some small victory/or laboured sullen under a defeat'.

Only when writing of her last illness and death does the depth of his feeling show through in 'On choosing some verses for my sister's cremation', when he responds to her request for a poem she would understand to be read at her funeral.

> I nodded my assent, my punished thought
> a chill black wind, a storm of screaming birds,
> not at that instant, to be quelled or caught
> in any net of comfortable words.

For once the stormy emotions overcome him and can only later be translated into 'comfortable words'. The writing of the poem for his sister does not so much express emotion as tame it and make it safe to live with. The restraint in feeling in Hewitt's poetry therefore does not rise from a lack of emotion but from the need to manage and subdue it to make life liveable. John Hewitt is no nineteenth century romantic who explores every nuance of feeling and bleeds upon the thorns of life. Rather he is a true son of a dissenting industrial community. Everything and everybody works and is useful and is valued for that usefulness as well as for sentiment – his sister 'shared what love and nurture both demand'. Love is there but overlaid with the rational demands of his upbringing. Already we see how his attitude to his mother and his sister casts them in the role of basic providers of the mental and physical necessities of life, background workers to the stage show which has himself and his father as the principal actors.

None of these is described in any physical detail, his mother was small and plump; his father had a moustache and wore pince-nez: but whether he was dark or fair, tall or thin we are not told and we are given no information at all about his sister Eileen's appearance. This seems to me rather odd for a man who devoted so much of his life to the visual arts. We know a good deal about what his family did, how they thought, about their turn of phrase and whether they were conventional or unconventional. So although we know how they might greet us if we met them in the street, we would not recognise them sufficiently to provoke any such response. Our knowledge of them is cerebral not physical.

When we come to Mrs Roberta Hewitt we are a little better off:

In brilliant colours dressed, her wide black brows
above her small pale face, with kerchief tied.
I thought of her as lovely as a rose,

he wrote of her in '*Kites in Spring*' and again he describes her as 'vivid being' laughing with him as they returned from a holiday in the Soviet Union.

'For Roberta in the Garden' and 'The Hedgehog' show his wife's mental attributes: private, protected by spines, timid and shy, making an untamed life of its own in the cultivated garden – a hedgehog and a person. In both poems and 'Last Summer, for Roberta' with the sonnets for Roberta, the only poems specifically dedicated to his wife, Hewitt pictures her as belonging to 'life's bright process' happiest in the garden, accepting the beauty of the flowers and the fact that they will fade and die. The brightness and love of gardening are Roberta's alone. The shyness and retreat into privacy belong to both of them. So too is the identification with the untamed and unpredicted presence of the hedgehog who lives his life on the edges of mankind. In both John and Roberta Hewitt there is an element which kept them separate from the organised mainstream life of their time and place, to pursue their own course independently. In Hewitt's case this is best exemplified by the poem 'A Mobile Mollusc' and in Roberta's by 'Hedgehog'. Hewitt describes himself as a freemoving shellfish moving through the water, feeding where he will and not heeding signals 'from Rome, Moscow, Peking or anywhere'. The mollusc is protected by its shell, the hedgehog by its spines from intrusions into their privacy. Neither allow any degree of intimacy with fellow-dwellers on land or sea. John Hewitt, the poet, protects himself by his 'net of words' from revealing more than he chooses of himself and his feelings.

It would be easy at this point to take up a feminist stance and dismiss Hewitt as totally chauvinist in his attitude since it would seem that the women in his life were valued mainly for those qualities which were useful to him or which echoed his own. The five 'Sonnets for Roberta (1954)' however change this view fundamentally. The date 1954 appears in the title but these poems were not published until after her death in the collection, *The Rain Dance* (1978). They were obviously written at a time when the poet felt that his marriage was under strain but he could not then bring himself to make his intimate feelings known to the public. The sestet begins:

Then you had lived as other women live,
warmed by a touch, responsive to a glance,
glad to endure, so that endurance give
the right to share each changing circumstance
and this form of living would have come about,
if I had given you that love and care.

What a strange view of the role of woman for a liberal thinker to have taken up even thirty years ago. It creates a picture of women's lives only having meaning when responsive to a man's love. When looked at in the context of the whole sequence of five poems the poet's intention becomes clearer and the poems stand as a searching detailed examination of the relationship of husband and wife at a difficult period after twenty years of marriage. It was in 1953 that John Hewitt had been turned down for the directorship of the Museum and Art Gallery, a decision which plunged him into a period of depression. So comparative failure in his profession was accompanied by what we can interpret as a temporary failure in human relationships. These poems, then, represent the poet's searching through his own psyche to explain his own inability to handle emotion and to ask for help from his wife as the stronger partner in the marriage. Far from condescending to her, he is looking to her to provide the strength to rebuild their equal partnership. If one looks at the five sonnets in order certain common themes and images become clear.

In sonnet one, for instance, the tone is set by laying the blame squarely upon his own shoulders, 'How have I served you?' he asks and I think the word 'served' has to be interpreted not as having a chivalrous, romantic meaning of service but with the idea of usefulness – what use have I been to you? is the question he means to ask. Because he has been no use to her she had been down-graded from woman to mere chattel, a thing of cloth and wood who performs the household tasks. While he, pompously dutiful, busies himself with words, she is sorry for him, not for herself even though his involvements have left her lonely. He has substituted words for emotion and both of them are the poorer for it.

In the second sonnet he goes on to contrast life enhancing love with the sterility of his ideas – dry thoughts, harsh loyalty and blurred and unreal concepts while her feelings are warm, responsive and alive in every pulse and tone. The right which he has denied her is the right to share in his thoughts – to be a real partner to him. As the bread and wine at communion put the living God into religion so true sharing would have brought life into their relationship. The last lines show great insight – 'you were true to me, as I to something less than you'. By confining himself to abstractions he has been faithful to the idea of partnership but has not seen his wife as a real living partner, a whole person.

The third sonnet is central to the whole sequence and to emphasise this, is written in a different rhyme scheme – all the others are Shakespearean sonnets. He has accused himself, accepted blame, acknowledged his weakness and now goes on to show that by undervaluing the contribution of love and feeling he has impoverished himself and his art. Relationships with people are more important than 'twig, feather or figured stone' and add to our appreciation of these objects which remain lifeless unless they are seen through the eyes of the emotionally mature. By giving more of himself to his wife he would have received the benefit of her warmth and richness. After blaming himself and acknowledging his weakness the fourth sonnet goes on to describe the breakdown in communication between himself and Roberta when even words which are unsaid are interpreted as hostile: 'till silence is no more than bitter truce'. Did Roberta Hewitt read these words in 1954 and did they help to heal the breach which had obviously been widening between them? The description of the breakdown leads into an acceptance of responsibilty and thence into a beautiful description of Roberta's place in all his life. Here we have once again Hewitt the skilled tradesman. First of all he shapes the blade and edge to drive the blow. Then he turns from carpentry to an image drawn from his knowledge of the textile trade and his friendship with damask designers. Roberta was, he felt, secure from hurt as she was so much part of himself that her life was interwoven with his, providing brightness like a damask pattern on a dull background. This pattern is immune from the ravages of time too, as even in middle age the rememberance of youth still warms his life.

The sequence ends with a plea to Roberta to forgive him and add blessing to forgiveness so that together they can rebuild their life and their marriage will become both a haven and a beacon to guide them through life's difficulties. Hewitt's reference to mercy and blessing is reminiscent of the situation in the 'Bloody Brae' where Hill asks for blessing as well as forgiveness from the ghost of the woman he murdered. This final sonnet has something of the air of a Methodist hymn in its imagery and tone. *Intention, wiser, foolishness, bless, mortal, mortality, grace, peace, mercy, blessing beacon, haven, guilt, love* – these words from the poem Hewitt would have been familiar with from childhood and they create a strong feeling almost of revivalism. He has acknowledged his guilt, explored the depth of his error and now, purged and renewed through love, can go forward again in partnership into a better future.

The 'Sonnets for Roberta' mark a watershed in Hewitt's writing. The earlier poems are concerned with nature and the poet's own identity – as a part of family tradition, as a poet, a craftsman, a socialist and a Northern Irishman. In all of these there is an accurate observation of physical detail and an analysis of mental processes. The lack of an emotional link, however, and commitment to the living as well as to the dead has made the poetry rather arid and lightweight. Disappointment in his job, the death of his father and the strained relationship with his wife all made him think more of feeling without dismissing fact, so that the later poems achieve a much greater range and depth. His exploration of his relationship with Roberta comes to him like a religious conversion as he writes out of an emotional identification with others and no longer relegates people to the background scenery of his life.

Writing 'Clogh Oir' in September 1971, Hewitt describes how, on a visit to Clogher to give a lecture, Roberta is reminded of the time she spent there as a child on a long farmhouse holiday and how seeing it through her eyes changes his view until

Time truant, all the past foregathered
myth, legend, history, yours, mine, ours,
but strongest whisper, it was your own
that answered you and stirred for me, with love,
who seldom name such stirrings, or yield words
for the dialectic of the heart.
Standing there, I saw the lonely child
with the black tossing head, the dark brows,
as intense and definite as now,
as palpable,now, musing by my side,
close in a vivid murmuring congregation
among queens, heroes, hands, kneeling peasants,
immortally assembled, that child's face

known before time struck, known forever
stuff of the fabric whereof I am made.

This love encompasses all that his wife is and he can acknowledge this love which is so great that it can make her part of himself – 'stuff of the fabric', from which he is made. I mentioned at the beginning the small number of the poems which dealt with the women in John Hewitt's life and the difficulties to which this gave rise. What was Hewitt's attitude to women? John Hewitt was, as we have seen in the poems to his family and wife, a representative of his 'own kind' – the hard working, dissenting skilled tradesmen of Ulster. There is no trace of the veneration, the emotional attachment, the setting apart of womanhood which is found in Roman Catholic writers who have made famous the figure of the Irish Mother, Mother Machree or Cathleen ni Houlihan. Instead in Hewitt's poetry there is a Calvinist respect for the elders of the family, an almost biblical emphasis on the continuation of a family name (which he, alas, did not pass on) a strong appreciation of the function of the woman in family life and, most striking of all, the admission of his wife not just to equal partnership but to a place right inside himself – her character woven into his to make both part of the same fabric. It is this identification which makes the 'Sonnets for Roberta' (1954) one of the most powerful poems on marriage. John Hewitt's final poem on his wife's death 'October Sonnets' (*Mosaic* 1981), is one of the most touching memorials I have ever read:

My dear spouse died – a tumour on the brain –
I gazed with pity on that shaven head,
so nun-like, quiet, on the smooth white bed,
We watched her breathing faintly. It was plain
she would not stay, would never more regain
that vivid being who so recently
had paced the Asian lanes and laughed with me
when hurtling back from Russia in the plane.
We sat together in the silent room
our nephew Keith and I, both well aware
this was the end. We had few words to share.
This was the end, I thought, an end for whom?
For me, of love that living had increased
these more than forty years. The breathing ceased.

CHAPTER 19

A Stirring in the Dry Bones: John Hewitt's Regionialism

by

Tom Clyde

It is not my intention here to debate the abstractions of regionalist theory, or analyse regionalist movements from around the world, but simply to outline as clearly as I can the reasons why John Hewitt gravitated towards regionalism, to define what Hewitt meant by that term, and analyse some of the reasons for the movement's apparent failure.

The period we are talking about began around 1939, but of course local writers had been working in an Ulster Idiom before that date, most notably the comic dramatists like Rutherford Mayne, but also the occasional poet such as Richard Rowley. However, this fell a long way short of constituting any kind of regionalist 'Ulster School' as no serious attempt was made to encapsulate the character of the province or its people, or to address its problems, and even the dialect was rendered very imperfectly. In fact the Ulster elements in the work of these writers rarely amounts to anything more than local colour, more often (especially in the plays) descending to the level of the stage Ulsterman, an occasion for unthinking sentimentality and humour.

The natural next stage in development began in the mid-1930's with a new generation of writers committed to writing about their local environment more directly, more honestly, and with a greater attention to detail than any since the last of the peasant poets was silenced a century before. The nature lyrics of the young John Hewitt, and the robust prose of Michael MacLaverty and Sam Hanna Bell, began to appear in magazines, and obviously struck a new note. The first substantial achievement was the publication of MacLaverty's *Call My Brother Back* in 1939. The influences which are strongest in these writings include John Clare, Robert Frost and Thomas Hardy, from whom local Ulster writers first learnt to look more closely at the countryside and its inhabitants, the intimate details of the rhythm and tenor of rural life.

At this stage there was no thought of any over-riding regionalist agenda, and no attempt to enlist their art in any campaign with any wider social and political objectives. Nevertheless, however unconsciously, these writers were laying the foundations for the developments in the 1940s. Ulster Regionalism did not spring fully-formed from the brow of John Hewitt, but was rather the result of a slow process of growth which was given a new and radical boost by a particular set of circumstances.

The question then is 'What happened to force an awareness upon these writers, and particularly Hewitt, of what they were doing, and set them upon the route of self-consciously analysing their work and its objectives in the context of their province?' 'What happened' was a complex web of international, national, regional and personal factors. Undoubtedly the most important of these was the outbreak of war, which transformed the scene on two levels, one practical and physical, the other political and philosophical. Firstly, Northern Ireland was very isolated during the war years – hostility towards the Free State was, if anything, increased after the government's decision to stay neutral, and travel there required an official pass; interestingly, access to Britain was even harder to obtain. The continent was of course not an option.

The people of the province were thrown back upon their own resources in a way which had never happened before, forced to take their holidays in Northern Ireland and to look to themselves to a much greater extent for entertainment and cultural nourishment. This situation, combined with the natural increase in feelings of solidarity and respect for community which occurs in any people during wartime, led to a boom period for readings, lectures, concerts, plays; the theatres and concert-halls of the province were packed as never before. Such good fortune increased in intensity as the war progressed, since the government had decided to set up CEMA, the first body for the public funding of the arts, mainly as a measure to maintain morale, including the increasing number of bored military personnel, including the Americans who were stationed in the north. After decades of the kind of misunderstanding and neglect which Hewitt has catalogued in a number of essays, suddenly cash was flowing, interest was high, and writers could (if they chose) fill their diaries with engagements.

One of the greatest problems of the province has always been that it was a neglected backwater, untroubled by foreign visitors and foreign ideas, so the presence of so many outsiders must have forced upon people an awareness of their identity, as distinct from these others, and of what it is that makes them different.

On a deeper, more internalised level, the war precipitated one of those great turning points in ideas, and encouraged people all over Europe to think deeply about the problems associated with nationalism, which for nearly a century had seemed a positive, progressive force, but which recent events had tainted forever. The horror of nationalism gone mad and mutated into fascism, the plight of small nations threatened by the more powerful, and the tragedy of states which contained within their borders more than one national or racial grouping, all tarnished nationalism's image and led some to look for valid alternatives to the monolithic state. At the same time another new idea was maturing: for the previous two centuries (at least) the twin, unrestrained, developments of bureaucracy and capitalism had led to an ever-increasing degree of centralisation, a concentration of power, influence and prestige in the hands of a relatively small number of people in a relatively small area of each country. This applied equally to the empires of the USSR and of the capitalist countries, and the fear and feeling of powerlessness engendered by this meant that bureaucracy – a word only coined a century earlier – suddenly became the dirtiest in the vocabulary. People began to cast around for alternatives.

On a much more mundane level: during the Second World War the loyal Orange brethern were requested to suspend or scale down their annual festival of triumphalism, and this they did for the duration of the conflict, and even a couple of years after. This must have had a considerable effect in reducing sectarian tensions and contributing to a more optimistic mood amongst those who wished to see the drums silenced forever.

Another factor which must have influenced writers was the success in Britain of two local poets, Louis MacNeice and W.R. Rodgers. The impact of Rodger's first collection *Awake! and Other Poems*[1] in particular, was phenomenal; this contributed to the increase in pride and confidence in the ranks at home. It also focused, for the first time, the attention of the British literary establishment on the province, an interest which manifested itself in, for instance, a survey of literary activity in Northern Ireland which appeared in the *Times Literary Supplement*. Brief and superficial as the survey was, it treated 'Ulster' as a discreet region (in the context of articles on Scotland, South Africa and so on), and treated the emerging northern writers seriously.

Since a level of descriptive pastoral had been achieved in the works of poets like Roy McFadden and John Hewitt, it is reasonable to propose that, under the influence of the kind of events and movements as outlined above, those authors who had the ability, wished to move their work ambitiously from description to meditation. There is the need for a larger canvas. And it is clear that this is what actually did happen. The nature of that transition from pastoralism to regionalism is what happened in Hewitt's writing.

Although there was a loose grouping involved in the development of Ulster Regionalism, with members maintaining various degrees of commitment and evolving through a number of stages, there was no one else, as Hewitt himself recognised, who was so involved and who needed it so much. I would like to suggest a number of personal characteristics which might explain the importance of these ideas for him.

Firstly, there was the development in his poetry of what John Montague has called 'the tug from description to comment [which] demanded a larger form than the brief nature lyric'.[2] Hewitt's model in this was William Wordsworth. The series of longer poems, meditating on his personal growth, his poetry, family and environment which John Hewitt produced during these years, such as *Conacre* and *Freehold*, were a conscious attempt to produce his own Prelude and achieve some larger, encompassing vision.

Secondly, there is the problem and conflict in Hewitt's stance in his nature lyrics; a conflict of which he was only too aware. The stance has been described as 'ironic pastoral', and the problem is the knowledge of his own difference which stops him short of total identification with his subject matter. Hewitt never pretended to be a part of the rural scene, and time and again he worried over this problem: 'Your nature poets', he says, 'mostly live in town'; or 'maybe I shall learn to wear dung on my heel'.[3] He knew that when they both looked at a field, he saw image and symbol as an embodiment of spiritual values, while a farmer saw money. Regionalism was a strategy for reconciling this conflict, a way of dissolving his alienation in corporate social action and of reconciling his head and his heart.

On a less elevated level, we should not forget the influence of Hewitt's day job. His work in the Ulster Museum researching, maintaining, cataloguing, and assessing the 'portraits and relics of notable men of Planter stock' was a very gradual and practical induction course into the basic principles of Regionalism. His own words, from 'No Rootless Colonist' paint a vivid picture: 'The sad, long-jawed painting of James Hope and the faded daguerrotype of Mary Ann

McCracken proved themselves icons [an important word] of greater charismatic power. I was led by the likenesses back to the records . . . So, unintentionally, I was becoming equipped with a local imaginative mythology'.

Finally, I would like to point to Hewitt's isolation, which is quite difficult to appreciate fully now, but which at times he felt keenly. He began to write seriously in the mid-1920s, and for nearly 15 years felt himself to be ploughing a very lonely furrow indeed. We know of the initial relief he felt when Roy McFadden emerged, evident in his habit of introducing McFadden, for a time, as 'the other poet'.

Hewitt's incessant search for artistic 'ancestors' has become an undervalued *cliché* among those who study his work, but it is important to remind ourselves of the painful personal circumstances which gave it birth. Initially he began by looking for the validation, support and even companionship he needed among the writers of the past. Regionalism gave him an organising structure to satisfy this need, but it also provided him with the hope that it might conjure the non-existent artistic community into being in the here-and-now. One reason why Hewitt felt it so important to record the history of the lost generations of isolated, undervalued, forgotten Ulster poets is that he was the link between them and the new era of the last fifty years. For a long time he must have feared that he would be the last of the line, and much of this work was directed toward making sure he was not! But what did John Hewitt and his contemporaries mean by the term 'Regionalism'? One of the problems is that the definitions they put forward at the time were particularly precise.

> Howard Sergeant, in an article entitled 'Ulster Regionalism' which was published in Rann in 1953, laid out a set of guidelines. Despite the aspirations of dialect societies and Village Institutes . . . true regionalism is a movement towards a future in which a balanced life in every community has become the source of local self-respect and human dignity. It arises out of a natural affection for or an attachment, conscious or unconscious, to a particular environment; and finds expression through a language, outlook and manner of life, of the people concerned, adapted to the intellectual and emotional experience of the individual. It follows that, to achieve this equilibrium the complexities of existing conditions must be taken fully into account. The poet who neglects or is unable to do so will probably find himself isolated in a mental backwater, at best a local colourist, at worst a sentimentalist looking to a past that has never existed.

Sergeant emphasises the uniqueness of Ulster. No other Irish province, he says, 'is so well defined, geographically, politically, or in its ancestry'. He uses the Ulster cycle to illustrate this uniqueness and Deirdre's flight to Scotland to emphasise the close connections between the two areas.

Since our main concern is with John Hewitt, I will not question Sergeant's article in depth, but simply make in passing a couple of points. The vagueness is evident in phrases like 'a balanced life in every community'. One of Ulster Regionalism's weaknesses was the lack of an agreed definition even amongst the inner circle, and we can see areas of disagreement here with Hewitt who would, for example, not have been so arrogant about 'dialect societies and Village Institutes'. Sergeant's case for the uniqueness of Ulster continues: 'The colonisation of Ulster by Scottish and English protestants . . . was a contributing factor to this distinction, in idiom, temperament, sense of humour and religious propensity between the Northerner and his fellow Irishmen'; thereby omitting any recognition of the negative contribution such as disinheritence, division and distrust. Sergeant makes the Plantation sound like a pleasant outing. He also criticises the nationalist impulse of lowering artistic standards and making ideological correctness the excuse for accepting bad verse. The nationalist ideal is also criticised for being confined to a small and unrepresentative minority. Yet he seems completely unaware that others might apply precisely the same criticisms to Regionalism. Sergeant concludes with the equally dubious assertion that 'the principal difference between (nationalism and regionalism) is that while regionalism offers its contribution to the whole culture of a nation . . . nationalism is more conducive to cultural isolation'.

John Hewitt made many references to his blueprint for his 'Townland of Peace': in 'No Rootless Colonist' to 'the region, an area of size and significance we could hold in our hearts'; or in 'The Bitter Gourd' where he claimed that, 'If writers in an isolated group or in individual segregation are for too long disassociated from the social matrix their work will inevitably grow thin and tenuous . . . He [the regionalist writer] must be a rooted man, must carry the native tang of his idiom like the native dust on his sleeve'.

The seminal text here is 'Regionalism: The Last Chance' (1947), the most urgent and rhetorical essay Hewitt produced:

> Regionalism is based upon the conviction that, as man is a social being, he must, now that the nation has become an enormously complicated organisation, find some smaller unit to which to give

> his loyalty. This unit, since the day of the clan is over and that of the large family is passing, must be grounded on something more than kinship. Between these limits lies the region; an area which possesses geographical and economic coherence, which has had some sort of traditional and historic identity and which still, in some measure, demonstrates cultural and linguistic individuality.

Hewitt claims that Regionalism will cure the diseased condition of the state 'which is defined by Lewis Mumford as 'apoplexy at the centre and paralysis at the extremities'; and that the establishment of this more 'conveniently manageable unit . . . will make possible more efficient planning and a more effective use of resources'. He concludes:

> Ulster, considered as a region and not as the symbol of any particular creed, can, I believe, command the loyalty of every one of its inhabitants. For regional identity does not preclude, rather it requires, membership of a larger association. And, whether that association be, as I hope, of a federated British Isles, or a federal Ireland, out of that loyalty to our own place, rooted in honest history, in familiar folkways and knowledge, phrased in our own dialect, there should emerge a culture and an attitude individual and distinctive, a fine contribution to the European inheritance and no mere echo of the thought and imagination of another people and another land.

Compared to Sergeant, Hewitt is considerably less vague, his tone is more practical, and he comes slightly closer to addressing directly the problem of religious conflict. The essay makes clear that the driving force of his regionalism is not tribalism or parochialism, but a concern with over-centralisation, standardisation and dogma. As Terence Brown remarks, Hewitt's 'fundamental interest is not, as it would seem, Ulster, but the relation of man to his environment, the shaping and controlling of consciousness by locale, climate and topography. The region provides a ready-formed laboratory for observing these processes at work'.[4] Brown's laboratory image is, however, too tepid to convey Hewitt's conviction at that time.

It is worth examining in this context the three theorists whom Hewitt cites as important influences on his thought: Frederick Le Play (1806–1881), Patrick Geddes (born half a century later in 1854), and Lewis Mumford (half a century after that again, in 1895). None of these writers was a poet, or even a politician; instead all three are remembered, out of a host of other preoccupations, for their contributions as the founding fathers of sociology and town planning. They developed systematic methods for analysing the structures and dynamics of a community, and the latter two in particular went on to suggest prototypes of the small-scale, decentralised Regionalist agenda outlined by Hewitt.

In conclusion, I would like to point to what I see as some flaws in this vision of Ulster Regionalism and also indicate how the movement was an apparent failure. The flaws and the failure are not necessarily connected beause an idea can fail in the real world, even if virtually flawless. What is more, several elements of his Regionalist programme were realised by Hewitt when he looked back at the project from a much later date.

It is obvious that any protest eventually fades: people die, move away, get seduced by other ideas and, if no obvious progress is being made, simply fade away. Related to this process is the fact of the end of the War. The troops in Northern Ireland left, taking their money with them; artists were able to travel again and new artistic influences developed on the liberated European continent, recalling Winston Churchill's infamous phrase, the old quarrels re-emerged undiminished.

With the gift of hindsight it is possible to discover many flaws in Hewitt's analysis. In 'Regionalism: The Last Chance' he quotes Mumford: 'Regionalism . . . begins with a revival of poetry and language: it ends with plans for the economic invigoration of regional agriculture and industry, with proposals for a more autonomous political life, with an effort to build up local centres of learning and culture'. This chronology is not necessarily accurate; in our own country's closest precedent (the movement for more freedom and independence of the whole country from Britain) we see no such civilised progress. For example, the 1880's saw the establishment of the Royal University of Ireland, the Phoenix Park Murders, Parnell's assumption of full control over the Irish Parliamentary party and the National League, and the publication of *The Wanderings of Oisin*: in other words, the simultaneous emergence of all streams of activity subversive, political, educational, economic, cultural. The very simultaneity was what made the period in Ireland so powerful. There was no such movement in Ulster during the 1940's. In the same essay Hewitt wrote: 'Unless an awakened popular consciousness rises to rally and mobilise these activities at once, the projected political measures will fail to reach the legislative stage, the painters will emigrate, the journals will cease publication, the old severing prejudices will trouble again, and we shall be left once more precariously perched upon our 'melting iceberg'. This is precisely what happened: not a single local politician embraced the Regionalist cause, and the momentum was lost.

AE's question, which Hewitt quotes ('Name, if you can, a single Unionist writer of genius?') is well asked; but one is tempted to throw it back at him: Name (yourself excluded) a single Ulster Regionalist writer of genius? For even the ancestors Hewitt employs are far from impressive. Hewitt's own words reveal the 'dismal heritage' of the Rhyming Weavers, whom he categorises in 'The Bitter Gourd' 'almost indistinguishable from the host of Burns imitators', the journalist-poets' ('not very high craft') or William Sydney Mount, his paradigm of a Regionalist artist yet one whom he faintly praises as 'not a great master, obviously, but a sincere craftsman'. None of these figures were likely to inspire a new generation of artists, let alone the public at large. Another unfortunate reference, this time in 'Regionalism: The Last Chance', is to Frederic Mistral; the only Felibrist to successfully update the Provencal tradition was Mistral himself, and even his success was purely literary, striking no chord in the people of his region. His only outstanding follower was Charles Maurras, who went on to become a guiding light of the extreme right-wing chauvnist group Action Francaise.

Parallels made between the situation in Ulster and that in Scotland or Wales are misleading. Although there are many different political strains in these countries, including a Unionist one, there is no argument over the territorial definition of Scotland, for instance, or of whom can be called Scottish. The regional and national boundaries coincide, so regionalism and nationalism amount to variations on the same theme, differing only in degree, but not in kind.

Perhaps the most important failing in Hewitt's Regionalism is his tactical decision not to tackle head-on the core of our problems. Writing anonymously in *The Bell* in 1942, WR Rodgers wrote: 'It is impossible to convince an Ulster Protestant farmer, that, in the event of an all-Ireland govenment being formed, independent of Westminster, his farm will not be taken away from him, and given to his Catholic neighbour. And, mark you, it is equally impossible to convince the Catholic neighbour that he will not be given the farm. That is the core of the problem, no matter how it is covered up'.[5] Rodgers' analysis may be brutal and over-simplistic, but we can all recognise the truth in it, relevant to all attempts to change the status quo. Beside this bluntness, many of Hewitt's presciptions seem lightweight and irrelevent. Part of the problem was that John Hewitt, unfortunately, was just not a typical Ulsterman as Terence Brown noted; 'he remains . . . a man of liberal, humane sympathies, whose primary instinct is to live in harmony with nature and with his neighbours, earnestly debating with himself how on earth this can be managed'. The bitterness, piety, tribal warmth and understanding of revenge which number among most Ulster people's characteristics appeared only in his poems, not in the man, and even then as puzzling, illogical influences, to be examined and dealt with dispassionately.

Let me end positively by saying that I do not regard Hewitt's Ulster Regionalism as a 'failed' concept. It would be stretching credulity too far to believe that the fact that so many of his practical prescriptions have been met is simply due to coincidence; rather I feel that this proves how accurate his original diagnosis was, and also hints that perhaps a quiet minority absorbed his ideas and were convinced of their importance. The local BBC station has slowly crawled its way toward immersion in the province; the staff at Queen's University, especially in departments such as Politics, History and English, have turned their formidable forensic talents upon the North; and the Belfast Museum and Art Gallery has become the Ulster Museum and moved considerably closer toward representing the history and culture of the whole province. CEMA has been replaced by the much-criticised Arts Council, but the quantum leap achieved in the intelligence, range and sheer amount of public funding of all the arts should be acknowledged.

On a different level, the groundwork done by Hewitt in the 1940's means that no Ulster poet since that time has found his or her self so confused, isolated and burdened by cultural cringe as Hewitt and his predecessors did. An emerging Ulster poet now has a tradition and a canon which he or she can accept, modify or rebel against, just like writers in other countries and cultures.

Finally, it has to be said that John Hewitt was not a politician, a sociologist or an agitator; he was a poet. If we want to see the real success of Ulster Regionalism, that is as a personal artistic strategy, then we should look not at the constitutional position of the province, but at 'The Bloody Brae'; 'The Colony'; 'Conacre'; 'One Alien Here'; 'Freehold'; 'Sunset Over Glenaan'; the poems that John Hewitt wrote.

CHAPTER 20

Uses of History among Ulster Protestants

by

Anthony Buckley

It is old but it is beautiful.
Its colours they are fine.
It was worn at Derry, Aughrim,
Enniskillen and the Boyne.
My father wore it as a youth
As in bygone days of yore.
On the Twelfth of July I long to wear
The Sash my father wore.
(traditional song)

. . . we Ulster people have an identity of our own, separate from the so-called Irish identity that everybody's trying to foist upon us against our will . . . We just drifted on. We were neither English or Irish or anything, and we lost our own identity, and our own culture, our own folk-heritage . . . And we've a part to play . . . by showing them our origins.
(Alan Campbell, leader of the Covenant People's Fellowship).

In Ulster there are to be found several specifically 'Protestant' versions of history explicitly related to the present conflict between Catholics and Protestants, nationalists and unionists. One such tradition is associated with the various 'Orange' brotherhoods. Another is a prophetic tradition found chiefly among fundamentalists. Among this group are the 'British Israelites' who claim to be descended from Abraham and Jacob. And there are also people who claim that Ulster Protestants are descended from the Pictish 'Cruthin' who inhabited prehistoric Ireland. All of these groups and individuals (and my list is not exhaustive) are competing to achieve a degree of political or intellectual leadership in specific segments of Ulster Protestant society.

This article will examine something of the breadth of Ulster Protestant attitudes to history.[1] My suggestion is that when this history is directly related to ethnicity it is used in at least three differentiable ways: as a rhetorical commentary that either justifies or condemns; as a blueprint or 'charter' for action; and as a focus for allegiance. Not all popular history in Ulster is directly intended to uphold the interests of one ethnic group against another, and in concrete situations a supposedly sectarian history can often be used for quite a variety of diverse purposes. Nevertheless, there are to be found in Ulster widely known versions of history identified with specific ethnic groups, and it is these that will be considered here.

When history is used as a political rhetoric, it typically upholds the claims of one's own 'side' to power, prestige, and influence in the present while stigmatizing one's opponents. Rhetoric of this kind seems usually to have one of two forms. The first consists of a list of past grievances awaiting redress. The second makes an assertion of the superiority of one's own group. Here the implication may be that because one's group is superior (in talents, divine favour, culture, etc.), it makes a greater contribution to the general welfare, and it is therefore entitled to greater rewards. It is tempting to dismiss such ideology as 'deceit'. Sometimes, indeed, there may be dishonesty, and criteria of truth employed by one faction are not always acceptable to another. Often, however, such historical discussion takes place within earshot of rivals or possible allies who demand some degree of plausibility according to the locally universal standards.

History's second major use is as a 'charter'. Here, a set of archetypical situations provides rules or guidelines for acting in the present. Such a charter may indeed have a simultaneous purpose as a rhetoric. In this case, however, the history is less of a commentary upon the present, and more of a practical pattern that may be imitated.

In the third of these uses of history, commemorations of historical events in, for example, processions or rituals, can provide a focus for ethnic allegiance. They thus form part of the interactive process whereby ethnic boundaries are daily defined and recreated. The definition of Ulster's ethnicities is complex, but it includes both descent and religious 'belief'. Of these, the first is the more important. It depends largely upon what is sometimes called 'endogamy' – the rule which forbids intermarriage between the two sides.

Endogamy effectively defines the two groups in Ulster both practically and intellectually. Practically, it restricts important kinship-based activities to one's own 'side'. Intellectually, it gives substance to the idea that modern Protestants and Catholics are lineal descendants of, respectively, the seventeenth-century 'planters' and 'Gaels'. Definition by 'belief', however, identifies Ulster's ethnic groups with such categories of person as British or continental co-religionists past and present, and indeed with others such as Old Testament figures, with whom there is not necessarily any alleged or real biological kinship.

Versions of history that are explicitly 'Protestant' reflect the interests of the sometimes divergent Protestant factions that propound or might be interested in them. The views examined here reflect one of the more important (but not always clearly defined) disagreements among Ulster Protestants: that between fundamentalists, and those people whom fundamentalists disparage as merely 'religious'. This distinction is reflected (though again not precisely) in the active membership of the two main unionist political parties. The sectional claims of these and other groups, however, are made by propounding justifications for the goals of the Protestant ethnic group considered as a whole.

Irish History: Seventeenth Century and Beyond

As Ulster Protestant ethnicity is irredeemably linked to Catholic ethnicity, so is loyalist history related to nationalist history. Nationalist history classically portrays an opposition between Britain and Ireland, planter and Gael as one between oppressor and oppressed. Scholarly nationalist histories have appeared throughout this century, whence their ideas have passed into school textbooks and the general consciousness. Modern historians still think them important enough to be worth systematic 'revision'.[2]

The central events of this nationalist history arise out of succesive invasions of Ireland, the most important of which was by Britain in the sixteenth and seventeenth centuries.[3] These invasions were undertaken with great ferocity,[4] replacing Irish landownership with British. The British removed the rights of tenants.[5] They systematically disrupted Irish industry and trade.[6] Legal restrictions were imposed upon Catholics. And England is popularly blamed for the 'decline' of the Irish 'culture' found in the Irish language, in ancient texts and in folklore.[7] Injustices continued into the nineteenth century. Independence was the solution, but even this was spoiled by the partition of Ireland and by the discriminatory laws and practices of the artifically created 'majority' in the north.

Irish nationalist history, therefore, contains a catalogue of grievances whose rhetorical force lies in the reciprocity principle. Since the British (or 'planters') stole the land of their Irish forefathers; since they destroyed Ireland's trade, despoiled its culture, and suppressed its religion, then Irish people have at least the right to claim their land back, to press for the reunification of their island, and to claim fair and equal treatment. In short, Irish history is seen to contain so many injustices perpetrated against native Irishmen by successive generations of British governments and planters, that the nationalists who are their heirs can lay claim to the rhetorical high ground of moral advantage against the putative descendants of their oppressors.

Irish nationalist history has also generated a pantheon of heroes who have withstood this oppression. Among them are O'More, Sarsfield, Grattan, O'Connell, Parnell, Connolly, the Defenders, Ribbonmen, Land Leaguers, and many others. History, therefore, provides Irish nationalism not only with a range of historic ills requiring redress in the present, but also with 'inspiration', i.e. a plethora of legitimated charters or blueprints from which to choose actions appropriate to their remedy.

As the seventeenth century is important to nationalists, so also is it to Protestants. Not least this is because the celebration of its events provides them with their most politically charged folk festivals. These are associated with the different Orange brotherhoods, although the parades and their significance are widely and popularly known. Most famously, on the Twelfth of July, the Protestant Orange Order celebrates the defeat of the Catholic James II at the hands of William III. On the 13th of July, County Armagh Royal Black Institution, whose members are drawn from the Orange Order, hold a well-attended 'Sham Fight' in which, with much shotgun fire and mock sword-fighting, James II is similarly 'defeated'. And in August and December, the 'Apprentice Boys of Derry' celebrate the victorious siege of Derry, by marching around the city's walls.

Of all these historical events, this siege has the greatest symbolic significance. It occurred when, in the face of indecision by the city governor, Lundy, Apprentice Boys shut the gates against the advancing James. Lundy escaped by stealth, in consequence of which his huge 16-ft effigy is burned as part of the celebrations each December.

Although it is not central, the rhetorical element in all this cannot be ignored. The narrative of the siege can readily be portrayed as a structure of opposites, in which the wicked, uncivilized, tyrannical, and 'rough' people outside the walls confront the good, civilized, freedom-loving, 'religious' people within. In the siege, the 'rough' behaviour of the Apprentice Boys (and by implication that of their successors} is justified by the fact that it is undertaken in defence of civilization, freedom, religion, and other high ideals.

The implied rhetoric here is consonant with another idea that I have heard many individuals separately state, viz. 'nobody expects that America should be given back to the Indians' (or Australia to the Aborigines). In part, this familiar statement is a plea to let bygones be bygones: 'it all happened a long time ago'. In part, however, it also contains an imperialist rhetoric, that Protestants in Ireland, like white people in America, Australia, and elsewhere in the British Empire, have been the bringers of Christianity and civilization. It is an old argument found, for example in Harrison's *The Scot in Ulster*, but it is also found in modern publications.[8]

Despite the existence of this implied rhetoric, this is not really to be regarded as the main purpose of these important commemorative processions. For rhetorical purposes, Protestants tend to emphasize more recent history. They therefore argue that since the 1920s Catholics have failed to accept the democratic will of the majority,[9] and have instead subverted the state using even violent means. Thus Protestants, too, have a catalogue of grievances against nationalists, some of them deeply felt, but the list that they nowadays use tends to start in the 1920s.

More important than their implied rhetoric, these celebrations also embody a set of rules or guidelines for action. The events being remembered are the ones that, above all, established a 'Protestant ascendancy' in Ireland. They therefore provide practical models for the reaffirmation of Protestant power. The guidelines are most succinctly contained in such slogans as 'Not an Inch' or 'No Surrender', frequently quoted from political platforms, and identified with the Williamite Wars. They evoke, too, memories of lesser battles, of the Diamond, Glencoe, Machen, and Dolly's Brae, and especially the campaigns of Carson and the Ulster Volunteers, which kept Ulster from the Irish Republic. These lesser incidents, like the stories of the Williamite Wars themselves, do not seriously attempt to justify Protestant claims except by the mildest of implication. They are used, rather, as 'charters', as models for action.

The various processions are also a focus for group loyalty. Solidarity is affirmed between bystanders and marchers and their putative ancestors who shared a concern to uphold Protestant monarch. This demonstration of cohesion is also intended to show strength and determination against others. In many Orange halls hangs the portrait of William Johnston of Ballykilbeg. Johnston, in 1864, broke a government ban on Orange processions and his memory is evoked whenever attempts are made to reroute or prohibit processions (as happened, for example in 1985–6). As the gates of Derry were slammed against the wishes of the governor, and as William Johnston defied the government by marching, so, today, Ulster loyalists strive to resist 'Rome Rule' (an echo of Carson's campaign) by resisting compromise by British governments and by other waverers. The processions not only commemorate, but are themselves examples of the defiant strength modelled upon that exhibited in the past.

Biblical History: the Chosen Few

The Orange Order, the Royal Arch Purple Chapter and the Royal Black Institution are comparable in organizational structure to the different bodies within Freemasonry. When a man has been initiated into a lodge of the Orange Order, he may be invited to enter the corresponding chapter of the Royal Arch Purple, whence he may be asked to enter a Black preceptory where he will be initiated into each of eleven degrees. Membership of the Orange Order has long been recruited from a wide cross-section of Protestant men. Until recently, no unionist politician could have become a member of either the Stormont or Imperial Parliaments without being a member. The Black Institution is almost universally regarded as more 'respectable' than the Orange Order, and is drawn from Orangemen of a somewhat higher social status than the average.

The initiation rites of the Arch Purple and Black Institutions consist centrally in the retelling and re-enactment of prescribed Bible stories, and such stories, usually, but not always those used in the rituals, are also painted on the banners carried by Black preceptories on their parades. In a representative sample of banner paintings and other materials relating to Black symbolism and ritual (discussed in much greater detail elsewhere),[10] I discovered that of seventeen different texts employed in these various contexts, fourteen had remarkably similar themes.[11] The dominant framework is of an individual or group in favour with God confronting alien peoples. Some of these 'aliens' are wicked people, as in the story of Noah; some uphold a rival religion, as in the contest of Elijah with the prophets of Baal; others are mainly foreigners. The stories emphasize faithfulness. Someone who is loyal to god is likely to prosper or be rescued from his enemies or from God's wrath. He may gain a victory as did David against the overwhelming strength of Goliath. When a heathen or foreigner changes allegiance and turns to God, as did Rahab or Ruth, that person may also be saved from destruction or become prosperous. But where, as with Ahab, one of God's chosen people turns to foreign gods, he must expect ruin. Thus do the different texts explore variations upon the same theme. This theme is the encounter between heathens or foreigners and God's chosen people. Though it is never stated as a dogma, the metaphorical implication here is that, like Israel and Judah, Ulster Protestants are 'God's Chosen Few'.

It is clear that, like the Williamite Wars, the biblical texts provide a set of practical models useful to those who confront the alien, apostate, or merely wicked. By obvious implications the stories recommend that Protestants should avoid marrying the daughters of their enemies; be loyal to their religion; welcome heathens who turn to the true religion; fight against all the odds; and trust in God.

If, however, these Williamite and biblical histories have similarities one to another, they are not identical. The siege of Derry, for example, is similar to that of Jericho, but its details are quite different. It is not useful to think of Ulster Protestants as somehow 'trapped by their history', for their history provides them with not one 'historical charter', but a whole range of practical blueprints for dealing with their opponents. The Blackman, in particular, who is already familiar with the history of King William, who has also 'been through', and taken many others 'through' the rites of the Arch Purple and Black Institutions, has acquired from this history much 'food for thought'.

There is a multitude of small Protestant denominations in Ulster whose theology can be classified as 'fundamentalist'. Fundamentalists are also to be found in many 'mainline' churches (Church of Ireland, Presbyterian, Methodist). Commonly, individuals from different denominations gather together for weekday meetings in the 'Mission Halls' found in most towns and villages. Fundamentalists distinguish themselves from both 'modernists' and 'charismatics' who are inclined to be sympathetic to Catholicism. They also differentiate themselves from the merely 'religious' people who typically attend church but who have not been 'saved', who 'think that just by being good they can get to heaven', and who look askance at over-eager attempts to interpret the more difficult portions of the Bible.

Politically, the opposition between the two Protestant parties, the Reverend Ian Paisley's Democratic Unionists, and the Ulster Unionists led by James Molyneaux, reflects that between fundamentalists and the 'merely religious'; activists in the DUP tend to be fundamentalists, while, with sometimes significant exceptions, fundamentalists are rarer in the UUP. Similarly, though there are DUP members in Orange lodges and even in Black preceptories, the DUP leadership and most fundamentalists are somewhat cool towards these institutions. On the other hand, the present Orange Grand Master, the Reverend Martin Smyth, is an UUP Member of Parliament, while the Imperial Sovereign Grand Master of the Black Institution is the leader of the UUP, Mr Molyneaux himself. By a paradox, the DUP achieves important electoral strength from working-class people who are well represented in Orange lodges, but who tend to be non-church going.

Whereas in the Black institution, the image of 'God's chosen people' emerges from metaphorical stories that provide merely 'food for thought', for fundamentalists it is more explicitly a doctrine. Its mildest form is found where an individual is said to have been 'chosen' to do God's work. 'Conservative' Presbyterians, Free Presbyterians, and other Calvinists sometimes say they are of the 'elect', but this view blends into the Arminian theology prevalent among fundamentalists who nevertheless say that they act by the 'grace of God'.

These ideas impinge most directly upon both history and ethnicity in millenarian thought. Of this, the most important form in Ulster is a type of 'premillenialism', which asserts that Christians will be taken up (raptured) to meet Jesus in the air before the 'Tribulation', which heralds the one thousand years of Christ's rule. There is much speculation about the events predicted by biblical prophecy. A very common view, or example, is that the ten-horned beast of Revelation 13:1 is identical with the feet of the statue (with ten toes) in Nebuchadnezzar's dream (Daniel 2:31–5), and the fourth beast in Daniel's own vision (Daniel 7). These all refer to the last Roman Empire constituted by the ten kingdoms (as there were in 1981) of the European Economic Community, whose False Prophet is the Pope. There are many disagreements between fundamentalists about the precise roles of middle-eastern countries, the Soviet Union, the Common Market, and Rome in the events outlined in Revelation. On one matter, however, most fundamentalists agree. For them, the Pope actually is the Devil, the Anti-Christ, or the False Prophet as described in scripture.

Such views seriously affect fundamentalist church history. Ministers commonly refer in sermons to those martyrs who died upholding Protestantism against Rome. The name of Dr Paisley's church in Belfast, 'Martyrs Memorial', reflects this interest. And modern editions of classic descriptions of Catholic butchery are readily available in evangelical bookshops.[12] The steadfastness of these saints is, of course, directly comparable to that of the heroes of the Bible and of Derry, the Boyne, the Diamond, and the Ulster Volunteers. More than this, fundamentalists see themselves as called by God to spread

His Word in the face of a Church inimical to God's purposes. Fundamentalists will readily claim that they 'love Catholics' as sinners who need salvation. They nevertheless oppose not only Catholic theology, but also Catholic power, manifested in the IRA, the Irish Government, the Common Market, and also the Soviet Union with all of which the Church of Rome is said to be in league.

British Israelism is found throughout the United Kingdom and elsewhere. In Northern Ireland, BI forms a small but significant strand within fundamentalist debate. Locally prominent political figures are said to be privately sympathetic. A former Orange Grand Master, John Bryans, and the late Reverend Robert Bradford, former Vanguard assemblyman and later OUP Member of Parliament, were vociferous BI supporters. From the 1960s, there existed a paramilitary group called Tara, which upheld BI principles. In the 1950s, BI meetings are said to have filled the spacious Ulster Hall in Belfast. Nowadays, BI is organized as the Covenant Peoples' Fellowship, holding small weekly gatherings in and around Belfast. In churches of all sorts there are individuals who agree with BI ideas, but its main strength is in the Churches of God, pentecostalist congregations whose official teachings include BI. The largest of these in Belfast in the early 1980s had 2,000 people at its Sunday services.

The essence of BI teaching is that the people of the United Kingdom and hence of the USA and the White Commonwealth are the descendants of ancient Israelites. Following the death of Solomon, the kingdom of Israel was divided. The people of the Northern kingdom, it is said, found their way to northern Europe where, as Angles, Saxons, Jutes, Vikings, and Normans, they reassembled to form the British people. The kingdom of Judah was conquered by the Babylonians, and their history is recounted in the later Bible. Except for some Benjaminites living near Galilee, among them Jesus and eleven of his disciples, the Jews became corrupted by intermarriage. At the time of the Babylonian exile, the prophet Jeremiah, carrying the Ark of the Covenant and the Stone, which had once formed Jacob's pillow at Bethel, travelled with the daughters of Zedekiah, last pre-exilic king of Judah, to County Antrim. One of these daughters, Tamar-Tephi, married the Israelitish Irish High King, Eochaidu. The Ark is believed still to rest at Tara where the High Kings of Ireland were once crowned. The Stone, however, was taken to Iona and thence to Scone and it now rests beneath the Coronation Chair in Westminster Abbey. The descent of Elizabeth II is traceable through James I and the Irish King Fergus the Great, to Eochaidu and Tamar-Tephi, and thence to King David.

Because the British are, in an Old Testament sense, God's chosen people, they have a responsibility to bring Christianity and civilization to the world. The collapse of the British Empire is for them a tragedy, and they support White rule in South Africa. British Israelites believe that non-White races are capable of civilization and salvation, but that Israelites have the task of helping them get there.

Adherents of BI are aware of the similarity of their doctrine to the symbolism of the Black Institution. But whereas Blackmen can see their similarity to certain biblical heroes, British Israelites say they are descended from them. The British Isles, according to BI, is the land promised to Abraham and Jacob, but they claim that even foreign lands (America, Australia, Africa) may be occupied, thus benefiting the aboriginal inhabitants.

Apart from providing a generalized justification for British rule in Ireland as elsewhere, this doctrine has a special Irish significance. Even before Jeremiah and Zedekiah, they say, Ireland was inhabited by Israelites. These were, however, driven into Scotland by invading Gaels, who were Phoenicians, half Canaanite, half Israelitish, from Tyre. This admixture of Canaanite blood, I was told, explains the 'instinctive hostility' between southern Ireland and the remainder of the British Isles, and why, for example, Ulster-Scots settlers in America could absorb themselves into the rest of the Israelitish people, while southern Irish people in America have remained a separate ethnic group.

The idea that the Israelites who now live in Scotland were once the inhabitants of Ireland until the Gaels expelled them calls into question much of the rhetoric of Irish nationalism. It implies that the subsequent invasions of Ireland, and especially those of the seventeenth century by the Scottish and other British were merely a reconquest by its former inhabitants. I have heard this argument stated explicitly by British Israelites, but its form is more widely used and has recently been given great prominence.

The Cruthin

The final version of history to be considered here is contained in two books. *The Cruthin* and *The Identity of Ulster* were written by a Belfast hospital doctor, Ian Adamson.[13] His thesis in outline is neither new nor intellectually disreputable,[14] but these books are striking because they explicity relate this ancient history to modern political issues. When he wrote his first book, Adamson lectured to various groups including members of the paramilitary organization, the

Ulster Defence Association, who later officially adopted his ideas. The second printing of this book has an introductory preface by Glen Barr, then an officer in the UDA, who became leader of the Ulster Workers Council, which co-ordinated the loyalist general strike that destroyed the 'power-sharing executive' in 1974. Adamson's books have had an appeal elsewhere. In 1986, a pamphlet was published by the junior wing of the Ulster Unionist Party, presenting Adamson's views in simplified form,[15] and, indeed, his work is now being more widely popularized.

Adamson argues that the earliest inhabitants of Ireland were not the Gaels, but the Cruthin, who were closely related to the Scottish Picts. After the Cruthin, came the Fir Bolg (from Britain), other tribes from Gaul, and finally the Gaels. The Gaels established a hegemony everywhere in Ireland except the north-east, where the Fir Bolg tribes of Dalriata and Ulaid formed with the Cruthin an Ulster confederacy. He writes, 'The descendants of the two races are the Ulster Scots'.[16] Significantly, he also adds that 'through the kings of the Dalriata are all the kings of Scotland descended, and through this line is descended the present Queen of the British Peoples'. By the fifth century, this mainly Cruthinic kingdom of Ulaid (later corrupted to Ulster) was pushed back into Antrim and Down until their defeat at Moira in A.D. 637 resulted in a gradual emigration of the Cruthin into lowland Scotland.

Adamson's attack is on at least three fronts. First, he challenges the naive assumption that all ancient Irish culture is Gaelic. He suggests, for example, that the Book of Darrow and the Book of Kells are Pictish or Scottish-Irish in inspiration. More damning, he appropriates Cuchulainn, hero of the (Gaelic language) epic *Táin Bó Cuailnge* to the Cruthin. Cuchulainn's statue famously stands in Dublin Central Post Office as a memorial to the nationalist dead of 1916, whose actions precipitated Irish independence. Placed in Adamson's context, however, Cuchulainn clearly personified the struggle of Ulster against the invading Gael. This idea is used with much rhetorical effect in the Young Unionists' pamphlet. Second, Adamson is able to appropriate St Patrick to the Cruthin: 'Patrick makes a clear distinction between the Scotti (Gaels) and the ordinary peoples, the Hibernians (Cruthin and Ulaid)'.[17] It is the latter, he says, that Patrick first converted. Thus in a manner comparable to the British Israelites, Adamson argues that the Cruthin are responsible for spreading Christianity. And third, Adamson denies 'the claim of the Gael to Ireland'. This is 'by the sword only, and by the sword was it reclaimed in later days by the descendants of those Ancient People

. . . of these two Ulster Peoples, the paramount claim belongs to the Cruthin, Last of the Picts'.[18] Or, as the Young Unionists urge, 'when the Plantation of Ulster got underway, in the seventeenth century, those Scots who came over from the lowlands were in fact members of the Cruthin race returning to the land of their birthright'.

In short, the Cruthin argument addresses directly the rhetorical challenge of Irish nationalist history. It makes the claim that Ulster Protestants, and particularly those who emigrated from Scotland, have at least as much right to live in Ireland as do Irish Catholics. Second, it takes from the nationalist heritage many of its most treasured traits by arguing their Cruthinic rather than Gaelic origins. And finally, the historical lynch-pin of Irish nationalism, the Plantation of Ireland, is transformed from a conquest by an oppressive people into a reconquest by a people who had formerly been forcefully expelled.

Conclusion

The different forms of history found here appeal to different groups of people in different ways. Many of the biblically orientated theories appeal to a fairly small but significant body of people, the fundamentalists. These people often make claim to represent the essence of Ulster Protestantism, a claim provisionally accepted among the largely non-religious working class, which accepts leadership from the DUP. Among fundamentalists, British Israelism has a rather limited appeal. Its advantage is that, if true, it wholly refutes Irish nationalism, giving Ulster Protestants a valuable place both in Ireland and in the cosmic scheme. However, many fundamentalists (and others) have doubts about its historicity – it is, perhaps, just a little too exotic. More important, its claim that the British are chosen by God by virtue of their descent from Jacob seems to question the doctrine of 'justification by faith', the cornerstone of fundamentalist Protestantism itself.

It is appropriate that a secularized and abbreviated version of the BI message, Adamson's Cruthin, should be espoused on the one hand by the UDA and, on the other by Official Unionists, both of whom have long been known to be antagonistic to the fundamentalist leadership of the DUP. One form of religious history, that found in the Arch Purple and Black institutions, has an appeal to respectable church-going unionists, especially Official Unionists, who are not, however, fundamentalists. For these people, the implied message that Ulster Protestants are God's chosen people is acceptable as long as it is not stated as a dogma, but is available merely as a set of useful metaphorical images. In a loose kind of way, they can see themselves as defenders of Protestantism or Christianity without being trapped into the rigorous life style and commitments of fundamentalism.

I have suggested, however, that not all of the history directly related to Protestant ethnicity has a rhetorical function: much of it is useful in generating strategems and tactics for action or as an expression and focus for allegiance. In this very generalized survey, I have not attempted to place the uses of history in immediate small-scale, concrete circumstances. My concern has been to explore the themes themselves in the broader context of Northern Ireland politics, and to indicate loosely the uses to which these histories are put.

Ulster Protestant histories reflect a very similar quest to that described by Boyce among Irish nationalists, namely that for a comprehensive concept of identity that transcends the pluralist nature of Irish (or Ulster) society.[19] The rhetorical histories that aspire to justify the claims of Ulster Protestants as a whole and give them a satisfactory identity seem doomed, at least at the moment, to reflect the partisan concerns of specific unionist factions.

CHAPTER 21

John Hewitt's Hierarchy of Values.

by

Paul Arthur

I

I come to Hewitt as a student of politics and as such I want to consider him as a political actor. In that respect I will be suggesting that he was both an amateur and an innocent but that his heritage – his hierarchy of values – is of immense importance. My analysis of his work will be centred on the following three quotations:

> . . . man's political life is more intimately an expression of the general quality of his imaginative life than we are in the habit of noticing. And those who are concerned with man's imaginative life are therefore concerned with the area in which his political concepts are shaped. Are shaped: they do not shape themselves, but are shaped, in his imagination, not only by man's mortal destiny and the metaphysical questions to which it gives rise, but also by the particular contexts of nation, doctrine, class and race . . . the study of politics must neither neglect the fact that man is an imagining and myth-making animal, nor fail to make explicit allowances for the necessary entry of imagination and myth-making into the study itself.
>
> Conor Cruise O'Brien.

> Unless we insist that politics is imagination and mind, we will learn that imagination and mind are politics, and of a kind that we will not like.
>
> Lionel Trilling.

> And now, fumbling, faltering, some of us in our varying crafts and with our uneven skills, not all knowing each other by name, are

> endeavouring to recreate that story, that art, that enchancement, drawn from and firmly rooted in what Ulster was and is, and playing our part in helping to make her what, first in fitful glimpses but now more and more by a steady light, we realise she should and can become.
>
> John Hewitt.

I wasn't sufficiently aware of Hewitt's contribution to political discussion until I read his contribution to a discussion arranged by Eavan Boland and printed in *The Irish Times* on 4 and 5 July, 1974. The discussion centred on 'The Clash of Identities' and, besides Hewitt, the group included the novelists Francis Stuart and James Plunkett, the poet Thomas Kinsella, Ruairi O'Bradaigh of Provisional Sinn Fein and two UDA representatives. A recent rereading suggests that it is rather thin in its discussion of the fundamental issues. It may have been the disparate nature of the group or it may have been a matter of timing, i.e. it was conducted within two months of the Ulster Workers' Council stike. Whatever the reason the following quote from Hewitt himself illuminates a fairly barren dialogue. It is, of course, Hewitt's own hierarchy of values:

> I'm an Ulsterman of planter stock. I was born in the island of Ireland, so secondarily I'm an Irishman. I was born in the British archipelago and English is my native tongue, so I am British. The British archipelago is offshore to the continent of Europe, so I'm European. This is my hierarchy of values and as far as I'm concerned, anyone who omits one step in that sequence of values is falsifying the situation.

I have no difficulty in identifying and empathising with that hierarchy but it is in converting the sequence into the concrete where I see problems arising, and I suggest that Hewitt himself was conscious of this fact. It is there later in the interview when he says that he cannot 'avoid the fact that my Ulster includes two strains of thought': one represented by Jemmy Hope and the other by Hewitt's personal heritage.

One way round this difficulty might be to look at another aspect of the Identity discussion. This is supplied by Francis Stuart with his self-description as 'a writer of dissent' and a 'ghetto writer': 'I wrote for the people of the ghetto, not the political and religious ghetto, but simply for the people who are distanced, oppressed and despised'. This is a more fruitful avenue in which to study Hewitt. He says as much himself: 'I have tremendous sympathy for men like Henry Joy McCracken. I believe we can only retain our identity if we retain the right to protest'.

So it is as a 'protestant' writer (upper and lower case 'p') that I want to examine Hewitt. In other words I use 'protestant' in two senses. The first, the more fundamental, is divorced from religion. In 1953 Hewitt wrote: 'spiritually I have felt myself to be my own man, the ultimate Protestant . . . I have often felt myself doubly free from the twin disciplines of organised religion and science. In argument this has been advantageous, as I can quite honestly cry plague on both their houses, and, unimplicated, set up my own mythology and magic in opposition to either . . .'.[1] In that sense he is at one with Stuart. In a piece the latter wrote for *The Irish Times* (7 October, 1976) on the 'soft centre of Irish writing', Stuart was critical of those who reflected 'more flatteringly, its habits and thought modes . . . They quickly become integrated into their society and serve a civic function in the same way as do lawyers, doctors and civil servants . . . they might be said to preserve common cultural standards and present the national identity'. Stuart cites Frank O'Connor as a typical representative. Seamus Deane adds to the list by condemning the aesthetic heritage of men like Yeats, Synge and Austin Clarke whose work 'clearly harbors the desire to obliterate or render nugatory the problems of class, economics, bureaucratic systems and the like, concentrating instead upon the essences of self, nationhood and Zeitgeist'.[2]

Clearly Hewitt stood outside the system – and paid the price. It is painfully and patently displayed, of course, in 'From Chairmen and Committee Men, Good Lord Deliver Us'[3] and is graphically illustrated in his description of the fate of Dr Alexander Irvine in 1934. In one short passage he depicts the levels of hypocrisy in public life in Northern Ireland: 'He had savaged the ideals of his sponsors, the YMCA and the Presbyterian Church. He had violated the Rotarian code. He had taken the Lord's name in vain. He had consorted with atheists and communists; and' (the greatest crime of all) 'the newspapers had reported it'.[4] He tells how he gave the story of Irvine's descent into non-personhood to a BBC producer but it wasn't used in the subsequent radio portrait: 'When this happened I was not even indignant. Rather I felt reassured that my old assessment of the dominant circles in Northern Ireland was still valid, and that Irvine's and my own battle still remain to be fought again and again'.

Hewitt's was an adversarial role in the Stuart mould: 'It is only those few writers capable of imagining alternative societies', said Stuart in the *Irish Times* discussion, 'who can enter into a serious and mutually advantageous relationship with their own. But, being deeply critical of it, their society fears to enter into a dialogue with them'. Hewitt's professional life was about imagining alternative societies but transferring the imaginative into the practical was to present him – constantly – with difficulties. The stamina, artistically, socially and, just as importantly, financially, to maintain this independence is remarkably draining. I am reminded of Heaney's poem, 'Exposure':

> I am neither internee nor informer;
> An inner émigré, grown long-haired
> And thoughtful; a wood-kerne
>
> Escaped from the massacre,
> Taking protective colouring
> From bole and bark, feeling
> Every wind that blows

Hewitt was an inner émigré who didn't have the political guile to take protective colouring. If I had to draw parallels it would be with the novelist, Forrest Reid. In his autobiography *Midnight Oil*, V.S. Pritchett paints an incredibly poignant picture of Reid in his garret in 'that awful, rainy and smoky Presbyterian city'. He describes him as 'a very distinguished writer – now forgotten and lost because he buried himself in Belfast'; and, significantly: 'Of his generation almost the only important writer who stayed at home, emotionally he lived far away'. Of Reid's work Pritchett writes: 'his few novels have an element of pagan symbolism . . . The idea of a ghost or revenant, some shade of a lost culture or a guilt appearing out of the past is often found in Irish literature . . . he was a genuine pagan. He stayed there as if in hiding, I used to think . . . I may exaggerate Reid's isolation . . . but it was odd to find a mystic, deep in Blake and Yeats among the linen mills'. The parallels between the 'ultimate Protestant' and the 'genuine pagan' are too obvious although Pritchett follows it with an exasperating liberal refrain: 'Why didn't he go South? perhaps because of some core of Ulster obstinacy or of family chains that are so powerful in Ireland'.

II

When we turn to John Hewitt's public life we find an individual whose political credentials are impeccably socialist: his work with the

Labour Party in the 1920s, with the National Council for Civil Liberties in its investigation of the Special Powers Act, and with the Peace League. And when we scour wider horizons we have a testimony of his cultural heritage: 'My mother tongue is English, instrument and tool of my thought and expression; John Ball, the Diggers, the Levellers, the Chartists, Paine, Cobbett, Morris, a strong thread in the fabric of my philosophy'.[5] His (English) radical credentials are impeccable.

But two problems arise when we attempt to transfer this very impressive political credo into political influence. In 'Planter's Gothic' Hewitt demonstrates that he is aware of both. 'I realised the difficulty of the transition from the public to the private face and back again' is an expression of the personalised difficulty. To complement that he makes the more valid generalised point in the same essay: '. . . when I make what I think is a free act of choice, I still wonder what distant bugle's echo is beckoning or in what mass movement I shall shortly find myself. I have only to examine the history of my personal opinions to have revealed to me the fluctuating climate of general ideas over the same period'.

The 'distant bugle's echo' is what I wish to concentrate on and I suggest that a possible approach is to examine the influence of the Left on the politics of the province before I look at the more general political climate in which all activists operate. There is a clash between provincial politics and what is loosely called the 'national question'. It can be seen in the careers of such as William Walker and Harry Midgley (whose 1985 biography by Graham Walker is aptly entitled *The Politics of Frustration*). Walker's book traces sensitively Midgley's explorations within the Labour tradition from his explicit anti-partitionism in the 1921 general election to his self-styled role of 'Unionist evangelist' by the late 1940s via municipal and Commonwealth socialism. And in attempting to give Midgley the benefit of the doubt he can do no more than reach the tentative conclusion that 'over the span of his long and chequered career his overall influence was arguably for relative good'. Such qualified praise speaks for itself. At the United Kingdom level activists had to confront the reality that Northern Ireland presented Labour with a major psychological problem. The province did not fit into the wider scheme of things. Labour is part of what L.J. Sharpe calls the 'overwhelming centralist spirit of the British political and administrative system'. In electoral terms three of the five Labour national victories since 1950 have depended on the seats it won in Scotland and Wales. In this respect Northern Ireland didn't count unless its domino effect was recognised during the devolution debate in the 1970s. Labour saw that as an unnecessary diversion from its egalitarian mission best pursued in a centralized United Kingdom.

So what to do about Ireland? As Home Secretary in the late 1960s Jim Callaghan worked on a policy of political incorporation (which might mean positive discrimination for the Catholic community). But as a beleaguered Prime Minister after 1976 he was prepared to contemplate creeping integration through the concession of extra seats. And in the post-Callaghan days of socialist contrition, the National Executive Council adopted a policy document for the 1981 conference which acknowledged 'a long and deeply held belief in the Labour Party that Ireland should, by peaceful means, and on the basis of consent, be united . . .'. At the very least this policy inconsistency revealed 'the fluctuating climate of general ideas' over a particular period; and more importantly, it clashed with Hewitt's hierarchy of values by omitting more than one step in that sequence of values.

At a more personal level it illustrates John Hewitt's political innocence. Take the late 1930s as an example. One of the better documented incidents during this period was the attempt by certain sections inside the Catholic community to destroy Harry Midgley for his stance on the Spanish Civil War. This doesn't appear to have registered on Hewitt. He writes in 'No Rootless Colonist': 'The Spanish Civil War and the mounting of fascism on the continent kept my gaze fixed away from local political affairs'. It may well have been this tendency to fix his gaze on larger issues which failed to alert him to the fate of his own professional career. I am astounded that *he* was astounded by the decision on the Directorship of the Museum in 1953. That may say more about the age in which we live than it does about John Hewitt but I want to pursue that by examining the political climate in which Hewitt operated.

His own disdain for the political establishment could not have been made more plain than it was in his 'Bitter Gourd' article in 1945 – and the date is significant. He writes (admittedly he is addressing the nineteenth century) of 'an extroverted, stubborn inarticulate society with well-defined material values and, for the most part, a rigid creed'; of 'that very inarticulateness of the Protestant block' which 'had this strange consequence that the best articulators of the general passion that Ulster was and should persist as a separate entity were not themselves Ulstermen' – Randolph Churchill, F.E. Smith and Sir Edward Carson. He bemoaned 'our absurdly vaunted material values' and the fact that the 'Ulster ideology . . . offered the writer no inspiration. The Ulster public offered him no livelihood'.[6]

Before we examine his response to this political despair I want to continue for a few moments with this checklist of our political inadequacies. Patrick Buckland has asserted that 'no constructive philosophy had been developed over the years of struggle to equip Ulster Unionists to govern a state they had neither expected nor wanted'.[7] Tom Nairn explains it thus:

> The unacknowledged kernel of the real problem is the character of Protestant Ulster. Hidden under its bowler hat, the physiognomy of this particular band of tonguetied sons of bastards' ghosts has remained curiously unknown. The inarticulacy is not some racial trait: five minutes in the Shankill Road will show anyone that. Like its opposite, the undrainable eloquence of Southern Ireland, it reflects certain aspects of the community's past cultural development.[8]

In these circumstances it isn't easy to categorise Protestant Ulster. Peter Gibbon, Richard Rose and J.C.Beckett all allow for the emergence of an embryonic Ulster nationalism. Tom Nairn writes exasperatingly of the 'peculiar, fractured development of the Ulster Protestant nationality' which is 'like a mad "variable" which falsifies every reasonable strategy of escape . . . there is only one direction in which this change can now occur – that is, towards the formulation of a more than nominal 'Ulster nationalism'. And finally, and devastatingly, Tom Paulin discerns 'very little in the way of an indigenous cultural tradition of its own' in Ulster Protestantism; and refers to 'the contradictory, self-pitying, childish and festering sense of grievance which is at the centre of the Loyalist mentality'.[9]

Why that particular checklist and why the concentration on Protestant Ulster? The checklist is a fairly representative sample of the academics' approach and of those who are not unsympathetic to Ulster Protestantism. All are united in agreeing on Protestant Ulster's political underdevelopment. And I concentrate on Protestant Ulster because we are concerned with John Hewitt.

III

Despite his rejection of formal religion, Hewitt was conscious that his heritage was an Ulster Protestant heritage with his Uncle Johnny in the UVF, with the 'large and pervasive role' which Methodism played in his life, and with his father as 'a lifelong abstainer, with the rigidity that marked his early attitude and coloured his behaviour all his days'. (I don't underestimate the significance of the temperance movement in unionist politics: in 1934, for example, the Moderator of the Presbyterian Church in Ireland, Rev. Dr. T.M.Johnstone, refused to attend a garden party at Buckingham Palace in connection with King George V's Silver Jubilee when he learned that two brewery horses were to draw the Speaker's coach in the procession.) But, it might be objected that Hewitt offered a wider vision than this. Didn't he write that 'The faith I have always sought has been inclusive, not exclusive'? In his concept of rootedness and regionalism and, indeed, in his life work there can be little doubt about that. But it is in moving from the personal to the collective that problems arise:

> We are a little people, but we will be heard,
> for we are lucky, can either grow or die,
> but the great have no alternative to dying.

He was not totally unsympathetic to the Irish language: 'The Irish language had no obvious effect upon our tradition, except where it has lingered in place-names or in the ears of those who have an affection for the odd dialect word or phrase wherein Irish keeps company with the lowland Scots and Tudor or Jacobean English'.[10] But compare this with Seamus Heaney's lecture 'Among Schoolchildren' (*Preoccupations*) where he speaks of Irish as being 'a fortification and an enrichment' and there you have the distance between colliding views on culture. In any case I would enter a second caveat.

As we have seen already Hewitt knew that he could not discount his own family background and its place in the wider scheme of things. Tom Paulin is another example of the conflct between the familial and the societal. Paulin, who has been excoriating in his criticism of Unionism, is also the author of 'Settlers', his account of UVF gunrunning:

> They cross from Glasgow to a black city
> Of gantries, mills and steeples. They begin to belong.
> He manages the Iceworks, is an elder of the Kirk;
> She becomes, briefly, a cook in Carson's Army.
> Some mornings, walking through the company gate,
> He touches the bonnet of a brown lorry.
> It is warm. The men watch and say nothing.
> 'Queer, how it runs off in the night',
> He says to McCullough, then climbs to his office.
> He stores a warm knowledge in his palm.

There is an intimacy and a proprietorial air about that 'warm knowledge' which belongs, of course, only to one tradition. Hewitt was in but not of that tradition. Indeed he was decidely outside, one of Stuart's ghetto writers. As his 'From Chairmen and Committee Men' essay and other writing demonstrates, he must have been galled by the political underdevelopment he witnessed in his own community. Probably he would have been at one with Sir James Craig when in his meetings with Michael Collins in London in 1922 he suggested that the proposed Council of Ireland be replaced by joint meetings of both cabinets and that 'in all matters under the purview of the Council' each government consult each other 'on terms of equality' because terms of equality implies a sense of communal dignity.

But there the mutuality would have ended. Hewitt could not have been happy with the co-optive and closed society which developed. Three examples will suffice. The first comes from the second Station Director appointed by the BBC in Belfast: 'When I arrived in Nothern Ireland I was made to feel for the first time in my life that I was a person of some public importance ... I was invited to become a member of the Ulster Club, where almost daily I met members of the Government; the Governor, the Duke of Abercorn, who was immensely helpful and friendly, and Lord Craigavon, the Prime Minister, was a keen supporter of our work. In effect I was made a member of the Establishment'.[11] The second appears in 'No Rootless colonist': '... nobody went as far as I did in analysis, definition, assertion. Indeed I met with strong criticism from fellow writers, had my encounters with the vice chancellor of the university and the then Minister of Education'. The establishment moved in. The third I borrow from A.T. Marshall, the Town Planning Officer for Londonderry County Borough (the first such person to be appointed in Northern Ireland). He was replying to an article, 'The Londonderry Air' by Jack McGougan which appeared in the journal, *Town and Country Planning*, Autumn 1948, complaining about unemployment, socio-economic conditions and the lack of planning in Derry. Writing in the next issue as 'a stranger in the City' Marshall stated that 'no physical planning can possibly erase the deepseated bigotry prevalent in the citizens of Derry' – a rather strange attitude towards central planning with Clement Attlee's government in office: 'It is up to the City, which has great potential, to stand on its own feet and not be spoon-fed by the Ulster or the British Government'. And in a final piece of pre-Thatcherite mumbling Marshall demonstrated that he may actually have been the founder of the school of creative accountancy when he commented on the male unemployment figures: '... of

2400 adult males at present unemployed, a very substantial number are self-employed in the greyhound industry'.

Above all Hewitt would have been depressed by the lack of vision and of movement in Unionist political thinking. The sixty odd years between Craig's offer to Collins in seeking terms of equality and the post-Hillsborough reaction to the Anglo-Irish Agreement movement can be measured by an observation about the latter: 'if . . . there was a greater equality of esteem as between Belfast and Dublin, then the situation would be different'.[12] What he would have detected was a largely reactive element in loyalism. It was evident just at the time that he was writing one of his most influential essays, 'The Bitter Gourd'. The Unionist establishment was in a funk because a socialist government was in power in London. One historian says that it led 'to something like a crisis of identity at Stormont' and he demonstrates how the Unionist cabinet began to survey its options lest the union was endangered. At a cabinet meeting on 15 November Sir Basil Brooke wondered 'whether any changes could be made to avert such a situation. Two possibilities were dominion status for Northern Ireland and a return to Westminster'. But cabinet soon reached the conclusion that a Labour government posed no threats since it was 'staffed by practical and experienced men who are personally friendly to Ulster'. And Unionists recognised that they had secured the best of all possible worlds in their desire for autonomy of decision-making within the constraints imposed by economic dependence.[13] End of another political crisis and a return to 'normality' . . . until the next crisis arrived.

Hewitt offered an alternative to this hand-to-mouth politics. (I am not here going to discuss this aspect of loyalism: David Miller's *Queen's Rebels: Ulster Loyalism in Historical Perspective*, 1978, is the best source). It differed from the official version in the breadth of its vision and in the fact that it was pro- rather than reactive. In an address to a Corrymeela conference in 1976 John Hewitt asserted that 'our best hope will be to "invent the myth", invent the metaphor for Ulster, which will give our peoples, at whatever stage in history they came here, identity with the region'; and he suggested that 'what makes a nation is the Myth of a Nation. Each nation subsists on a fiction derived from folklore and history. It is that unifying myth which gives coherence to a people's ideology and a people's feeling'. And although he cited Jemmy Hope, John Toland and Mary Ann McCracken who 'represent three strands of Ulster life, represent for me the epitome and apotheosis of my region' I would suggest that a better mentor might be Sir Samuel Ferguson.

Oliver MacDonagh has said of Ferguson that it is 'not too much to hail him as the discoverer of the ancient Irish literature in which the later literary renaissance was to be based. Nor is it an exaggeration to speak of him as the inventor of a new sort of Anglo-Irish nationality'.[14] Ferguson was motivated in part by this seeking after identity. Irish Protestants had suffered a series of legislative blows between 1825 and 1845 and southern Irish Protestants were well on their way to an identity crisis. The advantage of an escape into a Gaelic past was that it was an escape to the indigenous civilisation with its pre-Christian origins. Gaelicism was neither Catholic nor Protestant, North nor South, Unionist nor Nationalist. Irish Anglicans had been alienated by an Irish nationalism which implicitly identified nationality with Catholicism whereas a nationalism rooted in an immemorial past could break this particular connection; e.g. the most important collection of heroic sagas, the Ulster Cycle, was first committed to writing in the great northern monastic centres such as Bangor, Moville, Armagh, etc.

We must be careful not to make too much of the connection with Ferguson. That Hewitt was conscious of Ferguson's legacy goes without saying. It is there in the title of his 1972 *Aquarius* essay, 'No Rootless Colonist'. It's there in their separate ventures in mythmaking to evolve an inclusive identity which goes beyond the territory of Ireland. And it may be there in the manner in which both have been interpreted by certain strata in the loyalist community. Since the outbreak of the present conflict Ferguson has been reinterpreted to explain that 'the real enemy of British Ireland was not the Roman Catholic Church . . . but the rise of a Gaelic Nationalism and its identification with Irish Nationalism'.[15] His epic poem, *Congal, an Account of the Battle of Moira* is cited to demonstrate that 'a cultural unity of Ulster, Western Scotland and the Isle of Man was maintained until modern times. The tales of Cuchulainn and the Sons of Usnach as well as later sagas could be collected from among the common people of the Highlands and Islands of Scotland long after they had disappeared from the greater part of Scotland'.[16]

I cite the above not because I want to give it particular credence but because it represents an attempt to create the myth of the nation. But I find it interesting that those who have gone down this particular road have had some connection with militant loyalism and have expressed their opinions in 'Beyond The Religious Divide' and in 'Common Sense', the latter owing allegiance to the memory of Tom Paine.[17] These particular people will have had only a tenuous connection with John Hewitt. He stressed at Corrymeela in 1976 that 'those who are pressing for independence want most of all to break the link with Britain. This, in my view, falsifies the position, as any break would'. In the same lecture he noted that 'our myth is more vulnerable than the Irish myth. The Apprentice Boys . . . were subsequently driven from their homes by rack-renting landlords, while the landlords remained to sit in the halls of power right up to the closing of Stormont; but their expulsion is no part of our myth'.

In any case in his latter years he may have decided that he was not a political activist. His 'No Rootless Colonist' was no more than 'the chart of a highly personal journey. . .I have not offered a routing for another's setting out, for I do not know of anyone to whom it may now be relevant . . . I have proposed no immediate tactics or strategies which might resolve the tragic confusion of this heart-breaking present'.

IV

I have attempted to place Hewitt in the social, cultural and political milieu in which he operated. The (relative) despair in the lines I have quoted immediately above owes more to the desperation of the political impasse – they were written after all in 1972 – than to any loss in political faith: we should remember that they were followed by a decade of flowering poetic creativity. Two points need to be made about this passing despair. Hewitt's influence was and is much more complete than he has acknowledged. It has manifested itself, not in terms of a political movement, but in the electricity of an idea, his personal manifesto, his hierarchy of values. And, secondly, it is astonishing that he was able to produce such electricity given the society in which he chose to live and work. Hewitt offered a centre from which people could grow outwards and upwards. Few have grasped it. The vacuum has been occupied and, in the short term at least, it has marginalised the ancestors of his Uncle Johnny.

It has been the architects of the Anglo-Irish Agreement, with their shrewder sense of the archipelago and their vision of a new Europe, who have demonstrated a greater understanding of John Hewitt than the rest of the community. In doing so they have challenged the dictatorship of the 'distant bugle's echo' and cleared the political undergrowth to allow Hewitt's hierarchy of values to flourish.

CHAPTER 22

Scotland and the United Kingdom

by

Bernard Crick

I

There are many reasons why in Northern Ireland the concern with identity can be so obsessive, and therefore why we should celebrate someone who could, like John Hewitt, understand the cross-currents so profoundly and react to them so tolerantly.[1] But the concern is not entirely peculiar to the north of Ireland.

'I am a citizen of a state with no agreed colloquial name', I began a recent essay in the *Irish Review*.[2] I reflected on the difficulty we Brits (to use an Aussie expletive now favoured by both persuasions in Northern Ireland, where both Scots and Welsh are 'Brits' too) have in responding to the peremptory 'Nationality?' in a foreign hotel register. Few people, I've observed, write 'British'; most mistakenly take the question literally, not as asking for one's legal citizenship. The question was framed not for us Ukanians but for those in what are held to be normal happy lands where one nation is one state; or so it is believed, but that belief is itself a nationalist assumption.[3] The word 'British' doesn't, to paraphrase Catullus, 'warm the blood like wine', as 'English' can, and 'Scottish', 'Welsh' and 'Irish' do. 'British is best' sounds to my ear either commercial or evasive of the question of identity. Those who write in the register 'citizen of the United Kingdom' invariably turn out to be Ulster Loyalists, occasionally an aggressive and pedantic Scottish Tory.

The majority, of course, write 'English' for the good enough reason that they are English. But some do so in the mistaken belief that 'English' is the adjective corresponding to 'citizen of the United Kingdom of Great Britain and Northern Ireland'. The full title of the Union is a mouthful. One needs a sense of history to digest it. But many English men and women, high and low, now seem to have lost just such a sense of history, and are only left with a vague, warm, nostalgic and evasive mental mist called 'English heritage'. Even to speak of 'the Union' could risk, in some contexts, sounding either anti-Catholic or opposed to a Parliament in Scotland. But is a description of the foundations of our modern constitution to surrender to partisan rhetoric? I am a modern democratic socialist, but if ever public political banquets came back in fashion, I would lift my glass, like an eighteenth-century Whig, and drink 'to the Union, God bless it' (although not if construed to favour the suppression of the Parliament of Ireland in 1800).

A personal explanation is needed. I am a deliberate immigrant to Scotland because I came to love the country. But so different is the culture, and so strong my Englishness, that however Scottish my political and constitutional views have become (for good reasons, as I'll argue), I am now too old to believe that I'll ever think of myself or be thought of as Scottish, as my student friends in the late 1940s, whose Jewish parents had sent them from Germany as children, were already English. For at the heart of the matter there is, what Mrs Thatcher could never grasp, or only in an English context, national feeling, indeed nationalism. But nationalism does not necessarily imply separatism, or that for each nation there must be a state. There are multi-national states and there are also many areas of the world where nationalism (we need look no further than Ireland, or Israel/ Palestine or South Africa) is part of the problem and not of any 'solution' – the word 'resolution' is usually better.

Most Scots, like most Welsh, have an intense sense of dual identity, and for most purposes live with it comfortably, more so than most people in Northern Ireland; indeed, they find an enhanced quality of life in being able to live in two worlds, enjoy two cultures and their hybrids. But they perceive this, of course (except in mixed marriages), as being Scottish and British, not Scottish and English. 'British' can be sensibly used to convey not a whole cultural identity, like 'Scottish' or 'English' or, more ambiguously 'Welsh', but simply the political and legal elements of the culture, both customs and institutions, which are shared in common among the four main regions of the United Kingdom.

Much of the sub-text of Scottish constitutional nationalism is, I suspect, an implicit if seldom stated contrast with Northern Ireland. Both separatists and federalists in Scotland can pursue a political path to somewhat different ends because, they feel, those ends are not so different as in Northern Ireland, nor have they a long tradition of violence. But this does depend on how both sides behave. The

English provocations or insensitivities of the 1960s and 1970s were of a kind more easily discounted, overcome or tolerated than Mrs Thatcher's abrasive, confrontational, stridently Unionist politics of the 1980s when confronted with even the mildest devolutionary Scottish demands. A reasonable sense of dual identity is not shared by most of the English, and it depends on historically sensitive behaviour by the English towards the other nations in the Union, on their not misusing the quantum of power that lies all too easily to hand both in the institutions and the doctrines of the states.

This power has been abused (or so most people in Scotland think) and a constitutional crisis is likely to result, however this is dismissed south of the border due to the appalling lack of interest in and under-reporting of Scotland in the quality London press and broadcasting media. Editors and political writers read the press wires for events in foreign countries, but they think they know all about Scotland already; their knowledge is, in fact, a knowledge of political opinion in London from daily talk with people in London. They meet Scottish Labour and SLD MPs, of course, but they think they are exaggerating; and the Scots go home at weekends and in the recess, so are not much present on the London scene. How else can one explain that the Mori polls in The Scotsman go unreported in the London press although they showed in the summer of 1989 (and similarly since) 34 per cent favouring independence, 49 per cent for 'Home Rule' (a subsidiary Parliament but with substantial and residual powers including taxation), and only 15 per cent favouring 'no change', with an incredibly low 2 per cent with 'no opinion'. Of course, put to the test of a referendum campaign, say, as in 1979, the 'no change' or misnamed 'unionist' vote would undoubtedly increase; but the figures, and the intensity of feeling, are far greater than ten years ago. Thatcherism has fanned the fire but the fire never went out. It is only that politicians and their captive audience of London political writers are mainly impressed by events, not trends and tendencies.

One event brought the Scottish Parliamentary Labour Party out of a luke-warm and divided support for 1978 style devolution into an apparently unequivocal enthusiasm for Home Rule – the Govan by-election when Jim Sillars for the Scottish Nationalist Party destroyed an impregnable 19,000 Labour majority. Their rank and file had already reached the same position. The Campaign for a Scottish Assembly, a body of great influence in Scotland virtually unreported South of the border, had set up a committee which produced what is likely in future to be regarded as a classic statement of the Scottish political mind, *A Claim of Right for Scotland*.[4] Leave aside, for the moment, some rather old-fashioned romantic history picturing the Act or Treaty of Union as a great betrayal (rather than as a hard bargain, grudgingly conceded), and a dubious claim for a dubious doctrine – that Scottish constitutional law embodied a belief in 'the sovereignty of the people'; none-the-less the truculent moderation of its argument that the Scottish people have a right to choose, gained wide assent. The device for the choosing was to be a Constitutional Convention and the implication was that neither a Convention nor a referendum was likely to show a separatist majority but rather one for Home Rule or, in effect, if not in name, for a federal system. Certainly it swept opinion in the Constituency Labour Parties and the Scottish TUC (The Liberals or the SLD were already in that position, and had been since the 1900s).

The SNP refused to commit itself to a majority report, understandably favouring a referendum on the three obvious broad alternatives (independence, 'devolution', no change) before a proposal was drafted; so they withdrew, hoping to leave Labour holding the baby and being punished for not being able to do anything with it. Post-Govan euphoria helped their decision. But their standing in the polls declined almost at once.[5] The true message of Govan was not easy for either of the two main Scottish parties. The electorate is extremely volatile and will punish drastically either party if they do not appear (as depth interviews reveal) 'to be doing enough for Scotland': Labour was punished at Govan and the SNP by refusing to join the Convention. But this means that the Scottish Labour Party are committed to a radical report and to fight for it. But they also have to appear as leaders of a national movement, not a Labour Party whose status is simply that of a regional organisation of the national (London) Labour Party. This means, in practice, that the SLD tail at the Convention can wag the Labour dog on the issue of proportional representation (whatever Mr Kinnock and Mr Hattersley might want), just as collectively the Scottish Labour MPs would have Mr Kinnock, after a Labour General Election victory, in much the same position that Parnell had Gladstone.

II

Forgive this raw and speculative politics in a symposium mainly on cultural identities. But I am making the point that the Scottish tail is likely to wag the English dog and force general constitutional reform with repercussions for Northern Ireland as well. Without the Scottish initiative general reform of the United Kingdom constitution might otherwise simply remain what Mr Kinnock called the Charter 88 movement, an affair of the 'chattering classes'. But Charter 88 is itself (if one of its early signers may cheerfully confess) a symptom quite as much as a cause. Several books and many articles and editorials, at almost all levels, have been raising the issues of a Bill of Rights, electoral reform, freedom of information, indeed of the possible need for comprehensive constitutional reform, possibly a written constitution, as if the old informal, conventional constitutional order was breaking down.[6] So I want to consider the consequences of *A Claim of Right* for the constitution of the United Kingdom as a whole.

It does, indeed, call into question the whole character of the constitutional settlement that followed 1688 and 1707. And this is precisely why many English Conservatives so vehemently oppose any Devolution or Home Rule, as well as why most Scots and a growing minority of English (I mean a majority of the thoughtful) now favour it. The very name and nature of the Act or Treaty of Union of 1707 is still in dispute. The canny Scottish Lords of Appeal have never been drawn into judgement in any case fabricated to test whether alleged breaches of the Treaty of Union by Act of Parliament could be illegal (even the Poll tax). The response of English judges would be more robust and less equivocal: that Parliament has absolute power to legislate on anything it chooses, therefore no Parliament can be bound by Acts of its predecessors, however solemn; so the Act or Treaty of Union is simply an ordinary enactment, and even if it was a treaty, treaty obligations can be overridden by future enactments of Parliament (presumably even the Treaty of Rome).

But this English ideology of parliamentary sovereignty was never as clear as it sounded. Sir Edward Coke (1552–1634) held that the king had a veto and should be prepared on rare occasions to use it, so that the 'transcendent and absolute' power of Parliament, as he had styled it, was only when Crown and Parliament acted together, as in the royal assent to make Bills into Acts. Further, Coke explicitly, if somewhat vaguely, believed that there were 'laws of God and of nature' which Parliament could not override, as also some aspects 'of the Ancient Constitution'. Not even Parliament itself could (should?) override these things.

Practical men of both kingdoms in 1688 and 1707 saw the new abstract doctrine of parliamentary sovereignty as a gigantic bluff (a Leviathan indeed) to maintain order, to ensure the Protestant succession and the end of religious and dynastic civil war, to ensure the predominance of Parliament over the Crown, and to maintain the unity of the United Kingdom. Power was to be checked and balanced within Parliament, but if divided among the kingdoms, even under one crown, was to risk anarchy. And men felt that they had come close to 'anarchy' or perpetual civil war in all three kingdoms. Yet every man of affairs in Scotland and England knew that the claim to absolute power was a legal fiction tempered by political reality and mediated by skilled statecraft, sometimes by good or ill fortune.

Did prudence or corruption predominate in the last debates of the old Scottish Parliament? *A Claim of Right* (1988) is still coloured by an old romantic nationalist view of history, in a specific 19th century form: that a Parliament must embody the life of a nation. 'The nation was not conquered', they say, 'but it did not freely agree to the Union of Parliaments in 1707' (Para 2.5). Certainly there was bribery and corruption in Edinburgh, just as there was in Westminster to get the Bill through the English House of Lords with the Bishops in uproar. Yet modern historians suggest that most Scots believed that a hard bargain had been driven. 'The matters on which the Treaty guaranteed the Scots their own institutions and policies represented the bulk of civil life and government at the time: the Church, the Law and Education' (Para 2.6). And add to that, commercial union and military security against the Highlands, two overridingly important and urgent matters. True, 'the nation' was not consulted, but nations never were until modern democratic times, and only then most rarely in often rigged or procrustian referenda. And Parliament itself was not as respected at the time as it became in legend or aspiration. It is always easier to respect an imaginary parliament than an actual one. Much public opinion in Scotland saw the old Parliament not as the national institution and the nation's pride, but as a corrupt entity mainly serving the interests of the landowning class.

But there was a national institution in which both the middle classes and the common people took pride; the Church of Scotland itself, the Kirk. And by the standards of the time it was a remarkably representative institution; at least the elect proceeded by elections. The elected Church Assembly had at least as strong a claim to be seen as the national institution as the Parliament. That is why its establishment was so bitterly fought in the English Upper Chamber.

It was not the case that Scotland suddenly became directly governed by England, but that what government there was at that time (leaving aside trade and foreign affairs) was mainly local government, and it remained largely in the hands of the Kirk and the legal profession. And with the growth of the modern Scottish Office,

Scotland still exhibits the astonishing spectacle in an allegedly unitary state of almost complete administrative devolution, and one, moreover, mainly in Scottish hands. English migrants have recently come to dominate some Scottish universities and to penetrate business and the arts to an unprecedented degree – what some call 'the Englishing of Scotland'; but the civil service remains almost wholly a native preserve. And that is, of course, the minimum case for a representative institution in Scotland: that all this existing machinery should be subject to democratic control. What happened was less that Scotland 'lost' its Parliament, than that the established church it gained gradually lost its dominance over the nation's life and its role as the national institution.[7]

Scotland is full of what the eighteenth century called 'peculiar institutions' but it now lacks an elected national institution: the Kirk has withered away. Therefore the commonsense argument, as in Northern Ireland, is for some form of subsidiary or even federal Parliament (even if not recognised by all as a final solution), but it is not a wholly commonsense or rational matter. On the one hand, there is nationalism – Scotland is a unique culture and has its own history, it is not a meccano set of institutional arrangements that can be adjusted into the 'greatest happiness' equilibrium position; and on the other hand there is what I have called the English ideology of parliamentary sovereignty. It may have outlived its usefulness, but it has left behind deep fears that the creation of any national representative institution in Scotland will lead to the breakup of the United Kingdom. No ideology is held more tenaciously and irrationally than by people who believe that they are purely practical men and women, with no time for theory, without an abstract idea in their heads.

This English ideology of parliamentary sovereignty arose because from the end of the seventeenth century right up until the Government of Ireland Act (1920) the major business of English politics was holding the United Kingdom together.

III

Scotland was once almost as worrying to the English as as Ireland. Memories of 'the '45' lived long. The maintenance of law and order and the preservation of the Union were inseparable concepts to both the English and Scottish political classes through the Napoleonic wars. After the wars, the old memories and fears were still strong enough for the Government to feel the need to play cards from the other hand: conciliation. There was the ludicrous state charade of George IV's visit to Edinburgh produced by Sir Walter Scott and commissioned by the Cabinet. Only for political necessity did the dropsical Prinny wear the kilt that immortal once.[8] And in the next reign the young Queen was persuaded by Melbourne, at first reluctantly, of the desirability of spending 'an appreciable part of the year in Scotland'. Luckily she liked it. And at that time there was virtually a state cult of Celtic song, poetry and dance. Victoria's children wore tartan plaid and the children of a Viceroy of Ireland wore the green. It was later called 'cultural politics' in other contexts, but it was not then an insensitive and centralising imposition of southern English culture and values.

By the last quarter of the nineteenth century any residual English fears that Scotland might become Ireland had vanished, though there were lesser fears that Liverpool and Glasgow were becoming Catholic Irish colonies. Yet this very time saw the creation of the office of Secretary for Scotland in 1885 and the beginning of the gradual process which led to the modern Scottish Office in Edinburgh. This was part of, once again, an instinctive, almost routine, English conciliatory politics, triggered more by dubious analogies with Ireland than by any actual threats or immediate pressures in Scotland. There was a Scottish Home Rule Association from the 1880s. Its ideas were prescient but its influence, unless one is desperate for ancestors, appears to have been minimal. And when Liberal leaders in 1910 and 1911 began to talk of 'Home Rule All Round', and Asquith discussed in cabinet whether to bring in one Bill, or to take the difficult or the easy one first, again the impetus was analogy with Ireland, a preemptive or reflex action rather than something dictated by the political power of the Scottish Home Rule movement. Also many ministers of the day, not just thinkers, were coming round to the federalist position of Gladstone's *The Irish Question* pamphlet of 1886. They were beginning to see the drawbacks in 'sovereignty of Parliament' and the constitutionless constitution it entailed. They were influenced by Canadian and Australian experience, by American experience of course, and more immediately by the federal settlement in South Africa after the Boer War. Even a few Tories played with ideas of an Imperial federation. Only the Great War brought an end to such speculations, as to so much else.

Thus the old English political class could exercise sovereign power with more flexibility, restraint and conciliation than they are usually given credit for. The inner paradox of the legal theory of sovereign power is the need for good political judgement in when not to use it.

Holding the United Kingdom together called for all kinds of restraints. Among the most of them was the dog that did not bark. Consider then a huge literature of Scottish, Irish and Welsh nationalism, well charted in bibliographies and library subject-indexes; there are virtually no books of English nationalism. The fact is startling but the explanation is simple. An explicit and triumphalist English nationalism would have been as disruptive as Austrian-German nationalism was to the Austro-Hungarian Empire. What there was, of course, was a huge literature and cult of imperialism; but that was open to all the nations of the British Isles, indeed both the historian of Empire, Seeley, and the bard of imperialism, Kipling, boasted of the fact. The Scots-Irish figured not least in imperial epic and legend.

The older English ruling class actually knew the component parts of the United Kingdom. Perhaps the basic political problem is that we now have a generation of English Conservatives in power, not just Mrs Thatcher and her successor, whose ignorance about 'the other nations' is monumental. Enough of the old guard were left, however, for the party to change its rigid ways in one important area where the going was hard and obviously most un-English. Since 1980 some very unlikely Northern Ireland Office ministers (seemingly) sent there for punishment or to destroy themselves have worked the subject up, talked to the right people, got quite a feel for the ground, and have done, in the circumstances, reasonably well. And things inherently inimical and contrary to the British Constitution suddenly become possible, indeed necessary: statutory referenda, power-sharing, proportional representation and 'conditional sovereignty', even. The Anglo-Irish Agreement of 1985 stated: 'The two Governments ... declare that if in the future a majority of the people of Northern Ireland clearly wish for and formally consent to the establishment of a United Ireland, they will introduce and support in their respective Parliaments legislation to give effect to that wish'. And such language and provision for such a poll or referendum was already in the Northern Ireland Constitution Act of 1973. It should give heart to the SNP.

Why cannot this flexible attitude to the Union be extended to Scotland and Wales, though a majority of Scots and Welsh might wish to vote for something different? The answer must be that while most Conservatives are firm that Northern Ireland is part of the United Kingdom, yet it is sufficiently different that this membership is not absolute but conditional on the wishes of even a bare majority of its inhabitants. But when devolution proposals are suggested for Scotland, it is somehow thought that her membership of the United

Kingdom is unconditionally mandatory, even to the extent that the terms of membership cannot be changed, even towards the kind of devolved Parliament already on offer to Northern Ireland. English Conservatives must somehow believe that the Scots are not merely British but are somehow 'really' English, whereas even Ulster Loyalists (to the anger of some of them) are quite plainly not. Or does the willingness to take seriously other national identities within the United Kingdom now need unhappy stimulants of civil disobedience or violence?

Edmund Burke in his great speeches on Conciliation with America and on American Taxation was to rail at Lord North's claim that the American refusal to pay taxes threatened the sovereignty of Parliament. Do not ask, he said, 'whether you have a right to make them miserable, have you not rather an interest to make them happy?'

> Leave America, if she has taxable matter in her, to tax herself, I am not going into the distinctions of rights, nor attempting to mark their boundaries. I do not enter into these metaphysical distinctions; I hate the very sound of them. Leave the Americans as they anciently stood . . . They and we, and their and our ancestors, have been happy under that system . . . Be content to bind Americans by laws of trade; you have always done that. Do not burden them by taxes, you were not used to do that from the beginning. Let this be your reason for not taxing. These are the arguments of states and kingdoms. Leave the rest to schools; for there they may be discussed with safety. But if intemperately, unwisely, fatally, you sophisticate and poison the very source of government, by urging subtle deductions and consequences odious to those you govern, from the unlimited and illimitable nature of supreme sovereignty, you will teach them by these means to call that sovereignty itself into question.[9]

And that was precisely what happened, and could happen again now. By opposing all concessions and slamming the door on any discussions of change (even within her own party in Scotland), Margaret Thatcher, very like Lord North, may have raised the stakes dramatically and foolishly and actually strengthened the hands and hearts of separatist nationalists in Scotland. But I think it more likely that her intransigence swept mere devolution off the agenda and turned, almost overnight, devolutionists into federalists in the Scottish Labour party (as shown in the final demands of the Scottish Constitutional Convention on St Andrew's Day 1990).

The whole constitution of the United Kingdom is now called into question, and there is no secure way forward for Scotland unless it is. Unhappily while Mrs Thatcher has turned her back on Burke, Labour's leaders still echo him. They plead for and rely upon a prudence which is not there. They seek vigorously, like Mr Hattersley, to fudge the sovereignty issue. They can sound equally magnificent, perhaps, but the impact could prove equally futile. Like Burke, they are hedging the fundamental issue. For Burke, as is clear in the above passage, was not attacking sovereignty as such, but its imprudent abuse in bad policies. Labour's present leaders also believe in 'unlimited and supreme . . . sovereignty' but want it in their own good hands, and might, indeed, if it falls to them, exercise it more prudently and benignly, truly chock full of radiant and sincere concern. But by the time Burke spoke it was too late. The Americans did not just want better treatment, they wanted constitutional guarantees for a defined area of self-government. They were not prepared to wait for a more friendly government, and to trust for restraint, like good English politicians, to friendship alone. So also the Scots. Those in London who take Scotland seriously at all continue to talk of the demand for devolution. So do many in Scotland, for want of a better concept – though 'Home Rule' is catching on. But most Scots now want, as the Constitutional Convention will almost certainly demand, devolution with entrenched powers. And as we all know, that is impossible in the present traditional, informal, conventional and unwritten constitution.

IV

It used to be argued, in private, by the main draughtsman of the Scotland Act of 1978 before he retired from the Scottish Office, that the details of the 1978 Bill were of secondary importance. Many pro-devolutionists at the time shared this view. Not to worry, get an Assembly of some kind off the ground and as its authority grows so new powers will be added, or simply assumed. Such a process would be politically, even if not legally, irreversible. But Jim Ross has recently seen the catch in the Burkean argument for prudence and published an article which had considerable effect on the Scottish reformers, not least in the committees of the Convention.[10]

Ross simply argued that in 1978 'we were innocent enough' to suppose that future Ministers would not dare withdraw powers once granted. 'We now know better. We used to think that Governments under the British constitution were fussy and interfering but not fundamentally undemocratic. We now know that the British constitution is inherently authoritarian and is quite capable of spawning a Government to match'. So he concludes that the objective must be, however politically difficult, a constitutionally protected Scottish Parliament, such that only by some special and difficult procedure, involving that body too, could Parliament wind it up, change its powers or cut its funding (as has been done to local government).

The *Claim of Right* sees the English constitution as a barrier to Scottish rights to a national representative institution. But it is now widely canvassed, as never before (except within the old Liberal Party for most of this century!) that the constitution is an obstacle to all our British civil liberties. The lack of restraint upon government has reached epic proportions.

The *Political Quarterly*, a journal not famous for sensationalism, had a recent issue on 'Is Britain Becoming Authoritarian?'. Wyn Grant wrote comprehensively of 'The Erosion of Intermediary Institutions'.[11] And Mark Stallworthy wrote in the same place of 'Central Government and Local Government: the Uses and Abuses of Constitutional Hegemony'. It was an almost definitive listing of the extent to which powers and discretion of local government have been radically diminished (contrary to Tory tradition quite as much as to Labour's – in some respects more so). He sees it as a new, imposed constitutional settlement, and concludes: 'A constitutional settlement which is resistant to dialogue and which confers an unconditional legitimacy on imposed central solutions is antithetical to reasonable expectations within a purported liberal democracy'.

There has been a centralist tradition in the Labour Party. Old Fabianism had one thing in common with Leninism: that the party should act for the good through control of the central state, and a belief that most intermediary institutions were irrational, reactionary or obstructive. But there was also always a pluralist tradition, more concerned to do good through people, in ordinary social groups and communities, than to do good to them from however heavenly a height. This centralist tradition was unhappily apparent in the half-hearted support, if not open opposition, given both by Government Ministers and by many Scottish Labour MPs to the Devolution Bill of 1978. Things done by a Government simply for political survival carry little conviction among ordinary people. Yet the fear was real among Labour activists, in Scotland as well as in England and Wales, that the welfare state would suffer if central power declined, or if coalitions resulted from some form of proportional representation. But that was before Thatcher's massive demonstration of how much of social welfare, not merely in the personal social services and housing, depended on the strength of local government. So in the last ten years there has been an extraordinary conversion among Labour intellectuals and thinkers to constitutional reform. It is hard to think of any prominent intellectual or academic on the Left who now makes the old Footite defence of parliamentary sovereignty.

Constitutional traditionalists, of both Labour's Left and Right have, together with Liberals and Social Democrats, swelled the adherents of Charter 88's call for constitutional and electoral reform. Charter 88 arose in London, with no direct reference to Scottish conditions, but a remarkable cross-section of people have come together convinced that, because of a breakdown of traditional restraints on which civil liberties depended, a formal constitution is now needed.

How can my fellow English, once so skilled in statecraft, now be so obtuse as not to recognise that Scotland, for all the interconnections and friendliness, is a nation? And not to recognise, for that matter, that Northern Ireland is not one nation? Or so condescending as to think that what Texans, Bavarians, Quebecois, Gujaratis and Tasmanians do, cannot be done by Scots – that is, operate in a federal system without imperilling the stability of the state? And why should a federal solution be deemed impossible because of the numbers of English? It depends what constitutional guarantees are given and how and by whom they are guaranteed. Every federal system emerges from a different circumstance. Political institutions must be tailored to each peculiar circumstance. They do not come off-the-peg in a limited number of shapes and sizes.

What if the Government refuses (as is overwhelmingly likely) even to consider the report of the present Scottish constitutional Convention, let alone to empower a referendum? And what would happen if, as is at least possible under the present electoral system, the Conservatives retain office after the next election or if a Labour Prime Minister tries to avoid the commitment his party appears to have made to create a Scottish parliament? There is no knowing. Opinions might grow stronger but still not translate into appropriate, understandable, historically precedented behaviour. Or there could be widespread popular protest and real trouble. My vision of civil disobedience is neither of riots, nor of Jim Sillars and Donald Dewar politely disputing who shall cast the first symbolic stone at the windows of the Secretary of State for Scotland, but of respectable, worried, conventional local government officers all over Scotland beginning to ignore injunctions and to organise an election for a Scottish Parliament.

The heroic version of Irish independence and of Ulster maintaining the border centres on fighting, bloodshed, atrocities and 'the lads of the column' and the militias; while the realistic version centres on the resulting stalemate and war-weariness on both sides. But there is a civilian version also: that at some stage law-abiding and home-abiding family men in three-piece suits and watch chains began to post their official returns on this and that to Leinster House and not the Castle. Pray God Scotland's right can be obtained peaceably and without 'troubles'. Much will depend on the character of the response when propositions are made. It will be a test for the English political mind at a bad time. It is dangerous to affront the rights and pride of a nation for whom the present English Government has lost politically all right to speak. The matter of Scotland, as Burke said of the matter of taxation, 'goes to the heart of the whole constitution'; and it finds it wanting. And if the English come to accept in Scotland what will be, in fact if not in theory, a federal constitution, some ways forward, at present closed, will open up again in Northern Ireland, recognising the fact that the north of Ireland inherently faces both ways.

The key to the matter is, I honestly believe (if an English empiricist may risk sounding Hegelian) conceptual not practical: the English have to come to terms with the fact, as Hugh Kearney has so recently and so well argued, that the name of the state is 'the United Kingdom' not 'England' and its history is that of the intermingling and interindependence of four nations.[12]

CHAPTER 23

John Hewitt: an Ulster of the Mind

by

Terence Brown

> 'My cast of mind is such that I am moved by intuitions, intimations, imaginative realisations, epiphanies'
>
> John Hewitt.

A poet reveals the primary preoccupations of his life as much by his keywords as by his recurrent images. Few readers of Yeats fail to note how the word 'dream' recurs through his poetry like a verbal revenant from the land of sleep and shadows. The act of dreaming, the reverie, the dream itself become the stuff of poetry by which the apparently substantial life of humankind is measured and often found wanting. *In dreams begin responsibilities. Enough to know they dreamed and are dead. Mere dreams, nothing but dreams. This dream itself had all my thought and love.*

Hewitt's key word, surprisingly in one so apparently rooted in the material world is 'mind'. The word 'mind' tolls solemnly through his verse from beginning to end, usually qualified by adjective or adverb: 'lonely mind', comfortable mind', 'single mind', 'cynic mind', 'restless mind', 'troubled mind', 'the mind of truth'. This indeed is a poet obsessed by the reality of mental life, who is characteristically drawn to ponder the fact and nature of his own powers of consciousness. It is with Hewitt the mental traveller that I wish to journey in this essay, to discover how his conception of human personality, of its constituent parts with the mind in co-operative activity with the senses, the heart and the will, determine the ways in which he writes about his native place. The Hewitt joined on this excursion is a rather different poet from the poet of his popular reputation, altogether more philosphical than customarily realized, more involved in the problematics of selfhood and conscious of unfathomable mystery, than the current critical estimate would allow. The Hewitt with which criticism most now reckon I believe, especially as his later work comes more fully into focus in relationship with what went before, is more than the chronicler of a people's identity crisis, more than the pastoral poet of an Ulster landscape that is read for sociological and regionalist data.

The clue that Hewitt as man possessed surprising interests in psychoanalytic thought was offered to those of us so dull that we had not read the poetry aright, was supplied several years ago by Roy McFadden when he wrote in *Threshold* of the Hewitt household in Mount Charles in Belfast in the 1940's:

> The teaching of C.G.Jung dominated the Hewitt household during the Forties. In a letter written in 1945, complimenting me on my second book, *Flowers for a Lady* – 'quite honestly no recent book of verse by any of the younger moderns has so delighted me or interested me so immediately. Indeed most of what I want to say is in the sonnet I enclose: the verses occurred tonight after I had spent most of the evening reading and talking about your book' – he concludes: 'Ruby joins me in my enthusiasm. Together we agreed that in Jung's phraseology you are a fine 'feeling' poet – you know the quartering – sensation/feeling/intellect/intuition. I am satisfied that I can praise you objectively, as I am a 'sensation' type.[1]

And McFadden concludes by remembering how at Mount Charles 'Jungian allusions pervaded the room like the persistent aroma of herbal tobacco.'[2]

In writing in this fashion to McFadden, Hewitt was of course employing the notion of psychological types developed by Jung in his monumental work of that name in which he distinguishes between introverted and extraverted personalities and divides these into a further four groups or types: sensation, feeling, thinking and intuition. That Hewitt saw himself as a sensation type certainly is of a piece with the conventional estimate of his art as rooted in a realistic, even materialist grasp of the details of the physical world. For sensation in Jungian terms is the human function by which human beings come to know that a thing exists 'Sensation tells me that something is: it does not tell what it is and it does not tell me other things about that something; it only tells me that something is'.[3] But the Jungian would never see sensation as sufficient for healthy human existence, let alone for the production of art. Thinking is also necessary (the sensation type may have serious difficulty with feeling for these are opposites in Jung's scheme of things). And 'thinking' in Jungian terms is the function by which the human being can come to know what a thing is: 'It gives a name to the thing. It adds a concept, because thinking is perception and judgement'.[4] Accordingly in much of Hewitt's poetry of the 1940's which was collected in his first volume *No Rebel Word* (1948) the reader senses a dialectic between a landscape scrupulously itemised in its objective particulars and a mental life at work on the material world, giving it a local habitation and a name within the mental life of the poet. It was this that drew from Geoffrey Taylor, the critic and poet who encouraged Hewitt in his early career, the judgement that the poems in the book could not be 'subsumed under categories of sentiment and sensibility' For 'there is running through them, a tough intellectual quality that puts them outside the purely pastoral'.[5]

The first poem in the book makes my point and Taylor's with nice precision (the poem 'The Touch of Things' was excluded from the *Collected Poems* of 1968). The poem, admitting the man of sensation's thoughtful dialectic with the objective world, is also a plea for feeling and the insights of intuition. The first two stanzas set mind and world in strangely unsatisfying relationship. The final two posit a richer mode of consciousness than mere sensation and thinking:

> If life's to mean full fist and riper wisdom
> these things must turn to blood, to blood and muscle,
> till lash of eye is April rain transmuted
> and lift of knee the sun on Antrim cliffs.
>
> Then when I set a flock of dreams adrift
> they will be pigeons wandering at will,
> not paper-boats blown in among the reeds,
> nor helter-skelter down the spated streams,
> but have small eager beings of their own
> to plane or circle to any possible cloud,
> and then with homesick hearts come back to me.

Many of Hewitt's poems throughout his career continue this dialectical relationship between mind and matter, what he calls here 'the play of mind/upon the smooth or ragged surfaces'. His descriptive poems, the landscape poems of the Ulster countryside for which he is justly famous, are more therefore than works of the topographical impulse but poems which dramatise the mind in the act of perception, the heart finally fulfilled by what sensation and thought have offered to it, as in the remarkably achieved early poem 'Glenarriffe and Parkmore' with its resonant rhetoric:

so you have travelled far from Waterfoot
not marked in metres but in rhythm of pulse:
the heart uplifted with the mounting trees
and falling waters, scooped out of the air
and gapped beneath you as you stop to look;
and held at level of hushed ecstasy
as if with gull's straight heel you pass
to the vast silence of unmastered earth.

But what does Hewit mean by 'mind' in his poems and what is the thinking that the mind contributes to sensation, feeling and intuition? There is much evidence in the work that the poet means a great deal more than simply the mental capacity to engage in discursive, logical commentary on what eye and heart have observed and felt. Though at times reading Hewitt in bulk the reader may be deceived, for in the canon there are many poems which do not seem to rise above that. Indeed a central weakness of Hewitt as poet is his too frequent tendency to slip into an all too predictable tone of prosy comment on landscape and the life and times of his people. But in his most charged poems the mind is present as a synthesising agent, holding perception, feeling and intuitive understanding of symbolic, even mythical possibilities, in a composed harmony. 'First Honey', a late sonnet from the volume *Loose Ends* (1983) is one such poem. Here sensation, the details of landscape and the topography of an Ulster that had so often engaged Hewitt's poetic attention are rendered by the mind with a sense of particularity that does not prevent these things entering on the condition of personal allegory, one which hesitates on the verge of mythology.

My mind drifts back to those far days that bred
the heart-light lyric leaping off the thought
some flicking twig or wing provoked unsought
and easily nested in a rhyme-rife head.
Now strangely, from youth's hopes and hazards free,
the verses come much slower, with a tone,
closer to speech than song, their quality
of time's four seasons, this grave last alone.

Pulse-proven, wiser, maybe, but the mood
once lyric bright is now diffused and grey,
each blurred sun rises on a briefer day;

not green braird thrusting but rain darkened corn;
so I look back with ready gratitude
to the first honey won from blossomed thorn.

Carl Gustav Jung is obviously one source of this interest in myth, image, folklore and the symbolising powers of Man as maker which so preoccupies Hewitt in such poems as 'Freehold' and 'Those Swans Remember'. But the Hewitt of Marxist sympathies, of socialist conscience, the atheist who chose to donate his body to science and whose sensibility seems attracted by a materialist determination to resist mumbo jumbo of any sort is hard to read as a disciple of the Swiss image. Passages in 'Freehold' may hint at a belief in the Jungian version of the collective unconscious as when he admits:

For now I scorn no man's or child's belief
in any symbol that may succour grief
if we remember whence life first arose
and how within us yet that river flows;
and how the fabled shapes in dreams deep sea
still evidence our continuity
with being's seamless garment, web and thread.

But the tone even here is clear-minded and rational with none of Jung's cloudy religiosity, his suggestion of arcane, esoteric knowledge and power exercised. It is my sense that for Hewitt's philosophy of mind we have to look elsewhere, to another psychologist and aesthetician whose little known writings were I believe highly significant in the formation of Hewitt's sense of reality and art. I am referring to the Victorian, Eneas Sweetland Dallas (1828–1879) author of *Poetics* (1852) and *The Gay Science* (1866). John Hewitt himself in conversation alerted me to these works, speaking of them with that infectious enthusiasm about things which excited him, which was perhaps his primary charm as a human being.

The *Dictionary of National Biography* gives us the basic facts. Dallas was the elder son of John Dallas of Jamaica, a planter of Scottish parentage. One can imagine Hewitt's attention quickening at that word 'planter'. Dallas was educated at Edinburgh University under the philosopher and psychologist Sir William Hamilton (to whom his *Poetics is* dedicated) where, we are told, he 'acquired the habit of applying notions derived from electric psychology to the analysis of aesthetic effects in poetry, rhetoric and the fine arts'. Dallas spent most of his life working as a journalist in London; he worked on *The Times*. He must have died a saddened man for his most ambitious work in the two volumes I have cited never achieved much fame for their author. It might be some kind of consolation for his shade if it could know that the Scottish intellectual tradition in which he worked, with its humanistic interest in theories of personhood and in perception, the phenomenology of consciousness, gave through his own writings the intellectual stimulus which a twentieth century Irish poet required as he reflected on the nature of his own mental and imaginative life.

A few brief quotations suggest how sympathetic Dallas's writings must have been to Hewitt. 'The labour of ploughing up the soil of the mind is only undertaken in view of the coming harvest'.[6] 'The more natural and healthy state of the mind is to be self-forgetful'.[7] Imagination is 'the interpretor between sense and spirit'.[8] It is also 'the grand harmonist of life; it is the interpreter and peacemaker between mind and matter; it supplies the connecting link between thought and thought, it enters largely into the composition of faith and cemented by faith, it forms the pillars and the arches of society. Harmony is its chief end'.[9] All these from the *Poetics* suggest a shared sense of life, the same quietly moral imagination, the same serious-minded habit of categorisation and the establishing of hierarchies of value. But Dallas's influence on Hewitt was I think more than simply a matter of the poet finding confirmation of his habits of mind in the Scottish writer. I believe Hewitt adopted his art and developed his thinking about the human mind itself in line with Dallas's insights.

The most obvious manner in which Hewitt seems to have followed Dallas's poetic prescriptions is in the composition of landscape verse. Hewitt in his attempt to realize the landscape of his native region in language had of course models in the English poetic tradition, especially in the prospect poem of the English eighteenth-century.[10] But as a poet who could rarely separate his sense of landscape from his own awareness of observing eye and reflective mind which give the concept of landscape its significance, he must have found Dallas a cogent advisory voice. In *Poetics* Dallas writes of the poetic potential of topographical, descriptive verse:

> Of seeing it is nothing beyond a truism to observe that the mere view of any one thing, however agreeable to the eye is not poetical. Beauty is never a unit; it is a plural. Apart from the associations which belong to them, the sight of a cloudless sky, of a waveless sea, of a green grass plot, does not make poetry. But let any of these be combined with other objects – a sky with clouds or stars, a

> sea with ships, or porpoises, a grass plot with daisies or buttercups and there is a vision before you which, without help of imagination you cannot look at so truly to see it, that is so as to be able afterwards to picture it before your mind's eye. You cannot behold two things together and recognise them as joined, without imagination and it is for this reason, that with all their staring, many see so little . . . So that the mere survey of anything, especially anything beautiful, whose outline is filled with details not a few, is an act which requires so much imagination as will itself almost suffice to raise that act to the rank of poetry . . . No man can really behold a landscape, so that, when he turns away, it shall hang like a picture in his mind, and he could sketch it, if he had the art of pencilling, but the mood of his mind so engaged is entitled to the name of poetry.[11]

This intriguing passage, which must recall to us the Gaelic poets who were required in their long apprenticeship to summon to mind in their darkened cells the poetry of every significant place in the country, also reads like a recipe for much of the landscape verse of John Hewitt. For in paragraph after paragraph of careful verse he restores the rich detail of a particular place, allowing the mood of his mind, which Dallas identifies with imagination, to raise the act of mental recall to the condition of poetry. 'Glendun on a wet July Day', collected in *Out of My Time* is one such poem. A place and a moment are recalled in a mood of the mind in which detail is the controlling principle of composition:

> Today the misty hills are filled with water:
> the Dun runs brown round stones and over stones,
> or amber over gravel – a bleached branch
> stranded by spate beside a swaying foxglove
> rooted in stony splinters – loud it sounds,
> brimming the air with rush and splash and chatter,
> and, over, under these, an endless roar;
> foam-white at boulder's damming, ramming froth
> in the sharp crevices abrupt, it hurries
> along the glen-foot past the dripping trees
> and the combed grasses and the beaded whins.

There is in such writing both the express detail of a specific topography and the sense of the mind in the act of recall which Dallas reckoned the true power or imagination. Such recollection is accordingly an envisoning which finds expression in the orderly composure of the verse, a verse that gratefully accepts the poetic potential of the visible world and seeks only to charge that with the mind's recollective powers.

That Hewitt conceived of his topographical writings in this psychological, phenomenological manner is evidenced not only by such extensive descriptive passages which seem to proceed along principles which would have satisfied the Dallas of *Poetic*: a number of Hewitt's most complex poems in fact meditate upon the mysterious relationship which exists between landscape and mind when the poet seeks to make topography matter for verse. 'The Glen of Light' in what I consider Hewitt's most remarkable single collection, *The Rain Dance* (1978), supplies a telling text.

This open glen's so brimmed with air and light
that space itself has body, palpable;
between the steep fields rimming left and right,
this seems the deep cup of a crystal well,

ribbed by green hedges, shadow-sharpened clear,
grazing and grain their varied textures tilt;
the small sheep on the mountain flank appear
like rough burrs stitched into a billowed quilt.

Too full this sense. This eye's no mortal lens,
clouding with time and thought. Reality
must wear the colours of this innocence;
else how could creature man creation see?

This is in fact a poem in which Hewitt's unquestionable (but rarely discussed) mystical streak finds frank expression. For in such a poem Hewitt opens himself to the possibility that sensation, perception, the act of the mind in recall and creation, the phenomenon of consciousness itself, are not reductively to be comprehended in some simplistic materialism. Such a poem indeed suggests that what Hewitt can mean by 'mind' in the many poems in which he employs the term is something altogether more mysterious than scientistic rationalism can allow (and for Hewitt's attitude at one stage of his life to scientism and its works read 'The Ruins Answer', written between 1937 and 1944). 'The Glen of Light' attends to a moment in consciousness when consciousness itself realizes its own processes and therefore admits its own contingency in the order of being, its creaturely participation in perceptual activity which momentarily in the poem transcends time and thought. Call this secular mysticism if you like, but a form of mysticism it nevertheless remains (the imagery of air and light here are wonderfully bouyant, overflowing presences, redolent of transcendental possibilities). And the poem is an attempt to gain access to states of mind that lie beneath or above thought, free of time, in which sight and recall are elemental activities of the 'creature man'. 'Mind', not mentioned in the poem, is present as a state of abnormal consciousness ('too full this sense') which suggests its hidden powers of primal perception.

The Hewitt of 'The Glen of Light' is a poet who might well have interested himself at a stage in his life in the writings of Carl Gustav Jung, and not only in Jungian ideas about personality types and the process of individuation, but the Jung of the unconscious and the collective unconscious. For Hewitt, as such a poem indicates, clearly believes that mind is a more creative, collective and profound reality than any straightforward rationalist account of its capacities would suggest. The striking feature about the poems in which his mystical awarenesses of pre-conscious or unconscious mental processes is admitted, is their markedly a-religious, strictly profane attitude to what in Jung is invariably invested with the respect due to the sacred, the magical, the esoteric. I believe that Hewitt was encouraged to contemplate experience in the light of such a sanitised, secularised version of depth psychology by his readings in Dallas's second work *The Gay Science*.

A central chapter in that study is entitled 'The Hidden Soul'. By this term Dallas means not the spiritual essence of the human being which is imparted at birth by some divine agency and which will live on after death, but what we would now, after Jung, call the unconscious mind. He announces the burden of his argument in this chapter as follows:

> The object of this chapter is not so much to identify imagination with what may be called the hidden soul, as to show that there is a mental existence within us which may be so called – a secret flow which is no less energetic than the conscious flow, an absent mind which haunts us like a ghost or a dream and is an essential part of our lives.[12]

Dallas believes that this faculty is identical with imagination which in earlier chapters of his treatise he has categorised as a matter of memory, reason and passion. In addressing the hidden processes of a mental life which can be designated 'the hidden soul', Dallas admits that he is stepping into what must appear as he puts it, 'enchanted ground'[13] and that he is investigating what in the perennial philosophy of east and west has been the basis of mysticism. For 'the vast tracts of unconscious, but still active, mind existing within us, lies at the base of all the theories of the mystics'.[14] But Dallas in this work is at pains, and here I think his study must have been peculiarly sympathetic to the sceptical and materially inclined poet of sensation, John Hewitt, to distinguish such beliefs from metaphysical transcendentalism. This he dismisses as the 'absurdities and extravagances of transcendental philosophy'.[15] Furthermore as he gets down to show how imagination as memory, reason and passion has its unconscious as its conscious dimension he depends on demonstrable facets of mental life which constitute a taxonomy of psychological fact. To unconscious memory can be attributed all kinds of automatic unwilled acts of recall, to unconscious reason the fact that a person can perform acts quite unselfconsciously which require extraordinary feats of knowledge, technique and skill and to unconscious passion the fact that love and sympathy rise unbidden in the human heart driving the individual to deeds from which the conscious mind would shrink.

Dallas's chapter is a fascinating account of all sorts of odd mental events. There are tales of sleepwalkings, of solutions to problems that came in sleep, languages remembered unconsciously from childhood, automatic acts of skill, like children falling asleep over machines in factories and still functioning as unconscious hands. One example of the freaks of the unconscious mind is comic enough. 'We laugh to hear' says Dallas 'of the drunken Irish porter who forgot when sober what he had done when drunk, and had to get drunk again in order to remember any circumstances which was [sic] necessary for him to recall . . .'.[16] But Dallas's serious purpose is to give rational, defensible grounds for believing that mind is more than what it was in the Cartesian system where 'the essence of mind is thought; the mind is nothing unless it thinks, and to think is to be conscious'. And all his careful categorisation of mental processes and events is to demonstrate the sound Scottish sense of his conviction

> that consciousness is not our entire world, that the mind stretches in full play far beyond the bourne of consciousness. . .Outside consciousness there rolls a vast tide of life which is perhaps even more important to us than the little isle of our thoughts which lies within our ken . . . We live in two concentric worlds of thought – an inner ring, of which we are conscious, and which may be described

> as illuminated; an outer one of which we are unconscious, and which may be described as in the dark. Between the outer and inner ring, between our unconscious and our conscious existence there is a free and a constant but unobserved traffic forever carried on.[17]

Hewitt's poem 'The Response' could be read as a gloss on this fascinating chapter. It is the poem in which he most frankly admits of his interest in the unconscious, collective mind. An incident of shared, instinctive sympathy between the human and the animal provokes a philosophic speculation. A sleeping dog stirs in a dream. In the next room a sleeping girl who has spent the day in the hills with the dog picks up the signal of the dog's whimper in her unconscious mind. It is just the sort of incident Dallas would have lighted on and discussed in 'the Hidden Soul'. And Hewitt offers us an interpretation straight from the Scot's book:

> Some moments after the dog's cry
> the younger girl tossed restlessly
> and whistled a few straggling notes;
> and I, who have known mind to mind
> signal without the flags of speech,
> and took that as an added grace
> affection adds to sympathy,
> stood suddenly upon the shore
> of a new continent of sense
> that's mapped beneath our coarser world,
> where, not in the tormented throes
> in which the lonely spirit thrives
> with broken splinters of the self
> being, like water, finds its shape
> no longer bottled into selves,
> but flowing, tidal, out of time,
> and vast as ocean's unity.

I believe that when a full intellectual biography is written of John Hewitt, when we are given access to his papers, letters and other literary remains, the work of Dallas will come to be reckoned an important influence on his thought and poetic. What that influence was in all its aspects we can now only speculate. My sense of the matter, beyond what I have suggested already, is this. I imagine that Dallas's ideas about a hidden soul, or unconscious mind appealed greatly to an intelligence that found Jung an instructive guide to the divisions of the self and to the processes of individual growth but whose apparent, religiose transcendentalism was antithetical. Dallas offered the sceptical, materialist thinker a way to admit that the mind was more than intelligence and that poetic imagination (which Dallas indentified with the hidden soul or the mind at work in ways not readily available to conscious awareness) could have to do with myth, folklore, primary images, archetypes, without giving way to mystical obscurantism.

Dallas may well have given Hewitt leave to explore what is one of his most intriging subjects, what in the title of this essay I have called an Ulster of the mind. By that I mean that Hewitt through his work establishes an imaginary Ulster in which a set of private symbols – of birds, the swan and the heron, thorn trees, pathways, the fallen leaf – share a poetic space with the older mythology of the region, with Cuchulain, Ossian, the salmon of all knowledge of Celtic legend and with the folklore of the Ulster countryside – the hare in the last swathe, the May altar. A critical task remains therefore to examine fully Hewitt's use of private image and of mythology in his markedly mental poetry where he broods on the significance of the mythopoeic imagination in its Ulster setting.

For humankind in Hewitt's understanding is a symbol- and myth-making species, as well as a builder, farmer, worker, and social being. And as a generater of the symbolic, the unconscious mind with its roots in some collective human activity that lies beneath conscious awareness, has, in Hewitt's sense of things a powerful influence on the artist. Often Hewitt's poetic exploration of this intermediary territory between topography and the mythic faculty is somewhat vitiated as poetry by the very clear-headed lack of mystification which gave the poet personal licence to explore his subject. We expect our mythologists to give us the Yeatsian dream, the phantasmagoria. This Hewitt scarcely ever does although such poems as 'Swan', and 'Man Fish and Bird' touch what in another poem ('The Child, the Chair, the Leaf') Hewitt identified as the 'Drift of depth far deeper than the self'. What he does offer in some of his most interesting poems is consciousness in the act of composing an Ulster of the mind, in which sensation is held in the processes of thought like a chemical in a solution. But the processes of thought are also deemed in such poems to include activities of an unconscious which must declare itself in symbols and archetypes. And for Hewitt (the gallery man and art historian) it is in art, particularly in sculpture, that sensation, image and mythology achieve their fullest integration. His poem 'Substance and Shadow' (from *Time Enough*) supplies a conclusive instance where the Ulster landscape, sensation, the mind as an image-making faculty and images from the collective unconscious are reckoned to inform the peculiar energies of bronze and stone brought to consciousness from unconsciousness:

There is a bareness in the images
I temper time with in my mind's defence;
They hold their own, their stubborn secrecies;
no use to rage against their reticence:
a gannet's plunge, a heron by a pond,
the last rook homing as the sun goes down,
a spider squatting on a bracken-frond,
and thistles in a cornsheaf's tufted crown,

a boulder on a hillside, lichen-stained,
the sparks of sun on dripping icicles,
their durable signifigance contained
in texture, colour, shape, and nothing else.
All these are sharp, spare, simple, native to
this small republic I have charted out
as the sure acre where my sense is true,
while round its boundaries sprawl the screes of doubt.

My lamp lights up the kettle on the stove
and throws its shadow on the white-washed wall,
like some Assyrian profile with, above
a snake-, or bird-prowed helmet crested tall;
But this remains a shadow; when I shift
the lamp or move the kettle it is gone,
the substance and the shadow break adrift
that needed bronze to lock them, bronze or stone.

REFERENCES

Chapter 2
The Nine Glens of Antrim
CAHAL DALLAT

1. Dusty Rhodes [James Stoddard Moore], 'The Grey Man's Path' in *McCahan's Local Histories*, comp. Cahal Dallat (Cushendall: Glens of Antrim Historical Society, 1988).
2. Richard Dobbs, *A Briefe description of the County of Antrim in 1683*, appended to Rev. George Hill, *The MacDonnels of Antrim* (Belfast: Arche & Sons, 1873).
3. *Ordnance Survey Memoirs for the Parish of Layd* (1833), published as *Life in the Glens of Antrim in the 1830s* (Cushendall: Glens of Antrim Society, 1968).
4. W.M. Thackeray, *Paris, Irish and Eastern Sketch Books* (London: Smith, Elder, 1872), 517.
5. Hill, 23.
6. P. Rhodes, *The Antrim Coast Road* (Belfast: Northern Ireland Tourist Board, c. 1963).
7. Miss Higginson was better known as Moira O'Neill, poetess of the Glens.
8. H.V. Morton, *In Search of Ireland* (London: Methuen, 1930, 21st ed. 1947), 248.

Chapter 3
The Iconography of the Antrim Coast
MARTYN ANGLESEA

1. *Kings in Conflict: Ireland in the 1690s* (exhibition catalogue), ed. Eileen Black (Belfast: Ulster Museum, 1990), 86.
2. Martyn Anglesea and John Preston, 'A Philosophical Landscape: Susanna Drury and the Giant's Causeway', *Art History* 3.3 (1980): 252–73.
3. Rev. William Hamilton, *Letters Concerning the Northern Coast of the County of Antrim with the Natural History of the Basaltes* (Belfast: T. Mairs, 1822), Part II, letter I, 101–2.
4. See Christie's sale catalogue, *Original Drawings and Sketches by John Nixon (Part I) Sold by Order of the Governor and Directors of the French Hospital of La Providence* (Nov. 6 1973). See also Huon Mallalieu, 'John Nixon and his Circle', *Country Life* (May 12, 1977): 1260.

5. Robert L. Raley, 'John James Barralet in Dublin and Philadelphia', *Irish Arts Review* 2.3 (1985): 19; Samuel Redgrave, *A Dictionary of Artists of the English School* (1878; rpt. Bath: Kingsmead Reprints, 1970); Iolo Aneurin Williams, *Early English Watercolours* (London: Connoisseur, 1952).
6. Eileen Black, *Paintings, Sculptures and Bronzes in the Collection of the Belfast Harbour Commissioners* (Belfast, 1983), 52.
7. John Wilson Foster, 'The Topographical Tradition in Anglo-Irish Poetry', *Irish University Review* 4.2 (1974): 169–87.
8. Anne Plumptre, *Narrative of a Residence in Ireland during the Summer of 1814, and that of 1815* (London: Henry Colburn, 1817), 98.
9. *Transactions of the Geological Society* (1st series) 3 (1816): 196–216.
10. Martyn Anglesea, 'Andrew Nicholl and his Patrons in Ireland and Ceylon', Studies 71 (1982): 130; Martyn Anglesea, Introduction to *Andrew Nicholl's Views of the Antrim Coast in 1828* (Belfast: Glens of Antrim Historical Society, 1982).
11. James Moore 1819–1883 (exhibition catalogue), ed. Martyn Anglesea (Belfast: Ulster Museum, 1973); *Portraits and Prospects: British and Irish Drawings and Watercolours from the Collection of the Ulster Museum* (exhibition catalogue), ed. Martyn Anglesea (Belfast: Ulster Museum and Smithsonian Institution Traveling Exhibition Service, 1989), 98–100.
12. *The Irish Naturalists' Journal* 6.6 (1936) contains obituaries and reminiscences of Welch written by Robert Lloyd Praeger (naturalist), A.W. Stelfox (conchologist), A.R. Hogg (photographer) and J. Wilfrid Jackson of the Manchester Museum. See also E. Estyn Evans and Brian S. Turner, Ireland's Eye: *The Photographs of Robert John Welch* (Belfast: Blackstaff Press, 1977) and Kenneth James, 'A Hungry Lens', *Belfast Review* 10 (1985): 18.
13. Martyn Anglesea, *The Royal Ulster Academy of Arts: A Centennial History* (Belfast: RUAA, 1981).
14. Joseph Beuys, *The Secret Block for a Secret Person in Ireland* (Ulster Museum, Nov. 1974).

Chapter 4
Settlement and Society in Eighteenth Century Ireland
KEVIN WHELAN

1. L. Cullen, 'Man, Landscape, and Roads; the Changing Eighteenth Century', in *The Shaping of Ireland*, ed. W. Nolan (Cork: Mercier Press, 1986), 124.
2. E. Evans, *The Personality of Ireland* (Cambridge: Cambridge University Press, 1973), passim.

3. J. Andrews, 'The Ethnic Factor in Irish Historical Geography' (1974); 'The Geographic Study of the Irish Past' (1977), papers delivered to the Conference of Irish Geographers.
4. T. Jones Hughes, 'Society and Settlement in Nineteenth-Century Ireland' in *Irish Geography* V (1965): 79–96.
5. C. O'Hara, 'An account of County Sligo in the Eighteenth Century', N.L.I. MS 20, 397.
6. E. McParlan, *A Statistical Survey of County Mayo* (Dublin: Royal Dublin Society, 1802), 122.
7. K. Whelan, 'Catholic Mobilisation 1750–1850' in *Culture et Pratiques en France et en Irlande xvie – xviiie Siecle*, ed. P. Bergeron and L. Cullen (Paris: Centre De Recherches Historiques, 1991), 235–58.
8. T. Truxes, *Irish-American Trade 1650–1783* (Cambridge: Cambridge University Press, 1988), 86.
9. For Waterford, see J. Mannion, 'The Maritime Trade of Waterford in the Eighteenth Century' in *Common Ground: Essays on the Historical Geography of Ireland*, ed. W. Smyth and K. Whelan (Cork: Cork University Press, 1988), 208–25; for Cork see D. Dickson, 'An Economic History of the Cork Region in the Eighteenth Century', diss., T.C.D., 1977.
10. J. Mockler, 'A Report on the District around Mallow in 1775', *Cork Hist. Arch. Soc. Jn.* 33 (1915): 261.
11. K. Whelan, 'The Regional Impact of Irish Catholicism 1700–1850' in Smyth and Whelan, 252–71.
12. K. Whelan, 'The Catholic Community in Eighteenth Century County Wexford' in *Endurance and Emergence: Catholics in Ireland in the Eighteenth Century*, ed. T. Power and K. Whelan (Dublin: Irish Academic Press, 1990), 129–70.
13. R. Bell, *A Description of the Conditions and Manners of the Peasantry of Ireland such as they were between the Years 1780 and 1850*, in Smyth and Whelan, 252–71.
14. K. Whelan, in Power and Whelan, passim.
15. T. Jones Hughes, 'The Large Farm in Nineteenth-Century Ireland' in *Gold under the Furze*, ed. A. Gailey and D. O. hOgain (Dublin: Glendale Press, 1982), 92–100.
16. K. Whelan, 'Politicisation in County Wexford and the Origins of the 1798 Rebellion' in *Ireland and the French Revolution*, ed. H. Gough and D. Dickson (Dublin; Irish Academic Press, 1990), 156–78.
17. L. Cullen, 'Catholic Social Classes under the Penal Laws' in Power and Whelan, 57–84; K. Whelan, in Smyth and Whelan; K. Whelan, 'Gaelic Survivals', *The Irish Review*, 7 (1989); 139–43.
18. R. Dodgshon, 'The Ecological Base of Highland Peasant Farming 1500–1800' in *The Cultural Landscape: Past, Present and Future*, ed. H. Birks et al (Cambridge: Cambridge University Press, 1989), 139–51.
19. A. Nicholson, *Ireland's Welcome to the Stranger* (London: Bible Society, 1846), 153.

20. The following section is based largely on the pioneering work of W. Crawford. For a general summary, see W. Crawford, 'The Political Economy of Linen: Ulster in the Eighteenth Century', in *Ulster: An illustrated History*, ed. C. Brady, M. O'Dowd and B. Walker (London: Batsford Books, 1989), 134–57.
21. D. Miller, *Peep O'Day Boys and Defenders: Selected Documents on the County Armagh Disturbances 1784–96* (Belfast: P.R.O.N.I., 1990), 46.
22. W. Crawford, 'The Evolution of the Linen Trade in Ulster before Industrialisation', *Ir. Ec. Soc. Hist.*, xv (1988): 32–53.
23. K. Whelan, 'Catholics, Politicisation and the 1798 Rebellion', *Seanchas Ardmhacha* (forthcoming).
24. J. Andrews, 'Land and People c.1780' in *New History of Ireland*, vol. iv (Oxford: Oxford University Press, 1986), 236–64.
25. D. Dickson, 'The Demographic Implications of Dublin's Growth 1650–1850' in *Urban Population Growth and Development in Western Europe*, ed. R. Lawton and R. Lee (Liverpool: Liverpool University Press, 1989), 178–89.
26. J. Whitelaw, *An Essay on the Population of Dublin being the Result of an Actual Survey taken in 1798* (Dublin: Graisberry and Campbell, 1805).
27. T. Jones Hughes, 'Historical Geography since 1700' in *Irish Geography 1934–1984*, ed. G. Davies (Dublin: Geographical Society of Ireland, 1984), 139.

Chapter 5

Landscape and Locality in the Work of the Rhyming Weavers

IVAN HERBISON

1. The fullest account of these poets is John Hewitt's pioneering study *Rhyming Weavers and other Country poets of Antrim and Down* (Belfast, 1974), See also I. Herbison, *John Hewitt's Rhyming Weavers; Presbyterianism, Politics and Poetry in Nineteenth-century Ulster*, forthcoming.
2. J. Fullarton, 'Sketches of Ulster Poets — Andrew MacKenzie', *Ulster Magazine*: 2 [No.20] (August 1861): 374. This is the main source of biographical information on McKenzie.
3. 'To George Dugan, Esq.', *The Select Works of David Herbison* (Belfast and Ballymena, [1883]), 9 (SW; 'On the Death of Andrew M'Kenzie', SW, 66–67.
4. J. Fullarton, 'Sketches of Ulster Poets — Andrew MacKenzie', *Ulster Magazine* 2 [No.20]: 378.
5. For an account of Thomas Beggs, see J. Fullarton, 'Sketches of Ulster Poets — Thomas Beggs', *Ulster Magazine* 2 [No. 18] (June 1861): 243–

49. This was reprinted as the introduction to *The Poetical Works of Thomas Beggs* (Ballyclare, nd [1876]), i–xiv.

6. On James McHenry, see D.J. O'Donoghue, *The Poets of Ireland: A Biographical Dictionary with Bibliographical Particulars* (London, 1892); on John Smyth, see David Herbison, 'On the Death of John Smith', *SW*, 99–100, and also Herbison's biographical sketch, 'John Smith — 'Magowan', *Ulster Magazine*, 2 [No 23] (November 1861): 441–44; on Henry McD. Flecher, see David Herbison, 'To Mr Henry McD Flecher, on his informing me that he was on the eve of leaving this country for America', SW, 209–10.
7. For fuller accounts of David Herbison, see the introduction to my edition of a selection of his poems, *Webs of Fancy: Poems of David Herbison, The Bard of Dunclug* (Ballymena, 1980) and my article 'David Herbison, The Bard of Dunclug: a poet and his community 1800–1880' in *Mid Antrim 1983: Articles on the History of Ballymena and District*, edited Eull Dunlop (Ballymena, 1983), 102–130. This article was reissued separately as a publication of the Dunclug Press, to mark the occasion of the first John Hewitt International Summer School, held at St MacNissi's College, Garron Tower, 30 July – 5 August 1988.
8. *Rhyming Weavers*, 21.
9. See Archibald M'Dowell's 'Sketch of the Author's Life' prefacing *The Posthumous Works of James Orr of Ballycarry* (Belfast, 1817), 185–91. References are to the reprint of Orr's collected poems (Belfast, 1935).
10. *The Second Part of the Minstrel's Offering*, [3].
11. For a convenient treatment, see Kurt Wittig, *The Scottish Tradition in Literature* (Edinburgh, 1958).
12. See J. Fullarton, 'Sketches of Ulster Poets — David Herbison, The Bard of Dunclug', *Ulster Magazine*, 2 [No.23] (August 1861): 457–64.
13. *Minstrelsy of the Scottish Border* (1802–03).
14. J. Fullarton, 'Sketches of Ulster Poets — David Herbison': 460. On the issue of language and cultural identity, see I. Herbison, *Language, Literature and Cultural Identity: An Ulster-Scots Perspective* (Ballymena, 1989).
15. His editors also cut a stanza from "The Exile's Lament", *SW*, 30.
16. For example, 'The Exile's Lament', *SW*, 30; 'The Exile's Farewell to Glenariff', SW, 32; 'The Patriot's Death', *SW*, 99; 'The Patriot's Wife', *SW*, 121–22.
17. See 'Day-break in Glenariff', *SW*, 180; 'The Yarrow', *SW*, 125; 'The Clougher', *SW*, 134–35; 'Lines on the death of William John Mullan', *SW*, 152; 'Stanzas in Memory of the Rev. Hugh Smyth Cumming', *SW*, 159; 'A Few Lines addressed to the Electors of Antrim', *SW*, 292; 'Advertisement', *SW*, 302; 'To Mrs John Sloan, Rath Cottage, on her sending me down a cake of her own baking', *SW*, 309; 'A Poetical Endorsement', *SW*, 285
18. A different version of a section of this article appears in *Mid-Antrim 2*, edited Eull Dunlop.

Chapter 6
The Lonely Rebellion of William Drennan
ADRIAN RICE

1. This information can be found in the permanent Irish historical exhibition of the Ulster Museum.
2. Public Records Office of Northern Ireland (PRONI), D.729/43d.
3. Margaret MacCurtain and Mark Tierney, *The Birth of Modern Ireland* (Dublin: Gill and Macmillan, 1969), 86–87.
4. PRONI, D.729/43e. The rest of the quotations in the first section of my essay are from, respectively, PRONI, D.729/44, 43i, 43f, 43h, 46, 48a and 48b.
5. Maureen Wall, 'The United Irish Movement', *Historical Studies* V (1965), ed. J.L. McCracken, 122–140.
6. A.T.Q. Stewart, *The Narrow Ground: Patterns of Ulster History* (Belfast: Pretani Press, 1986), 106.
7. Stewart, 107.
8. Patrick G. Curley, 'William Drennan and the Young Samuel Ferguson: Liberty, Patriotism, and the Union in Ulster Poetry between 1778 and 1848', diss., Queen's U (Belfast), 1987, 3, 6.
9. Curley, 4.
10. Curley, 68.
11. Ted Hughes in his Afterword to *A Choice of Shakespeare's Verse*, cited in Seamus Heaney, *Preoccupations: Selected Prose* (London: Faber, 1980), 91.
12. This poem, and the ballad 'Erin' (1795) can be found in William Drennan, *Fugitive Pieces in Verse and Prose* (Belfast: Finlay, 1815), 79f.
13. PRONI, D. 531/6, 440.
14. Leerssen, 347.
15. PRONI, T.965/2–5 contains a newspaper report which carries these remarks.
16. PRONI, T.765/2/7, letter 1010, Drennan to M. McTier, October 27, 1802.
17. PRONI, T. 965/2–5.
18. PRONI, T. 765.2.5, letter 641, Drennan to M. McTier, December 1796.
19. PRONI, T. 765/2/5, Drennan to M. McTier, January 14, 1797.
20. Drennan (under the pseud. A.P.), preface to his poem 'Erin', *Belfast Monthly Magazine* 9 (1812): 301.
21. For this letter and subsequent letters from which I have quoted, see, respectively, PRONI T.765/2/ (letter 334), T.765/2/5 (letters 701 and 697), T.765/2/4 (letter 598), T.765/2/5 (letters 678 and 715) and T. 765/2/4 (letter 598).
22. 'To Ireland', *Fugitive Pieces*, 12f.
23. 'Juvenal, Eighth Satire', *Fugitive Pieces*, 87f.

24. *Poetry and Ireland: Essays by W.B. Yeats and Lionel Johnson* (Cork: University Press, 1970), 43.
25. Cited in John Hewitt, 'Regionalism: The Last Chance' (1947), in *Ancestral Voices: The Selected Prose of John Hewitt*, ed. Tom Clyde (Belfast: Blackstaff Press, 1987).

Chapter 7
Samuel Ferguson: A Tourist in Antrim
EVE PATTEN

Sources

Ferguson, S.	*Hibernian Nights' Entertainments.* (3 vols) Dublin: Sealy, Briers & Walker, 1897. These stories were originally published in *Blackwoods Magazine* and the *Dublin University Magazine* between 1833 and 1836.
Ferguson, S.	'The Black Monday of the Glens'. *Dublin University Magazine* VI (Sept 1835.)
Ferguson, S.	'The Attractions of Ireland'. *Dublin University Magazine* VIII (July, Sept, Dec 1836.)
Ferguson, M.C.	*Sir Samuel Ferguson in the Ireland Of His Day*. (2 vols) Edinburgh: Blackwood, 1896.
Andrews, J.H.	*A Paper Landscape: Ordnance Survey in Nineteenth Century Ireland.* Oxford: Clarendon Press, 1975.

References

1. Raymond Williams, *The Country and the City* (London: Chatto & Windus, 1973), 120.
2. William Gilpin, *Essays on Picturesque Beauty, Picturesque Travel and Sketching Landscape*. 2nd ed. London: R. Blamire 1794. Essay 3 p.67.
3. George Petrie *Letters*. N.L.I. Ms. 789–94: Letter from J. Prior 1835.
4. William Wordsworth, *Letters: Irish Tour 1829* cited McCormack, *Ascendancy and Tradition* (Oxford: Clarendon Press, 1985), 36.

Chapter 8
No Rootless Colonists: Samuel Ferguson and John Hewitt
GRÉAGOIR O'DUILL

1. Recent work on Ferguson includes Malcolm Brown, *Sir Samuel Ferguson* (Lewisburg: Bucknell University Press, 1973); Robert O'Driscoll, *An Ascendancy of the Heart* (Dublin: Dolmen Press, 1976); Terence Brown and Barbara Hayley (eds.), *Sir Samuel Ferguson: A Centenary Tribute*

(Dublin: Royal Irish Academy, 1987). The key published source for biographical detail is his widow's unsatisfactory biography: Lady Mary Catherine Ferguson, *Sir Samuel Ferguson in the Ireland of his Day* (Edinburgh: Blackwood, 1896). His major collections are *Lays of the Western Gael* (1865), *Congal* (1872) and *Poems* (1880).
2. 'My Grandmother's Garter'. Most of the Hewitt poems I quote can be found in his *Collected Poems 1932–67* (London: MacGibbon & Kee, 1968).
3. 'The Northern Athens and After', in J.C. Beckett *et al.*, *Belfast: The Making of the City 1800–1914* (Belfast: Appletree, 1983), 79.
4. Robert Bernard Martin, *Tennyson: The Unquiet Heart* (Oxford: Clarendon, 1980), 111.
5. 'The Course of Writing in Ulster', *Rann* 20 (1953): 69–70; repr. in *Ancestral Voices: The Selected Prose of John Hewitt*, ed. Tom Clyde (Belfast: Blackstaff Press, 1987).
6. 'The Bitter Gourd', *Lagan* 3 (1945): 93–105; repr. Clyde.
7. 'Irish Poets Learn Your Trade', *Threshold* (1958); repr. Clyde.
8. Hewitt cites as his evidence Alexander McDowell, *Posthumous Works of James Orr* (1817).
9. 'The Attractions of Ireland', *Dublin University Magazine* (1836), cited in John Hewitt, *Rhyming Weavers and Other Country Poets of Antrim and Down* (Belfast: Blackstaff, 1974), 38.
10. *Rhyming Weavers*, 4.
11. Austin Clarke, *The Celtic Twilight and the Nineties* (Dublin: Dolmen, 1969), 87.
12. In *Sir Samuel Ferguson: A Centenary Tribute*, 73. Kenner's question is posed in his *A Colder Eye: The Modern Irish Writers* (London: Allen Lane), 68; for Rafroidi see his *Irish Literature in English* (Gerrards Cross; Colin Smythe, 1980), 194–96.
13. *Rhyming Weavers*, 12–13.
14. J.A., *A Brief Historical Notice of the Parish and People of Donegore 1632–1832*.
15. 'The Northern Athens and After', in Beckett *et al.*, 73.
16. Dónall Ó Luanaigh, 'Contemporary Irish Comment Concerning the Revolution of 1830 in France', *Eire-Ireland* (Summer 1987): 96– 115.
17. W.H. Crawford and Brian Trainor, *Aspects of Irish Social History 1750–1800* (Belfast: H.M.S.O., 1969), 187.
18. Jonathan Bardon, *Belfast: A Thousand Years* (Belfast: Blackstaff, 1985), 14.
19. Allan D. McKillop, 'Local Attachment and Cosmopolitanism', in *From Sensibility to Romanticism*, eds. F.W. Hilles and Harold Bloom (New York: Oxford University Press, 1965), 204.
20. Martin Mooney, 'A Native Mode: Language and Regionalism in Poetry', *The Irish Review* 3 (1988): 67–73.
21. Gréagóir O Dúill, 'Ferguson, an Stát agus an Léann Dúchais', *Studia Hibernica* 19 (1979): 102–111.

Chapter 9
Natural History, Science and Irish Culture
JOHN WILSON FOSTER

Sources

Allen, David Elliston. *The Naturalist in Britain: A Social History*. London: Allen Lane, 1976.

Barber, Lynn. *The Heyday of Natural History London*: Cape, 1980.

Brooke, Peter. 'Religion and Secular Thought 1850–75'. *Belfast: The Making of the City 1800–1914*. Belfast: Appletree Press, 1983.

Campbell, A. Albert. *Belfast Naturalists' Field Club: Its Origin and Progress*. Belfast: Hugh Greer, 1938.

Collins, Philip. *Dickens and Education*. London: Macmillan, 1965.

Davies, Gordon L. Herries. 'Irish Thought in Science'. *The Irish Mind*. Ed. Richard Kearney. Dublin: Wolfhound Press, 1985.

Deane, Arthur, ed. *The Belfast Natural History and Philosophical Society: Centenary Volume, 1821–1921*. Belfast: BNHPS, 1924.

Gray, William. *Science and Art in Belfast*. Belfast: *The Northern Whig*, 1904.

Outram, Dorinda, 'Heavenly Bodies and Logical Minds'. *Graph* (Spring 1988): 9–11.

Praeger, R. Lloyd. *Some Irish Naturalists: A Biographical Note-Book*. Dundalk: Dundalgan Press, 1949.

Ross, Helena C.G. and Robert Nash. 'The Development of Natural History in Early Nineteenth Century Ireland'. *From Linaeus to Darwin*. London: Society for the History of Natural History, 1985.

Chapter 12
Modern Gaelic Poetry
CAOMHIN MAC GIOLLA LITH

1. See Reg Hindley, *The Death of the Irish Language* (Dublin: Routledge, 1990) for a discussion of the available statistics.
2. See Hindley, 225–7; also Charles Withers, *Gaelic in Scotland 1698–1981: the Geographical History of a Language* (John Donald, 1984).
3. 'The Background of Early Irish Literature', *Studia Hibernica* 1 (1961): 11–12.
4. 'A Historical Inventory of the *Dindshenchas' Studia Celtica* 10/11 (1975/76) 115. This discussion of *dinnshenchas* is greatly indebted to Bowen's useful survey article.
5. Bowen, 115.
6. Bowen, 116.
7. Bowen, 116.

8. R. Baumgarten, 'Placenames, Etymology, and the Structure of *Fianaigecht', The Heroic Process: Form, Function and Fantasy in Folk Epic*, edited B. Almqvist, Séamas O Catháin and Pádraig O Héalaí (The Glendale Press, 1987), 2.
9. The Prose Tales in the Rennes Dindshenchas', *Revue Celtique* 15 (1894): 279–80.
10. Bowen, 117.
11. Baumgarten, 24.
12. *The Figure in the Cave and Other Essays* (Dublin: The Lilliput Press, 1989), 43.
13. *Belfast Confetti* (Dublin: Gallery Press, 1989), 48.
14. 'Roots of Melancholy in the Troubled Earth of Ireland'. *The Independent on Sunday*, 14/6/1990.
15. 'Out from Skye to the World: Literature, History and the Poet', in *Sorley Maclean: Critical Essays* edited R.J. Ross and J. Hendry (Scottish Academic Press, 1986), 53.
16. 'Introduction', *Sorley Maclean: Critical Essays*, 3.
17. *O Choille gu Bearradh: Dàin Chruinnichte/From Wood to Ridge: Collected Poems* (Carcanet, 1989), 226–9.
18. Language, Metre and Diction in the Poetry of Sorley Maclean', *Sorley Maclean: Critical Essays*.
19. Heaney, 2.
20. 'Continuing the Link: an Aspect of Contemporary Irish Poetry', *The Irish Review* 3 (1988): 50.
21. See my 'Contemporary Gaelic Poetry: Divided Loyalties and the Chimera of Continuity', *The Irish Review* 6 (Spring 1989): 46–64.
22. *Selected Poems/Rogha Dánta* (Raven Arts Press, 1988), 152–3.
23. Cited by J.H. Delargy in *The Gaelic Storyteller* (The University of Chicago, 1969), 7. In some areas it was believed that the gift was lost to a family for seven generations when inherited by a woman.
24. *Innti* 11 (1988): 31. The translation is by the present writer.
25. "Pap for the Dispossessed". Seamus Heaney and the Poetics of Identity'. *Boundary* 13. 2–3 (Winter/Spring 1985): p.330.
26. See, for instance Gerald Dawe, 'Undermining Assumptions 2. The Irish Poet: Anecdotes over a Jar', *The Irish Review* 9 (Autumn 1990): 58. Reprinted in *How's The Poetry Going?* (Belfaast: Lagan, 1991).
27. 'The Divided Mind', *Irish Poets in English*, edited Seán Lucy (Mercier Press, 1972) 209.

Chapter 14

The Note of Exile: Michael McLaverty's Rathlin Island

SOPHIA HILLAN KING

1. Wallace Clark, *Rathlin: Disputed Island* (Portlaw, Waterford: Volturna Press, 1971), 20–21.

2. 'Leavetaking', *Ireland Today* 11 (1937): 45–51; republished in *In Quiet Places: The Uncollected Stories, Letters and Critical Prose of Michael McLaverty*, ed. Sophia Hillan King (Dublin: Poolbeg, 1989).
3. This letter is in the possession of the McLaverty family.
4. 'The Wild Duck's Nest', *Irish Monthly* 62 (1934): 236–240; republished in *In Quiet Places*.
5. 'The Wild Duck's Nest' (later version) in *The Game Cock and Other Stories* (New York: Devin Adair, 1948); republished in *Michael McLaverty: Collected Short Stories* (Dublin: Poolbeg, 1978).
6. 'The Grey Goat', *Irish Monthly* 61 (1933): 516–520; republished in *In Quiet Places*.
7. 'The Prophet', Irish Monthly 64 (1936): 95–101; republished in *Collected Short Stories*.
8. 'Stone', *Collected Short Stories*, 43–44.
9. In conversation with S.H. King; *Call My Brother Back* (New York and London: Longmans, 1939).
10. John Wilson Foster, 'McLaverty's People', *Eire-Ireland* IV (1971): 92–105.
11. *Call my Brother Back* (Dublin: Poolbeg, 1979), 17–18.
12. McLaverty to V. Mercier, November 1964; letter in possession of the McLaverty family.
13. *Truth in the Night* (New York: Macmillan, 1951), 215.
14. 'The Sea' (later 'Look at the Boats'), *Capuchin Annual* (1939): 150–175.
15. *Call My Brother Back* (Dublin: Poolbeg, 1979), 36.

Chapter 15

History and Poetry: Derek Mahon and Tom Paulin

PETER McDONALD

1. Mahon, *Poems 1962–1978* (Oxford, 1979), 4.
2. *Poems*, 75–6.
3. *Poems*, 6.
4. *The Collected Poems of Louis MacNeice*, ed. Dodds (London, 1966), 62.
5. 'The Man from No Part: Louis MacNeice', *Ireland and The English Crisis* (Newcastle-upon-Tyne, 1984), 78–9.
6. Mahon, *Poems*, 49.
7. Paulin, *Liberty Tree* (London, 1983), 16.
8. Mahon, *The Hunt by Night* (Oxford, 1982), 20.
9. Mahon, *Poems*, 68.
10. Mahon, *Courtyards in Delft* (Dublin, 1981), 17.
11. Mahon, *Poems*, 79–80.
12. Paulin, Introduction to *The Faber Book of Political Verse* (London, 1986), 51.
13. Paulin, 17.

14. Paulin, *Liberty Tree*, 32.
15. *Liberty Tree*, 55–6.
16. *Viewpoints: Poets in Conversation With John Haffenden* (London, 1981), 159.
17. Paulin, *Ireland and The English Crisis*, 17.
18. Paulin, *Fivemiletown* (London, 1987), 4.
19. It is worth adding that Bowden Beggs is the name of a school contemporary of Paulin's, although the poem does not in fact refer to him specifically.
20. Paulin, *Fivemiletown*, 54.
21. *Fivemiletown*, 8.
22. Louis MacNeice, *The Strings Are False: An Unfinished Autobiography* (London, 1965), 78–9.
23. Paulin, *Ireland and The English Crisis*, 18.
24. T.S. Eliot, 'Little Gidding' III, *Complete Poems and Plays* (London, 1969), 195.

Chapter 16
Against Piety: A Reading of John Hewitt's Poetry
GERALD DAWE

1. An interview entitled 'Beyond the Planter and the Gael', *The Crane Bag* 4.2 (1980–1): 722–29.
2. 'Including the North', *Texts and Contexts* 3 (1988): 17–24.
3. Unless otherwise indicated, references to Hewitt's writing are taken from *The Selected John Hewitt*, ed. Alan Warner (Belfast: Blackstaff, 1981), *Collected Poems 1932–67* (London: MacGibbon and Kee, 1988) and *Ancestral Voices: The Selected Prose of John Hewitt*, ed. Tom Clyde (Belfast: Blackstaff, 1987).
4. *Preoccupations: Selected Prose 1968–1978* (London: Faber, 1980), 56–7.
5. *Fortnight* (Feb. 1985).
6. *Poetry Ireland*, repr. in John Montague, *The Figure in the Cave and Other Essays* (Dublin: Lilliput, 1989).
7. *A Gathered Church* (London: Routledge & Kegan Paul, 1978), 26.
8. 'An Englishman Considers his Passport', *The Irish Review* 5 (1988): 10.
9. *Games with Shadows* (London: Radius, 1988), 62.

Chapter 19
A Stirring in Dry Bones: John Hewitt's Regionalism
TOM CLYDE

1. *Awake! and Other Poems* (London: Secker & Warburg, 1941).
2. 'John Hewitt: Regionalism into Reconciliation', *Poetry Ireland* 3, (Spring 1964).

3. 'O Country People'.
4. 'John Hewitt: Land and People', *Northern Voices* (Dublin: Gill and Macmillan), 1975.
5. 'An Ulster Protestant', Bell 4.5 (Aug 1942).

Chapter 20
Uses of History among Ulster Protestants
Anthony Buckley

1. A fuller, more anthropological version of this article appeared in *History and Ethnicity*, eds. E. Tonkin, M. McDonald and M. Chapman (London: Routledge, 1989). Thanks are due to Routledge for permission to abridge it, and to Dr I. Adamson, Mr A. Campbell, members of the Covenant People's Fellowship, church members in south Antrim and Belfast, and innumerable Orangemen and others who helped my fieldwork. Thanks are particularly due to Mrs L.J. Buckley and Dr P.S. Robinson for their unswerving support.
2. For example, D. Bowen, *Souperism: Myth or Reality* (Cork: Mercier, 1970); K.H. Connell, *Irish Peasant Society* (Oxford: Oxford University Press, 1968); S.E. Connolly, *Priests and People in Pre-Famine Ireland 1780–1845* (Dublin: Gill and Macmillan, 1982).
3. For example, F.J. Biggar, *The Ulster Land War of 1790* (*The Hearts of Steel*) (Dublin: Sealy Byers and Walker, 1910); A.S. Green, *The Making of Ireland and its Undoing* (London: Macmillan, 1908); G.O'Brien, *Economic History of Ireland in the 18th Century*. 1918. (Philadelphia, Porcupine Press, 1977); P.S. O'Hegarty, *A History of Ireland Under the Union, 1802–1922* (London: Methuen, 1949).
4. Green, 114.
5. Biggar, 5–6; Green, 118ff.
6. Green, 123ff; O'Brien, 383ff.
7. J.W. Foster, 'Yeats and the Folklore of the Irish Revival', *Eire-Ireland* XVII (1982): 6–18; J.H. Delargy, *The Gaelic Story-Teller: With Some Notes on Gaelic Folk-tales* (Oxford: Oxford University Press, 1945), 187; P. Kennedy, *Legendary Fictions of the Irish Celts* (Detroit: Singing Tree Press, 1891); S. O'Sullivan, *Folktales of Ireland* (Chicago: University of Chicago Press, 1966).
8. J. Harrison, *The Scot in Ulster: Sketch of the History of the Scottish Population in Ulster* (Edinburgh: Blackwood, 1888), 33ff, 48. *Cuchulain, the Last Legend: Ulster, the Lost Culture?* (Belfast: Ulster Young Unionist Council, 1986).
9. There are difficulties with the concept of a 'majority' in Ireland. In Northern Ireland, Protestants are in a majority; in the island as a whole Catholics predominate. Legitimacy based on majorities is, therefore, permanently questionable. See M. Poole, 'The Demography of Violence',

Northern Ireland: The Background to the Conflict, ed. J. Darby (Belfast: Appletree Press, 1983).
10. A.D. Buckley, 'The Chosen Few: Biblical Texts in the Regalia of an Ulster Secret Society', *Folk Life* 24 (19): 5–24.
11. The texts are: 1. Adam and Eve (Genesis: 2–3); 2. Noah's Ark (Genesis: 6–9); 3. Abraham and Isaac (Genesis: 22); 4. Jacob's dream (Genesis: 25–28); Joseph (Genesis: 37–50); 6. Moses and the Exodus (Book of Exodus); 7. Rahab and the Battle of Jericho (Joshua: 2–6); 8. The Two-and-a-half Tribes (Joshua: 22); 9. Gideon (Judges: 6–7); 10. Ruth (The Book of Ruth); 11. David and Goliath (1 Samuel: 17–18); 12. The building of the Temple (1 Kings: 5–8; 13. Elijah and the prophets of Baal (1 Kings: 16–19); 14. Jehu's purge (2 Kings: 10–12); 15. Daniel (Daniel: 2–3, 5–6); 16. New Testament references (Matthew: 3; John: 19–21; Revelation: 21); 17. Melchizedek (Exodus: 28; Hebrews: 7; Genesis: 14, 18ff; Revelation: 5).
12. J. Foxe, *The Book of Martyrs*. 1563. Ed. W.G. Berry (Grand Rapids: Baker Books, 1985); C.B. Tayler, *Memorials of the English Martyrs*. ca. 1850. (Toronto; Wittenberg, 1984).
13. I. Adamson, *The Cruthin: The Ancient Kindred* (Belfast: Donard Press, 1974); I. Adamson, *The Identity of Ulster: The Land, the Language and the People* (Belfast: Pretani Press, 1982).
14. See T.F. O'Rahilly, *Early Irish History and Mythology* (Dublin: Institute for Advanced Studies, 1957).
15. *Cuchulain, the Last Legend.*
16. *The Cruthin*, 12.
17. *The Cruthin*, 42.
18. *The Cruthin*, 15.
19. D.G. Boyce, *Nationalism in Ireland* (London: Croom Helm, 1982), 193.

Chapter 21
John Hewitt's Hierarchy of Values.
PAUL ARTHUR

1. 'Planter's Gothic', repr. in *Ancestral Voices: The Selected Prose of John Hewitt*, ed. Tom Clyde (Belfast: Blackstaff, 1987), 1–33.
2. 'The Literary Myths of the Revival: A Case for their Abandonment' in *Myth and Reality in Irish Literature*, ed. Joseph Ronsley (Waterloo, Ontario: Wilfrid Laurier Press, 1977), 322.
3. Repr. in *Ancestral Voices*, 48–55.
4. 'Alec of the Chimney Corner', repr. in *Ancestral Voices*, 38–47.
5. 'No Rootless Colonist' (1972), repr. in *Ancestral Voices*, 146–57.
6. 'The Bitter Gourd', repr. in *Ancestral Voices*, 108–21.
7. *The Factory of Grievances: Devolved Government in Northern Ireland 1921–1939* (Dublin: Gill and Macmillan, 1979), 5.

8. *The Break-Up of Britain: Crisis and Neo-Nationalism* (London: Verso, 1981), 233.
9. *Ireland and the English Crisis* (Newcastle-upon-Tyne: Bloodaxe, 1984), 17, 119.
10. 'The Course of Writing in Ulster', repr. in *Ancestral Voices*, 64–76.
11. Rex Cathcart, *The Most Contrary Region: The BBC in Northern Ireland 1924–84* (Belfast: Blackstaff, 1984), 36.
12. David Trimble, 'A Unionist Perspective', in *Consensus in Ireland: Approaches and Recessions*, ed. C. Townshend (Oxford: Clarendon Press, 1988), 83.
13. David Harkness, *Northern Ireland Since 1920* (Dublin: Helicon, 1983), 106, 108.
14. *States of Mind: A Study in Anglo-Irish Conflict 1780–1980* (London: Allen and Unwin, 1983), 109.
15. Ian Adamson, *The Cruthin* (Belfast: Donard, 1974), 89.
16. Ian Adamson, Introduction to *The Battle of Moira being the Epic Poem 'Congal'* by Samuel Ferguson (Belfast: Nosmada, 1980), xxxi.
17. These are pamphlets published in Belfast in (respectively) 1979 and 1986 by the 'think tank' of the UDA: the Ulster Political Research Group.

Chapter 22
Scotland and the United Kingdom
BERNARD CRICK

1. This version of Professor Crick's talk at the 1989 John Hewitt Summer School is a scaling down of the talk's amplified version as 'The Sovereignty of Parliament and the Scottish Question' in Gordon Lewis (ed.), *Happy and Glorious: The Constitution in Transition* (Milton Keynes: Open University Press, 1990). (Eds.)
2. 'An Englishman Considers his Passport', *The Irish Review* 5 (1988), reprinted in my *Political Thoughts and Polemics* (Edinburgh: Edinburgh University Press, 1990).
3. Elie Kedourie famously argued that nationalism as a doctrine is the disruptive claim that for every nation there must be a state: *Nationalism* (London: Hutchinson, 1960). But in that case national identity or cultural nationalism may sometimes, at least, stop short of being a 'doctrine' demanding a state, or one needs to distinguish between national identity and (such) nationalism: for there can be stable multi-national states.
4. Campaign for a Scottish Assembly, *A Claim of Right for Scotland* (Edinburgh, 1988) and reprinted in a book of essays and commentaries of the same title, edited by Owen Dudley Edwards (Edinburgh: Edinburgh University Press, 1989).
5. Key opinion polls are reprinted in my pamphlet, *Labour and Scotland's Right* (Tranent: East Lothian Labour Party, 1989).

6. See especially Ian Harden and Norman Lewis, *The Noble Lie* (London: Hutchinson, 1986); Richard Holme and Michael Elliott (eds.), *1688–1988: Time for a New Constitution* (London: Macmillan, 1988); Antony Wright, 'The Politics of Constitutional Reform', *The Political Quarterly* (Oct. 1986): 414–25. And to these should be added editorial campaigns for reform in the *Independent, Guardian, New Statesman* and *Observer*.
7. The 'Church and Nation' report in *Reports to the General Assembly* (Church of Scotland, 1989): 144–52 contains an interesting account of the historical role of the Church in Scottish life and a claim that it has always opposed on theological grounds 'the alien English constitutional doctrine of the unlimited sovereignty of the British Parliament'.
8. See John Prebble, *The King's Jaunt: George IV in Scotland, 1822* (London: Collins, 1988).
9. From 'American Taxation' in *Speeches and Letters on American Affairs* (London: Dent, 1908), 57–61.
10. 'A Fond Farewell to Devolution', *Radical Scotland* (Dec. 1988).
11. *The Political Quarterly* (Jan. 1989): 10–21.
12. *The British Isles: A History of Four Nations* (Cambridge: Cambridge University Press, 1989): perhaps the first truly British (and Irish) rather than English history.

Chapter 23

John Hewitt: An Ulster of the Mind

TERENCE BROWN

1. Roy McFadden, 'No Dusty Pioneer', Threshold, 38 (Winter, 1986/87): 9.
2. 'No Dusty Pioneer', 9.
3. Cited by Anthony Storr, *Jung* (London: Fontana/Collins, 1973), 76.
4. Storr, 76.
5. Geoffrey Taylor, Preface to John Hewitt, *No Rebel Word* (London: Frederick Muller, 1948).
6. E.S. Dallas, *Poetics* (London: Smith Elder and Co., 1852), 33.
7. Dallas, 35.
8. Dallas, 48.
9. Dallas, 51.
10. In another conversation Hewitt told me of his interest in and admiration for John Barrell's book *John Clare and the Idea of Landscape*.
11. Dallas, 56–7.
12. E.S. Dallas, *The Gay Science* Vol.I (London: Chapman and Hall, 1866), 199.
13. Dallas, 201.
14. Dallas, 205.
15. Dallas, 202.
16. Dallas, 231.
17. Dallas, 207.

LIST OF CONTRIBUTORS

Martyn Anglesea is curator of prints and drawings at the Ulster Museum. He is author of *Portraits and Prospects: drawings and water colours from the Ulster Museum* (Belfast, 1989).

Paul Arthur is senior lecturer in politics at the University of Ulster and is author of *Government and politics in Northern Ireland* (London, 1984).

Terence Brown is associate professor of English at Trinity College, Dublin. Among his publications is *Ireland's literature* (Mullingar, 1988).

Ronald Buchanan is director of the Institute of Irish Studies at the Queen's University of Belfast. He is co-editor (with B. M. Walker) of *Province, city and people* (Antrim, 1987).

Anthony Buckley is curator of anthropology at the Ulster Folk and Transport Museum.

Tom Clyde is a civil servant and editor of *Ancestral voices: selected prose of John Hewitt* (Belfast, 1987).

Timothy Collins is librarian of the science library at University College, Galway.

Patricia Craig is a freelance writer and critic. Among recent work is *The Oxford Book of detective stories* (Oxford, 1990).

Bernard Crick was formerly professor of politics at Birkbeck College, London University.

Gerald Dawe is a poet and critic. Recent works include *Sunday School* (Dublin, 1991) and *How's the poetry going?* (Belfast 1991).

Cahal Dallat is a local historian. Among recent work is *A road to the Glens* (Belfast, 1990).

John Wilson Foster lectures in English at the University of British Columbia, Vancouver, Canada. His latest book is *Colonial consequences* (Dublin, 1991).

Ivan Herbison lectures in the department of English at Queen's University, Belfast.

Sophia Hillan King is a part-time lecturer at the Institute of Irish Studies at the Queen's University of Belfast. She has edited *In quiet places: the uncollected stories, letters and critical prose of Michael McLaverty* (Dublin, 1989).

Peter McDonald lectures in English at the University of Bristol and is the author of *Louis MacNeice: the poet in his contexts* (Oxford, 1991).

Roy McFadden is a poet whose latest work is *After Seymour's funeral* (Belfast, 1990).

Caomhin Mac Giolla Leith lectures in Irish at University College, Dublin.

Gréagóir Ó Dúill is an archivist.

Eve Patten is a research fellow at the Institute of Irish Studies, the Queen's University of Belfast.

Adrian Rice is a poet.

George Watson lectures in English at Aberdeen University and is the author of *Irish identity and the literary revival.*

Geraldine Watts of Trinity College Dublin is presently engaged in researching the life and work of John Hewitt.

Kevin Whelan is the Newman Fellow in the Geography department at University College, Dublin. He recently edited (with W. J. Smyth) *Common Ground: essays on the historical geography of Ireland, presented to Professor T. Jones Hughes* (Cork, 1988).